HOME REMODELING
A HOW-TO
MONEY-SAVING HANDBOOK

Other TAB Books by the Author

No. 1068 *Successful Sandy Soil Gardening*
No. 1415 *The Energy Efficient Home—101 Money-Saving Ideas*

No. 1515
$24.95

HOME REMODELING
A HOW-TO
MONEY-SAVING HANDBOOK

BY BETTE GALMAN WAHLFELDT

TAB BOOKS Inc.
BLUE RIDGE SUMMIT, PA 17214

"We shape our buildings;
thereafter they shape us."
. . . . Winston Churchill
No better words could describe do-it-yourself builders/
remodelers . . . . . .

Bette Galman Wahlfeldt

Dedicated to
Carole and Ed Gillette
For Their Friendship and Support
in My Endeavors

FIRST EDITION

THIRD PRINTING

Printed in the United States of America

Copyright © 1984 by TAB BOOKS Inc.

Library of Congress Cataloging in Publication Data

Wahlfeldt, Bette G. (Bette Galman)
Home remodeling—a how-to, money-saving handbook.

Includes index.
1. Dwellings—Remodeling. I. Title.
TH4816.W335 1984   643'.7   84-8520
ISBN 0-8306-0215-1
ISBN 0-8306-1515-6 (pbk.)

Contents

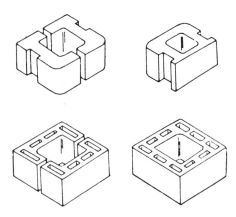

Preface

Save it! How many times have we all heard that phrase in the last decade?

Save what? Where? How?

It is the 1980s, and while we may not be living in the type of depression as those who lived through the Great Depression visualize, we are, nevertheless definitely in an era where it seems that we must take a few steps backward in order that we can go forward and continue to live up to the standards to which we, as Americans, have become accustomed.

We are being hurt by the demands of higher taxes, lesser services, and our individual needs; so we must all put our minds, and our backs, into becoming do-it-yourselfers, not only for the sheer joy of it, but yes, to save!

The "American dream" is owning your own home. For those between 25 and 45 it doesn't need to be just a dream, even with high interest rates and high labor costs. Now is the time for those people who were not interested in owning their own home in the 1950s and 1960s to learn how they can now, in the 1980s, afford their "American dream."

This book has been written in the hope that the younger generation will rehabilitate older homes, thereby preserving the architectural beauty of a bygone era and, most importantly, providing themselves with a home that will provide them with joys through the years, besides immediate monetary savings. It will also make their American dream come true.

Let's put new life back into old dwellings.

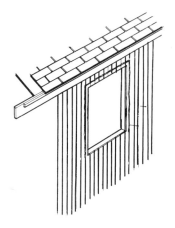

Introduction

The key words in the 1980s are rehabilitation and recycling, and today more than ever is the time for the generation having "funding" difficulties to use those words to their benefit. The high cost of financing, coupled with the high cost of labor, is bringing to life a "new breed" of homeowner/builder. They are the do-it-yourselfers. While you may not be able nor wish to build your home from scratch, you can, in this day of ever rising inflation, have available to you the knowledge whereby you can remodel all or part of an existing structure yourself.

If you are new to home building, don't let it scare you. Don't give up before you begin. Once you have found "your house," which, undoubtedly, will be in need of many repairs, remember, the important thing is that you want to save money. Overall, while the cost of buying the many materials which will be needed will not necessarily provide much savings when you do it yourself, major savings factors will be involved in the cost of labor. If you do all of the paneling, weather stripping, caulking, and insulating, you will save up to 75 percent of the total

cost of having it done entirely by outside labor. Conversely, if you are remodeling your kitchen and are purchasing new major appliances, such as refrigerator, stove, and cabinetry, then your savings would be as low as 25 percent. It is safe to say, then, that by remodeling your newly found "old" dwelling you will save approximately 50-60 percent. Again, that is a lot of money!

Where do you begin? How do you go about all the needed repairs which will be made? If you are in no hurry, then undoubtedly you will find that you are able to do the majority of the remodeling yourself, with perhaps the help of friends and family. If, however, you do not have the time and you must hire labor, there is little doubt that you will still ultimately save tremendously while looking forward to the day when you can sit comfortably in your new surrounding and have the satisfaction that you have put new life into an old dwelling.

Where you start will, of course, depends on the type of structure you have purchased and its individual needs. Whatever the type, the following chapters outline dozens of areas which require knowledge and instruction. First, however, you must find the home. Since you are making the biggest investment you will ever make, don't rush into it. Look around.

Chapter 1

The Remodeling Decision

Unlike most objects, a well-built home that has been reasonably well maintained does not wear out for many years—several hundred in fact, as can be attested to by the thousands you see as you travel throughout the country. True, it may become outmoded, but it does not wear out.

Tests conducted by the Forest Products Laboratory show that when decay or other abnormal environmental factors are not present, wood does not deteriorate in strength or stiffness from age alone for 100 or more years.

The place for you, the prospective remodeler, to begin is to appraise your future purchase (Fig. 1-1).

KEY POINTS

Financial. Will the cost of improvement be less than 60 percent of the cost to build a new home of equal quality? Will the value of the house after improvements be less than 20 percent greater than the average home in the neighborhood?

Location. Is the neighborhood attractive, pleasing, and well maintained? Is the neighborhood free from heavy traffic, dust, noise, and other forms of pollution? Is the neighborhood free from the threat of flooding?

Lot. Is the property graded so moisture will drain away from the house? Is the house oriented so maximum benefit is provided from sunlight and maximum protection is provided from wind and rain? Is the view from the house pleasant and likely to remain unchanged? Is access by pedestrians and automobiles direct, simple, and easy?

Foundation. Does the alignment of the foundation appear to be straight and sure? Is the foundation free from large cracks and deterioration? Is siding at least 8 inches above the outside soil and free from decay?

Structure. Are floors sturdy and even? To check, jump up and down; the floor should not shake. Are doors and windows tightly fitted and snug, yet easy to open and close? Are the exterior walls free from excessive paint blistering and cracking (possible signs of an improperly installed vapor barrier)? Does the house have at least 3 inches of insulation in exterior walls and at least 6

1

inches in the ceiling? Is the roof free from sagging, bowed surfaces, or missing shingles? Are the flashing, gutters, and downspouts in good repair, and free from rust and holes? Is the house free from termite infestation?

Utilities. Does the electrical system include 100 amp service or more (200 amps preferred), 12 or more 110-volt circuits, at least one 110-volt outlet on each wall, and enough 220-volt outlets for major appliances?

Does the water pressure remain adequate when the toilet is flushed and the bathroom faucets are turned on at the same time? Will the water heater be satisfactory after remodeling (at least 40 gallons for a family of four with a washing machine)? Will the source of water be adequate, especially if it is from a well and if a washing machine or dishwasher is added?

Will the existing method of sewage disposal be adequate, especially if a dishwasher, garbage disposal, or washing machine are added? Are the plumbing fixtures in good condition? Will the present method of cooling and heating be adequate and efficient after improvements? Check with the utility company on rates for the area.

Arrangement and Appearance. The value of the house to be remodeled is strongly affected by the layout and appearance. Many houses, however, will not lend themselves to an ideal arrangement without excessive cost, but adequate living conditions may be possible with some sacrifice in arrangement.

Is the house large enough to meet the family's needs? Does the house provide all the different kinds of living space your family needs? Does the house have rooms arranged in three areas—kitchen, living, and sleeping? Is the traffic pattern through the house direct and uncluttered with a minimum of floor space devoted to traffic lanes? Are the rooms large enough? Is there adequate, well-planned storage space? Is the appearance of the house pleasing to you?

Final Evaluation. Now review your answers. If you have answered "no" quite a few times, either remodeling is of questionable value, or you are willing to spend a great deal of money and time

to achieve personal satisfaction alone. If many answers were "yes", remodeling will benefit you; however, your no answers may indicate items that you should consider improving, repairing, or remodeling.

Major Reasons for Rejection

—The foundation is completely unrepairable.

—The entire frame of the house is considerably out of square.

—The house is generally decayed or termite infested.

—Many items must be replaced, repaired, or remodeled.

BEFORE YOU BUY AN OLD HOUSE

To provide a systematic approach for your remodeling project, be it one room or the entire house, let us examine typical elements with which you will be involved, each of which will be outlined in detail in their own chapter.

Masonry and Concrete

The most important component of a house from the standpoint of remodeling is its foundation. Since it supports the entire house, failure of the foundation can have far-reaching effects.

Make sure that you check the foundation for general deterioration which may allow moisture or water to enter the basement, if there is one, and may require expensive repairs. More importantly, check for uneven settlement. (Fig. 1-2). Not only can uneven settlement distort the frame, it can pull it apart. This situation could result in the racking of window and door frames out of plumb, and in cracks, which permits infiltration of cold or hot air.

In instances where there is only a single localized failure or minor settlement, you can relevel beams or floor joists, so don't reject the purchase of the house on this basis, nor, for that matter on the basis of a more distorted frame. Certainly it is a major problem and must be considered in the overall budgeting of your remodeling plan, however, of course, you should not buy a house of this nature until you have thoroughly investigated the cost,

Fig. 1-1. Old homes can be renovated (courtesy USDA Forestry Service).

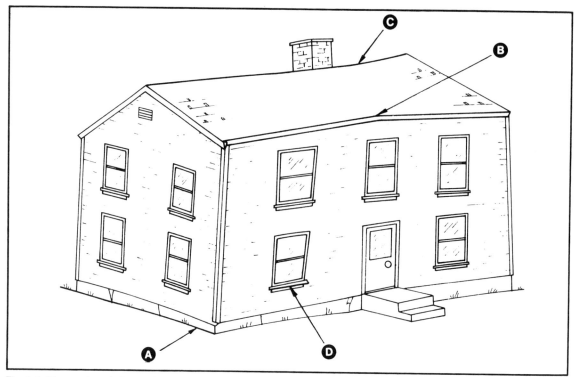

Fig. 1-2. Uneven foundation settlement (A) may result in a house badly out of square. Evidences may include (B) eaveline distortion, (C) sagging roof ridge, or (D) loose-fitting frames or binding windows or doors (courtesy USDA Forestry Service).

since you may need a new foundation, or the house may be so critically unstable that it would not be a good buy.

Many older homes have stone or brick foundations; some are supported on masonry piers. Be sure to check the masonry foundation for cracks and crumbling mortar. Simple defects are repairable; more excessive deterioration may indicate the need for major repair or replacement of the entire foundation.

Houses which have crawl spaces usually have a foundation wall or piers supporting floor joists. Check these supports for cracks and settlement, also.

There are also houses built on pier-type wood post foundations. These foundations are more common in certain areas of the country, and they provide excellent foundation service if the wood has been properly treated with a preservative. Upon inspection of them look for decay and insect damage.

In checking foundation walls you will find that most are of poured concrete and have little effect on the structure; however, open cracks indicate a failure that may get progressively worse. Whether a crack is active or dormant can be determined only by observation over several months; so you should not rush into buying the first house that appeals to you. Shop around.

In parts of the country where basements are prevalent, be sure to check if the basement is damp or leaks. If so, the walls may require major repairs, especially if you intend to use the basement in the future. Usually the cause of deterioration in a basement comes from a clogged drain tile, clogged or broken downspouts, cracks in walls, lack of slope of the finished grade away from the house foundation, or a higher water table. If you look at this type of property on a dry day, go back after a rain and check again.

The most common source of dampness is surface water, such as from downspouts discharging directly at the foundation wall or from surface drainage flowing directly against the foundation wall. The solution is proper grading.

Masonry Veneers

Although uneven settlement of the foundation will cause cracks in brick or stone veneer, these cracks can be grouted and joints repointed. Large or numerous cracks will be unsightly even after they are patched, however. The mortar also may be weak and crumbling, and joints may be incompletely filled or poorly finished. If these conditions are limited to a small area, regrouting or repointing is feasible. To improve the appearance, the veneer can be cleaned with water or chemicals.

It is extremely important to prevent water from entering the masonry wall or flowing over the face of the wall in any quantity. Scrutinize flashing or caulking at all projecting trim, copings, sills, and intersections of roof and walls.

Chimneys and Fireplaces

Most older homes already have fireplaces. The most obvious defects to look for in the chimney are cracks in the masonry and loose mortar. Cracks are usually the result of foundation settlement or the attachment of television antennas or other items that put undue stress on the chimney.

It is wise to support the chimney by its own footing and not with the framework of the house when you remodel.

While you are doing an overall check of the fireplace to see how much, if any, remodeling will be required, here, check to see if it has an operating damper. If no damper exists, you will need to place one to prevent heat loss up the flue when the fireplace is not in use. If the fireplace looks as though it has had a lot of use, it probably draws well; however, you can check by lighting a few sheets of newspaper on the hearth. A good fireplace will draw immediately; a usable one will draw after about a minute.

Structural Wood Frame

The building frame should be examined carefully to determine whether it is distorted from foundation failure or from improper or inadequate framing. It should also be checked for decay and insect damage.

Decay thrives in a mild temperature and in wood with a high moisture content. Look for decay in any part of the house that is subject to prolonged wetting.

Indications of decay in wood are abnormal color and loss of sheen. The brown color may be deeper than normal (Fig. 1-3), and in advanced stages cubical checking and collapse occur (Fig. 1-4). The abnormal color may also be a lightening which eventually progresses to a bleached appearance (Fig. 1-5). Fine black lines may be present with the bleached appearance.

Fungal growths appearing as strandlike or cottony masses on the surface of wood indicate excessive water and consequently the presence of decay (Fig. 1-6).

Visual methods of detecting decay do not, however, show the extent of the damage. The two strength properties severely reduced by decay are hardness and toughness. Prod the wood with a sharp tool and observe the resistance to marring. The loss of hardness is determined by comparing this resistance with that of sound wood. Sound wood tends to lift out as one or two relatively long slivers, and breaks are splintery. You can determine loss of toughness by using a pointed tool to jab the wood and pry out a sliver. If toughness has been greatly reduced by decay, the wood will break squarely across the grain with minimal splintering and will lift out with little resistance.

While decay may exist in any part of the house, some areas are more vulnerable. Following are major areas which should be given special attention when looking for decay.

Foundation and Flooring. Decay often begins in framing members near the foundation. It can be detected by papery, fanlike growths that are initially white with a yellow tinge and turn brown or black with age. Look for these growths between the subfloor and finished floor, also between the joists and subfloor. They can become exposed by shrinkage of flooring during dry weather. They also exist

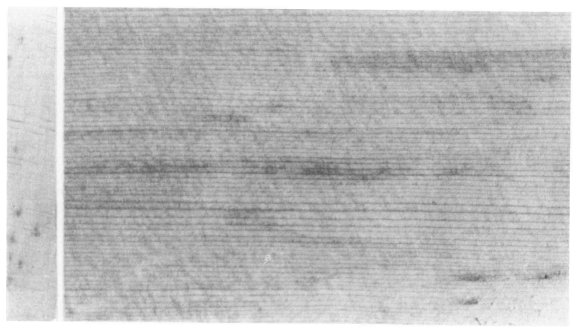

Fig. 1-3. Discolored wood shows advanced stages of decay (courtesy USDA Forestry Service).

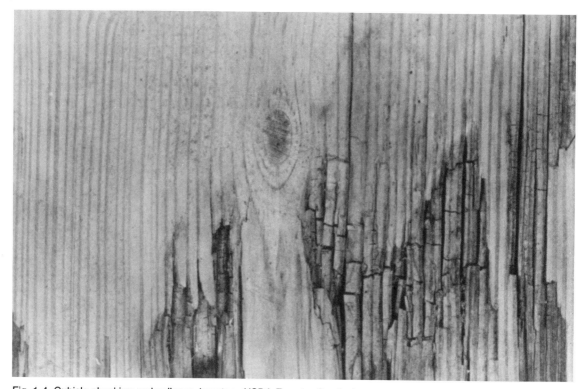

Fig. 1-4. Cubicle checking and collapse (courtesy USDA Forestry Service).

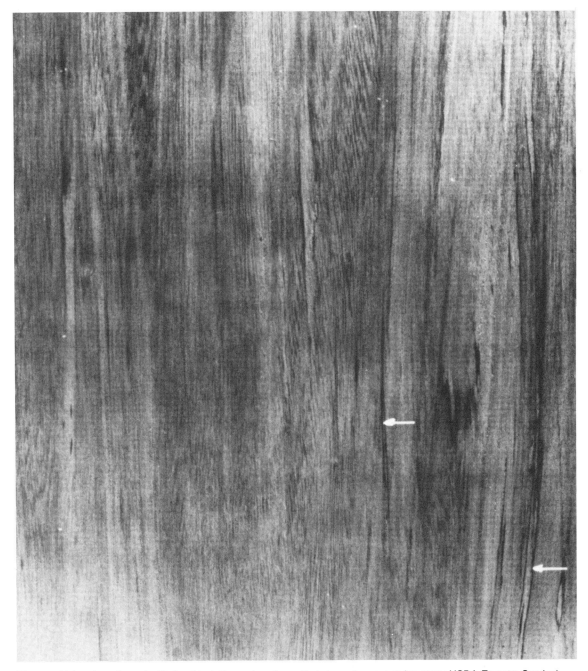

Fig. 1-5. Lightening of wood with fine black lines also shows that decay is present (courtesy USDA Forestry Service).

under carpets, in cupboards, or in other protected areas that tend to stay damp.

Siding and Exterior Trim. Where siding is close to the ground, look for discoloration, checking, or softening. Check for decay where siding ends butt against each other or against trim.

Fig. 1-6. Fungi surface growth in crawl space area under joist. The pen shows comparative size (courtesy USDA Forestry Service).

Roof. Inspect wood roof shingles for cubical checking, softening, and breaking of the exposed ends. Asphalt shingles have deteriorated if they can be easily pulled apart between the fingers. Roof edges are particularly vulnerable to decay if they were not properly *flashed*, or protected against rain by being covered with sheet metal or other material. If the roofing is deteriorating, check the underside of the roof sheathing for evidence of condensation or decay.

Porches. Pay particular attention to porch step treads or deck surfaces that are checked or concavely worn, and so able to trap water. Check joints in railings or posts. Check enclosed porches for condensation on the underside of the deck and framing. Check the crawl space for signs of dampness and examine areas where these signs occur.

Windows and Doors. Look for brown or black discoloration near joints of windows and doors or flaking of nearby paint (Fig. 1-7). These are signs of possible decay. Check the inside for water stains on the sash and sill resulting from condensation running down the glass. Where you find such stains, check for softening and molding.

Insect Problems. Three major kinds of insects attack wood and cause problems in wood-frame houses: termites, powder-post beetles, and carpenter ants. Where there is any indication of one of these insects, probe the wood with a sharp tool to determine the extent of damage.

There are two major classifications of termites: subterranean termites, which have access to the ground or other water source; and nonsubterranean, which do not require direct access to water.

To determine if there are subterranean termites, examine all areas close to the ground. One of the more obvious signs is earthen tubes built over the surface of foundation walls to provide runways from the soil to the wood above. Termites may also enter through cracks or voids in the foundations or concrete floors. They do not require runways to the soil where there is a source of water, such as a plumbing leak.

Another sign of the presence of termites is the swarming of winged adults early in the spring or fall. Termites resemble ants, but they have much longer wings and do not have the thin waist of an ant. Where there is an indication of termites, look for galleries that follow the grain of the wood, usually leaving a shell of sound wood.

Damp or dry wood without outside moisture or contact with the ground is the home of nonsubterranean termites. They are found only in narrow coastal strip regions which extend from central California to Virginia and Hawaii. An early sign of these termites is sandlike excretory pellets that are discarded outside the wood.

Nonsubterranean termites can also be identified by the presence of swarming winged forms. They cut freely across the grain of the wood rather than following the grain as the subterranean termites do.

Fig. 1-7. Stain or decay may occur at joists in a window frame (courtesy USDA Forestry Service).

Powder-post beetles are most easily recognized by their borings, which are about the consistency of flour. Many borings remain inside the wood. The adults leave the wood through a hole about the diameter of a pencil lead, giving the wood the appearance of having been hit by birdshot. Such holes may be just the result of a previous infestation, so check for fresh, clean sawdust as a sign of current activity. Activity may also be recognized by the rasping sound the beetles make while tunneling.

Humid locations, such as near the ground, are usually the most prevalent areas for powder-post beetles. They can be destroyed with approved insecticides, but in severe cases, as with termites, it is well worth the cost of a professional exterminator.

Carpenter ants are often discovered by the wood on which they have chewed, which resembles coarse sawdust and is placed in piles outside the wood. Carpenter ants do not eat the wood, but only nest in it. Working ants may be as long as 1/2 inch. They make a rustling noise in walls, floors, or woodwork. Look for signs of carpenter ants in softwood in high humidity locations.

An approved insecticide blown into the galleries will destroy carpenter ants. Eliminate the high moisture situation to prevent a recurrence.

Floor Supports

If the house you are remodeling has a basement, interior support is usually provided by wood or steel girders supported on wood or steel posts. Wood posts should be supported on pedestals and not be embedded in the concrete floor, where they may take on moisture and decay. Examine the base of the wood posts for decay even if they are set above the floor slab. Steel posts are normally supported on metal plates.

Check the wood girders for sag and also for decay at the exterior wall bearings. Sag is a permanent deflection which can be noted especially near the middle of a structural member (Fig. 1-8). Some sag is common in permanently loaded wood beams and is not a problem unless parts of the house are

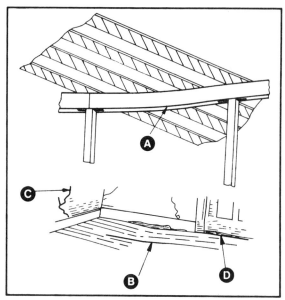

Fig. 1-8. A sagging horizontal member (A) has resulted in: (B) uneven floor, (C) cracked plaster, and (D) poorly fitted door (courtesy USDA Forestry Service).

obviously distorted. Sag is usually a surface rather than a structural problem. Some deflection is normal, about 3/8 inch in a 10-foot girder is acceptable.

Floor Framing

Sill plates or joists and headers rest on top of the foundation; so they are exposed to moisture and are vulnerable to decay or insect attack. Specific examination should be made of these members as well as the entire floor framing system for decay and insect damage, particularly if the basement or crawl space is very damp.

Joists, like girders, should be examined for sag. Here, too, some sag can be expected and is not a sign of structural damage. It is usually not a serious problem in floor joists unless the foundation has settled unevenly, causing excessive deflection in parts of the floor structure. Look for local deflection from inadequate support of a heavy partition load that runs parallel to the joists. Sag might be considered excessive if it is readily apparent from a visual examination of the floor.

If a floor is springy when you walk across it, you can add extra joists or girders to increase stiffness.

Of particular concern is the framing of the floor joists around stair openings. Some builders estimate that 50 percent of houses have inadequate framing around stairs. Check floors around the opening for levelness. Where floors are sagging, you will need to carefully level and reinforce the framing.

Flooring

Wood Floors. When you check wood floors look for buckling or cupping of boards which can result from a high moisture content of the boards or a wetting of the floor. See if separation of the boards is due to shrinkage. This shrinkage is more probable if the flooring boards are wide. If the floor is generally smooth and without excessive separation between boards, refinishing may put it in good condition; however, be sure there is sufficient thickness left in the flooring to permit sanding. Most flooring cannot be sanded more than two or three times; if it is softwood flooring without a subfloor, even one sanding might weaken the floor too much. Sanding of plywood block floors should also be limited. If floors have wide cracks or are too thin to sand, some type of new flooring should be considered. Carpeting is now the most popular choice for remodeling living areas.

Resilient Tile. Examine floors with resilient tile for loose tile, cracks between tile, broken corners, and chipped edges. Look to see if any ridges or unevenness in the underlay are showing through. Replacement of any tile in a room may necessitate the replacement of the flooring in the whole room because tile changes color with age, and new tile will not match the old.

Wall Framing

Stud walls normally have more then adequate strength. They may be distorted, however. Check openings for squareness by operating doors and windows and observing the fit. Some adjustments are possible, but large distortions will require new framing. Check for sag in headers over wide window openings or wide openings between rooms. Where the sag is visually noticeable, new headers will be required.

Walls and Ceilings

Interior Covering. The interior wall covering in old houses is usually plaster, but it may be gypsum board in more recently built homes. Wood paneling may also be found, but it is usually limited to one room or to a single wall or accent area.

Plaster almost always has some hairline cracks, even when it is in good condition. Minor cracks and holes can be patched, but a new wall covering should be applied if large cracks and holes are prevalent, if the surface is generally uneven and bulging, or if the plaster is loose in spots. The same general rule applies to ceilings.

If walls have been papered, check the thickness of the paper. If more than two or three layers of paper are present, they should be removed before applying new paper. All wallpaper should be removed before painting.

Painted Surfaces. Paint on surfaces may have been built up to excessive thickness. It may be chipped due to mechanical damage, to incompatibility between successive layers, or to improper surface preparation prior to repainting. Old calsimine surfaces may require considerable labor to recondition them; so a new wall covering should be considered. Paint failures may be due to application of paint over calsimine.

Roof Framing

Examine the roof for sagging of the ridge, rafters, and sheathing. If the ridge line is not straight, or the roof does not appear to be in a uniform plane, some repair may be necessary. The ridge will sag from improper support, inadequate ties at the plate level, or even from sagging of the rafters. Rafters will sag because of inadequate stiffness or because they were not well seasoned. Sheathing sag may indicate too wide a spacing between rafters or strip sheathing, or plywood that is too thin or has delaminated.

Roof

A leaky roof will be obvious by inspecting the damage inside the house. Look in the attic where water stains on the rafters will indicate small leaks that will eventually cause damage. Damage inside the house is not always attributable to roofing, however; it could be caused by faulty flashing or condensation.

Wood Shingles. Wood shingles also are used considerably to cover pitched roofs and are most commonly made of durable woods. A good wood shingle roof should look like a perfect mosaic, whereas a roof with worn shingles has an allover ragged appearance. Individual shingles on worn roofs are broken, warped, and upturned. This type of roof needs to be replaced even if there is no evidence of leaking. Excessive shade may cause fungal growth and early shingle deterioration. A good wood shingle roof will last up to 30 years under favorable conditions.

Built-up Roofing. Examine built-up roofing on flat or low-sloped roofs by going onto the roof and looking for bare spots in the surfacing and for separations and breaks in the felt. Bubbles, blisters, or soft spots also indicate that the roof needs major repairs. Alligator patterns on smooth-surfaced, built-up roofs may not be a failure of the roof. The life span of a built-up roof ranges from 15 to 30 years, depending on the number of layers of felt and the quality of application.

Flashing. Flashing should be evident where the roof intersects walls, chimneys, or vents, and where two roofs intersect to form a valley. Corroded flashing should be replaced to prevent future problems. Likewise, check and replace corroded gutters and downspouts.

Overhang. If the house was built with no roof overhang, the addition of an overhang should be considered in the remodeling plan. It will greatly reduce maintenance on siding and window trim, and prolong the life of both.

Asphalt Shingles. Asphalt shingles are the most common roof covering and are made in a wide range of weights and thicknesses. The most obvious deterioration of asphalt shingles is loss of the surface granules. The shingles may also become quite brittle. More important, however, is the wear that occurs in the narrow grooves between the tabs or sections of the shingle, or between two consecutive shingles in a row. This wear may extend completely through to the roof boards without being apparent from a casual visual inspection. A good asphalt shingle should last 18 to 20 years.

Siding and Trim

Major problems with siding and trim stem from excessive moisture. One main contributor to this problem is the lack of roof overhang, allowing rain to run down the face of the wall. Moisture may also enter from the inside if there is no vapor barrier, and subsequently condense within the wall.

Check for space between horizontal siding boards by standing very close and sighting along the wall. Some cracks can be caulked, but a general gapping or looseness may indicate new siding is necessary. If the boards are not badly warped, re-nailing may solve the problem. Look for decay on siding where two boards are butted end to end, at corners, and around window and door frames.

Decorative trim can present unusual decay and maintenance problems, particularly where water may be trapped. Good shingle siding has a mosaic appearance. Worn shingles have an allover ragged appearance, and close examination will show individual shingles to be broken, warped, and upturned. New siding will be required if shingles are badly weathered or worn.

Finish failures may be caused by poor paints, improper application of good paints, poor surface preparation, or incompatible successive coatings. Excessive peeling (Fig. 1-9) may require complete removal of the paint. You may want to consider residing instead of painting.

Windows

One of the more difficult problems of old woodframe houses is found in its windows (Fig. 1-10). Loose fitting windows that are not weatherstripped will be a major source of uncomfortable drafts and cause large heating and cooling loss. Check the tightness of fit and examine the sash and sill for decay. Check the operation of the window,

Fig. 1-9. Excessive paint peeling on siding (courtesy USDA Forestry Service).

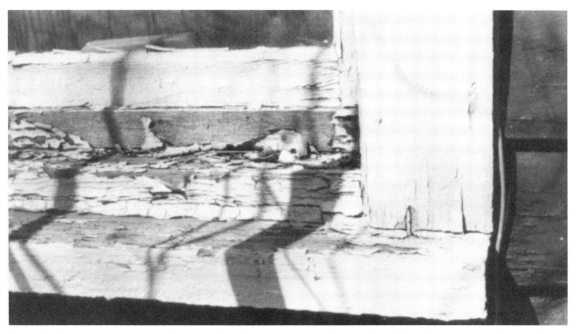

Fig. 1-10. Signs or excessive water damage are evident in the paint peeling on this window sill and sash and broken caulking around the window (courtesy USDA Forestry Service).

also. Casement windows should be checked for warp at the top and bottom.

If window replacement is planned, check the window dimensions. If the window is not of a standard size, or if a different size is desired, the opening must be reframed or new sash must be made, both of which can be expensive. It is best, therefore, to stay with the original dimensions as far as possible.

Double glazing of windows is as important in warm climates as it is in cold climates to retain heat and/or cooling and to reduce condensation.

Doors

Exterior doors should fit well without sticking. They should be weather stripped to avoid air infiltration. If you find difficulty latching a door, it can usually be attributed to warping. A simple adjustment of the latch keeper will solve the problem in some instances. Badly warped doors should be replaced.

Storm doors serve their purpose, again, in both cold and warm climates, not only for heat and cooling saving and comfort, but also to avoid moisture condensation on or in the door and to protect the door from severe weather.

If the door frame is out of square due to foundation settlement or other racking of the house frame, the opening will probably need to be reframed.

The lower paths of exterior doors and storm doors are particularly susceptible to decay and should be carefully checked. Also observe the condition of the threshold, which may be worn, weathered, or decayed, and so require replacement.

Porches

An open porch is very vulnerable to decay and insect attack since it is open to windblown rain or snow. Steps are often placed in direct contact with the soil—a poor practice unless the wood is treated.

Check all wood for decay and insect damage, paying particular attention to the base of posts or any place where two members join and water could get into the joint. Decay often occurs where posts

are not raised above the porch floor to allow air to dry out the base of the post. You may need to replace a few members, but it will be worthwhile if you plan to keep the porch as it is.

Trim, Cabinets, and Doors

Trim should have tight joints and fit closely to walls. If the finish is worn, but the surface is smooth, refinishing may be feasible. If the finish is badly chipped or checked, removing it will be laborious regardless of whether the new finish is to be clear sealer or paint. Trim or cabinetry of plain design will be less difficult to prepare for refinishing than ornately carved designs.

If any trim is damaged, or it is necessary to move doors or windows, all trim in the room may need to be replaced because existing trim may be difficult to match. Small sections of special trim can be custom-made, but the cost should be compared with complete replacement.

The problems with interior doors are much the same as those for exterior doors except there are no decay or threshold problems.

Insulation and Moisture Control

Good insulation cuts heating costs and adds to comfort by making the temperature in the house more uniform. Humidification increases comfort and saves fuel by reducing the temperature level required for comfort. While both insulation and humidification are desirable, their addition to older homes without vapor barriers in walls and ceilings may create moisture condensation problems. Where large differences exist between indoor and outdoor temperatures, pressure forces water vapor out through the walls.

In the uninsulated house this vapor usually moves on to the outside without any problem. Where insulation is added, the dew point often occurs within the insulation; so water vapor condenses into free water with consequent wet insulation and siding. In some instances where indoor relative humidities are low, and the outside covering material allows moisture in the walls to escape readily, no moisture problems may result. Mechanical humidification amplifies moisture problems; however, because the water vapor pressure drive is increased and consequently so is the rate of moisture movement into the walls. Vapor barriers in walls and ceilings reduce the rate of moisture movement into these areas and thus help to control the moisture problems created by insulation or humidification.

Insulation. Look in the attic to determine the amount of ceiling insulation present. The ceiling represents the greatest source of heat loss on cool days and heat gain on warm days.

Vapor Barriers. Provide vapor barriers on the warm side of all insulation. Most houses built before the mid-1960s do not have vapor barriers. If the ceiling insulation is in blanket form with a covering around it, the covering material may resist the passage of moisture. If the ceiling is loose fill, look under it for a separate vapor barrier of coated or laminated paper, aluminum foil, or plastic film. The same is true of insulated walls, where the vapor barrier should be on the inside of the walls.

Check in crawl spaces for a vapor barrier laid on top of the soil. If there is none and the crawl space seems quite damp, you should add a vapor barrier.

If the house you are inspecting for possible renovation has been built on a concrete slab, there is no convenient way to determine if there are vapor barriers under the slabs. If the floor stays damp, there probably is no vapor barrier. A barrier should then be added on top of the slab, and a dry finish floor applied over it.

Ventilation. The two major areas where good ventilation is required are the crawl space and the attic, or roof joist spaces if the house has a cathedral ceiling or flat roof. The general adequacy of existing ventilation can be observed from the degree of dampness.

Moisture passes into the attic from the house and condenses as the air cools down or when the moist air contacts the cold roof members. Both inlet and outlet vents must be located properly for good air circulation through the entire attic. These vents not only help keep the attic dry in winter, but keep hot air moving from the attic during summer and help to cool the house.

Look at the size and location of crawl space vents. There should be at least four vents located near building corners for optimum cross ventilation and minimum dead air space.

Plumbing

Because many of the plumbing, heating, and wiring systems in a house are concealed, it may be difficult to determine their adequacy when you initially evaluate your proposed purchase.

In a very old house some of the systems may need to be replaced entirely; in others only modified. One such bonus could be the dramatic recovery of space and improvements in the appearance and future use of a basement when you replace an old-fashioned "octopus" gravity warm air heating system with a modern forced-air system.

Water Supply System. Water pressure is important. Check several faucets to see if the flow is adequate. Low pressure can result from various causes. A 3/4-inch inside diameter service is adequate.

The main distribution pipes should have 3/4 inch inside diameter, but branch lines may have 1/2 inch inside diameter. Sizes can be checked easily. Copper pipes 1/2 inch inside diameter are 5/8 inch outside diameter, and 3/4-inch inside diameter pipes are 7/8-inch outside diameter. Galavanized pipes 1/2 inch inside diameter are 7/8 inch outside diameter and pipes 3/4 inch inside diameter are 1/8 inch outside diameter.

To ascertain if the supply pressure system is inadequate, if the house has its own water system, check the gauge on the pressure tank, which should read a minimum of 20 pounds and preferably 40 to 50 pounds. Anything less will indicate the pump is not operating properly, or the pressure setting is too low. If the supply is from a municipal system, the pressure in the mains may be too low, although this situation is unlikely.

Check shutoff valves at the service entrance and at various points in the system to determine if they have become frozen with age or little use.

Check for leaks in the water supply system. Rust or white or greenish crusting of pipe or joints may indicate leaks.

Water hammer, the concussion of moving water against the sides of a containing pipe may also be a problem. It results from a stop in the water flow in the pipe by the abrupt closing of a faucet. Air chambers placed on the supply lines at the fixtures usually absorb the shock and prevent water hammer. If there is a water hammer, air chambers may be waterlogged. If there are no air chambers, you can add them.

The water from any private well should be tested even though the well has been in continuous use.

Plumbing Drainage System. The drainage system consists of the sewer lateral, the drains under the floor, the drainage pipes above the floor, and the vents. Pipes may have become clogged or broken, or they may be of inadequate size. Venting in particular may be inadequate and far below code requirements.

Flux fixtures to see if drains are sluggish. If so, check for the following:

☐ Old laterals are commonly of vitreous bell tile. These tiles may have been poorly installed or have become broken, allowing tree roots to enter at the breaks or through the joints. Roots can be removed mechanically, but this operation may need to be repeated every few years.

☐ The underfloor drains may be of tile or steel and could be broken or rusted out. They may have become clogged and only need cleaning.

☐ The drainage system above the basement floor or within the house should be checked for adequacy and leaks.

☐ Vents may be inadequate or may have become clogged. In extreme cases they may cause the water in the traps to be siphoned out, allowing sewer gas to enter the house. Note any excessive suction when a toilet is flushed.

During the course of remodeling you may find that additional supply and drain lines may be desirable. New lines may be required for automatic washers, additional bathrooms, adequate sill cocks, or to reorganize the entire layout of the house.

Water Heater. With a hot water heating system, water may also be heated satisfactorily for cooking, bathing, and other personal needs. In a hot air furnace, however, the water heating coil seldom provides enough hot water. Furthermore, during summer months when the hot air heating is not needed, a separate system is required to provide hot water. A gas water heater should have at least a 30-gallon capacity, and preferably more. An electric water heater should have a capacity of 50 gallons or more.

Fixtures. Plumbing fixtures that are quite old may be rusted and stained and require complete replacement, or it may be desirable to replace them for their general appearance.

Heating

Heating system advances and concepts of comfort outdate the heating systems in most old houses. Most of the time this is one area where the remodeler puts in an entire central system.

Electrical

Obviously an old home will not be equipped to accommodate the modern way of living with all of our new appliances; thus an older home undoubtedly will have insufficient electrical wiring.

Wiring should be examined wherever possible so that you can make a materials/cost evaluation of your remodeling needs. Wall receptacles or fixtures may be in a liveable condition, enabling you to concentrate on more important remodeling projects. If any armored cable or conduit is badly rusted, or if wiring or cable insulation is deteriorated, damaged, brittle, or crumbly, however, the overall house wiring has probably deteriorated from age or overloading and will need to be completely replaced.

GENERAL CONSIDERATIONS

The value of the house you are renovating and the convenience and pleasure of using it over many years will be affected by the layout and appearance.

Several points to consider are:

—The relationship and convenience of areas to each other.
—Traffic circulation.

—Privacy.
—Adequacy of room size.

Conceivably, some houses will not lend themselves to an ideal arrangement without excessive cost, but, keeping in mind that we are concerned with a low budget, most of us can live without the "ideal" arrangement.

There are some, though very few, older homes which cannot lend themselves to some of these important physical aspects. These are worth mentioning so you can see what your house has to offer.

Circulation

Observe circulation or traffic patterns. For good circulation, keep through traffic from all rooms or at least at one side of a room rather than through its center.

Layout

Ideally, houses should have rooms arranged as follows:

—The private or bedroom area.
—The work area, consisting of kitchen and utility rooms.
—The relaxation area, consisting of dining and living rooms.
—The den or family room, also relaxing areas.

The den should, however, be out of the general circulation areas. If it is part of the bedroom area, it can double as a guest room. If you have a basement this, too, can double as a play room/guest room.

Work Area. The location of the kitchen in relation to other areas of the house is one of the most critical. It should have direct access to the dining room area for unloading groceries. Nearness to the utility room is also convenient since the housewife often has work in progress in the kitchen and utility room at the same time. Traffic should not pass through the kitchen work area, i.e., the range-refrigerator-sink triangle.

The size of the kitchen is important, and older homes usually have larger kitchen areas, but they must be updated to accommodate the many modern kitchen appliances which now exist.

Private Area. The bedroom and bathroom area should be separated as much as possible, both visually and acoustically, from the living and work areas.

Bedrooms should be accessible to bathrooms without going through another room, and, if possible, one bathroom should be accessible to work and relaxation areas without going through a bedroom. One of the basic rules of privacy is to avoid traffic through one bedroom to another. If this privacy is not presently provided, some changes in layout may be desirable.

Relaxation Area. The relaxation area usually is at the front of older homes, but rooms at the side or rear may be used through renovation, particularly if they provide a view into a landscaped yard.

Appearance

Taste is largely an individual matter; so only basic guidelines can be provided. Simplicity and unity are major considerations; however, a house possessing the quality commonly referred to as *charm* may be appraised somewhat higher than plainer ones. Older homes that have historic or architectural significance are in a special category, and while they are more expensive to purchase and rejuvenate, if you are able to do so certainly they add an extra spice.

Simplicity is one of the first principles. Observe the main lines of the house. Some variety adds interest, but numerous roof lines at a variety of slopes present a busy, confused appearance. Strong horizontal lines are usually desirable in a conventional residence to give the appearance of being tied to the ground. Strong vertical lines tend to make a house look tall and unstable.

List the number of materials used as siding. There should never be more than three, and not more than two is preferable. Look at the trim and see if it seems to belong with the house or is just stuck on as ornamentation.

Unity is as important as simplicity. The house should appear as a unit, not as a cluster of unrelated components. Windows and trim should be in keeping with the style of the house. Windows should be of the same type and of a very limited number of sizes. Shutters should be 1/2 the width of the window so that when closed they cover the window. Porches and garages should blend with the house, rather than appear as attachments.

If you see a dwelling as unattractive at first glance, consider how paint and landscaping may affect it. Even an attractive house will not look good without being properly painted or landscaped.

REHABILITATION

Now that you have an insight into what you should look for while searching for your home, I will take you through the rehabilitation of a basic house so that you can get some ideas as to how you should remodel your home. The rehabilitation will carry you through the major sections of renovating all phases, from the development of a plan to the installation of bathtub framing. It is designed to help you begin making important decisions as to how much of the work you wish to do completely yourself, and what changes you might want to make in any given area.

It will also provide you time to go to the lumber yard and get estimates on lumber, and to hardware and other suppliers for cost estimates on any other fixture you may use. Take notes as you read through this hypothetical rehabilitation process; they will help when you begin your project.

I will discuss rehabilitation in a way that will be applicable to a broad range of individual interests and capabilities. Much will depend on you: how much you intend doing yourself, and how much you want to learn about each individual phase of renovating your low budget home. Keep in mind, however, that the major way you are going to be able to renovate a home on a low budget is by doing it yourself. The more you can do, the less labor you pay out, which means the more you will have to spend on the extras that otherwise you might forego.

There will doubtless be many areas, regardless of how adept you are at doing it yourself, where you will save time, money, and energy by calling in outside help. It can be done on a piecemeal basis.

Maybe you would want to put up new siding, but not paint; maybe you can tackle the electrical wiring, yet do not wish to hang all the fixtures; all you need to do then is subcontract for the areas you don't wish to handle yourself, especially updating critical structural items or making major structural changes.

With the proper help, remodeling can be much easier. It is up to you to choose which is best for your needs. Whether you choose to do all or part, though, the more you learn about the overall aspects with which you will be faced, the easier will be the job.

Developing the Plan

You have by now found your house to remodel. You are ready to plan the improvements—the layout (if you plan to change it), additional space, modern conveniences, and the overall appearance inside and out. Special attention and effort should be given toward achieving a proper layout for your particular family. Each house, each family is an individual entity.

Remember that whatever you do your remodeled home will make it yours for as long as you live in it. By keeping your budget low now and by doing as much of the work as you can yourself, your home, when it is completely refurbished, will be one which has increased in value besides being convenient and liveable for as long as you own it.

Before making any changes, if you are doing all or part of the work yourself, obtain a building permit from the local building department. One is required in most areas of the country.

Regardless of the plan you eventually choose, it is desirable to provide separate zones for various family activities and to provide good traffic circulation through and between areas. Naturally, if you are remodeling an older home you will need to compromise. Inability to fully satisfy your individual goals should not prevent restoration.

Area Living

In many families with young children one section of the house can be centered on the adults and the other on the children. This holds true with both privacy and recreational areas.

Regardless of how you decide to zone your house, each zone should be located for good relationship to outdoor areas. If outdoor living in the backyard is desirable, perhaps the living room should be at the back of the house. The working zone should have good access to the garage, the dining room, and outdoor work areas. The main entrance to the house should have good access to the driveway or usual guest parking area, which may be on either the front or side of the house. In deciding where to locate rooms and entrances, past arrangements should not be binding, but consider convenience in the particular situation.

Traffic Circulation

Traffic circulation is one of the most important aspects in the layout of the house. Ideally there should be no traffic through any room, but this is difficult to accomplish in the living and work areas. You can, however, keep traffic from cutting through the middle of the room. Many older homes have doors centered in the wall of a room; which not only

directs traffic through the middle of the room, but also cuts the wall space in half, making furniture arrangements difficult.

Study the plan to see where a door might be moved from the middle of a wall to a corner of the room; however, movement of doors is not the easiest job and should be limited in a moderate renovation program. Also consider where doors might be eliminated to prevent traffic through a room. Figure 1-11 shows an improved layout through the relocation of doors.

Changing Partitions

Changing partitions is one way of making rooms into more desirable sizes. It is not difficult to do if the partition is not load bearing, and plumbing, electrical, or heating services are not concealed in the partition. It is possible to move even load-bearing partitions by adding a beam to support the ceiling where the partition is removed.

To determine whether a partition is load bearing or not:

—Check the span direction of ceiling joists.

—If joists are parallel to the partition, the

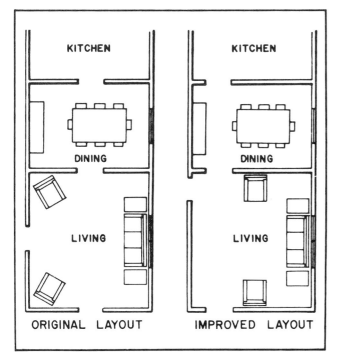

KITCHEN

KITCHEN

DINING

DINING

LIVING

LIVING

ORIGINAL LAYOUT

IMPROVED LAYOUT

Fig. 1-11. Relocation of the doors directs traffic to one side of the rooms (courtesy USDA Forestry Service).

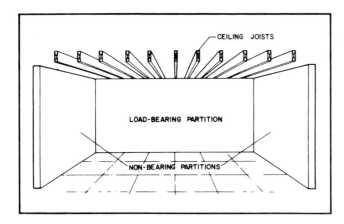

Fig. 1-12. Load-bearing and non-load-bearing partitions. A second-floor load may place a load on any partition (courtesy USDA Forestry Service).

CEILING JOISTS

LOAD-BEARING PARTITION

NON-BEARING PARTITIONS

partition is usually load bearing (Fig. 1-12).

—Check to see if the partition is supporting a second-floor load.

In most construction where the second floor joists are perpendicular to the partition, they do require support; so the partition is load bearing. An exception would occur when trusses span the width of the building; in this case no partition would be load bearing.

If you decide to move partitions, although the removal of a non-bearing partition will not require a structural modification, the wall, ceiling, and floor will require repairs where the partitions inter-sected them. It is, therefore, important that you consider the decision to move any partition in any room before you decide how you plan to finish the walls, floors, and ceiling.

In many older homes, rooms might be smaller than desired; therefore, removing partitions will provide not only more spaciousness but a more airy atmosphere, as well as making furniture placement and rearrangements easier (Fig. 1-13).

In some instances unneeded bedrooms adjacent to the living area can be used to increase needed living space by removing a partition. Removing a partition between a hallway and a room in

Fig. 1-13. The removal of a partition creates better space utilization (courtesy USDA Forestry Service).

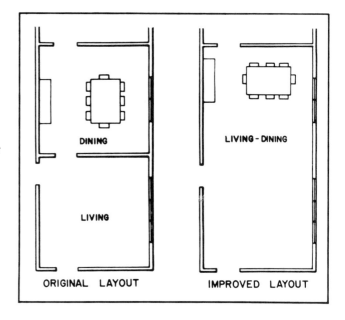

DINING

LIVING

ORIGINAL LAYOUT

LIVING - DINING

IMPROVED LAYOUT

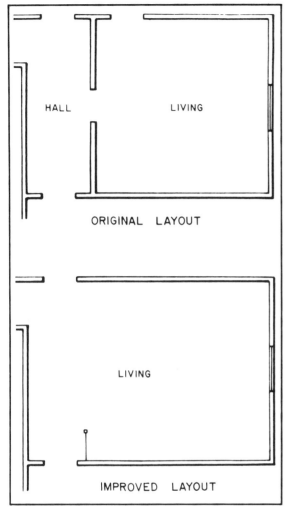

HALL   LIVING

ORIGINAL LAYOUT

LIVING

IMPROVED LAYOUT

Fig. 1-14. The removal of a partition gives a more spacious feeling (courtesy USDA Forestry Service).

the living area gives a more spacious feeling even though traffic continues through the hallway (Fig. 1-14).

Placement of Windows

The general arrangement and appearance of the house is greatly influenced by window placement. Moving windows, however, could be costly, and it involves changes in studs, headers, interior and exterior finish, and trim. For this reason the number of windows relocated should be very limited but, where changes are practical, properly placed windows can enhance the liveability of a house.

Where possible, avoid small windows scattered over a large wall, since they cut up the wall space and make it hard to decorate. Every attempt should be made to group windows into one or two large areas, thus leaving more wall space undisturbed (Fig. 1-15). Where there is a choice of outside walls for window placement, south walls rank first in cold climates. Winter sun shines into the room through a south window and heats the house, and in the summer, when the sun is at a higher angle, even a small overhang shades the window. In extremely warm climates, north windows may be preferable to south windows to avoid heat gain even in the winter. West windows should be avoided as much as possible because the late afternoon sun is so low that there is no way of shading the window.

Windows provide three major functions: they admit daylight and sunlight; they allow ventilation of the house; and they provide a view.

Other points to consider in planning for each of these functions, and some general practices to ensure adequate light, are:

—Provide glass areas in excess of 10 percent of the floor area of each room.

—Group window openings in the wall to eliminate undesirable contrasts in brightness.

—Screen only those parts of the window that open for ventilation.

— Mount draperies, curtain, shades, and other window hangings above the head of the window and to the side of the window frame to free the entire glass area.

To ensure good ventilation:

—Provide ventilation in excess of five percent of the floor area of a room.

—Locate the ventilation openings to take full advantage of prevailing breezes.

—Locate windows to get the best movement of air across the room and within the level where occupants sit or stand.

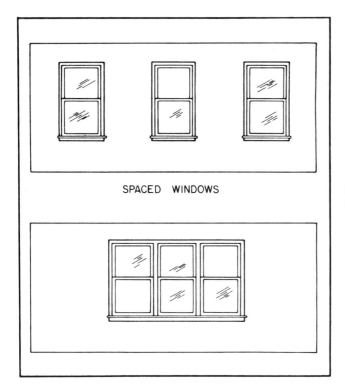

SPACED WINDOWS

Fig. 1-15. Window spacing—spaced and grouped (courtesy USDA Forestry Service).

—Ventilation openings should be in the lower part of the wall unless the window swings inward in a manner to direct air downward.

To provide the best view:

—Minimize obstructions in the line of sight for sitting or standing, depending on the use of the room.

—Determine sill heights on the basis of room use and furniture arrangement.

Closets

It seems no matter how new or old a house is, you never have enough closet space. Remodeling is your opportunity not only to make additional space, but to place closets in more convenient locations. Plan for a coat closet near both the front and rear entrances. A cleaning closet is extremely beneficial in the work area. A linen closet works well in all bedrooms, or put a central closet in the hall to house major linens and individual, under-the-sink closets in the bathrooms.

Look for waste space, such as the end of a hallway or at a wall offset. If the front door opens directly into the living room, a coat closet can sometimes be built beside or in front of the door to form an entry (Fig. 1-16). In a 1 1/2 story house, closets can often be built into the attic space where the headroom is too limited for occupancy.

Closets used for hanging clothes should be at least 24 inches deep, but shallower closets are also practical. Other closets can vary in depth depending on their use, but a depth greater than 24 inches is usually impractical. The exception is the walk-in storage or dressing-room closet, which is very useful and should be considered if space is available. Where existing closets are narrow and deep, hanging rods that can roll out can make them very usable. To make the best use of closet space, plan for a full-front opening.

In many remodeling situations, plywood wardrobes may be more practical than conventional closets. More elaborate closets can be built by dividing the wardrobe into a variety of spaces for various types of storage and installing appropriate doors or drawers.

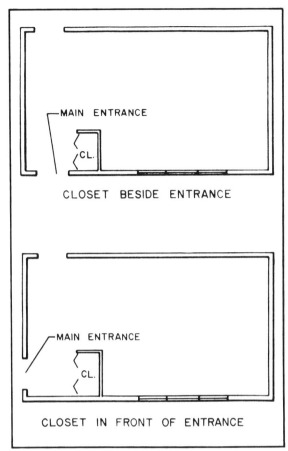

MAIN ENTRANCE

CL.

CLOSET BESIDE ENTRANCE

MAIN ENTRANCE

CL.

CLOSET IN FRONT OF ENTRANCE

Fig. 1-16. Entry formed by a coat closet (courtesy USDA Forestry Service).

Porches

On older homes porches are usually quite narrow, have sloping floors, and cannot easily be enlarged. They do not lend themselves well to the outdoor dining and entertaining usually desired today. You will probably want to completely redo this area and, in fact, expand it from its original environs. There are exciting innovations to be applied, from adding a lean-to greenhouse to closing in the porch with bifold doors for a greenhouse effect.

EXPANSION WITHIN THE HOUSE

Regardless of the size of a house, there always seems to be a need for more space, for storage,

work, recreation, and other informal living. Family rooms are seldom found in older houses. Furthermore, in some houses rooms may be small, or additional bedrooms may be needed. Many older houses have only one bathroom sometimes none; so bathroom additions are often required. Often you can use existing unfinished space, such as the attic, basement, or garage. If expansion into these areas is not practical, an addition can be built directly onto the main structure itself.

Attic

A house with a relatively steep roof slope may have some very usable attic space going to waste. It can be made accessible for storage by the addition of a fold-down staircase. If this space is usable for a living area and has an available stairway, it may be finished to form additional bedrooms, a den, study, or hobby room, or an apartment for a relative.

If the attic is on the third floor, local codes should be checked. Some do not permit use of the third floor for living areas; others require a fire escape.

The headroom requirements for attic rooms are a minimum ceiling height of 7 feet 6 inches over at least half of the room (Fig. 1-17). The space with a lower ceiling height could be used for bunks or other built-in furniture or as storage space.

If there is sufficient headroom only in a narrow strip at the center of the attic, consider building a large shed dormer to increase the usable space (Fig. 1-18). Dormers may be required for windows even though they are not needed to increase space.

It is important that insulation, vapor barriers, and ventilation be considered when finishing attic space, because this space can be particularly hot in the summer. Insulate and install vapor barriers completely around the walls and ceiling of the finished space.

An item often overlooked when expanding into the attic area is the stairway. The usual straight-run stairway requires a space 3 feet wide and at least 11 feet long, as well as a landing at both top and bottom. There must also be a minimum overhead clearance of 6 feet 8 inches at any point on the stairs.

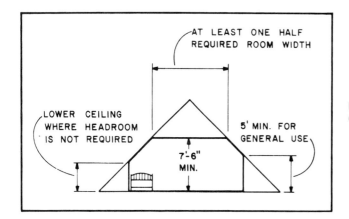

Fig. 1-17. Headroom requirement for attic rooms (courtesy USDA Forestry Service).

Image labels: AT LEAST ONE HALF REQUIRED ROOM WIDTH; LOWER CEILING WHERE HEADROOM IS NOT REQUIRED; 5' MIN. FOR GENERAL USE; 7'-6" MIN.

If space is quite limited, a low budget, aesthetic, wrought iron spiral staircase provides the answer to this problem. Some spiral stairs can be installed in a space as small as 4 feet in diameter; however, code limitations should be checked. Since moving furniture up or down spiral stairways is quite difficult, some other entry for furniture should be provided.

Basement

One of the easiest places for expansion is the basement. There are, as with all areas, conditions which must be met if the basement is to be used for habitable rooms. A habitable room is defined as one which is used for living, sleeping, eating, or cooking. Rooms not included and, therefore, not bound by the requirements of habitable rooms include bathrooms, toilet compartments, closets, halls, storage rooms, laundry and utility rooms, and basement recreation rooms. These rooms can still

be included when remodeling your basement.

The average finish grade elevation at the exterior walls of habitable rooms should not be more than 48 inches above the finish floor. Average ceiling height for habitable rooms should be not less than 7 feet 6 inches. Other basement rooms should have a minimum ceiling height of 6 feet 9 inches.

Dampness in the basement can be partially overcome by installing vapor barriers on the floor and walls, if they were not installed at the time of construction. In an extremely damp basement, plan to use a dehumidifier for summer comfort.

In many basements one main disadvantage is the lack of natural light and view. If the house is on a sloping lot or is graded to permit large basement windows above the ground, the basement is much more usable than when the basement has only a few inches of the top of the wall above the ground. Even the completely sunken basement can have natural light if large area ways are built for windows (Fig.

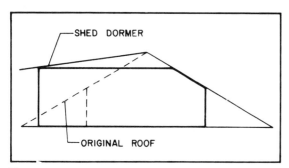

Fig. 1-18. A shed dormer can be built to give additional attic space (courtesy USDA Forestry Service).

Fig. 1-19. A large basement window areaway with sloped sides (courtesy USDA Forestry Service).

1-19). At least one window large enough to serve as a fire exit is recommended and often required by code.

The usefulness of the basement may also be increased by adding a direct outside entrance. It also adds to fire safety by giving an alternate exit, and it is particularly desirable if the basement is to be used as a shop or for storing lawn and garden equipment.

Garage

Another place for expansion is a garage that was built as an integral part of the house. If the garage was well built, the only work is in finishing, which is much less costly than adding to the house. The main consideration is whether the additional finished space is needed more than the garage itself. Much depends on the locale in which you live. For instance, in northern climates, garages are much more in use to store vehicles than in southern climates where, much of the time, people use them as storage rooms or finish them and use them as room additions.

The garage is often adjacent to the kitchen, so that it is an ideal location for a large family room. It could also be used for additional bedrooms and possibly another bathroom.

The walls and ceiling of the garage can be finished in any conventional material. The floor will probably require a vapor barrier, insulation, and a new subfloor. It may be convenient to use the existing garage door opening to install large windows or a series of windows, otherwise the door opening can be completely closed and windows added at other points.

ADDITIONS

After considering all the possibilities of expanding into the attic, basement, or garage, if space requirements are not met the only alternative left is to construct an addition. A house on a small lot may have minimum setback limitations that will present problems. Local zoning and lot restrictions must be checked. The distance from the front of the house to the street is usually kept the same for all houses on a particular street; so expanding to the front may

not be permitted. Often the house also has a minimum setback on the sides, preventing expansion on either side. Thus, the only alternative is to add on behind the house. A house in the country usually can be expanded in any direction without restrictions.

Use the addition for the most critical need. If the need is for more bedrooms, but a much larger living room is also desirable, the present living room can be used as a bedroom and a large living room can be added. If the main requirement is a large modern kitchen, add on a new kitchen and use the old kitchen as a utility room, bathroom, or some other type of living or work space.

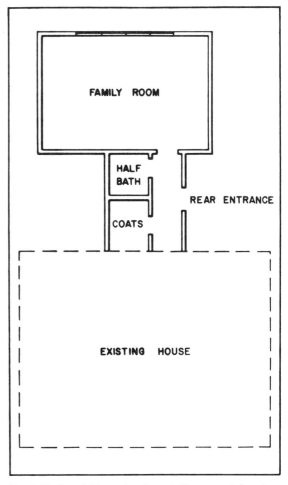

Fig. 1-20. An addition using the satellite concept (courtesy USDA Forestry Service).

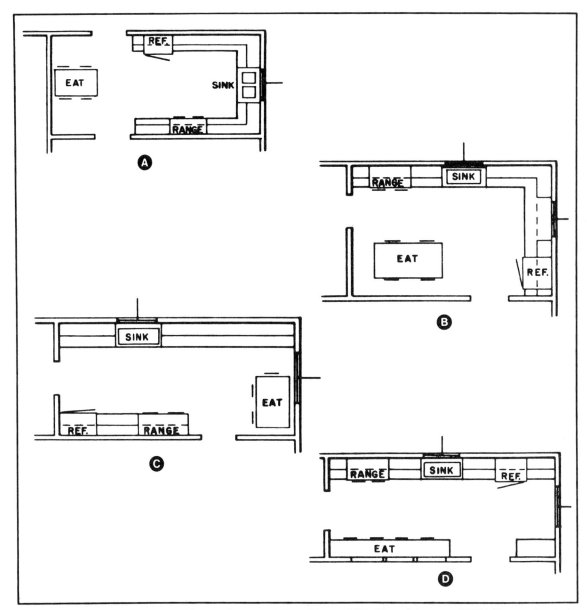

Fig. 1-21. Kitchen arrangements: (A) U-type, (B) L-type, (C) corridor, and (D) side wall (courtesy USDA Forestry Service).

The important thing for good appearance is that the addition be in keeping with the style of the house. Roof lines, siding, and windows should all match the original structure as closely as possible to give the house continuity, rather than giving the appearance that something has just been stuck on it.

One of the most difficult problems is in con-necting the addition to the original house. In some constructions it may be well to use the satellite concept, in which the addition is built as a separate building and connected to the original house by a narrow section which could serve as an entry or mudroom, and which include closets or possibly a bathroom (Fig. 1-20). One disadvantage of this concept is the resulting large exterior wall area with proportionate heat loss and maintenance cost.

REMODELING THE KITCHEN

New appliances and present concepts of convenience have revolutionized the kitchen in recent years. More space is required for the numerous appliances now considered necessary.

The basic movements in food preparation are from the refrigerator to the sink, and then to the range. The four generally recognized arrangements for kitchens are: the "U" and "L" types, the corridor, and side wall (Fig. 1-21). The arrangement selected depends on the amount of space, the shape of the space, and the location of doors. If the kitchen will be entirely new, select the layout you prefer. The work triangle is smallest in the "U" and corridor layouts. The side-wall arrangement is preferred where space is quite limited, and the "L" arrangement is used in a relatively square kitchen that must have a dining table in it.

If kitchen cabinet space is adequate and well arranged, updating the cabinets may be the only desirable change. New doors and drawer fronts can be added to the old cabinet framing. Even refinishing or painting the old cabinets and adding new hardware can do much to improve an old kitchen at little cost.

The single most important improvement will be the countertops which, in older homes, will definitely need to be rejuvenated. Tops could be fabricated and installed by a good custom counter shop. Easy, do-it-yourself tiles which come in 12-inch squares are quick and easy to install in only a few hours. The hardest part of this job is removing the older countertop material. With certain ceramic tiles, however, this procedure is not always necessary; so look for the type that can be placed directly on any surface.

Doorways should be located to avoid traffic through the work triangle. Generally doorways in corners should be avoided, and door swings should avoid conflict with the use of appliances, cabinets, or other doors. If a door would be in the path of travel in a hall or other activity area when it is swing out, consider using a sliding or folding door. The purchase and installation of sliding doors are more expensive, but may be worth the expense in certain situations, and you can stay within your budget if you do the work yourself.

Windows should be adequate to make the kitchen a light, cheerful place. The current trend toward indoor-outdoor living has fostered the *patio kitchen*, with large windows over a counter which extends to the outside to provide an outdoor eating counter. This arrangement is particulary useful in warmer climates, but it is also convenient for summer use in any climate.

Fig. 1-22. An island counter divides the kitchen and family room (courtesy USDA Forestry Service).

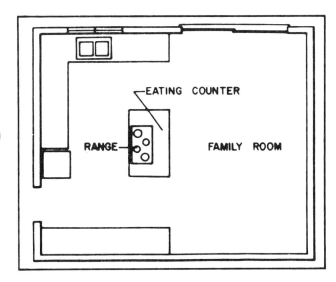

EATING COUNTER

RANGE

FAMILY ROOM

The placement of the sink in relation to windows is a matter of individual preference. Keep in mind, however, that installing the sink along an interior plumbing partition is usually less costly than on an outside wall.

If the kitchen is quite large, it may be convenient to use part as a family room. The combined kitchen-family room concept can also be met by removing a partition to expand the kitchen or by adding on a large room. One method of arranging work space conveniently in such a room is by using an island counter (Fig. 1-22) which can also serve as an eating counter for informal dining.

ADDING A BATH

Improved bathroom facilities should be one of the main considerations in the planning stages of remodeling. There should be plans to add a bath where there is none, and a half bath or second bath should be considered for houses with only one bath.

It is often quite difficult to locate a convenient area in an older home to add a bath. Adding a room especially for this purpose, is of course, possible, yet seldom a good solution because it is usually desirable to have access to the bath from a bedroom hallway. A half bath near the main entrance or in the work area is desirable. One consideration in locating a bath economically is to keep all piping runs as short as possible. Also, all fixtures on one plumbing wall can use a common vent.

One prevalent mistake in adding a bath in an older house has been to place it in any unused space without regard to convenience. They have been placed in what was once the pantry, a large closet, or under a stairway. This usually means the only access to the bathroom is totally removed from the bedroom area. If you are buying an older home where this mistake has been made, while it would

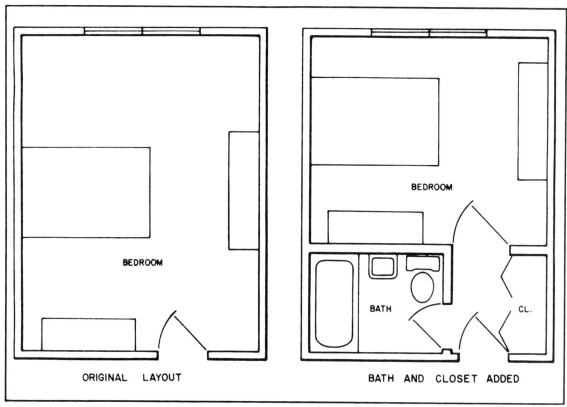

Fig. 1-23. A portion of a large bedroom can be used to add a bath (courtesy USDA Forestry Service).

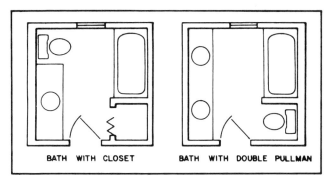

Fig. 1-24. Increase size to provide space for a closet or double sink. Note that plumbing is on two walls in these drawings (courtesy USDA Forestry Service).

BATH WITH CLOSET   BATH WITH DOUBLE PULLMAN

not be budget wise to tear out the obvious error, it would be feasible to simply add another bath in a good location.

In a house with large bedrooms, a portion of one bedroom can be used for a bath (Fig. 1-23). Such a bedroom should be at least 16 feet in one dimension so that it will still be no less than 10 feet in the least dimension after the bath is built. If the bedrooms are small and all are needed, you may have no choice except to build an addition. If, however, you don't need a lot of little bedrooms, which often has been the case in older homes, it may be advantageous to make a small bedroom into one or even two baths and add on another bedroom. In a 1 1/2-story house you can add a bath in the area under the shed dormer. Remember, however, that the wall containing the plumbing must have a wall below it on the first floor through which piping can run. This situations applies to 2-story houses also.

While larger bathrooms are certainly more desirable, the minimum size for a bathroom is 5 feet by 7 feet, and larger sizes are certainly more advantageous. Increasing the size even slightly makes the bathroom less cramped and could provide space for a storage closet for towels, cleaning equipment, or supplies (Fig. 1-24).

If your plan is for only one bath, (highly unlikely in today's bathroom concepts), consider making it in compartments for use by more than one person at a time (Fig. 1-25). Two baths are more economical to build and really help on your bathroom budget since the fixtures can be installed back to back (Fig. 1-26), but do not sacrifice convenience of location to accomplish this objective. Bathrooms built on both floors of a two-story house are most economically built with the second-floor bath directly over the first-floor bath.

Bathroom fixtures vary in size, style, and

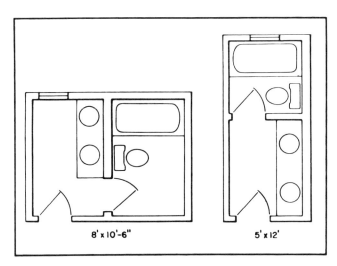

8' x 10'-6"   5' x 12'

Fig. 1-25. Compartmented bathroom (courtesy USDA Forestry Service).

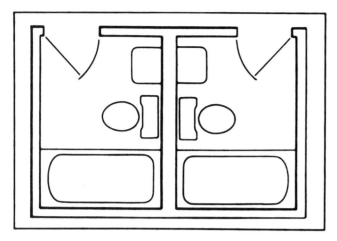

Fig. 1-26. Two bathrooms with economical back-to-back arrangement (courtesy USDA Forestry Service).

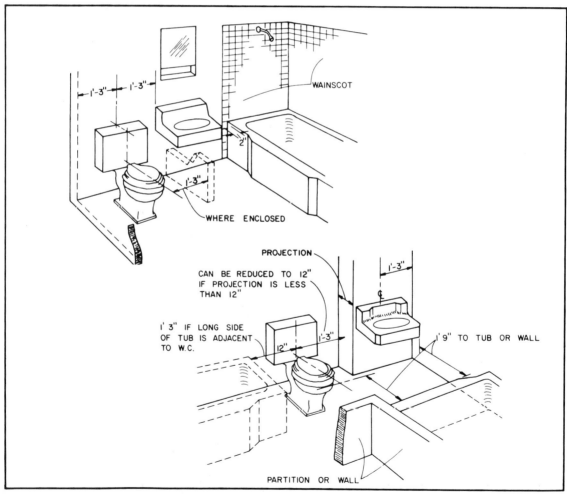

WAINSCOT

1'-3" 1'-3"

2"

1'-3"

WHERE ENCLOSED

PROJECTION

CAN BE REDUCED TO 12"
IF PROJECTION IS LESS
THAN 12"

1' 3" IF LONG SIDE
OF TUB IS ADJACENT
TO W.C.

12" 1'-3"

1'-3"

1' 9" TO TUB OR WALL

PARTITION OR WALL

Fig. 1-27. Recommended dimensions for fixture spacing (courtesy USDA Forestry Service).

shape; so detailed dimensions will be needed to work with your building supplier. Minimum dimensions between and around fixtures are shown in Fig. 1-27.

APPEARANCE

Many new homes today copy styles of the past in an attempt to capture the dignity of the two-story Colonial, the quaintness of the Victorian house, the charm of the old English cottage, the look of solid comfort of the Midwestern farmhouse, or the rustic informality of the ranch house. If the older dwelling you have purchased possesses any of these or other qualities, you may want to avoid any change of appearance. Keep any changes, such as adding windows, doors, and covering materials, in character with the original design.

There should be a roof overhang of at least 1 square foot and preferably 2 feet all around the house to protect the siding and windows, as well as to give a good appearance. If this overhang is lacking, consider adding an overhang during your remodeling (Fig. 1-28). It should pay for itself in reduced maintenance in addition to improving the appearance of the house.

For the house that is exceptionally plain, one of the best places to add interest is at the main entrance. It is the natural focal point for the house, and an attractive door, a raised planter, or interesting steps can do much to enhance overall appearance. One caution is to keep the entrance in scale and in character with the house, and to avoid an overly grand appearance.

The house that appears too tall can often be improved by adding strong horizontal lines at porch or carpet roofs. Painting the first and second story different colors can also produce a lower appearance. Color can also affect the apparent size of the house; a light color will make it appear much smaller.

Consider interior appearance before finishing materials are selected. The most convenient materials do not always produce the desired character. Ceiling tile that is attractive in a recreation room may not be suitable in a living room. Paneling comes in various types and qualities, which result

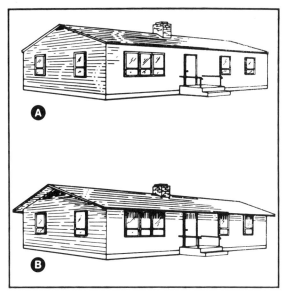

Fig. 1-28. Improved appearance can be achieved by adding a roof overhang (courtesy USDA Forestry Service).

in major differences in the dignity and charm of a room. Keep the ultimate desired effect in mind as plans are made.

RECONDITIONING DETAILS

You are now in a position to begin actual renovation. In locations where termites are a particular problem (Fig. 1-29) and are prevalent in and around the house, soil poisoning may be advisable before you begin work. Contact your local County Extension Office or your local termite control company for advice.

The order in which components of the house are remodeled will vary with each individual and each situation, but there is a primary step applying to all: making sure that the house and floor system is level. A level form from which to work is essential to a good remodeling project. Before any interior work is begun, roof repairs and changes in windows and exterior doors should be made, and all changes in plumbing, electrical wiring, and heating should be completed.

General information useful in reconditioning wood frame construction follows.

☐ Moisture content of framing material

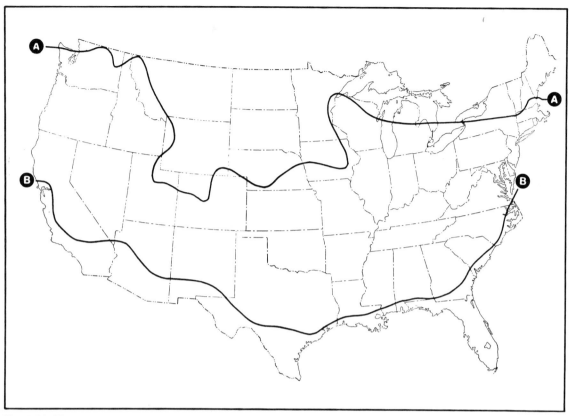

Fig. 1-29. The northern limit of damage in the United States by subterranean termites (line A); and by dry-wood, or nonsubterranean, termites (line B) (courtesy USDA Forestry Service).

should not exceed 19 percent, and a maximum of 15 percent would be better in most areas of the United States.

☐ Recommended moisture content for interior finish woodwork varies from 6 to 11 percent depending on your locale. A map showing the average moisture contents is shown in Fig. 1-30. Plywood should be of the exterior type anywhere it will be exposed to moisture during construction or use.

☐ Recommended nailing for assembly of framing and application of covering materials is listed in Table 1-1. Sizes of common nails are shown in Fig. 1-31.

Soil Poisoning

Crawl-Space Houses. To treat buildings with crawl spaces for protection against insects, dig trenches adjacent to and around all piers and pipes and along the sides of foundation walls (Fig. 1-32). Around solid concrete foundations the trenches should be 6 to 8 inches deep and wide. A chemical is poured into the trench, and as the excavated soil is put back into the trench it also is treated. The soil is tamped and the trench filled to a level above the surrounding soil to provide good drainage away from the foundation.

In brick, hollow-block, or concrete foundations that have cracked, dig the trench to, but not below, the footing. As the trench is refilled, treat the soil. Treat voids in hollow-block foundations by applying the chemical to the voids at or near the footing.

Slab Construction. Treatment of soil under slab-on-ground construction is difficult. One method consists of drilling holes about a foot apart through the concrete slab adjacent to all cracks and

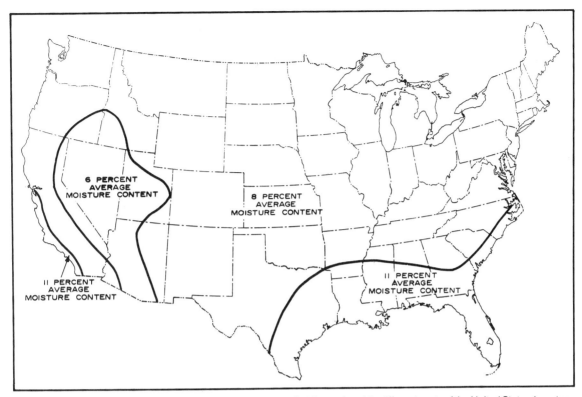

Fig. 1-30. Recommended average moisture content for interior finish woodwork in different parts of the United States (courtesy USDA Forestry Service).

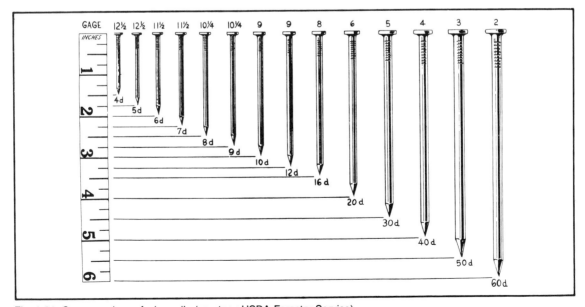

Fig. 1-31. Common sizes of wire nails (courtesy USDA Forestry Service).

TABLE 1-1. NAILING THE FRAMING AND SHEATHING.

Joining	Nailing Method	Nails		
		Number	Size	Placement
Header to joist	End nail	3	16d	—
Joist to sill or girder	Toenail	2	10d or 8d	—
Header and stringer joist to sill	Toenail	—	10d	16 in. on center
Bridging to joist	Toenail each end	2	8d	—
Ledger strip to beam, 2 in. thick	—	3	16d	At each joist
Subfloor, boards:				
1 by 6 in. and smaller	—	2	8d	To each joist
1 by 8 in.	—	3	8d	To each joist
Subfloor, plywood:				
At edges	—	—	8d	6 in. on center
At intermediate joists	—	—	8d	8 in. on center
Subfloor (2 by 6 in., T&G) to joist or girder	Blind nail (casing) and face nail	2	16d	—
Soleplate to stud, horizontal assembly	End nail	2	16d	At each stud
Top plate to stud	End nail	2	16d	—
Stud to soleplate	Toenail	4	8d	—
Soleplate to joist or blocking	Face nail	—	16d	16 in. on center
Doubled studs	Face nail, stagger	—	10d	16 in. on center
End stud of intersecting wall to exterior wall stud	Face nail	—	16d	16 in. on center
Upper top plate to lower top plate	Face nail	—	16d	16 in. on center
Upper top plate, laps, and intersections	Face nail	2	16d	—
Continuous header, two pieces, each edge	—	—	12d	12 in. on center
Ceiling joist to top wall plates	Toenail	3	8d	—
Ceiling joist laps at partition	Face nail	4	16d	—
Rafter to top plate	Toenail	2	8d	—
Rafter to ceiling joist	Face nail	5	10d	—
Rafter to valley or hip rafter	Toenail	3	10d	—
Ridge board to rafter	End nail	3	10d	—
Rafter to rafter through ridge board	Toenail	4	8d	—
	Edge nail	1	10d	—
Collar beam to rafter:				
2-in. member	Face nail	2	12d	—
1-in. member	Face nail	3	8d	—
1-in. diagonal let-in brace to each stud and plate (four nails at top)	—	2	8d	—
Built-up corner studs:				
Studs to blocking	Face nail	2	10d	Each side
Intersecting stud to corner studs	Face nail	—	16d	12 in. on center
Built-up girders and beams, three or more members	Face nail	—	20d	32 in. on center, each side
Wall sheathing:				
1 by 8 in. or less, horizontal	Face nail	2	8d	At each stud
1 by 6 in. or greater, diagonal	Face nail	3	8d	At each stud
Wall sheathing, vertically applied plywood:				
3/8 in. and less thick	Face nail	—	6d	6-in. edge and 12-in. intermediate
1/2 in. and over thick	Face nail	—	8d	
Wall sheathing, vertically applied fiberboard:				
1/2 in. thick	Face nail	—	(1)	3-in. edge and 6-in intermediate
25/32 in. thick	Face nail	—	(2)	
Roof sheathing, board, 4-, 6-, 8-in. width	Face nail	2	8d	At each rafter
Roof sheathing, plywood				
3/8 in. and less thick	Face nail	—	6d	6-in. edge and 12-in. intermediate
1/2 in. and over thick	Face nail	—	8d	

[1] 1 1/2-in. roofing nail.
[2] 1 3/4-in. roofing nail.

expansion joints, and injecting a chemical into the soil beneath the slab. Another method is to drill through the perimeter foundation walls from the outside and force the chemical just beneath the slab along the inside of the foundation and along all cracks and expansion joints.

Basement Houses. Application of soil poisoning for basement houses is much the same as for the slab-on-ground and crawl-space construction (Fig. 1-33). Treat the basement floor in the same way as for a slab-on-ground house.

Precaution. Chemicals for termite control are poisonous to people and animals. Be sure to use them properly and safely.

—Carefully read all labels and follow directions.

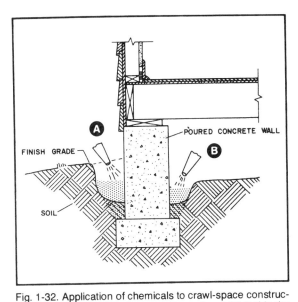

Fig. 1-32. Application of chemicals to crawl-space construction soil treatment: (A) along outside wall and (B) inside the foundation wall (courtesy USDA Forestry Service).

—Store insecticides in labeled containers out of reach of children and animals.

—Dispose of empty containers.

Fig. 1-33. Application of chemicals to the soil in and around a full basement: (A) along the outside of the foundation (B) pipe and rod hole from the bottom of the trench to the top of the footing to aid chemical distribution, (C) drill holes for the treatment of fill or soil beneath a concrete floor in the basement, and (D) position of the concrete slab (courtesy USDA Forestry Service).

—Wash contaminated parts of your body with warm, soapy water immediately after exposure.

Cracks in Concrete Foundation

Minor hairline cracks frequently occur in concrete walls during its curing process and usually require no repair. Open cracks should be repaired, but the type of repair depends on whether the crack is active or dormant and whether waterproofing is necessary. One of the simplest methods of determining if the crack is active is to place a mark at each end of the crack and check in the future to see if the crack extends beyond the marks.

If the crack is dormant, it can be repaired by routing and sealing. Routing is accomplished by following along the crack with a concrete saw or chipping with hand tools to enlarge the crack near the concrete surface. The crack is first routed 1/4 inch or more wide and deep; then the routed joint is rinsed clean and allowed to dry. A joint sealer such as an epoxy-cement compound should then be applied in accordance with the manufacturer's instructions.

Working cracks require an elastic sealant

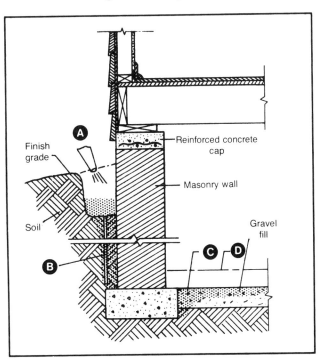

which should also be applied in accordance with the manufacturer's instructions. Sealants vary greatly in elasticity; so a good-quality sealant that will remain pliable should be used. The minimum depth of routing for these sealants is 3/4 to 1 inch, and the width is about the same. The elastic material can then conform with movement of the crack. Strip sealants which can be applied to the surface are also available, but these protrude from the surface and may be objectionable.

Crumbling Mortar. Crumbled mortar joints in masonry foundations or piers should be repaired. First chip out all loose mortar and brush thoroughly to remove all dust and loose particles. Before applying new mortar, dampen the clean surface so that it will not absorb water from the mixture. Mortar can be purchased premixed. It should have the consistency of putty and should be applied like a caulking material. For a good bond, force the mortar into the crack to contact all depressions; then smooth the surface with a trowel. Provide some protection from sun and wind for a few days to keep the mortar from drying out too fast.

Uneven Settlement. Uneven settlement in a concrete foundation due to poor footings or no footings at all usually damages the foundation to the point that precludes repair. In a pier foundation, the individual pier or piers could be replaced, or, if the

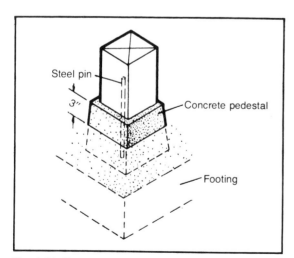

Fig. 1-34. Basement post on a pedestal above the floor (courtesy USDA Forestry Service).

pier has stopped settling, blocking could be added on top of the pier to level the house. In either situation, the girder or joists being supported must be jacked and held in a level position while the repairs are being made.

Basement Posts. Any type of basement post may have settled due to inadequate footings, or wood posts may have deteriorated due to decay or insect damage. To correct either problem, a well-supported jack must be used to raise the floor girder off the post in question. This releveling must be done slowly and carefully to avoid cracking the plaster in the house walls. Steel jack posts are convenient replacements. If a wood post is used, a pedestal should be built to raise the base of the post slightly above the floor surface (Fig. 1-34). This pedestal allows the end of the post to dry out if it becomes wet.

Floor Systems

If an examination of the floor framing reveals decay or insect damage in a limited number of framing members, the members affected must be replaced or the affected sections repaired. Large-scale damage would probably have resulted in classifying the house as not feasible to renovate; it is well, however, to know the basic ways of correcting any damage you find.

Replace damaged members with preservative-treated wood if exposure conditions are severe. To do so, the framing supported by the damaged member must be temporarily supported by jacks in a crawl-space house or jacks with blocking in a basement house. A heavy cross arm on top of the jack will support a width of house of 4 to 6 feet. Where additional support is necessary, more jacks are required. Raise the jacks carefully and slowly and only enough to take the weight off the member that is to be removed. Excessive jacking will pull the building frame out of square. After the new or repaired member is in place, gradually take the weight off the jack and remove it.

Sometimes decay may exist in only a small part of a member, such as at the end of a floor joist supported on a concrete foundation wall, where the wood contacts the concrete. After applying a

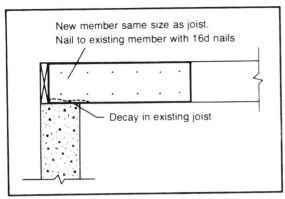

Fig. 1-35. Repair of a joist with decay in the end contacting the foundation (courtesy USDA Forestry Service).

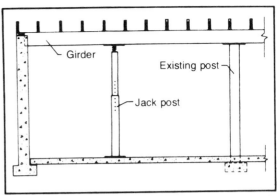

Fig. 1-37. A jack post is used to level a sagging girder in a basement house (courtesy USDA Forestry Service).

brushed-on preservative to the affected area, jack the existing joist into place and nail a short length of new material to the side of the joist (Fig. 1-35).

Leveling the Floor. After the foundation repairs have been properly made, the support points for the floor should be level; however, the floor may still sag. Where the floor joists have sagged excessively, permanent set may have occurred, and little

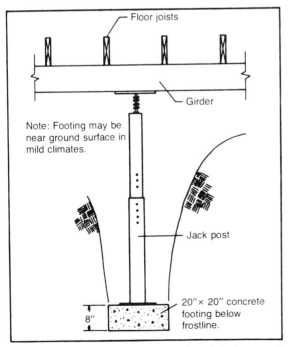

Fig. 1-36. A jack post supports a sagging girder in a crawl-space house (courtesy USDA Forestry Service).

can be done except by replacement of the floor joists. A slight sag can be overcome by nailing a new joist alongside alternate joists in the affected area. If the new joists are slightly bowed, place them crown up. Each joist must be jacked at both ends to force the ends to the same elevation as the existing joist. The same treatment can be used to stiffen springy floors.

Girders that sag excessively should be replaced, since excessive set cannot be removed. Jack posts can be used to level slightly sagged girders or to install intermediate girders, but unless the space is seldom used, or jack posts can be incorporated into a wall, they are generally in the way. Methods for installing jack posts are shown in Figs. 1-36 and 1-37.

When jack posts are used to stiffen a springy floor so that it can carry light loads, they can be set directly on the concrete floor slab. Where they are used to support heavy loads, a steel plate may be needed to distribute the load over a larger area of the floor slab. Do not use jack posts for heavy jacking; use a regular jack to carefully lift the load, and then put the jack post in place.

Eliminating Squeaks. Squeaks in flooring are frequently caused by the relative movement of the tongue of one flooring strip in the groove of the adjacent strip. You can remedy it by applying a small amount of mineral oil to the joints.

Sagging floor joists often pull away from the subfloor and result in excessive deflection of the floor. If this problem is the cause of squeaks,

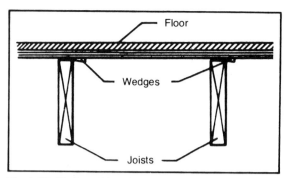

Fig. 1-38. Wedges driven between joists and subfloor stop squeaks (courtesy of USDA Forestry Service).

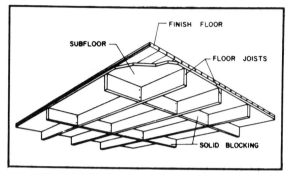

Fig. 1-39. Solid blocking between floor joists where the finished floor is laid parallel to the joist (courtesy USDA Forestry Service).

squeeze construction mastic tape into the open joints. Another remedy is to drive small wedges into the spaces between the joists and sub-floor (Fig. 1-38), but only far enough for a snug fit. This method of repair should be limited to a small area.

Undersized floor joists that deflect excessively are also a major cause of squeaks. The addition of girders to shorten the joint span is the best solution to this problem.

Strip flooring installed parallel to the joists may also deflect excessively. Solid blocking nailed between joists and fitted snugly against the subfloor (Fig. 1-39) will prevent this deflection if installed at relatively close spacing.

One of the most common causes of squeaking

is inadequate nailing. To correct this problem, drive a nail through the face of the flooring board near the tongue edge into the subfloor, preferably also into a joist. Set the nail and fill the hole. A less objectionable method from the standpoint of appearance is to work from under the floor using screws driven through the subfloor into the finished floor. This method will also bring warped flooring into a flat position.

The following chapters will discuss the many facets you will need to address to complete your remodeling. Some must be completed before you move into your home; many can wait until your budget allows for continued renovation, or time permits you to do them.

Chapter 2

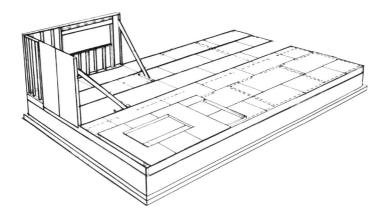

Framing

The guidelines outlined in this chapter apply equally to remodeling or adding on to existing structures and refer continually to the term "house plans." It is important that you have a set of plans. If you are renovating an older dwelling and are unable to locate the original house plans (which is more than likely, especially in much older houses), you should make a good working drawing of the entire structure before you begin renovations. Include in this set of plans the dimensions of all rooms, numbers and placements of windows, and present placements of electrical and plumbing outlets and fixtures.

You need not draw the house plan to "scale." A simple drawing, outlining the exterior and interior dimensions will be invaluable to you as you continue your renovations or additions.

NAILS

On any construction job, the cost of nails is so small, compared with their importance, that they should always be of the best quality. Even though you are renovating on a budget, this is not the place to cut costs! Sizes, or lengths, are indicated by "penny," abbreviated as "d." Lengths of all nails will be the same in a particular penny size, regardless of head or shank configuration. Only the diameter changes. Use nonstaining siding or casing nails to prevent siding from discoloring because of weathering or rusting nails.

Common and Box Nails. Common and box nails are for normal building construction, particularly framing. Smooth box nails of the same penny size will have a smaller diameter than common nails. Since this smaller diameter has less tendency to split the lumber, box nails are recommended for most uses. You also get more box nails per pound, as shown in Table 2-1. Figure 2-1 shows the common and box nails: 16d for general framing, 8d and 10d for toenailing; and 6d and 8d for subfloor, wall sheathing, and roof sheathing. Size depends on the thickness of panel sheathing.

Scaffold Nails. Scaffold, or "double-headed," nails can save you time and trouble in many operations where the fastener must later be removed, as

		Common			Box	
Size	Length (in.)	Diameter (in.)	No. per Pound	Diameter (in.)	No. per Pound	
4d	1 1/2	.102	316	.083	473	
5d	1 3/4	.102	271	.083	406	
6d	2	.115	181	.102	236	
7d	2 1/4	.115	161	.102	210	
8d	2 1/2	.131	106	.115	145	
10d	3	.148	69	.127	94	
12d	3 1/4	.148	63	.127	88	
16d	3 1/2	.165	49	.134	71	
20d	4	.203	31	.148	52	
30d	4 1/2	.220	24	.148	46	
40d	5	.238	18	.165	35	

TABLE 2-1. NAIL SIZE AND NUMBER PER POUND.

in scaffolding, bracing, concrete forms, and temporary fastening during framing layout. Sizes 8d and 10d are most common for scaffolds, bracing, and any temporary fastening that must be later removed.

Casing and Finishing Nails. When you do not want large nailheads visible, such as in interior and exterior trim nailing, interior paneling installation, and exterior siding application, use casing and finish nails. To further reduce visibility, both may

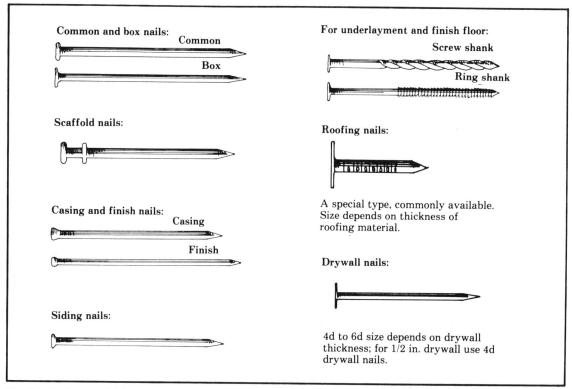

Fig. 2-1. Casing and finishing nails (courtesy American Plywood Association).

be driven deeper into the material with a nail-set and the holes filled with wood filler of matching color. Sizes 4d, 6d, and 8d are most common for exterior and interior trim and paneling where large nailheads should not show. Use casing nails for exterior siding.

Nonstaining Nails. For long service and freedom from staining, use nonstaining nails. They are necessary where exterior exposure is combined with the need for good appearance; for example, in siding, fascias, soffits, exterior trim, and wood decks. Hot-dipped, or hot-tumbled, galvanized is the most common nail coating, and offers good protection against staining. Nails also are made of metals or alloys not subject to corrosion, including aluminum, bronze, and stainless steel.

Deformed-Shank Nails. A variety of deformed-shank nail patterns, such as screw shank, ring shank, and barbed, are available. These all have greater holding power than smooth nails. Often, you may use a smaller size deformed-shank nail and still do the job satisfactorily. Ring-shank nails should always be used to install panel underlayment or subfloor/underlayment. Screw-shank nails should be used for wood strip flooring.

Roofing Nails. A special type of nail, commonly available, is the roofing nail. The needed size depends on the thickness of the roofing material.

Drywall Nails. Drywall nails come in sizes from 4d to 6d, depending on the drywall thickness. For 1/2-inch drywall, use 4d drywall nails.

FRAME THE WALLS

Wall framing refers to the vertical studs and horizontal members, including bottom and top plates, and window and door headers, of both exterior and interior walls that support the ceiling and roof. Wall framing in conventional house construction is generally of 2-×-4 lumber, with the exception of headers over windows and doors in walls that bear loads, which may be 2 × 6s or larger, or two or more 2 × 4s nailed together.

Before selecting or cutting wall-framing materials, check your house plan to determine whether the dimensions are drawn to the middle or the outside of the stud. Also check dimensions given for roughing in door and window openings against the millwork manufacturer's installation recommendations.

The wall framing described in this section is called *platform construction*. Wall sections are constructed flat on the subfloor when tilted up into position. The length of exterior wall sections must be determined by the number of people you have available to assist you in raising walls. If only two men are on hand, it may be wise to frame sections no longer than 24 feet.

☐ Lay out and mark on the subfloor the location of all exterior and interior walls. Then select 2-×-4 bottom plates for all exterior walls and cut them to length. Temporarily nail them in place to the subfloor, with the outside edge of the 2 × 4 flush with the edge of the floor header joist. Use 8d scaffold nails, since they permit easy withdrawal.

☐ Position the bottom of all interior wall partitions, again tacking them in place with 8d scaffold nails. By laying out all walls, both interior and exterior, you can identify all wall intersections and determine any special framing required (Fig. 2-2).

☐ While the bottom plates are still tacked in place, mark the location of all major openings on all plates. Make sure it's a rough, clear opening. Then lay out all stud locations, which are generally 16 inches on center. Start on one exterior corner, and measure and mark the locations of each stud (Fig. 2-3). Remember that most structural wood sheathing and siding panels are 48 inches wide; so the dimension from the outside of the corner to the centerline of the first stud from that corner should be 16 inches. Extra studs needed at wall intersec-

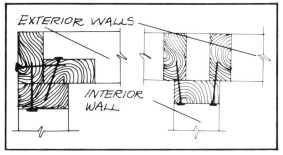

Fig. 2-2. Exterior/interior walls (courtesy American Plywood Association).

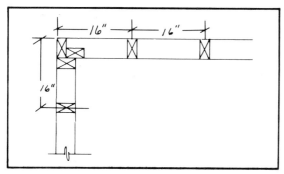

Fig. 2-3. Stud markings (courtesy American Plywood Association).

tions and those required to carry special loads at door openings should also be noted and marked.

□ After all bottom plates are marked, cut a second set of plates and mark them exactly like the bottom plates. These plates will be the lower of the doubled top plates.

□ Prepare to cut all wall-height stud framing members. To the floor-to-ceiling height dimension noted on your drawing plan, add about 1 inch for underlayment and ceiling material thickness. Subtract about 3 1/2 inches for three 2-×-4 plate thicknesses.

Measure and cut one stud to the proper length, and mark it as a stud pattern. Cut all the other studs

to this pattern to ensure standard stud height for all exterior and interior walls. You can also use precut studs, if you prefer. Then cut all cripples, jack studs, and headers, each time checking for proper length. Where several pieces of the same length are required, as in cripples, always use the same member as the pattern.

□ First assemble exterior wall sections for the long wall. Move the interior wall plates and exterior wall plates out of the way to clear the floor for working space. Make sure you have marked their location on both the plate and subfloor for later reference.

Remove the scaffold nails from the exterior wall bottom plates. Tip on edge and nail in place with 16d nails driven diagonally through the plate into the panel subfloor (Fig. 2-4). Nailing the bottom plate to the subfloor will keep the completed wall section from sliding off the floor deck when you tilt up the wall. Make sure the 16d nails are not driven into the edges of the 2 × 4 where a stud will be located or into a floor joist. Move the top plate of the same wall parallel to the bottom plate, a stud height apart.

□ Locate all full-height studs and nail them in place by driving nails through the bottom and top plates into the ends of the studs—two 16d nails in

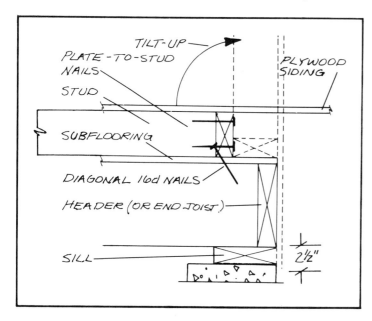

Fig. 2-4. A tilted wall (courtesy American Plywood Association).

each plate at each stud. You will add another top plate after the wall is erected. Where special wall-intersection framing is required, as at corners and where interior walls will join, nail it in place. Next nail all cripples in place. Then cut and install all bottom and doubled top headers. The following sizes are recommended:

Maximum Span (ft.) 3 1/2 - 5, 6 1/2 - 8
Header Size (in.) 2 × 6, 2 × 8, 2 × 10, 2 × 12

☐ Check the wall for squareness by measuring the diagonals from corner to corner. When the wall is square, the two diagonals will be exactly the same length.

☐ You have several options on the next installation step. The easiest is to apply American Plywood Association (APA) 303 plywood siding directly to framing, called the *APA Sturd-I-Wall or single-wall system,* or to apply APA-rated sheathing directly to framing while framing is still flat on the floor, called *double-wall construction.* If you elect to use Sturd-I-Wall construction, remember to allow the siding to extend far enough beyond the top plate to cover the additional top plate that is added after you tilt up the wall. Figure 2-4 shows the amount to allow at the bottom.

With either single or double walls, attach the 4-×-8 sheets according to recommended nailing schedules. Applying panels before you raise the wall ensures that wall squareness is maintained during the raising.

☐ Before raising the wall sections, cut several 1-×-4 or 1-×-6 diagonal braces that, once the wall is upright, can be used to attach the wall framing temporarily to the subfloor, to prevent the wall from tipping over (Fig. 2-5).

☐ Erect the wall sections, starting with the long wall. As you tilt the sections into place, the diagonally driven 16d nails will withdraw gradually from the floor. Use 16d nails spaced 16 inches on center to secure the wall sections to the floor; then build and raise the shorter end walls. Nail them to the floor and to the side walls at the corners.

☐ Frame the interior walls. Interior partitions are laid out exactly like exterior walls except that no sheathing or siding is attached. Interior walls should be braced diagonally during raising and, where necessary, nailed to exterior walls at their intersection.

When all walls are in place, apply a second layer of top plates throughout. Make sure that butt joints in the two layers are offset, and that the double plates are properly lapped to tie together all intersection walls (Fig. 2-6). Wall stud spacing may be 24 inches on center.

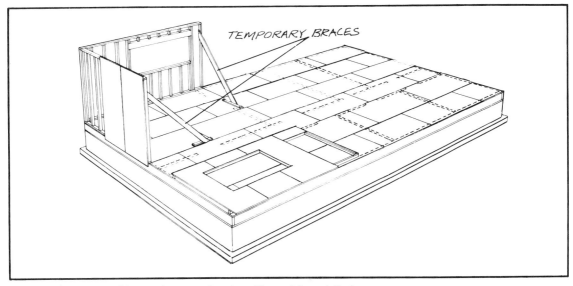

Fig. 2-5. Temporary wall braces (courtesy American Plywood Association).

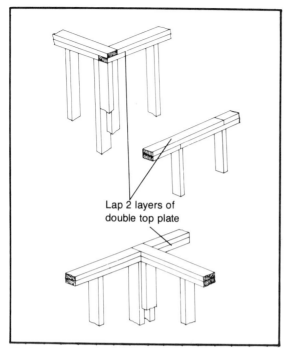

Fig. 2-6. Double plates (courtesy American Plywood Association).

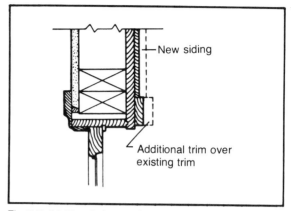

Fig. 2-7. Additional trim member over siding (courtesy USDA Forestry Service).

SIDING

The solution for wood siding problems often involves corrective measures in other components of the house. Failure of paint is frequently not the fault of the siding but can be attributed to moisture moving out through the wall or to water washing down the face of the wall. Corrective measures are made by vapor barriers and roof systems; siding may then only need to be refinished by painting.

Some of the permanent sidings that require no painting may cause serious difficulty in time by trapping moisture in the wall, thus creating a decay hazard. You should, therefore, have a siding that will let water vapor escape from inside the wall.

If new horizontal wood or nonwood siding is used, it will probably be best to remove old siding. Vertical board and panel-type siding can, however, be successfully applied over old siding.

The main difficulty in applying new siding over existing siding is in adjusting the window and door trim to compensate for the added wall thickness. The window sills on most houses extend far enough

beyond the siding so that new siding should not affect them; however, the casing may be nearly flush with the siding and so require some type of extension.

One method of extending the casing is by adding an additional trim member over the existing casing (Fig. 2-7); a wider drip cap may also be required. The drip cap could be replaced, or it could be reused with blocking behind it to hold it out from the walls a distance equal to the new siding thickness (Fig. 2-8).

Another method of extending the casing is to add a trim member to the edge of the existing casing

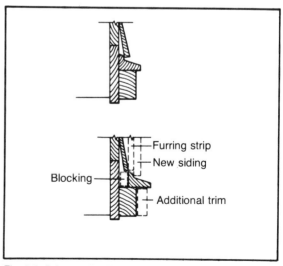

Fig. 2-8. Drip cap detail (courtesy USDA Forestry Service).

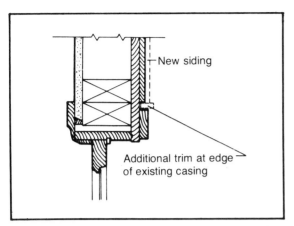

— New siding

Additional trim at edge
of existing casing

Fig. 2-9. Top view of a window casing (courtesy USDA Forestry Service).

and perpendicular to it, (Fig. 2-9). A wider drip cap will also be required. Exterior door trim can be extended by the same technique as used for the window trim.

Any of the conventional siding materials can be used for renovation, but some may be better than others; so check carefully at your lumberyard before you purchase it. Panel-type siding is probably one of the simplest to install and one of the most versatile. It can be applied over most surfaces, and will help to smooth out any unevenness in the existing walls. Nonwood sidings, such as aluminum, steel, or vinyl, are available in a variety of styles and colors.

Panel Siding

Panel siding is available in plywood, hardwood, and particleboard, as well as numerous nonwood materials. The most popular of these materials are probably plywood and hardboard. This chapter will explain how to install APA Sturd-I-Wall and siding over sheathing. Always specify the exterior type for both. The hardboard must be tempered. The grade of plywood depends on the quality of the finished surface you desire.

Plywood panel siding is available in a variety of textures and patterns. Sheets are simple to apply and finish by either brush painting or roller painting, although brush painting is recommended. Sheets are 4 feet wide and are often available in

lengths of 8, 9, and 10 feet on special order. Rough-textured plywood is particularly suited to finishing with water-repellent preservative stains. Smooth-surfaced plywood can be stained, but it will not absorb as much stain as rough-textured plywood, and, therefore, the finish will not be as long lasting. Paper-overlaid plywood is particularly good when you want a paint finish. The paper overlay not only provides a very smooth surface, but also minimizes expansion and contraction from moisture changes.

Most textures can be purchased with vertical grooves. The most popular spacings of grooves are 2, 3, and 8 inches. Battens are often used with plain panels. They are nailed over each joint between panels and they can be nailed over each stud to produce a board-and-batten effect.

In new construction, plywood applied directly over framing should be at least 3/8 inch thick for 16-inch stud spacing and 1/2 inch thick for 24-inch stud spacing. Grooved plywood is normally 5/8 inch thick with 3/8- × -1/4-inch deep grooves.

For installation over existing siding or sheathing, thinner plywood can be used; however, most of the available sidings will be in the thicknesses just listed. Nail the plywood around the perimeter and at each intermediate stud, using galvanized or other rust-resistant nails spaced 7 to 8 inches apart. Be sure the nails are longer than the ones you used for applying siding directly to studs.

Some plywood has shiplap joints. They should be treated with water-repellent preservatives, and the siding should be nailed at each side of the joint. See Fig. 2-10(A). Square-edge butt joints between plywood panels should be caulked with a sealant with the plywood nailed at each side of the joint. See Fig. 2-10(B). Where battens are used over the joint and at intermediate studs, nail them with 8d galvanized nails spaced 12 inches apart. Longer nails may be required where thick siding or sheathing must be penetrated. Nominal 1- × -2 inch battens are commonly used.

If existing siding on gable ends is flush with the siding below the gable, you will need to use furring strips when you apply panel siding so that the new siding at the gable extend over the siding below it

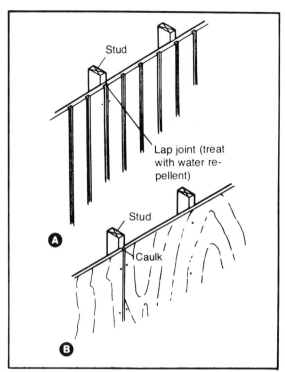

Fig. 2-10. Joints of plywood siding: (A) shiplap joint, (B) square-edge joint.

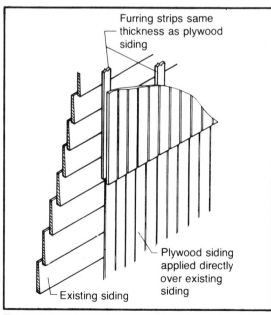

Fig. 2-11. Application of plywood siding at a gable end (courtesy USDA Forestry Service).

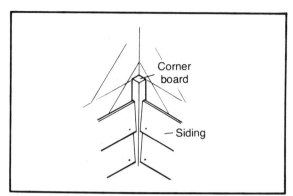

Fig. 2-12. Corner board for application of horizontal siding at the interior corner.

(Fig. 2-11). Furring must be the same thickness as the new siding applied below the gable. Nail a furring strip over the siding or sheathing to each stud and apply the siding over the furring strips the same way as you applied it directly to studs.

Plywood siding can be purchased with factory-applied coatings that are relatively maintenance free.

Hardboard siding is also available in panels 4 feet wide and up to 16 feet long. It is 1/4 inch thick, but may be thicker when grooved. Hardboard generally is factory primed, and finished coats of paint are applied after installation.

Corners are finished by butting the panel siding against corner boards as shown for horizontal siding in Figs. 2-12 and 2-13. Use a 1 1/8-inch-

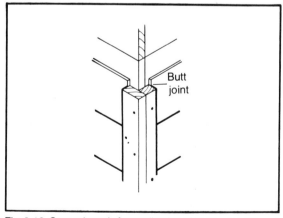

Fig. 2-13. Corner boards for application of horizontal siding at the exterior corner (courtesy USDA Forestry Service).

square corner board at interior corners and 1 1/8-×-1 1/2 or 1 1/8 × 2 1/2 boards at outside corners. Apply caulking wherever siding butts against corner boards, windows, or door casings, and trim boards at gable ends.

Horizontal Wood Siding

Bevel siding has been one of the most popular sidings for many years. It is available in 4- to 12- inch widths. The sawn face is exposed where a rough texture is desired and a stain finish is planned. The smooth face can be exposed for either paint or stain. Siding boards should have a minimum of 1-inch horizontal lap. In application, the exposed face should be adjusted so that the butt edges coincide with the bottom of the sill and the top of the drip cap of window frames (Fig. 2-14).

Horizontal siding must be applied over a

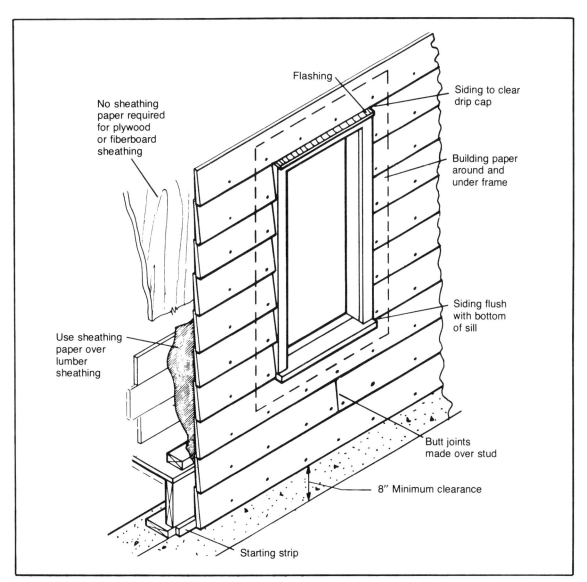

Fig. 2-14. Application of bevel siding to coincide with the window sill and drip cap (courtesy USDA Forestry Service).

smooth surface. If the old siding is left on, it should either be covered with panel sheathing or have turning strips nailed over each stud. Nail siding at each stud with a galvanized siding nail or other rust-resistant nail. Use 6d nails for thicker siding. Locate the nail to clear the top edge of the siding course below. Make butt joints over a stud. Interior corners are finished by butting the siding against a corner board 1 1/8 inches square or larger depending on the thickness of the siding. Exterior corners can be mitered and butted against corner boards 1 1/8 inches or more or thicker and 1 1/2 and 2 1/2 inches wide or covered with metal corners.

Strips of plywood or hardboard can be applied horizontally. The strips are lapped just as for bevel siding, but a starting strip is required at the base, and a shingle wedge is required at each vertical joint (Fig. 2-15). The starting strip should be the same thickness as the siding. Nail the siding at each vertical joint in the same manner as for bevel siding. Special clips are available from many fabricators for applying the siding. If you use these clips, be sure to follow the manufacturer's instructions.

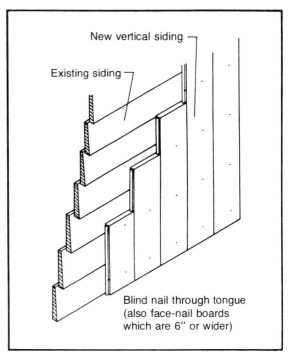

Fig. 2-16. Application of vertical siding (courtesy USDA Forestry Service).

Vertical Wood Siding

Vertical siding is available in a variety of patterns. Probably the most popular is matched or tongue-and-groove, boards. Vertical siding can be nailed to 1-inch sheathing boards or to 5/8- and 3/4-inch plywood. Furring strips must be used over thinner plywood because the plywood itself will not have sufficient nail-holding capacity.

When the existing sheathing is thinner than 5/8 inch, apply 1-×-4-inch nailers horizontally, spaced 16 to 24 inches apart vertically. Then nail the vertical siding to the nailers. Blind-nail through the tongue at each nailer with galvanized 7d finish nails. When boards are nominal 6 inches or wider, also face-nail at midwidth with an 8d galvanized nail (Fig. 2-16). Vertical siding can be applied over existing siding by nailing through the siding into the sheathing.

Various combinations of boards and battens comprise another popular vertical siding material. It must also be nailed to a thick sheathing or to horizontal nailers. Nail the first board or batten

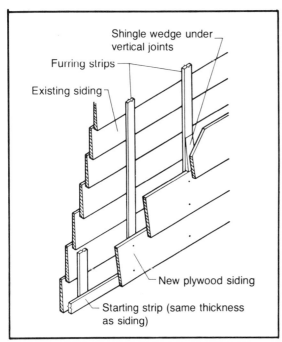

Fig. 2-15. Application of plywood as lap siding (courtesy USDA Forestry Service).

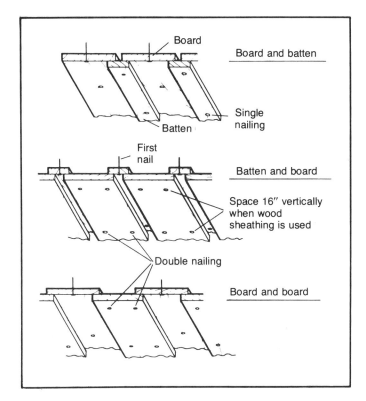

Fig. 2-17. Application of vertical wood siding (courtesy USDA Forestry Service).

with one galvanized 8d nail at center, or for wide boards, two nails spaced 1 inch each side of the center. It is important to achieve close spacing of the nails to prevent splitting if the boards shrink. Nail the top batten with 12d nails, being careful to miss the underboard and nail only through the space between adjacent boards (Fig. 2-17). Use only rust-resistant nails. Galvanized nails are not recommended for some materials; so be sure to follow siding manufacturer's instructions.

Wood Shingle and Shake Siding

Some architectural styles may be well suited to the use of shakes or shingles for siding. They give a rustic appearance and can be left unfinished, if desired, to weather naturally. They may be applied in single or double courses over wood or plywood sheathing.

Where shingles are applied over uneven siding or over a nonwood sheathing, apply 1-×-3- or 1-×-4-inch wood nailing strips horizontally as a base for the shingles. Spacing of the nailing strips will depend on the length and exposure of the shingles. Apply the shingles with about 1/8- to 1/3-inch space between adjacent shingles to allow for expansion during rainy weather.

For the single-course method, lay one course over the other similar to the way lap siding is applied. Second-grade shingles can be used because only 1/2 or less of the butt portion is exposed (Fig. 2-18).

For the double-course-method apply an undercourse and nail a top course directly over it with a 1/4- to 1/2-inch projection of the butt over the lower course shingle (Fig. 2-19). Using this method, less lap is used between courses. The undercourse shingles can be lower quality, such as third grade or undercourse grade. The top course should be first grade because of the exposed shingle length.

Recommended exposure distances for shingles and shakes are given in Table 2-2. Regardless of whether you use the shingle course or the double course in applying the shingles, all joints must be

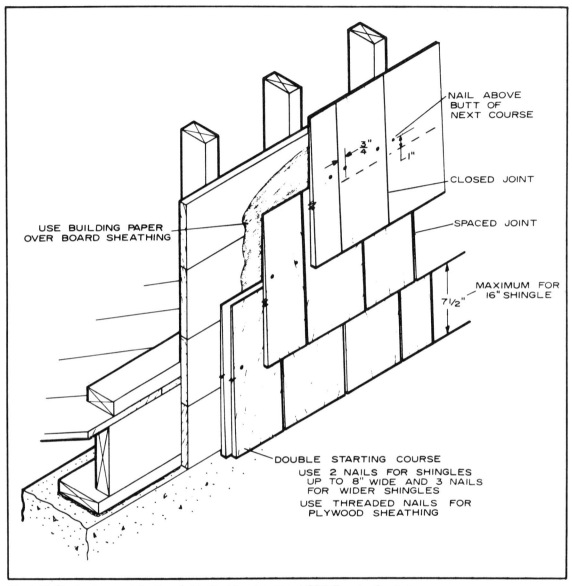

Fig. 2-18. Single-course application of shingle siding (courtesy USDA Forestry Service).

broken so that the vertical butt joints of the upper shingles are at least 1 1/2 inches from the under-shingle joint.

Be sure to use rust-resistant nails for all shingle applications. Shingles up to 8 inches wide should be nailed with two nails. Wider shingles should be secured with three nails. Zinc-coated "shingle" nails of 3d or 4d are commonly used in the single-course method. Zinc-coated nails with small flat heads are commonly used in the double-course method where nails are exposed. Use 5d nails for the top course and 3d or 4d for the undercourse. When plywood sheathing less than 3/4 inch thick is used, threaded nails are required to obtain suffi-cient holding power.

Nails shoud be 3/4 inch from the edge. They

should be 1 inch above the horizontal butt line of the next higher course in the single-course application and 2 inches above the bottom of the shingle or shake in the double-course application.

Masonry Veneer

Where brick or stone veneer is used as siding, mortar may become loose and crumble, or settlement may cause cracks. In either case, new mortar should be applied, both to keep out moisture and to improve appearance.

Repair is accomplished in much the same manner as for masonry foundations, except that more attention to appearance is necessary. After removing all loose mortar and brushing the joint to remove dust and loose particles, dampen the surface. Then apply mortar and tamp it well into the joint for a good bond. The points of joints should conform to

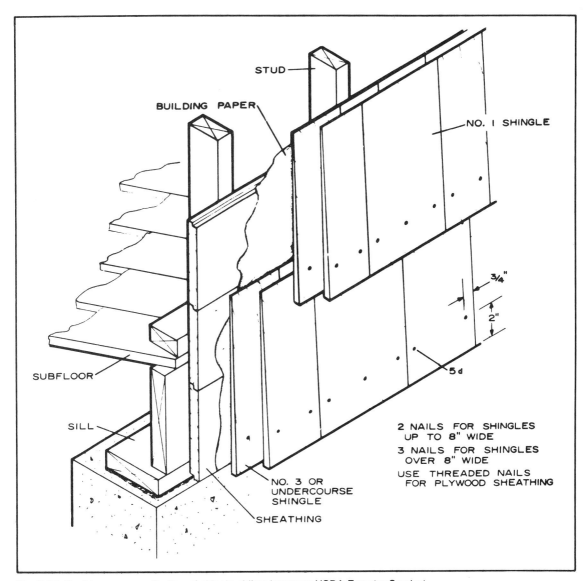

Fig. 2-19. Double-course application of shingle siding (courtesy USDA Forestry Service).

| Material | Length | Maximum Exposure | | |
| | | Single Coursing | Double Coursing | |
			No. 1 grade	No. 2 grade
	In.	In.	In.	In.
Shingles	16	7 1/2	12	10
	18	8 1/2	14	11
	24	11 1/2	16	14
Shakes (handsplit and re-sawn)	18	8 1/2	14	—
	24	11 1/2	20	—
	32	15	—	—

TABLE 2-2. EXPOSURE DISTANCES FOR WOOD SHINGLES, SHAKES ON SIDEWALLS

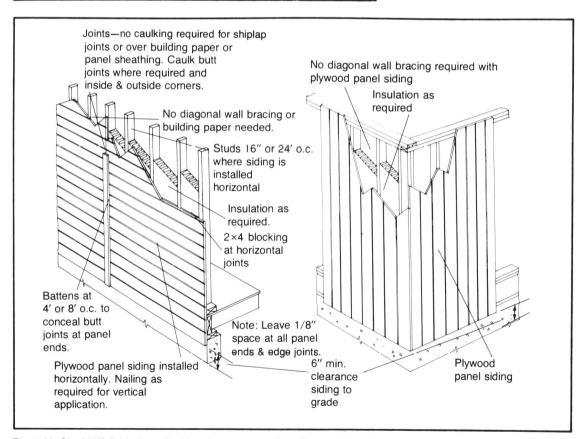

Fig. 2-20. Sturd-I-Wall (single wall) siding (courtesy American Plywood Association).

existing joints. Be careful to keep mortar off the face of the brick or stone unless the veneer is to be painted.

Brick or stone veneer should be cleaned gently, with water under low pressure and a soft-bristled brush, for example. When chemical cleaner is required, the services of a professional masonry cleaner are recommended.

INSTALLING SIDING

Directions for installing the various types of siding and sheathing follow.

Installing APA Sturd-I-Wall (Single Wall)

The APA Sturd-I-Wall system will save you time and money. Plywood panel siding bearing the APA 303 trademark—available in a wide variety of textures and patterns—is applied directly to the wall framing (Fig. 2-20) or over nonstructural sheathing, thus eliminating the costs of material and labor to installing structural sheathing required in conventional double-wall construction. Sturd-I-Wall construction meets all requirements for structural performance, as a combination siding and structural sheathing.

Plywood siding with the APA trademark comes in panels 3/8 to 3/4 inch thick and 4 feet by 8, 9, or 10 feet. Normally, panels are installed vertically, with the long dimension running parallel to the studs; however, they may be installed horizontally. Allowable stud spacing is marked on the APA trademark on the back of 303 plywood siding panels. For example, 303 plywood siding bearing a "303-24 o.c. Span" designation may be applied vertically to studs 16 or 24 inches on center, while panels marked "303-16 o.c. Span" may be applied vertically over stud spacing no more than 16 inches apart.

Texture 1-11 siding may be used vertically with studs 16 inches on center. Any APA 303 panel may be used on studs 24 inches on center when applied with the long dimension placed horizontally, provided horizontal joints are blocked. No extra corner bracing is needed with panel siding.

Before applying plywood siding, check your house plans to see if there are any special require-

ments. Panel thickness may be specified; or windows may need to be attached to framing before siding is applied. The plan also may call out particular butt-joint locations or give specific details for joints around door openings and at the top edge of the panel. No building paper is required if joints are shiplapped or to be covered with battens. Building paper is required, however, for unbattened square butt joints in single-wall construction.

Panel the side walls first, then the shorter end walls.

☐ Frame tilt-up walls, or erect 2-×-4 stud walls in place.

☐ Cut siding panels to the proper length. See Fig. 2-21. In determining length, allow for 1 inch to lap over the top of the foundation wall and 1 1/2 inch to cover the second top plate after the wall is raised.

☐ Place the first panel at one end of the wall framing section, making sure the edge of the panel is flush with the outside of the corner stud.

☐ Apply the panel to the wall framing. Use hot-dip galvanized, aluminum, or other nonstaining nails to prevent any staining of the siding from weathering and rusting nails. Use 6d box, siding, or casing nails for plywood siding 1/2 inch or less thick; use 8d nails for thicker panels. Drive nails every 6 inches along the panel ends and edges and every 12 inches at intermediate supports.

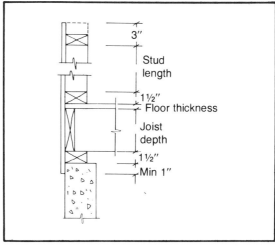

Fig. 2-21. Cut siding panels to proper length (courtesy American Plywood Association).

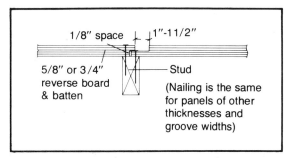

Fig. 2-22. Nailing shiplapped panels (courtesy American Plywood Association).

Figure 2-22 shows how to nail shiplapped panels. All edges of the panel siding must be backed by solid lumber framing or blocking.

In addition the spacing of panel edges and the use of straight studs, nailing sequence can also be a factor in maintaining a uniformly flat appearance of the finished wall.

You can install plywood siding without building in compression stress. Position the siding panel, maintaining recommended edge spacing, and lightly tack at each corner. Install the first row of second intermediate stud, and at the edge opposite the preceding panel. Complete the installation by fastening to the top and bottom plates.

☐ Apply additional panels in the same manner until the wall is finished. Remember to leave a 1/8-inch space between all ends and edges of panels. This spacing is necessary to ensure that panels will stay flat under all weather conditions.

☐ Tilt the side wall into position and fasten it through the subfloor to the sill plate and header joist.

☐ When both side walls are completed and in place, apply the siding to the shorter end walls. Place one panel at the end of each wall and temporarily tack it into position. Allow for overlap of the side wall framing and siding. See Fig. 2-23 for help in figuring the overlap (normally about 3 1/2 inches plus the panel thickness). It is usually easier to use corner trim pieces than to try to trim the edges to a perfect fit. Permanently fasten all remaining panels to the wall framing; do not apply panel at the other end of the wall. Remove the temporarily fastened panel from the wall. The open

framing at either end of the walls facilitates tilt-up and attachment to side walls.

☐ Tilt walls into position and nail to the side walls at the corners with 16d nails. Apply corner siding panels to complete the siding application.

☐ Caulk joints as required. No caulking is required for shiplapped joints or for joints backed by building paper. Caulk butt joints at all inside and outside wall corners, using any of the various high-performance polyurethane or Thiokol caulks. In some cases, a foam rod or other type of filler material may be used behind the sealant. Always follow the sealant manufacturer's recommendations.

☐ Apply battens and trim strips as desired for appearance, or as shown on your house plans. Lap corner trim strip over the siding joint so that there is no continuous joint through the corner trim and siding (Fig. 2-23). Where siding is applied with face grain across the studs, apply battens to conceal the vertical butt joints at the panel ends. Block behind the horizontal joint. Nails through battens must penetrate the studs at least 1 inch.

Installing Sheathing (Double Wall)

Conventional exterior wall covering consists of a structural sheathing material overlaid with siding. APA trademarked panels for both purposes provide strength, stiffness, durability, and distinctive appearance.

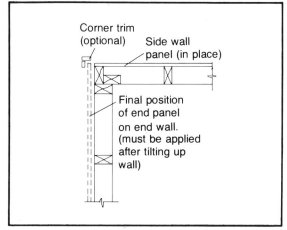

Fig. 2-23. Side wall panel in place and the final position of the end wall (courtesy American Plywood Association).

APA-rated sheathing 24/0 is recommended over studs spaced up to 24 inches on center. Sheathing may be applied vertically or horizontally. Be sure to check local building regulations to see if horizontal joints must be locked.

Apply sheathing to the tilt-up side walls first, and raise them; then sheathe shorter end walls. Before you apply sheathing, check your house plans for possible special requirements. The plans may also call out special details at door openings, wall corners, and at the top edge of the panel.

□ Frame tilt-up walls, or erect 2 × 4 stud walls in place.

□ For vertical application, position the first sheathing panel at one end of the wall framing section. Make sure the edge of the panel is flush with the outside edge of the corner stud. Allow the sheathing to overlap the top plate by 1 1/2 inch so that the panel will cover the second top plate when installed after the wall is raised. Since most floor-to-ceiling heights are 7 feet 6 inches to 7 feet 9 inches, the sheathing will also overlap the bottom plate. Do not trim. If the sheathing is applied with the face grain across the studs, be sure to make the same overlap allowances over the bottom plate.

□ Nail the sheathing to the wall frame. Use 6d box or common nails, spacing them 6 inches on center at panel edges and 12 inches on center over the intermediate studs.

□ Apply the rest of the sheathing to the wall section. Remember to leave a 1/8-inch space between all panel ends and 1/4 inch between panel edges.

□ Tilt the wall into position and fasten the bottom plate to the floor framing with 16d nails at 6 inches on center.

□ When both side walls are completed and in place, apply sheathing to the shorter end walls. Place one panel at the end of the wall framing and temporarily tack it into place. Allow for overlap of the side wall framing and sheathing. The overlap will be about 3 1/2 inches plus the sheathing thickness.

Permanently fasten all remaining panels to the wall framing; do not fasten the last panel at the other end of the wall. Remove the temporarily fas-

tened panel from the wall. The open framing at either end of the walls allows the end-wall panels to be tilted up past the side walls.

□ Tilt the walls into position and nail to the side walls at the corners with 16d nails. Attach the bottom plate and sheathing to the floor framing with 16d nails at 6 inches on center. Apply corner panels to complete the sheathing installation.

□ Add a sheathing filler strip, if necessary, below the sheathing to help tie the floor to the sill (Fig. 2-24). Nail this filler 6 inches on center to both header joist and sill.

□ Apply plywood siding to sheathed walls (Fig. 2-25). Texture 1-11, 303-16 on center sidings, and other exterior panels under 7/16 inch thick may be applied with the face grain parallel to the studs 24 inches on center when vertical rows of nails are

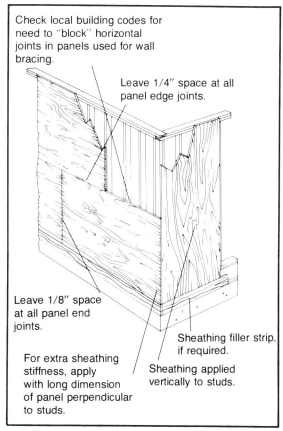

Fig. 2-24. Sheathing filler strip (courtesy American Plywood Association).

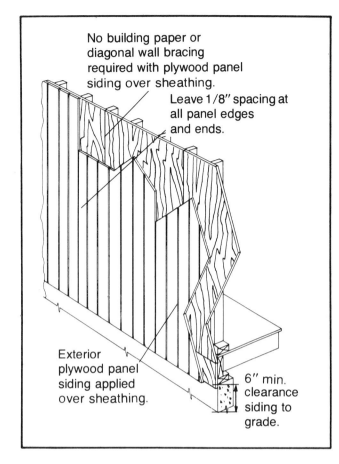

No building paper or diagonal wall bracing required with plywood panel siding over sheathing.

Leave 1/8" spacing at all panel edges and ends.

Exterior plywood panel siding applied over sheathing.

6" min. clearance siding to grade.

Fig. 2-25. Application of plywood to sheathing wall (courtesy American Plywood Association).

spaced 16 inches on center and nailing is into APA-rated sheathing. Use hot-dipped galvanized, aluminum, or other nonstaining nails to prevent the siding from staining because of weathering and rusting nails. Use 6d box, siding, or casing nails for plywood siding 1/2 inch or less thick; use 8d nails for thicker panels. Drive nails every 6 inches along panel ends and edges and every 12 minutes at intermediate supports. Nails through battens must penetrate studs at least 1 inch or be driven through the sheathings if the joint does not occur over a stud.

☐ Leave a 1/8-inch space between all ends and edges of siding panels.

☐ Caulk square-edged siding butt joints with any of the various high-performance polyurethane or Thiokol caulks. In some cases, a foam rod or other type of filler material may be used behind the sealant. Always follow the sealant manufacturer's recommendation. No caulking is needed for ship-lapped joints or for joints covered by battens.

After the exterior and interior walls are erected, plumbed for straightness, braced, and tied together with the second top plates, the ceiling framing can be installed.

FRAME THE CEILING

The basic construction of ceiling framing is similar to that of floors, except that header joists are not included.

Ceiling framing does three things. It ties together opposite walls and roof rafters to reduce the outward pressure imposed on the walls from the pitched roof; it supports the finished ceiling, and it supports a second story or an attic storage area.

Main framing members are called *joists*, and,

like flooring framing, their size is determined by spacing and length of span. Check your house plans for the correct size and spacing and your local building codes for agreement. Ceiling framing is generally 2-×-1 lumber.

To provide you with a working platform for building the roof, install the ceiling framing before the roof rafters. Lay out both ceiling framing and roof rafters at the same time, however, since the ceiling joists must lap the roof rafters and be securely nailed to them. Follow your house plans for the location of members. Space ceiling joists at the same spacing as roof rafters.

With panel sheathing and siding and with doubled top plates, ceiling joists and roof rafters need not line up over the wall studs. In fact, wall studs are usually placed at 16 inches on center, whereas roof rafters and ceilings joists can be placed at 24 inches on center.

If the load-bearing interior wall is not continuous, a beam will be needed to carry the inside ends of the ceiling joists. Check your house plans to determine the type, placement, and size of beam necessary to support the load. The beam may be located below, at the same level as, or even above the joists. If it is at the same level as, or above, the joists, it must support them with metal hangers.

☐ Lay out the position of the ceiling joists and roof rafters in approximately the same manner as was done for the floor joists, marking the location of each joist and rafter on both outside plates and the interior bearing wall. Note that the two roof rafters on opposite sides of the house will frame opposite each other at the center, but the ceiling joists will lap these rafters.

The easiest method for making everything line up is to use filler blocks over the interior bearing partition, as shown in Fig. 2-26. The two ceiling joists "meeting" over the center partition can then be placed one on each side of the roof rafter, with the filler block occupying the space of the roof rafter at the center joint.

☐ Begin installing ceiling rafters. Because the end rafter will be placed with its outside face flush with the outside of the wall, the ceiling joist at the end of the house will not lap its rafter (Figs. 2-27 and 2-28). For this reason, it is easier to place the end joist so it laps the first interior roof rafter, which will have its centerline 24 inches in from the face of the end wall. Succeeding joists and rafters are spaced 24 inches on center.

☐ Trim the corners of ceiling joists at the outer walls where they must match the rafter slope. You can find the slope by checking your house plan. If only a small amount must be removed, you can saw it off after the rafters are in place.

☐ Cut the ceiling joists to the proper length with the outer end flush with the outside of the wall and allowing for at least 4 inches overlap at the center.

☐ Install ceiling joists and toenail to the top plate of the exterior walls with two 10d nails on each side. At the center lap, nail the joists to the filler block, and then toenail to the plate of the load-bearing wall or beam (Fig. 2-29).

Since the ceiling rafters are supplying the tie across the building, they must be well spiked. For a building 24 feet wide with ceiling joists and roof rafters both at 24-inch spacings, four 16d nails are required from each ceiling joist into the filler block. Tie together ceiling joists and the nonbearing walls that run parallel to them, as in Fig. 2-30. As with

Fig. 2-26. Use filler blocks for alignment (courtesy American Plywood Association).

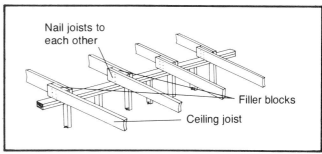

Nail joists to each other

Filler blocks

Ceiling joist

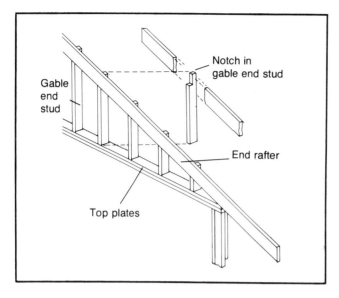

Fig. 2-27. End rafter detail (courtesy American Plywood Association).

floor framing, place ceiling joists with the crown facing up.

☐ Cut and frame the attic access in the same manner as the openings in the floor. Fire regulations and building codes usually list minimum size requirements, and your house plan shows locations. If the opening is small (2 to 3 feet square), doubling of the headers and joists is not necessary.

FRAME THE ROOF

Roof framing is a combination of rafters, ridge

board, collar beams, and cripple studs. In gable roof construction, all rafters are precut to the same length and pattern.

Each pair of rafters is fastened at the top to a ridge board, commonly a 2-×-8 or 2-×-6 rafter, which provides support and a nailing area for rafter ends.

Rafter location should be laid out at the same time as ceiling joists to establish a proper relationship between them.

☐ If not already done, mark rafter locations on the top plate of the side walls. The first rafter pair will be flush with the outside edge of the end wall. Space the first interior rafter at 24 inches measured from the end of the building to the center of the rafter. All succeeding rafter locations are measured

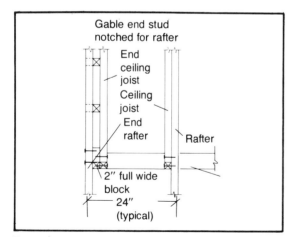

Fig. 2-28. End joist detail (courtesy American Plywood Association).

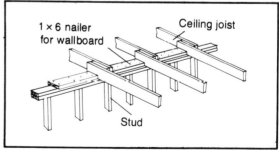

Fig. 2-29. Nailing ceiling joists (courtesy American Association).

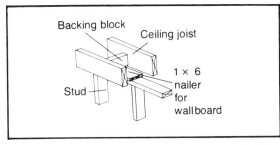

Fig. 2-30. Tie together ceiling joists (courtesy American Plywood Association).

24 inches center to center. They will be at the sides of ceiling-joist ends.

☐ Next, mark rafter locations on the ridge board, allowing for specified gable overhang. To achieve the required length of the ridge board, you may need to splice it (Fig. 2-1), but do not do so yet, since it is easier to erect in shorter sections.

☐ Check your house plan for roof slope. Four inches of rise in 12 inches of run is common, and is usually considered the minimum for asphalt or wood shingles (Fig. 2-32).

☐ Draw a full-size rafter pattern on the floor of the house, showing the actual slope. From this drawing you can determine the length of rafters including overhang, the angle of cut at the ridge and overhang, and the location of the notched seat cut to fit on the wall top plate. Remember to include the width of the ridge board in the drawing so that the rafter length will be accurate.

☐ Lay out one pair of rafters, marking the top and bottom angles and the seat cut location. Make the cuts and check the fit by setting them up at floor level. Once a good fit is achieved, marked this set of rafters and use it as a pattern for the remainder.

☐ Cut the remaining rafters. For a 48-foot house with rafters spaced 24 inches on center, you will need 24 more pairs cut to the pattern, (for a total of 25 pairs). You will also need two pairs of fascia rafters for the ends of the gable overhang (Fig. 2-33). Since they cover the end of the ridge board, they must be longer than the pattern rafters by 1/2 the width of the ridge board. Fascia rafters will have the same cuts at the top and bottom as the regular rafters, but they will not have a seat cut.

Getting started with the raising of the roof framing is the most complicated part of framing a house. Plan it carefully, making sure you have all the materials on hand/all the steps in your mind before you begin. It is best to make a "dry run" at ground level. Raising the roof will be much easier if you have at least two helpers. A considerable amount of temporary bracing will be required if the job must be done with only one or two men.

☐ Build temporary props of 2-×-4s to hold the rafters and ridge board in place during the installation. The props should be long enough to reach from the top plate to the bottom of the ridge board, and should be fitted with a plywood gusset at the bottom. When installed the plywood gusset is nailed temporarily to the top plate or to a ceiling joist. The props are also diagonally braced from about midpoint in both directions to maintain a true vertical line. Check with a plumb bob. See Fig. 2-34.

☐ Move the ridge board sections and rafters onto the ceiling framing. Lay panels over the ceiling joists for safer footing. First erect the ridge board and the rafters nearest its ends. If the ridge of the house is longer than the individual pieces of ridge board, you will find it easier to erect each piece separately, rather than splicing the ridge board full length first. Support the ridge board at both ends with the temporary props. Toenail the first rafter pair securely to the ridge board using at least two 8d nails on each side, then nail at the wall. Install the rafter pair for the other end in the same manner.

☐ Make the ridge board joints, using plywood gussets on each side of the joint and nailing them securely to the ridge board.

☐ Check the ridge board for level. Also check for straightness over the centerline of the house.

☐ After the full length of the ridge board is

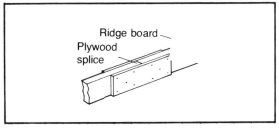

Fig. 2-31. Splicing ridge board (courtesy American Plywood Association).

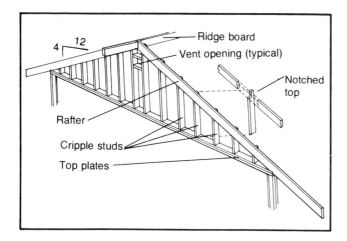

Fig. 2-32. Roof slope check (courtesy American Plywood Association).

erected, put up the remaining rafters in pairs, nailing them securely in place. Check occasionally to make sure the ridge board remains straight. If all rafters are cut and assembled accurately, the roof should be self-aligning.

☐ Toenail the rafters to the wall plate with 10d nails, using at least two for each side. Also nail the ceiling joists to the rafters. For a 24-foot-wide house, you will need four 16d nails at each lap. In high wind areas, it is a good idea to add metal-strap fasteners for extra uplift resistance.

☐ Cut and install 1-×-6 collar beams at every other pair of rafters 4 feet on center. See Fig. 2-33. Nail each end with four 8d nails. Collar beams should be in the upper third of the attic space. Remove the temporary props.

☐ Square a line across the end wall plate directly below the ridge board. If a vent is to be installed, measure half its width on each side of the center mark for the location of the first studs. Mark the positions for renailing studs at 16 inches on center, then measure and cut studs. Notch the top end to fit under the rafter so that the stud bottom will be flush with the top plate. Cut the cripple studs

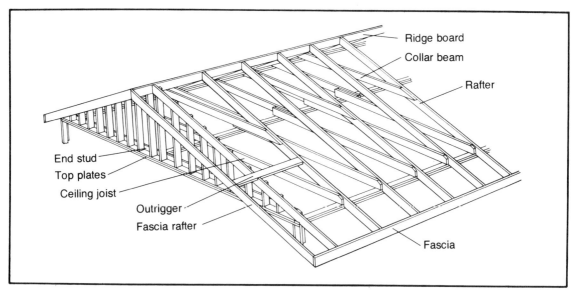

Fig. 2-33. Fascia rafters (courtesy American Plywood Association).

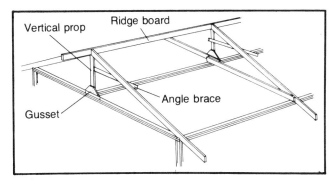

Fig. 2-34. Vertical props (courtesy American Plywood Association).

and headers to frame in the vent opening.

☐ Cut and install fascia board to the correct length of the ridge board. Bevel the top edge to the roof slope. Nail the board to the rafter ends, then install the fascia rafters. Fascia rafters cover the end of the ridge board. Where nails will be exposed to weather, use hot-dipped galvanized or other nonstaining nails.

Ready-made, lightweight, wood roof trusses are available at building supply dealers in lengths of 20 to 32 feet or more. Because they will span from one exterior wall to the other, with no interior bearing walls required, they allow greater flexibility in planning interior room arrangement. Trusses are most adaptable to houses with rectangular plans where the constant width requires only one type of truss.

INSTALLING ROOF SHEATHING

Roof sheathing, the covering over rafters or trusses, provides structural strength and rigidity and makes a solid base for fastening roofing material. APA-rated sheathing is marked with a *span rating*, which tells you the recommended rafter spacing for the panel thickness. For the sample house, with 24-inch spans between rafters, panels with a marking of 24/0 are adequate. Sheathing panels with this span rating are available in 3/8-, 7/16-, and 1/2-inch thickness.

Your renovation plan will show either "open soffits" or "closed or boxed soffits" (Fig. 2-35). If you have closed soffits, all of your roof sheathing can be APA-Rated Sheathing Exposure 1 or Exposure 2. With open soffits, all panels to be exposed at the overhang, either along the side or at the end of

the roof, must be marked exterior, exposure 1, or interior with exterior glue, and have a high enough appearance grade to permit painting or staining to blend well with the rest of the house.

To keep the roofing nails from showing through the underside, these exposed soffit panels must be at least 15/32 inches thick. You will also need to consider the length of roofing nails. Many of the textured-finish plywoods of 1/2 inch and 5/8 inch thickness can be used with the textured side down to provide attractive open soffits.

With either open or boxed soffits, you will need a roof sheathing layout.

☐ Draw your layout. You can do it freehand, but it should be relatively close to scale. The easiest method is to draw a simple rectangle representing half of the roof. The long side will represent the length of the ridge board. Make the short side equal to the length of your rafters, including overhangs.

If you have open soffits, draw a second line (possibly dotted) inside the ends and bottom, to show the area that must be covered by Exterior or Exposure 1 panels. Remember that this sketch represents only half of the roof, and that any cutting of panels on this side can be planned so that the cutoff portions will be used on the other side.

If your eave overhang is less than 2 feet, and you have an open soffit, you may wish to start with a panel of half the normal width; otherwise, start with a full 4-×-8-foot section of sheathing at the bottom of the roof, and work up toward the ridge, where you may have to cut the last row of panels. Stagger panels in succeeding rows.

☐ Complete your layout for the whole roof.

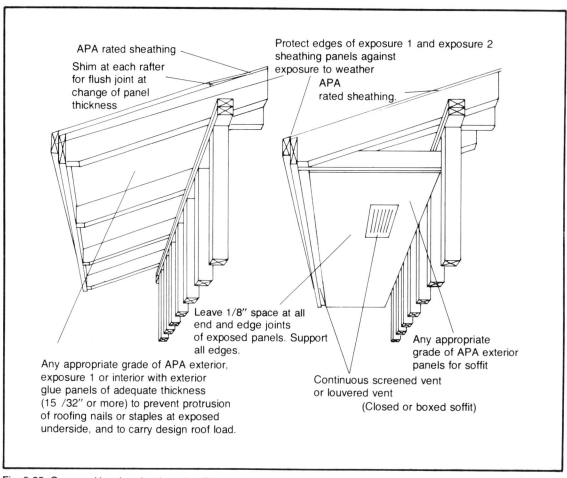

APA rated sheathing

Shim at each rafter for flush joint at change of panel thickness

Protect edges of exposure 1 and exposure 2 sheathing panels against exposure to weather

APA rated sheathing.

Leave 1/8" space at all end and edge joints of exposed panels. Support all edges.

Any appropriate grade of APA exterior, exposure 1 or interior with exterior glue panels of adequate thickness (15 /32" or more) to prevent protrusion of roofing nails or staples at exposed underside, and to carry design roof load.

Continuous screened vent or louvered vent

Any appropriate grade of APA exterior panels for soffit

(Closed or boxed soffit)

Fig. 2-35. Open and/or closed or boxed soffits (courtesy American Plywood Association).

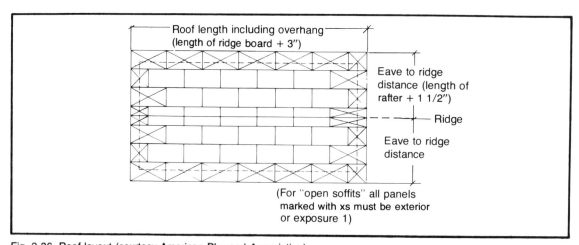

Roof length including overhang (length of ridge board + 3")

Eave to ridge distance (length of rafter + 1 1/2")

Ridge

Eave to ridge distance

(For "open soffits" all panels marked with xs must be exterior or exposure 1)

Fig. 2-36. Roof layout (courtesy American Plywood Association).

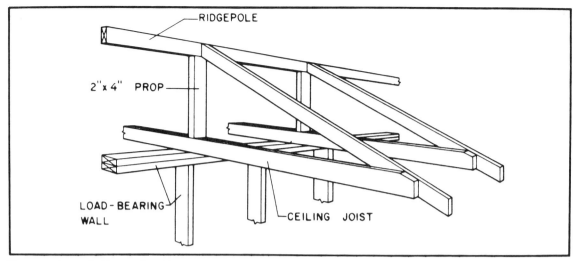

RIDGEPOLE

2" x 4" PROP

LOAD-BEARING WALL

CEILING JOIST

Fig. 2-37. A prop holds sagging ridge pole in a level position (courtesy USDA Forestry Service).

The layout in Fig. 2-36 shows panel size and placement as well as sheathing panel quantities needed. If your diagram shows that you will have excessive waste in cutting, you may be able to reduce the scrap by slightly shortening the rafter overhang at the eave, or the gable overhang.

For the sample house, nearly half of the panels are soffit panels. For such a case, rather than shimming to level up soffit and interior sheathing panels, you may want to use interior sheathing panels of the same thickness as your soffit panels, even though they might then be a little thicker than the minimum requirement.

☐ Cut the panels as required, marking the cutting lines first to ensure square corners.

☐ Begin the panel placement at any corner of the roof. If you are using special soffit panels, remember to place them textured side down.

☐ Fasten each panel in the first course, or row, in turn, to the roof framing using 6d common smooth, ring-shank, or spiral-thread nails. Space nails 6 inches on center along the panel ends and 12 inches on center at the intermediate supports.

☐ Leave 1/8 inch at the panel ends and 1/4 inch at the edge joints.

☐ Apply the second course, using a soffit half panel in the first, or overhang, position. If the main sheathing panels are thinner than the soffit

sheathing, install small shims to ease the joint transmission (Fig. 2-35).

☐ Apply the remaining courses as above.

☐ If your plans show closed soffits, the roof sheathing will be all the same grade and thickness. To apply panels to the underside of closed soffits, use nonstaining nails.

RENOVATING ROOF SYSTEMS

The first steps in repairing a roof system are to level sagging ridgepoles and to straighten rafters. Then the new roof covering can be applied to a smooth, flat surface.

Framing

A sagging ridgepole can sometimes be leveled by jacking it at points between supports and installing props to hold it in a level position. The jack must be located where the load can be traced down through the structure so the ultimate bearing is directly on the foundation. Where there is no conveniently located bearing partition, install a beam under the ridge and transfer the load to bearing points.

After the ridgepole is jacked to the level position, cut a 2 × 4 just long enough to fit between the ceiling joist and ridgepole or beam and nail it at both ends (Fig. 2-37). For a short ridgepole, one prop may be sufficient. Where rafters are sagging, nail a new rafter to the side of the old one after forcing the new rafter ends into their proper position. Permanent set in the old rafters cannot be removed.

Sheathing

Sheathing may have sagged between rafters, resulting in a wavy roof surface. Where this condition exists, new sheathing is required. Often the sheathing can be nailed over the old roofing. Where wood shingles are excessively cupped or otherwise warped, they should also be removed. Wood shingle and slate roofs of older houses were often installed on furring strips rather than on solid sheathing.

Sheathing nailed over existing sheathing or over sheathing and roofing must be secured with longer nails than would normally be used. Nails should penetrate the framing 1 1/4 to 1 1/2 inches. Nail the edges of plywood sheathing at 6-inch spacing and to intermediate framing members at 12-inch spacing. Apply the plywood with the length perpendicular to the rafters. For built-up roofs, if the plywood does not have tongue-and-groove edges, use clips at unsupported edges. Clips are commercially available and should be installed according to the fabricator's instructions. For 16-inch rafter spacing, 3/8-inch plywood is the minimum thickness to be used, and 1/2-inch thick plywood is preferable.

Adding a Roof Overhang

The addition of a roof overhang is most advantageous when renovating on a low budget since the end results will soon pay for themselves in the reduced amount of maintenance on siding and exterior trim. Without the overhang, water washes down the face of the wall, creating moisture problems in the siding and trim and, consequently, a need for more frequent painting. Additional roof overhang also does much to improve the appearance of the house.

☐ If you are adding new sheathing, extend it beyond the edge of the existing roof to provide some overhang. This is a minimum solution and the

extension should not be more than 12 inches where 1/2-inch plywood sheathing is used. Any greater extension would require some sort of framing.

☐ Framing can usually be extended at the eave by adding to each rafter.

☐ Remove the frieze board. In the case of a closed cornice, remove the fascia.

☐ Nail a 2 × 4 to the side of each rafter, letting it extend beyond the wall the amount of the desired overhang. The 2 × 4 should extend inside the wall a distance equal to the overhang. See Fig. 2-38(A).

☐ Framing for an overhang at the gable ends can be accomplished by adding a box frame. Extensions of the ridge beam and eave fascia are required to support this boxed framing.

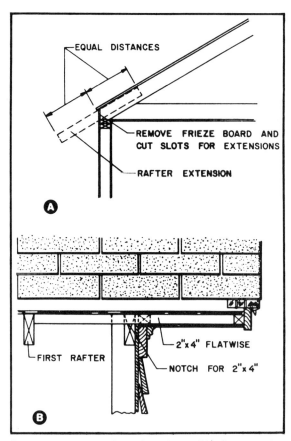

Fig. 2-38. Extension of a roof overhang: (A) rafter extension at eaves, (B) extension at the gable end (courtesy USDA Forestry Service).

☐ An alternative extension is possible by placing a plank flat, cutting into the gable framing, and extending it back to the first rafter. See Fig. 2-38(B).

Roof Coverings

A wide variety of roof coverings is available, and most can be used in renovating your home. Local code requirements for fire safety should be checked.

Before you choose a type of roof covering, first consider the budget that you have set; usually it will influence the choice. While the most popular covering materials for pitched roofs are wood, asphalt, and asbestos shingles, in most houses the roof is a major design element, and the covering material must fit the house design. Heavy materials such as tile or slate should not be used unless they replace the same material or unless the roof framing is strengthened to support the additional load.

If two layers of shingles exist from previous reroofing, you may want to remove the old roofing before applying your new roof.

Roll roofing is sometimes used for particularly low-cost applications or over porches with relative low-pitched roofs. The most common covering for flat or low-pitched roofs is built-up roof with a gravel topping; however, it is used mainly in the south and southwest; so your location will play a major role in this decision.

An underlay of 15- or 30-pound asphalt-saturated felt should be used in moderate- and low-slope roofs covered with asphalt, asbestos, or slate shingles, or tile roofing. It is not commonly used under wood shingles or shakes.

A 45-pound or heavier smooth-surfaced roll roofing should be used as a flashing along the eave line in areas where moderate to severe snowfalls occur. The flashing should extend to a point 36 inches inside the warm wall. If two strips are required, use mastic to seal the joint. Also use mastic to seal end joints.

Flashing gives protection from ice dams which are formed when melting snow runs down the roof and freezes at the colder cornice area (Fig. 2-39). The ice gradually forms a dam that backs up water under the shingles. The wide flashing at the eave will minimize the chances of this water entering the ceiling or the wall. Good attic ventilation and sufficient ceiling insulation are also important in eliminating ice dams. Roll roofing 36 inches wide is also required at all valleys.

Where shingle application is over old wood or asphalt shingles, industry recommendations include the following preparations.

☐ Remove 6-inch-wide strips of old shingles along the eaves and gables.

☐ Apply 1-inch board at these locations.

☐ Thinner boards may be necessary where the application is over old asphalt.

☐ Remove the old covering from ridges or hips and replace it with bevel siding with butt edges up.

☐ Place a strip of lumber over each valley to separate the old metal flashing from the new.

☐ Double the first shingle course.

Wood Shingles. Wood shingles used for house roofs should be No. 1 grade which are all heartwood, all edge grain, and tapered. Principal species used commercially are western red cedar and redwood, which have heartwood with high decay resistance and low shrinkage. Widths of shingles vary, and the narrower shingles are most often found in the lower grades. Table 2-3 indicates the recommended exposure for common shingle sizes. When you apply wood shingles:

☐ Extend shingles 1 1/2 to 2 inches beyond the eave line and about 3/4 inch beyond the rake, or gable, edge.

☐ Nail each shingle with two rust-resistant nails above the butt line of the next course. Use 3d nails for 16- and 18-inch shingles and 4d nails for 24-inch shingles. Where shingles are applied over old wood shingles, use longer nails to penetrate through the old roofing and into the sheathing. Use a ring-shank, threaded nail where the plywood sheathing is less than 1/2 inch thick.

☐ Allow a 1/8- to 1/4-inch space between each shingle for moisture expansion. Lap vertical joints at least 1 1/2 inches by the shingles in the course above it. Space the joints in succeeding

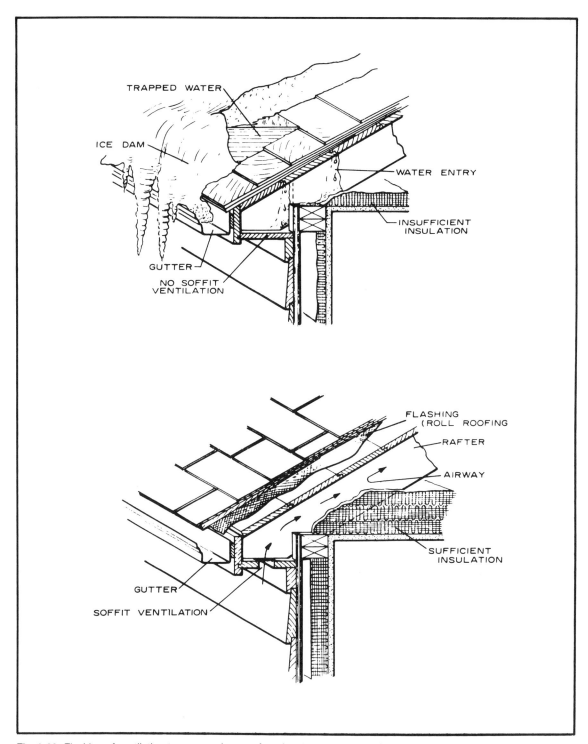

Fig. 2-39. Flashing of ventilation to prevent damage from ice dam (courtesy USDA Forestry Service).

TABLE 2-3. RECOMMENDED EXPOSURE FOR WOOD SHINGLES.

| Shingle Length | Shingle Thickness (green) | Maximum Exposure | |
		Slope less[1] than 4 in 12	Slope 4 in 12 and over
In.		In.	In.
16	5 butts in 2 in.	3 3/4	5
18	5 butts in 2 1/4 in.	4 1/4	5 1/2
24	4 butts in 2 in.	5 3/4	7 1/2

[1] Minimum slope for main roofs—4 in 12. Minimum slope for porch roofs—3 in 12.

courses so that the joint in one course is not in line with the joint in the course above it.

☐ Shingle away from valleys, selecting and precutting wide valley shingles. The valley should be 4 inches wide at the top and increase in width at the rate of 1/8 inch per foot from the top.

☐ Use valley flashing with a standing seam. Do not nail through the metal. Valley flashing

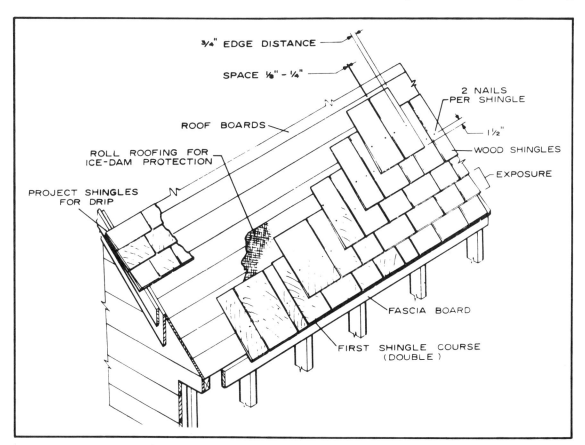

Fig. 2-40. Application of wood-shingle roofing over boards (courtesy USDA Forestry Service).

should be a minimum of 24 inches wide for roof slopes under 4 in 12, 18 inches wide for roof slopes of 4 in 12 to 7 in 12, and 12 inches wide for roof slopes of 7 in 12 and over.

☐ Place a metal edging along the gable end of the roof to help guide the water away from the end walls (Fig. 2-40).

Wood Shakes. Wood shakes are applied in much the same manner as shingles, but you must use longer nails because the shakes are thicker. Shakes have a greater exposure than shingles because of their length. Exposure distances are 8 inches for 18-inch shakes, 10 inches for 24-inch shakes, and 13 inches for 32-inch shakes. Butts are often laid unevenly to create a rustic appearance. Use an 18-inch wide underlay of 30-pound asphalt felt between the rough faces of the shakes. Position the underlay above the butt edge of the shakes a distance equal to double the weather exposure. Where exposure distance is less than 1/3 the total length, underlay is not usually required.

Asphalt Shingles. The square-butt strip shingle is the most common type of asphalt shingle. It is 12 × 36 inches, has three tabs, and is usually laid with 5 inches exposed to the weather. Pile bundles flat so that strips will not curl when the bundles are opened for use. An underlayment of 15-pound saturated felt is often used. Table 2-4 shows the requirements in applying underlayment.

☐ Apply a wood-shingle course or a metal edging along the eave line. See Fig. 2-41(A).

☐ The first course of asphalt shingles is doubled and extended downward beyond the wood shingles, or edging, about 1/2 inch to prevent the water from backing up under the shingles.

☐ Make a 1/2-inch projection at the rake. See Fig. 2-41(B).

☐ Make several chalk lines on the underlayment parallel to the roof slope to serve as guides in aligning the shingles' tabs. Follow the manufacturer's directions in securing the shingles.

☐ In areas of high winds, nail each 12-×-36-inch strip with six 1-inch galvanized roofing nails. Use seal-tab or lock shingles in these areas.

☐ When a nail penetrates a crack or knothole, remove the nail, seal the hole, and replace the nail in sound wood. If the nail is not in sound wood, it will gradually work out and cause a hump in the shingle above it.

Built-up Roof Coverings. Built-up roof coverings are limited to flat or low-pitched roofs and are installed by contractors that specialize in this work. The roof consists of three, four, or five layers of roofers' felt. Each layer is mopped down with tar or asphalt; the final surface is then coated with asphalt and usually covered with gravel embedded in asphalt or tar.

Other Roof Coverings. Other roof cover-

Underlayment[1]	Minimum Roof Slope	
	Double Coverage[2] Shingles	Triple Coverage[2] Shingles
Not required	7 in 12	[3]4 in 12
Single	[3]4 in 12	[4]3 in 12
Double	2 in 12	2 in 12

TABLE 2-4. UNDERLAYMENT REQUIREMENTS FOR ASPHALT SHINGLES.

[1]Headlap for single coverage of underlayment should be 2 in. and for double coverage 19 in.

[2]Double coverage for a 12- by 36-in. shingle is usually an exposure of about 5 in. and about 4 in. for triple coverage.

[3]May be 3 in 12 for porch roofs.

[4]May be 2 in 12 for porch roofs.

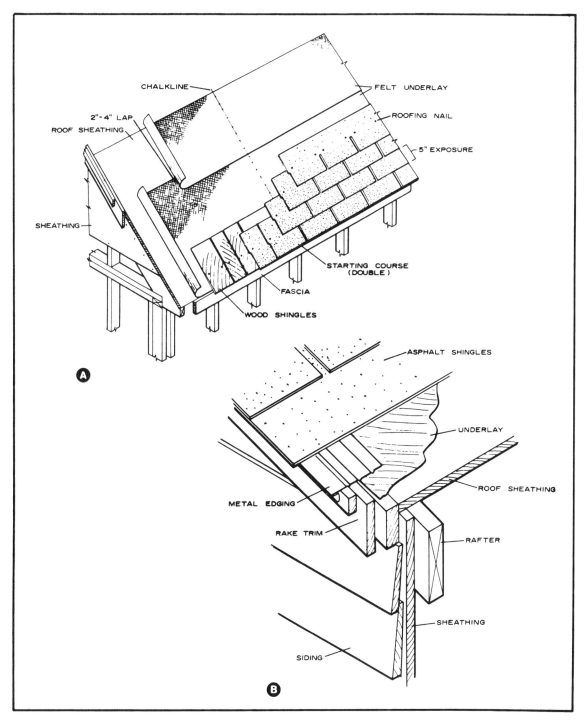

Fig. 2-41. Application of asphalt-shingle roofing over plywood: (A) with strip shingles, (B) metal edging at the gable end (courtesy USDA Forestry Service).

69

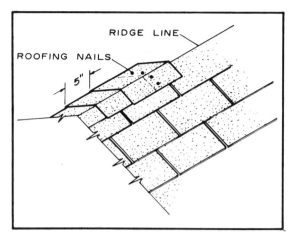

Fig. 2-42. Boston ridge using asphalt shingles (courtesy USDA Forestry Service).

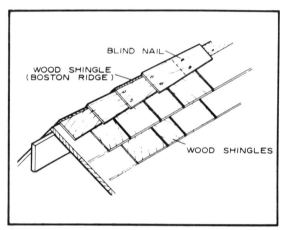

Fig. 2-43. Boston ridge using wood shingles (courtesy USDA Forestry Service).

ings, such as asbestos, slate, tile, and metal, require specialized applications; so their application is best left to a trained professional and is not recommended for remodeling on a low budget. Since each budget is an "individualized" part of your

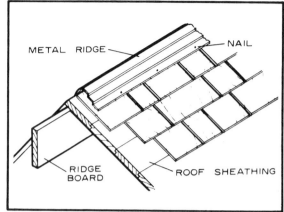

Fig. 2-44. Metal ridge roll (courtesy USDA Forestry Service).

renovating, however, if you desire any other than the commonly used materials as outlined, ask the advice of a contractor.

Roof Ridge

The Boston ridge is the most common method of treating the roof ridge and is also applicable to hips. Where asphalt shingles are used, cut the 12-×-36-inch strips into 12-×-12-inch sections. Bend them slightly and use in a lap fashion over the ridge with a 5-inch exposure distance (Fig. 2-42). Locate nails where they will be covered by the lap of the next section. A small spot of asphalt cement under each exposed edge will give a positive seal.

Wood-shingle roofs can also be finished with a Boston ridge. Flashing should first be placed over the ridge. Shingles 6 inches wide are alternately lapped, fitted, and blind-nailed (Fig. 2-43). Exposed shingle edges are alternately lapped.

A metal ridge roll can also be used on asphalt-shingle or wood-shingle roofs (Fig. 2-44). This ridge of copper, galvanized iron, or aluminum is formed to the roof slope.

Chapter 3

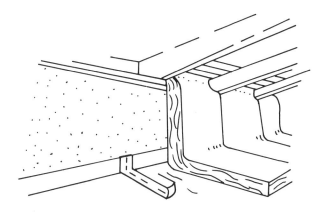

Insulation and Moisture Control

For years contractors, and the industry in general, focused their insulating attention on cold climates. Now we know that, regardless of the climate in which you live, insulation is important. Not only do you need to keep out the cold air and keep in the warm air in cold climates, but, in warm regions you must keep in the cold, air-conditioned air and keep out the hot, humid air.

During remodeling your first determination of where to insulate, what to use, and how to do it will be during your evaluation, which then will be transferred to your drawings and plans.

When you are planning to insulate, consider all the major causes of heat and/or cooling loss. Heat loss per unit is much greater through windows and exterior doors than through most wall materials. Another major loss is from air infiltration around doors and windows. Regardless of the type and location of insulation, vapor barriers are required on all warm sides of the insulation.

WHAT IS INSULATION?

All materials are capable of conducting heat; some allow it to pass more readily than others do. Materials that are poor heat conductors are known as *insulators*. These insulating materials are used as barriers wherever you want to reduce the flow of heat from one place to another.

Insulation is often placed in the walls of buildings to slow down the flow of heat from the space inside to the cold outside or, conversely, from the heat outside to the cold inside. Insulation does not produce any heating or cooling by itself; it simply helps to keep the heat where you want it—inside in winter and outside in summer.

A good insulating material must be light, dry, and resistant to moisture and fire. It must contain many spaces that trap air and reduce the passage of heat.

There is no best insulation. Many materials are easily handled by the do-it-yourselfer. Others, such as foamed or sprayed insulations, must be installed by professionals using special equipment. When remodeling you must first determine where and how much insulation is needed in specific areas of the house.

An insulating material's effectiveness in resisting the flow of heat is indicated by its *R-value*, or effective resistance value. The higher the R-value, the more resistant the material is to the passage of heat.

Some materials have higher R-values per inch of thickness than others. When shopping for insulation, always compare the cost per unit of resistance. The R-value of the insulation should be clearly indicated on the package. Divide the cost of the package by the number of square feet that the package will cover and then by the rated R-value to determine the cost per unit of resistance. (Table 3-1).

Suppose that you buy mineral wool batts with an R-value of 19 for 30¢ per square foot. By dividing 30¢ by 19 you can determine that each unit of resistance will cost 1.6¢ (30¢ ÷ 19 = 0016). Then by comparing the cost per unit of resistance for the different insulations, you can determine what material offers the best value.

TYPES OF INSULATION

Batts and Blankets. Mineral wool and glass fiber are made to fit exactly between studs and joists spaced either 16 or 24 inches apart (Fig. 3-1). They are available either unfaced or with an attached vapor-retardant facing and in a variety of thicknesses from 2 to 12 inches.

Rigid Board. Polystyrene, both beadboard and extruded, urethane and polyisocyanurate are used to insulate masonry walls, such as those found in basements and crawl spaces, and the edges of concrete floor slabs. Rigid glass fiber boards are frequently used under built-up roofs, on wood plank roofs, and in other locations when attic insulation cannot be used. Beadboard, urethane, polyisocyanurate, and glass fiber need a separate vapor retardant. Extruded polystyrene itself resists the passage of vapor, and therefore a separate vapor retardant is not needed. When used in occupied spaces, the polystyrenes and urethanes must be covered with gypsum board at least 1/2 inch thick to provide fire protection.

Foams or Sprayed-in-Place Insulation. Urethane or urea formaldehyde is normally installed in walls by contractors using special equipment. Sprayed urethane is combustible and is not allowed by some local residential codes. It should always be covered by gypsum board at least 1/2

TABLE 3-1. COST PER UNIT OF RESISTANCE R-VALUE.

| Insulating Material | Approx. R/Inch | Inches Needed for | | | | | Cost in Your Area | | |
		R11	R19	R22	R34	R38	$	R	$/R
Loose Fill									
Fiberglass	3.0-3.2	3.5	6	7	10.5	12			
Mineral Wool	3.0-3.2	3.5	6	7	10.5	12			
Cellulose	3.1-3.7	3	5.5	6	10	11			
Vermiculite	2.2	5	9	10	15.5	17			
Batts or Blankets									
Fiberglass	3.2	3.5	6	7	10.5	12			
Mineral Wood	3.2	3.5	6	7	10.5	12			
Rigid Board									
Polystyrene beadboard	3.6	3	5.5	6	9.5	10.5			
Extruded polystyrene	5.3	2	3.5	4	6.5	7			
Urethane	6.2	2	3	3.5	5.5	6			
Fiberglass	4.0	3	5	5.5	8.5	9.5			
Polyisocyanurate	8.0	1.5	2.5	3	4.5	5			
Foam									
Urea formaldehyde	4.8	2.5	4	4.5	7	8			
Polyurethane	6.2	2	3	3.5	5.5	6			

Fig. 3-1. Laying batt/blanket insulation (courtesy Owens-Corning).

inch thick for fire protection. Urea formaldehyde can give off a strong odor when not properly cured or when only partially cured. It may also shrink as it cures in the walls, resulting in void spaces.

SELECTING INSULATION

By installing adequate insulation, you may be able to save 20 to 30 percent of the energy used to heat your home during the winter and cool it during the summer. This saving fits in perfectly with your remodeling and building on a low budget. In addition, when your home is well insulated, the inside temperatures are more uniform, and your home is more comfortable.

Table 3-2 indicates the nominal R-values for various thicknesses of insulation. After you have determined the total R-Value recommended for your area, find out how much more insulation you

will need to add beyond what your home already has in order to bring it up to the recommended level.

Let's say that a home was constructed in St. Louis, Missouri, several years ago. To find out how much additional ceiling insulation is required for best results:

☐ Find the recommended R-Values for the St. Louis area. Figure 3-2 indicates these values to be R-30/19/19; it recommends R-30 for ceilings, R-19 for walls, and R-19 for floors. Therefore, for the ceiling, R-30 is the total insulating value to be achieved.

☐ Now measure the thickness and note the type of insulation already in the home. Use a ruler or yardstick. To determine the type of insulation, compare it with the description given in Table 3-3.

☐ Determine the R-Value of the existing insulation. From Table 3-4, which compares total

73

TABLE 3-2. NOMINAL R-VALUES FOR VARIOUS THICKNESS OF INSULATION.

	Batts or Blankets		Loose and Blown Fill				
R-Value	Glass fiber	Rock wool	Glass fiber	Rock wool	Celluloisic fiber	Vermiculite	Perlite
R-11	3 1/2	3	5	4	3	5	4
R-13	4	3 1/2	6	4 1/2	3 1/2	6	5
R-19	6	5	8 1/2	6 1/2	5	9	7
R-22	7	6	10	7 1/2	6	10 1/2	8
R-26	8	7	12	9	7	12 1/2	9 1/2
R-30	9 1/2	8	13 1/2	10	8	14	11
R-33	10 1/2	9	15	11	9	15 1/2	12
R-38	12	10 1/2	17	13	10	18	14

(Inches of Thickness)

The R-Value for urea-formaldehyde foam is 4.2 per inch of thickness. However, a bulletin (Use of Materials Bulletin No. 74, Sept. 15, 1977) from the Department of Housing and Urban Development (HUD) indicates that the effective R-Value of this type of fill is only 3.3 per inch when installed, due to a 6-percent average linear shrinkage. Therefore, urea-formaldehyde foam in a 3 1/2 inch wall cavity would have an R-Value of 10.5

insulation thickness, types, and R-values, you can see that 3 1/2 to 4 inches of fiberglass batt has an R-value of 11.

☐ Now determine how much more insulation is needed by subtracting what is already there (R-11) from the recommended amount (R-30) for the ceiling.

☐ Finally, determine the amount of insulation

TABLE 3-3. INSULATING R-VALUE EQUIVALENTS.

	Batts or Blankets		**Loose Fill			
	Glass fiber	Rock wool	Glass fiber	Rock wool	Cellulosic fiber	
R-11	3 1/2"-4"	3"	5"	4"	3"	R-11
R-19	6"-6 1/2"	5 1/4"	8"-9"	6"-7"	5"	R-19
R-22	6 1/2"	6"	10"	7"-8"	6"	R-22
R-30	9 1/2"-10 1/2"*	9"*	13"-14"	10"-11"	8"	R-30
R-38	12"-13"*	10 1/2"*	17"-18"	13"-14"	10"-11"	R-38

*Two batts or blankets required.
**Must be poured or blown to mfg. specification for correct density.

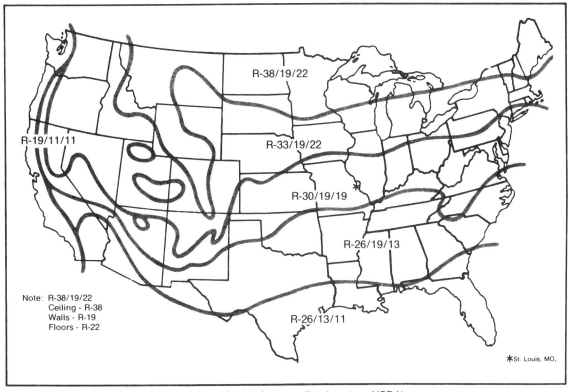

Fig. 3-2. How much insulation you need depends on where you live (courtesy USDA).

you must add to gain an additional R-19. Go to Table 3-3 and read across from R-19. You will have several choices:

—6-to-6 1/2-inch fiberglass batts or blankets;
—5 1/4-inch rock wool batts or blankets;
—8-to-9-inch blown or poured in fiberglass;
—6-to-7-inch blown or poured in rock wool; or
—5-inch blown or poured in cellulose

Any one of these choices would provide the total recommended insulation when added to the existing insulation. Your final decision may be based on which material is most economical, which is most readily available, or other requirements (Fig. 3-3).

CEILING/ATTIC INSULATION

The attic is one of the most important areas to insulate. If your attic is very large, as is the case in most older houses, insulate while you are remod-

eling so you will have it ready to use if you decide to turn the attic into another bedroom, sewing room, or hideaway room (Fig. 3-4).

Most houses have an accessible attic with exposed ceiling framing; so any type of insulation can easily be applied there. If batt or blanket insulation is used, get the width that conforms to your joist spacing, as indicated, either 16 or 24 inches. Loose fill can also be used by dumping the insulation between the joists and screening it off to the desired thickness; however, this type of insulation and installation is best done by a contractor with the correct equipment to "blow" the insulation into the ceiling and/or attic.

The first thing you should do is determine how much insulation you now have in the attic and, if possible, what kind. Take measurements at several locations, keeping in mind that the results may not be uniform. Refer to Fig. 3-2 for your zone.

In unfinished attics, the insulation is installed

TABLE 3-4. INSULATION METHODS, ADVANTAGES, AND WHERE APPLICABLE.

Form	Method of Installation	Where Applicable	Advantages	Materials
Blankets or batts	Fitted between wood-frame studs joists and beams	—All unfinished walls, floors, and ceilings	—Do-it-yourself —Best suited for standard stud and joist spacing, which is relatively free from obstructions —Blankets: Little waste because it's hand-cut —Batts: More waste, but easier to handle than large rolls	Rock wool Glass fiber
Loose fill (poured in)	Poured between attic joists	—Unfinished attic floors and hard-to-reach places —Irregularly shaped areas and around obstructions	—Do-it-yourself —Easy to use for irregularly shaped areas and around obstructions	Rock wool Glass fiber Cellulose fiber Vermiculite Perlite
Blown fill	Blown into place by special equipment	—Anywhere that frame is covered on both sides, such as side walls —Unfinished attic floors obstructions and hard-to-reach places	—The only insulation that can be used in finished areas —Easy to use for irregularly shaped areas and around obstructions	Rock wool Glass fiber Cellulose fiber Urea-formaldehyde foam (not recommended for unfinished areas)
Rigid insulation	Must be covered with 1/2-inch gypsum board or other finishing material for fire safety	—Basement masonry walls —Exterior walls under construction	—High insulating value for relatively little thickness	Polystyrene board Polystyrene board Isocyanurate board

between and over the joists. In unfinished attics that have a floor, the insulation is installed below the floor and between the joists. Either lift the floor boards to provide access or blow the insulation between the joists through holes drilled through the flooring. Be careful not to block the flow of air from the eave vents to the vents of the roof ridge (Figs. 3-5 through 3-8).

Preparation

Materials you will need include:

—Batts, glass fiber, or rock wool;
—Blankets, glass fiber, or rock wool;
—Loose fill, rock wool, cellulosic fiber, or vermiculite;

—Vapor barriers (probably attached to batts or blankets), and
—Four or six-mil polyethelene.

How much you will need is determined as follows:

☐ Accurately determine the attic area by measuring the rooms directly underneath the roof. Then, measure the distance between the beams in the attic. This distance will be either 15 inches or 23 inches.

☐ If the distance between the beams is 15 inches, multiply the area of your ceiling by .9 to find how many square feet of insulation you will need. If the distance between the beams is 23 inches multiply the ceiling area by .94 to find how many square

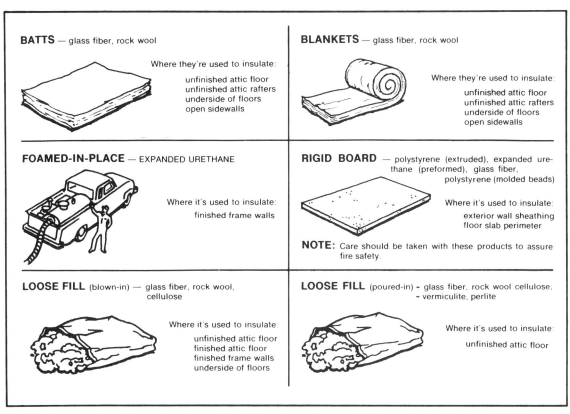

BATTS — glass fiber, rock wool

Where they're used to insulate:

    unfinished attic floor
    unfinished attic rafters
    underside of floors
    open sidewalls

BLANKETS — glass fiber, rock wool

Where they're used to insulate:

    unfinished attic floor
    unfinished attic rafters
    underside of floors
    open sidewalls

FOAMED-IN-PLACE — EXPANDED URETHANE

Where it's used to insulate:

    finished frame walls

RIGID BOARD — polystyrene (extruded), expanded ure-thane (preformed), glass fiber, polystyrene (molded beads)

Where it's used to insulate:

    exterior wall sheathing
    floor slab perimeter

NOTE: Care should be taken with these products to assure fire safety.

LOOSE FILL (blown-in) — glass fiber, rock wool, cellulose

Where it's used to insulate:

    unfinished attic floor
    finished attic floor
    finished frame walls
    underside of floors

LOOSE FILL (poured-in) - glass fiber, rock wool cellulose, - vermiculite, perlite

Where it's used to insulate:

    unfinished attic floor

Fig. 3-3. You can choose from various types of insulation, depending on what job needs done (courtesy USDA).

Fig. 3-4. Insulate your attic (courtesy USDA HUD).

77

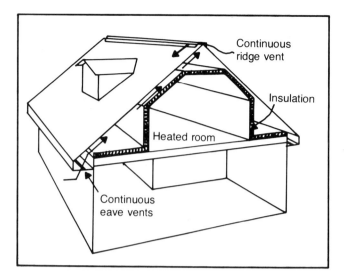

Fig. 3-5. Attic ventilation (courtesy Extension Service, University of Illinois).

feet of insulation you will need.

☐ Determine insulation thickness from Tables 3-2 and 3-4.

Procedure

☐ Install temporary footing and lights. Keep the insulation in the wrappers until you are ready to install it. Insulation comes wrapped in a compressed state and expands when the wrappers are removed.

☐ Check for leaks by looking for water stains or marks. If you find leakage, make repairs before you insulate. Wet insulation is ineffective and can damage the structure of your home (Fig. 3-9).

☐ Install a separate vapor barrier if needed. Lay in polyethylene strips between joists or trusses and staple or tack in place. Seal seams and holes with tape; seams may be overlapped 6 inches instead (Fig. 3-10).

☐ If you are using loose fill, install baffles at the inside of the eave vents so that the insulation won't block the flow of air from the vents into the attic. Be sure that insulation extends out far enough to cover the top plate (Fig. 3-11).

☐ Lay in blankets or batts between joists and trusses. Batts and blankets are slightly wider than joist spacing so they will fit snugly. If blankets are used, cut long runs first to conserve material and use leftovers for shorter spaces. Slide insulation

under wiring whenever possible. If you are using batts or blankets with a vapor barrier, place the barrier on the side toward the living area (Fig. 3-12).

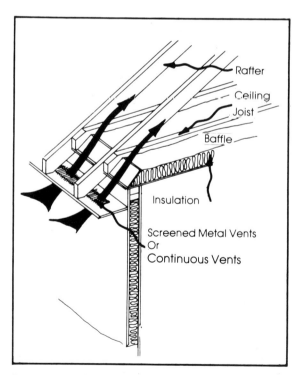

Fig. 3-6. Typical eave vent (courtesy Extension Service, University of Illinois).

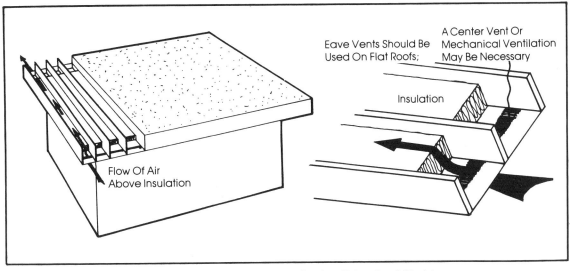

Fig. 3-7. Ventilation of a flat-roofed house (courtesy Extension Service, University of Illinois).

□ Pour in loose fill insulation between the joists up to the top of them. Use a board or a garden rake to level it. Fill all the nooks and crannies, but do not cover recessed light fixtures or exhaust fans (Fig. 3-13).

□ The space between the chimney and the wood framing should be filled with noncombustible material, perferably unfaced batts or blankets. Also, the National Electric Code requires that in-sulation be kept 3 inches away from light fixtures (Fig. 3-14).

WALL INSULATION

Wood-frame walls in existing houses are usually covered inside and out; so the application of batt or blanket insulation is impractical there. It is possible, however, to blow fill insulation into each of the stud spaces.

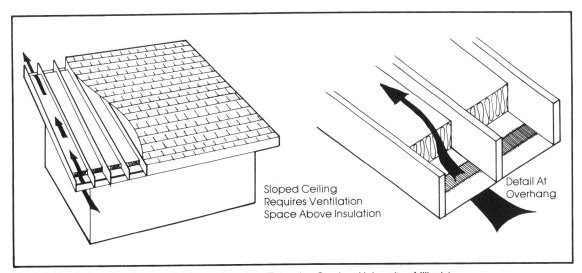

Fig. 3-8. Ventilation of a slope-roofed house (courtesy Extension Service, University of Illinois).

Fig. 3-9. Check for leaks (courtesy USDA HUD).

In houses with wood siding, the top strip just below the top plates and strips below each window are removed. Holes 2 inches in diameter are cut through the sheathing into each stud space. The depth of each stud space is determined by using a plumb bob, and additional holes are made below obstructions in the spaces. Insulation is forced under slight pressure through a hose and nozzle into the stud space until it is completely filled. Special care should be taken to insulate around doors and at intersections of partitions and outside walls.

Stucco, brick, and stone veneer walls can be insulated in a similar manner. The same method can also be used in attic and other roof spaces that are not accessible to other types of insulation.

Solid masonry walls, such as brick, stone, and concrete, can only be insulated in the interior surface. Remember that you will lose some space through this method. One method of installing such insulation is to adhesively bond insulation board directly to the interior surface. The insulating board can be plastered, covered with any desired finish material or left exposed. Thicker insulating board can be used for added effectiveness. Another method of installing insulation on the inside surface of masonry walls is through the attachment of 2-×-2-inch furring strips to the walls at 16-inch centers and the installation of 1-inch blanket insu-

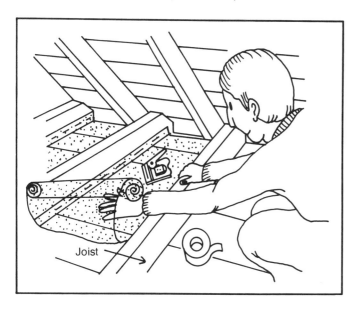

Joist

Fig. 3-10. Installing a vapor barrier (courtesy USDA HUD).

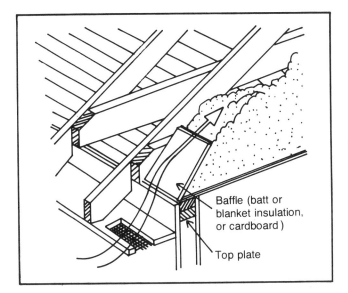

Fig. 3-11. Installing baffle (courtesy USDA HUD).

Baffle (batt or blanket insulation, or cardboard)

Top plate

Fig. 3-12. Laying in blankets (courtesy USDA HUD).

81

Fig. 3-13. Use a board to rake the insulation (courtesy USDA HUD).

lation between strips. Thicker furring strips would permit the use of thicker blanket insulation. The technique used on masonry walls above grade can also be applied to basement walls.

BASEMENT INSULATION

For the most part, especially in colder climates, older homes have basements. During remodeling the basement plays a major part since it means additional space for recreation, sewing, and, many times, sleeping. Whatever it will be used for it must be insulated. (Fig. 3-15).

The cost of insulating your basement will be minimal to the heat loss if you do not insulate. If you have a basement that has air outlets, radiators, or baseboard heating units, it will pay to add a layer of insulation to the inside of the wall. The cost figures in Table 3-5 do not include the cost of refinishing. Multiply the top number in the square you circled times the total length of the walls that you get from the measurements you will take.

Preparation

You will need the following tools:
—Saws,
—Hammer, nails,

Fig. 3-14. Wood framing around the chimney (courtesy USDA HUD).

Fig. 3-15. Insulate your basement walls (courtesy USDA HUD).

—Heavy duty staple gun, or hammer and tacks,
   —Tape measure,
   —Linoleum knife or heavy duty shears,
   —Level, and
   —Small sledge hammer, masonry nails.

Provide adequate temporary lighting. If you use glass fiber or rock wool, wear gloves and a breathing mask, and keep the material wrapped until you are ready to use it.

Materials you will need include 1-R11 (3 1/2-inch) batt or blanket insulation, glass fiber or rock wool, with a vapor barrier. Buy polyethylene if you can't get batts or blankets with a vapor barrier.

Measure the height and length of the walls you intend to insulate. Multiply these two figures to determine how many square feet of insulation you need.

Find the linear feet of studs you will need by multiplying the length of the walls you intend to insulate by six.

The area of wall covering equals the basement wall height times the length of wall you intend to finish.

Procedure

☐ Check to see whether or not moisture is coming through your basement walls from the ground outside. If it is and your walls are damp, eliminate the cause of the dampness so that the insulation you are going to install will not become wet and ineffective. To be sure, install the new studs and insulation slightly away from the wall.

☐ Nail the bottom plate to the floor 3/4 inches out from the base of the wall with a hammer and masonry nails. Install studs 16 or 24 inches apart after the top plate is nailed to the joists above. Where the wall runs parallel to the joists you might be able to fasten the top plate in this way, but you may need to fasten a 3/4-inch thick horizontal fur-

TABLE 3-5. AVERAGE HEIGHT ABOVE THE GROUND.

	0 feet	2 feet	4 feet	6 feet	8 feet
Do-it-Yourself	1.84	1.84	1.84	1.84	1.84 Cost Save Factor
	0.2	1.1	2.0	2.8	3.4
Contractor	4.84	4.84	4.84	4.84	4.84 Cost Save Factor
	.02	1.1	2.0	2.8	3.4

Fig. 3-16. Nail plates and studs to the masonry wall (courtesy USDA HUD).

ring strip to the wall near the top, and fasten the studs to it. Block between studs at the ceiling after the studs are in place if you need backing for the finish material (Fig. 3-16).

☐ Cut blankets into sections the height of the wall. Staple them into place, with the vapor barrier toward the living space (Fig. 13-17).

☐ Install another small piece of insulation above the new studs and against the sill to insulate the sill and band joist (Fig. 3-18).

☐ For a more finished look, install finish wall board or paneling over the insulation and studs (Fig. 3-19).

CRAWL SPACE INSULATION

Many older homes sit on top of a crawl space which can be tightly sealed off from the outside air in the winter. By insulating you will help keep in air-conditioned air during the summer.

Measure the distance around the outside of the heated part of your crawl space. Do not include areas underneath porches, and other unheated areas. Write this distance down in Fig. 3-20.

The cost depends on whether you want to do the work yourself or call a contractor. To estimate the cost if you are doing it yourself, multiply the total distance around your crawl space by $0.80, the

84

approximate cost per running foot. (Check with your local supplier to determine the specific cost in your area.)

To estimate the cost if a contractor is doing the work, multiply the distance around the crawl space by $1.10, the cost per running foot.

To get your saving factor, multiply the distance around your crawl space by .54.

Tools and materials you will need include:

—Staple gun,
—Heavy duty shears or linoleum knife,
—Temporary lighting,
—Portable fan or blower to provide ventilation,
—Tape measure,
—Duct or masking tape (2″ wide),
—R-11 (3″ to 3 1/2″ thick) blankets or rock wool or glass fiber; without a vapor barrier (Fig. 3-2).
—Six-mil-thick polyethylene plastic to lay on earth for vapor barrier.

To find out how much insulation you will need, determine the area to be insulated. Measure the length and average height of the wall to be insulated; add 3 feet to the height (for perimeter insulation). Multiply the total height by the length to find the total insulation area.

FLOOR INSULATION

Batt insulation will add much to your comfort

Fig. 3-17. Staple blankets into place (courtesy USDA HUD).

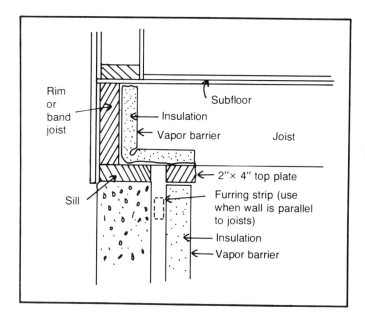

Rim or band joist

Subfloor

Insulation

Vapor barrier

Joist

2" × 4" top plate

Sill

Furring strip (use when wall is parallel to joists)

Insulation

Vapor barrier

Fig. 3-18. Insulate the sill and band joist (courtesy USDA HUD).

even in moderate climates. It is often used for floors, although blanket insulation can also be used. Friction batts fit tightly between joists, and are secured to the bottom side of the subfloor with an adhesive.

Batts that are not of the friction type require some support in addition to the adhesive. This sup-

port can be provided by wood strips cut slightly longer than the joist space so that they spring into place (Fig. 3-22). They should be about 3/16 × 3/4 inch or similar in size and spaced 24 to 36 inches apart, or as needed.

Another method of supporting floor insulation is by nailing or stapling wire netting between joists.

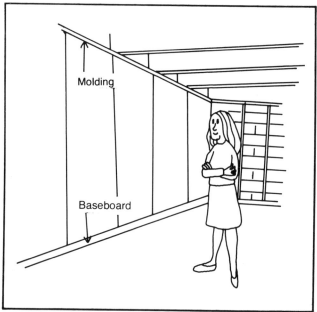

Molding

Baseboard

Fig. 3-19. Installed finish wallboard (courtesy USDA HUD).

86

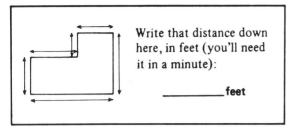

Write that distance down here, in feet (you'll need it in a minute):

_____feet

Fig. 3-20. Measure your crawl space area (courtesy USDA HUD).

This method can be used for blanket as well as batt insulation.

VAPOR BARRIERS

Vapor barriers, also known as moisture control barriers, are essential wherever insulation is used. Cooking, bathing, laundry, and respiration contribute to moisture inside a house. Vapor barriers are always placed near a warm surface and must be continuous over it in order to be effective.

Since insulation reduces heat flow, the cold surface of a wall or roof is colder if insulation is used than if it is not. This colder surface is likely to be below the dewpoint of the air inside the house, and so can cause condensation. Additional water vapor may be added if humidifiers are used during the winter. The high vapor pressure inside causes the vapor to move out through every available crack and even through most building materials. This water vapor condenses in the wall at the point where the temperature is below the dewpoint of the inside atmosphere. The purpose of a vapor barrier is to slow down the rate of vapor flowing into the wall to a rate lower than the outflow to the outside atmosphere.

Continuous Membrane

By far the most effective vapor barrier is a continuous membrane which is applied to the inside face of studs and joists in new construction. In renovating, such a membrane can be used only where interior covering materials are being applied.

The rate of vapor movement through a material is measured in perms. The lower the perm rating of a material, the more effective it is as a

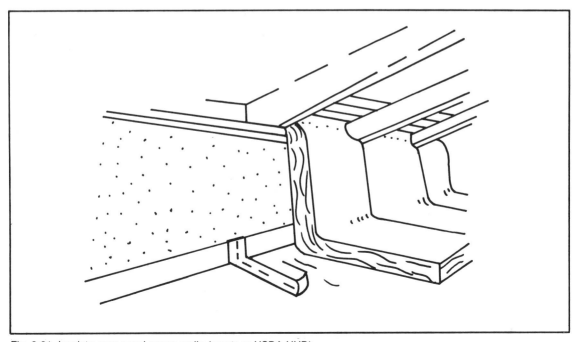

Fig. 3-21. Insulate your crawl space walls (courtesy USDA HUD).

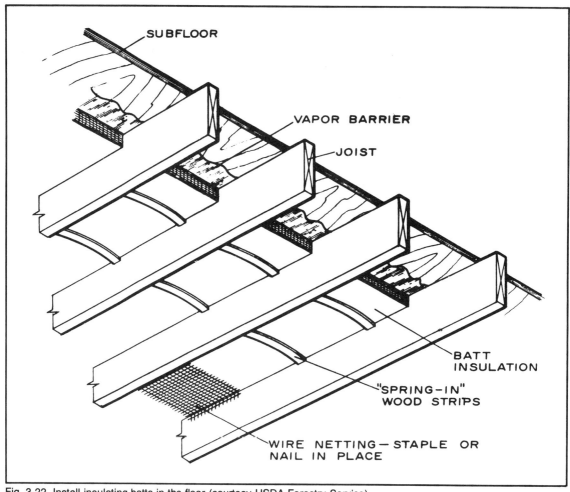

Fig. 3-22. Install insulating batts in the floor (courtesy USDA Forestry Service).

vapor barrier. Suitable materials for a membrane are polyethylene 2 mils or more in thickness, asphalt-impregnated and surface-coated kraft papers, and duplex, or laminated, paper consisting of two sheets of paper cemented together with asphalt.

These vapor barriers are stapled to furring strips before new ceiling or drywall is applied. If the old ceiling or wall finish is removed, staple the vapor barrier directly to the studs or joists. This type of barrier can also be laid on a subfloor directly under any finish floor or floor-covering material. When installing the membrane, be sure to lap all joints at least 2 inches and be careful not to puncture

it. Nail anchorages of finished floor will of course, puncture the barrier, however, they will not greatly reduce its effectiveness.

BLANKET INSULATION WITH VAPOR BARRIER

Most blanket insulation has a vapor barrier on one side. Place the insulation with the vapor barrier toward the warm surface. Tabs on the blanket must be stapled to the inside face of the stud or joist (Fig. 3-23), and adjacent tabs should lap each other. Tabs stapled to the side of stubs or joists in the cavity will be ineffective because vapor will move out between the tabs and framing members.

In remodeling, this type of vapor barrier can be

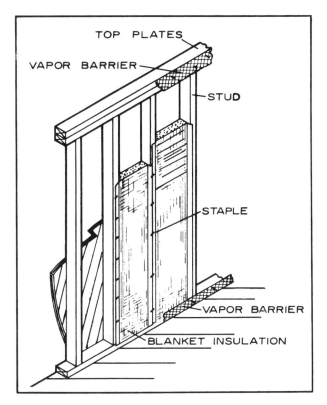

Fig. 3-23. Vapor barrier (courtesy USDA Forestry Service).

used only where the old interior covering materials are completely removed or where furring strips are added on the inside. Insulation is installed between furring strips in the same manner as between studs.

Vapor-Resistant Coating

Where loose fill insulation has been used in the walls and ceiling, and no new interior covering is planned, a vapor-resistant coating should be applied

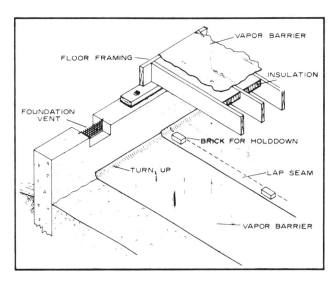

Fig. 3-24. A vapor barrier for a crawl space (courtesy USDA Forestry Service).

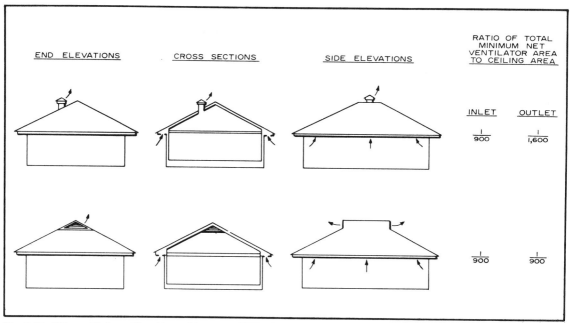

Fig. 3-25. Attic ventilation with a hip roof (courtesy USDA Forestry Service).

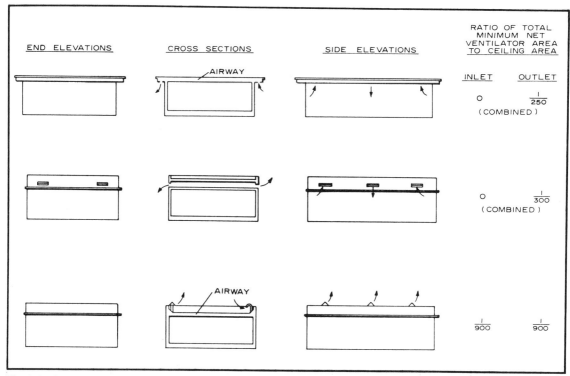

Fig. 3-26. Ventilation of ceiling space in a flat roof (courtesy USDA Forestry Service).

90

to the inside surface. One method of applying such a coating is to paint the interior surface of all outside walls with two coats of aluminum primer, which is subsequently covered with decorative paint. This coating does not offer as much resistance to vapor movement as a membrane, so it should be used only where other types cannot be used. If the exterior wall covering is permeable enough to allow moisture to escape from the wall, a vapor-resistant coating on the inside should be adequate.

Soil Cover

Crawl spaces can be ventilated to effectively remove most of the moisture, but a soil cover will prevent a lot of moisture from ever entering the crawl space. Any of the continuous membranes can be used. Lay the membrane so that it contacts the outside walls and has a lap of at least 2 inches at all joints (Fig. 3-24). Use brick or stones on top of the

membrane to hold it down and prevent curling. Ventilation requirements are greatly reduced where a soil cover is used.

VENTILATION

Ventilation of attics and crawl spaces is essential in all climates where the average January temperature is 35 degrees Fahrenheit or lower. Vapor barriers help to control moisture problems, but there are always places, such as around utility pipes, where the moisture escapes. In older houses without proper vapor barriers, ventilation is especially important.

Moisture escaping from the house into the attic tends to collect in the coldest part of the attic. Relatively impermeable roofing, such as asphalt, shingles, or a built-in roof, complicates the problem by preventing the moisture from escaping to the outside. The only way to get the moisture out is to

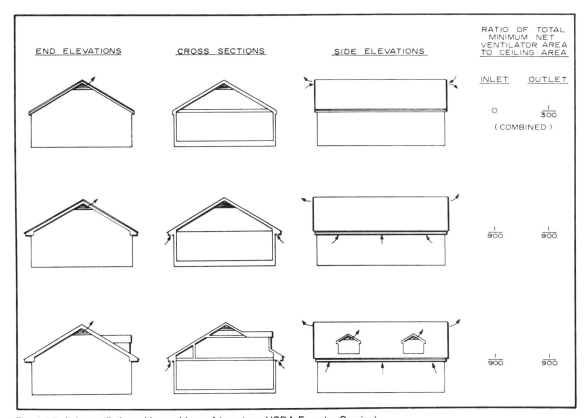

Fig. 3-27. Attic ventilation with a gable roof (courtesy USDA Forestry Service).

ventilate the attic. Attic ventilation also helps keep a house cool during hot weather.

Where possible, provide inlet vents in the soffit area and outlet vents near the ridge to give natural circulation regardless of wind direction. The warm air in the attic goes out the vents, and fresh air enters through the inlet vents to replace it.

In some attics only gable vents can be used. Air movement is then somewhat dependent on wind. The open area of the vent in these attics must be larger than in attics where both inlet and outlet vents are provided.

Hip roofs cannot have gable vents near the peak; so some other type of outlet ventilator must be provided (Fig. 3-25). It can be either a ventilation near the ridge, or a special flue in the chimney with openings into the attic space. Both types require inlet vents in the soffit area. The hip roof can also be modified to provide a small gable for a conventional louvered vent.

Flat roofs with no attic also require ventilation above the ceiling insulation. If this space is divided by joists, each joist space must be ventilated; you can use a continuous vent strip in the soffit. Drill through all headers that impede passage of air to the opposite eave. Figure 3-26 shows other methods of ventilation of ceiling space in flat roofs.

Cathedral ceilings require the same type of ventilation as flat roofs. A continuous ridge vent is also desirable because, even with holes in the ridge rafter, air movement through the rafter space is very sluggish if there is no ridge vent.

Figure 3-27 shows various methods of ventilating gable roofs and the amounts of ventilation required. Ratios shown for all ventilation should be multiplied by the total ceiling area to find the size of opening required for the vent. The open area required should be completely unobstructed. Where 16-inch mesh screen is used to cover the area, double the vent area.

Chapter 4

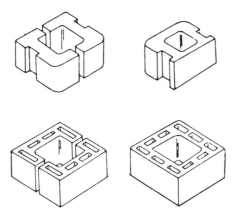

Concrete and Concrete Blocks

Sometime during your remodeling you will probably need to use concrete and/or concrete blocks. For the most part, do-it-yourselfers are quite familiar with the use of these products. For those who are new to doing-it-yourself, though, this chapter will help you learn the many uses of concrete, concrete blocks, and products.

Concrete home improvements can enhance the beauty and the value of your property. They can also make routine lawn maintenance easier, outdoor entertaining more enjoyable, and housecleaning of tracked-in dirt less burdensome.

MATERIALS

Ordinary tools and easily obtained materials are all that you need for concrete work. You will usually have three options for obtaining concrete:

—You can buy ready-mixed concrete;

—You can buy portland cement, sand, and coarse aggregate and mix your own concrete, or

—You can buy dry-mixed concrete by the bag and mix it with water.

Your choice depends on the size of the job and the amount of labor you wish to provide. In general, the more work you do, the less you will pay.

Terminology

People often confuse the words cement and concrete. Before you begin a project, you should know some basic facts and terminology with which you will be confronted.

Concrete is a building material widely used around the home for foundations, walls, patios, sidewalks, steps, fireplaces, and more. It is a versatile and popular building material because freshly mixed concrete can be formed into practically any shape, and hardened concrete is strong and durable.

Although ready-mixed concrete is widely used for large construction jobs, it is not always practical to use for small jobs. In some cases the amount of concrete you require might be less than 1 cubic yard, which is less than most producers will supply.

Quality concrete costs no more to make than poor concrete, and it is far more economical in the long run because of its greater durability. The rules for making good concrete are simple:

—Use proper ingredients;
—Proportion the ingredients correctly;
—Measure the ingredients accurately; and
—Mix the ingredients thoroughly.

Portland cement is an extremely fine powder that is manufactured in a cement plant. When it is mixed with water it forms a paste. This paste binds materials such as sand and gravel or crushed stone which are called *aggregate,* into concrete.

The quality of the paste determines the strength and durability of the finished concrete. Too much water makes the paste thin and weak. Water for mixing should be clean and free of oil, acid, and other injurious substances.

Fine aggregate consists of sand; coarse aggregate is made of gravel, crushed stone, or air-cooled slag. Good, sound aggregate is necessary for making quality concrete. Loam, clay, dirt, and vegetable matter are detrimental to concrete; so aggregate containing these materials should not be used.

Mortar is a mixture of mortar sand, masonry cement, and water. It is used for laying concrete block, brick, and stones.

Various types of cements are manufactured for every use. Normally portland cement is gray. If white concrete is needed or desired, use white portland cement.

Table 4-1 gives the approximate amount of materials needed for various amounts of concrete. It might be necessary to vary the amount of aggre-

gates slightly, depending on their characteristics.

You can determine the amount of concrete needed for any square or rectangular area by using this formula:

$$\text{Width} \times \text{length} \times \text{thickness}$$
$$\text{(in feet)} \quad \text{(in feet)} \quad \text{(in feet)}$$
$$= \text{cubic feet} - \frac{\text{cubic yards.}}{27}$$

Forms

Forms for concrete can be built with materials available from your local dealer (Fig. 4-1). Dimension lumber such as 2 × 4s or 2 × 5s, is used for most jobs. If large surfaces must be formed, like the sides of concrete steps, plywood is usually used. You should use either forming grade or exterior grade plywood that is undamaged by moisture. A light coat of oil on the forms will permit easier removal and help preserve the wood for possible reuse.

Reinforcing steel may or may not be needed. In general, flatwork, such as sidewalks, patios, stepping stones, and driveways, requires no reinforcement if proper attention is paid to jointing. Retaining walls and items subject to heavy loading will need to be reinforced, however.

You will need a strike-off board, a float of wood or light metal, a metal trowel, and edging tools to do concrete work.

REMODELING WITH CONCRETE

When planning a job, first calculate roughly the amount of concrete you will need according to the formula under the terminology section.

TABLE 4-1. WEIGHTS OF MATERIALS.

Maximum size Coarse Aggregate in.	Cement lb.	Sand lb.	Agg. lb.	Water lb.	Cement lb.	Sand lb.	Agg. lb.	Water lb.
3/8	29	53	45	10	29	59	45	11
1/2	27	46	55	10	27	53	55	11
3/4	26	42	65	10	25	47	65	10
1	24	39	70	9	24	45	70	10
11/2	23	38	75	9	23	43	75	9

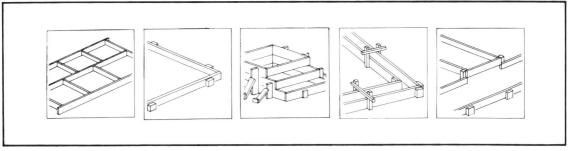

Fig. 4-1. Forming for common concrete jobs, precast work only (courtesy USDA).

Planning the Job

For flatwork, you can estimate the amount of concrete needed by using this simple rule: one cubic yard of concrete will cover approximately 300 square feet 1 inch thick, allowing for some waste. If the slab is 4 inches thick, a cubic yard will cover 300/4 square feet, or about 75 square feet.

Most ready mix producers specify a minimum volume that they will deliver, which may be as little as one cubic yard (27 cubic feet). If your job requires an amount smaller than the minimum order, you may wish to investigate other options; however, on large jobs such as patios and driveways, ready-mixed concrete usually is the best choice.

When you order ready-mixed concrete, ask for a mix that contains 550 pounds of cement, or about six bags, to the cubic yard. Also ask that the concrete be air entrained. Air entrainment gives hardened concrete increased resistance to salt action and cycles of freezing and thawing. It is a good practice to tell the producer what you plan to build so that he can furnish the mix best suited to your job.

For small jobs that you intend to do a piece at a time or when the quantity of concrete is less than the minimum order, you will need to mix your own. Once you have learned the generalities about concrete mixing your own cement is quite simple. Remember that variations in proportions between batches will result in minor color differences in hardened concrete. Therefore, if the job is all one piece, such as a patio, try to do it at one time rather than spreading the job out over several days.

Although most expensive, a poured concrete slab used for patios, for example is the most perma-

nent form. A major portion of the cost can be cut if you do the initial preparation and finishing yourself. Unlike blocks or bricks, pouring a slab is a nonstop operation. To make it an efficient procedure, some careful planning is required. Colored concrete is obtained by mixing pigment with the cement.

Mixing by hand in a wheelbarrow or mortar box works well for small jobs. For a large job, however, rent a small mixer to save back-breaking labor and provide better efficiency and end results.

To mix 1 cubic yard of concrete you will need:

—6 bags of Portland cement,
—1250 pounds of concrete sand,
—1000 pound of gravel or crushed stone, and
—Approximately 30 gallons of water.

Because sand and gravel vary, you will need to "reach" the desired consistency. To start mix 1 part cement, 1 1/2 parts sand, and 3 parts gravel or crushed stone. The key to good quality is the proportion of water to cement. Use about 5 gallons of water for each bag of cement and keep this proportion consistent. The amount of sand and gravel can be adjusted in order to attain the workability desired.

The stress of concrete can cause cracks. Divide the area into sections; the sections should be nearly square. Cut dummy groove joints in the fresh concrete to about 1/4 the concrete thickness.

For smaller jobs, such as the pouring of concrete stepping stones, bagged, dry-mixed concrete is ideal. It only needs to be mixed with water because the ingredients have been accurately proportioned at the factory.

Pouring the Concrete

For large jobs, it is a good idea to have extra help on hand to spread the concrete as it is poured from the truck, or from the small machine if you are mixing it yourself. In either case, once the concrete arrives speed is of the essence, and a continuous flow of spreading the concrete must be maintained.

Using shovels or rakes, spread concrete to the form's edge.

It is important not to overwork the concrete since overworking draws fine material to the surface and results in less durability. Strike the surface off to the desired level. Move the strike-off board across the surface as many times as needed. When the sheen has left the surface, it is ready for final finishing.

Finishing

Concrete should be kept moist for several days after it has set. To cure it, cover the new concrete with a waterproof material, such as a sheet of polyethelene.

After the mortar has set, at least overnight, wear rubber gloves and use a wire brush to clean any spilled mortar from bricks or concrete. Use a mixture of 1 part muriatic acid to 9 parts water. Remove the forms and the edging and hose down the area.

MIXING CONCRETE

The versatility of concrete masonry as a building material is demonstrated by the many sizes, shapes, patterns, and textures available. Blocks are readily available for structural purposes as well as for decorative uses. Some of the most common shapes and sizes are shown in Fig. 4-2.

Choosing Ingredients

Portland Cement. Portland cement is not a brand name of cement; it is a type of cement. Most portland cement is gray in color; however, some portland cement is manufactured from special raw materials that produce a pure white color. Because white portland cement is more expensive, regular portland cement is more widely used.

Cement suitable for use in concrete should be freeflowing. The presence of lumps that cannot be pulverized readily between your thumb and finger indicates that the cement has absorbed moisture. Such cement should never be used for important work. When the lumps have been screened out through an ordinary house screen, the cement can be used for some minor jobs.

Water. You can use almost any natural water that is drinkable and has a pronounced taste or odor to make concrete. Some kinds of water that are not suitable for drinking will also make satisfactory concrete. To be on the safe side, though, use only water fit to drink.

Air. Air is another important ingredient for making good concrete. In the late 1930s it was discovered that air, in the form of microscopic bubbles evenly dispersed throughout the concrete, improved concrete durability, virtually eliminating scaling from freeze-thaw and deicer salt action. Concrete containing such air bubbles is called *air-entrained concrete.*

Hardened concrete usually contains some water. When this water freezes, it expands and causes pressure which can rupture, or *scale,* the concrete surface. The tiny air bubbles act as reservoirs or relief valves for the expanding water. They relieve pressure and prevent damage to the concrete.

Air entrainment is also important for concrete exposed to alternate cycles of freezing and thawing or the use of deicers. In cold climates, and even in mild climates that have several cycles of freezing and thawing each year, air-entrained concrete should be used for all exterior concrete work, including patios.

Air entraining has another advantage. The tiny air bubbles act like ball bearings in the mix, increasing its workability, so that less mixing is required.

Aggregate. Aggregates are divided into two sizes: fine and coarse. Fine aggregate is always sand and natural sand is the most common. Manufactured sand, made by crushing gravel or stone, is also available in some areas. Sand should have particles ranging in sizes from 1/3 inch down to dust-

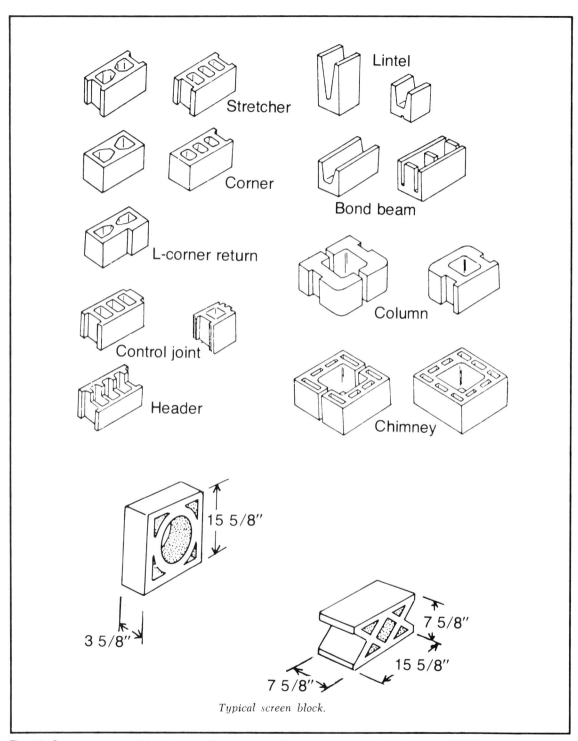

Stretcher

Lintel

Corner

Bond beam

L-corner return

Column

Control joint

Header

Chimney

15 5/8"

3 5/8"

7 5/8"

15 5/8"

7 5/8"

Typical screen block.

Fig. 4-2. Common concrete block shapes. The name usually relates to the function (courtesy USDA).

97

size particles small enough to pass through a No. 100 mesh sieve. Mortar sand should not be used for making concrete because it contains only small particles.

Gravel and crushing stone are the most commonly used coarse aggregates. They should consist of particles that are sound, hard, and durable, not soft or flaky, with a minimum of long, sliver-like pieces. Particles should range in size from 1/4 inch up to the maximum size used for the job. The common maximum sizes are 1/8, 1/2, 3/4, 1, or 1 1/2 inches.

Generally, the most economical mix is obtained by using the largest size coarse aggregate that is practical or available. Coarse aggregate up to 1 1/2 inch in size, for example, can be used in a thick foundation wall or heavy footing. In walls, the largest pieces should never be more than 1/5 the thickness of the finished wall section. For slabs, the maximum size should not exceed 1/3 the thickness of the slab.

All sizes of aggregates might not be available locally, but within the above limitations try to use the largest size aggregate readily available. Both fine and coarse aggregates used for concrete must be clean and free of excessive dirt, clay, silt, coal, or other organic matter, such as leaves and roots. These foreign materials prevent the cement from properly binding the aggregate particles resulting in porous concrete with low strength and durability.

If you suspect that the sand contains too much extremely fine material, such as clay and silt, check its suitability for use in making concrete through the *silt test.* Fill an ordinary quart canning jar or milk bottle to a depth of 2 inches with a representative sample of the sand in question. The sample should be taken from at least five different locations in the sand pile and thoroughly mixed together. Add clean water to the sand in the jar or bottle until it is about 3/4 full.

Shake the container vigorously for about a minute. Use the last few shakes to level off the sand. Allow the container to stand for an hour. Any clay or silt present will settle out in a layer above the sand (Fig. 4-3). If this layer is more than 1/16 inch thick, the sand is not satisfactory unless the clay and silt

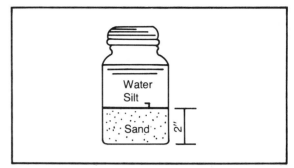

Fig. 4-3. Jar silt test (courtesy John Wahlfeldt).

are removed by washing.

Estimating Quantities

Before measuring and mixing the concrete, you will need to know just how much cement, sand, and coarse aggregate you need for your project. Use the following simple formula. It works for any square- or rectangular-shaped areas.

$$\frac{\text{Width (ft.)} \times \text{Length (ft.)} \times \text{Thickness (in)}}{12} = \text{Cubic Ft.}$$

For example: A 4-inch thick patio slab, 12 feet wide and 15 feet long, would require:

$$\frac{12 \times 15 \times 4}{12} = 60 \text{ cubic feet of concrete.}$$

A wall 3 feet high, 10 feet long and 8 inches thick would require

$$\frac{3 \times 10 \times 8}{12} = 20 \text{ cu. ft.}$$

The amount of concrete determined by the above formula does not allow for losses due to uneven subgrade, spillage, etc., so add 5 to 10 percent for such contingencies. In the wall example, the total amount of concrete required would be $20 + (0.10 \times 20) = 22$ cubic feet.

The quantities of material to buy can be calculated by multiplying the number of cubic feet of concrete (22 in this example) by the weights of materials needed for 1 cubic foot given in Table 4-1.

TABLE 4-2. CONCRETE REQUIREMENTS.

A 1:2 1/4: 3 mix = 1 part cement to 2 1/4 parts sand to 3 parts 1-inch maximum aggregate				
Concrete required cubic feet	Cement 1 lb.	Maximum amount of water to use gallon	Sand 1 pound	Coarse aggregate 1 pound
1	24	1 1/4	52	78
3	71	3 3/4	156	233
5	118	61 1/4	260	389
6 3/4 (1/4-cu. yd)	165	88	350	525
13 1/2 (1/2 cu. yd)	294	16	700	1050
27 (1 cu. yd)	588	32	1040	2100

If crushed stone is used, decrease the amount of coarse aggregate by 3 pounds, and increase the sand by 3 pounds.

Assuming the wall will require air-entrained concrete and the maximum size of available aggregate is 3/4 inch, the quantities of material needed would be:

— 22×25 = 550 pounds of cement,
— 22×42 = 924 pounds of sand,
— 22×65 = 1430 pounds of gravel,
—Plus a 10 percent allowance to cover normal waste.

Mixing Ingredients

Proper mixing is an essential step in making good concrete. It is not sufficient merely to intermingle the ingredients. They must be thoroughly mixed so that cement paste coats every particle of fine and coarse aggregate in the mix. Concrete can be machine or hand mixed.

Mixing Concrete. Make a trial mix using the amounts of material shown in Table 4-2. If this mix does not give satisfactory workability, vary the amounts of aggregate used. Do not vary the amounts of cement and water.

All concrete should be mixed thoroughly until it is uniform in appearance. Add some of the mixing water, then the gravel and cement, then sand and the balance of the mixing water. Each piece of aggregate should be completely coated with cement paste.

Concrete for small improvements can be mixed in a mortar box or wheelbarrow. A bag of cement weighs 94 pounds and is 1 cubic foot in volume (Fig. 4-4).

The following mix (expressed in parts by vol-

Fig. 4-4. Mixing mortar in a wheelbarrow (courtesy John Wahlfeldt).

ume) is recommended for improvements that will only require small batches of mortar:

—1 part portland cement,
—2 1/4 parts sand,
—3 parts gravel or crushed stone (1 1/4 maximum size), and
—2/3 parts water (5 gallons of water per sack of cement).

The proportions suggested are based on experience with typical aggregates. The key to quality concrete is the amount of cement and water used; therefore, the proportions of cement and water recommended should not be changed. If, after mixing the first batch the concrete is too stiff, use less sand and coarse aggregate in subsequent batches. When the mix is too soupy, add more sand and coarse aggregate until the desired consistency is obtained. To make 1 cubic yard of concrete you will need:

—6 1/4 bags of portland cement,
—14 cubic feet of sand (1260 pounds),
—19 cubic feet of gravel or crushed stone (1900 pounds),
—31 1/2 gallons of water, and
—10 percent extra for waste.

Ready-Mixed Concrete. For larger jobs consider using ready-mixed concrete which eliminates the work of mixing and proportioning. Ready-mixed concrete is sold by the cubic yard. When ordering remember the numbers 6-6-6: 6 bags of cement per cubic yard, 6 gallons of water per bag of cement, and 6 percent entrained air. Air-entrained portland cement contains an agent that forms billions of microscopic air bubbles in concrete.

Machine Mixing. The best way to mix concrete is with a concrete mixer. It ensures thorough mixing of the ingredients and is the only way to produce air-entrained concrete. For best results, follow this sequence:

☐ With the mixer stopped, add all the coarse aggregate and 1/2 the mixing water. If an air-entraining agent is used, mix it with this part of the mixing water.

☐ Start the mixer and add the sand, cement, and remaining water while the mixer is running.

☐ After all the ingredients are in the mixer, continue mixing for at least three minutes or until all materials are thoroughly mixed, and the concrete has a uniform color.

A workable mix should look like Fig. 4-5. The concrete should be just wet enough to stick together without crumbling. It should "slide" down, not run off a shovel. In a workable mix, there is sufficient cement paste to bind the pieces of aggregate so that they will not separate.

Hand Mixing. For very small jobs where the volume of concrete required is less than a few cubic feet it is sometimes more convenient, though less efficient, to mix by hand. Hand mixing is not vigorous enough to make air-entrained concrete, however, even if you use air-entraining cement or an air-entraining agent.

Jobs small enough for hand mixing usually can be done with convenient, prepackaged concrete mix. You can find it at building materials stores and hardware stores. All of the necessary ingredients—portland cement, dry sand, and dry coarse aggregate—are combined in the bag in the correct premeasured proportions. Packages are available in different weights, but the most common sizes are 45- and 90-pound bags. A 90-pound package makes 2/3 cubic foot of concrete. All you need to do is add the water and mix. Directions for mixing and the correct amount of water to add are given on the bag; read them carefully.

To ensure that you get good quality from prepackaged concrete mixes, the American Society for Testing and Materials has adopted specifications for packaged, dry, combined materials for mortar and concrete. They cover the quality of the ingredients and the type of bag in which the ingredients are packaged.

CONCRETE BLOCK

The size of a concrete masonry unit is usually described by listing its thickness or width first, followed by its height and then its length. There-

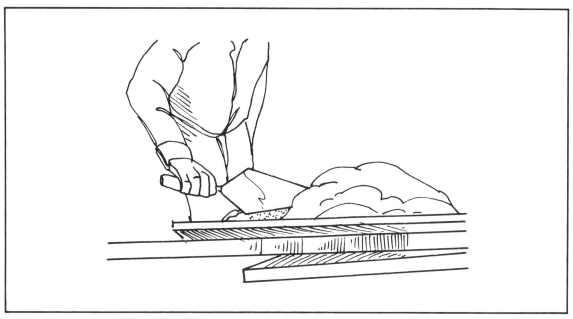

Fig. 4-5. Workable mortar (courtesy John Wahlfeldt).

fore, a 4-×-8-×-16-block has a nominal width of 4 inches, a height of 8 inches, and a length of 16 inches.

The nominal dimension includes a 3/8-inch allowance for the thickness of a standard mortar joint. The actual dimensions of the well-known 8-×-8-×-16-inch unit are manufactured as 7 5/8 × 7 5/8 × 15 5/8 inches.

Concrete masonry units offer a vast array of natural faces and finishes for walls. They range from the wide variety that come at no extra cost to the highly unusual, more expensive blocks that give luxurious effects.

Customized or architectural facing concrete masonry units are designed and manufactured to provide the finished surface of a wall without the addition of opaque coatings or treatments which would appreciably change its appearance.

Using these units, a wall can be built as an exterior wall that is not load bearing. It can be designed of "through-wall" units where only one masonry unit comprises the wall section. The wall section can consist of architectural facing concrete masonry units as a veneer backed up with concrete masonry or other materials. The units could instead be the facing portion of the structural composite or cavity wall.

Fluted and scored or ribbed units provide the architectural design with raised striations which can be developed into many kinds of patterns. The accuracy achieved in machine production of these units makes it possible to produce the effect of long, continuous, vertical lines even when the blocks are laid in running bond.

Shadowwall block, developed and introduced by the National Concrete Masonry Association, are units with creased corners that can be put together in such a limitless variety of patterns that this product has been called the "block of 1000 faces." Hi-Lite block, another type of raised pattern, can be used similarly. Interesting changing shadow effects can be obtained with such units when they are used on exteriors.

Open-faced block of many patterns is available for decorative uses or to partially screen walls or yards from either the sun or outside views. Some manufacturers produce block with colorful, hard, glossy, mar-resistant surfaces that resemble ceramic tile, and are durable and easy to clean. Surfaces may be made of epoxy or polyester resins and could contain fine sand or other fillers. Ceramic or porcelainized glazes, mineral glazes, and cement like finishes have also been used.

A number of rapid-assembly systems have come into use in the past 20 years. These systems are designed for assembly by the unskilled or partially skilled. They include:

☐ Tongue-and-groove interlocking systems which are assembled dry and then bonded together by grout which flows through horizontal and vertical channels.

☐ Wedge-shaped blocks that interlock and are self-plumbing.

☐ Surface bonding application, which involves stacking the block up without mortar and then troweling both sides with a plaster containing strands of fiberglass. The result is a waterproof wall with good lateral strength.

Estimating

Before any work is started, you should estimate the amount of blocks and mortar you will need.

Block. First, determine the number of courses by multiplying the height of the wall in feet by 1 1/2 for an 8-inch high block. Multiply the wall height by 3 for a 4-inch high block. Find the number of blocks in each course by multiplying the length of the wall in feet by 3/4 inches. The total number of blocks is the number of blocks in each course multiplied by the number of courses. Each end of the wall requires a half block for every other course. To determine the number of corner blocks, multiply the number of corners by the number of courses in the wall.

Mortar. For each 100 of the 8-×-8-×-16-inch blocks use 2 1/2 sacks of type II masonry concrete and 667 pounds of sand. For a 6-foot high garden wall that is 50 feet long on each of the three sides you would need:

—6 (height in feet) × 1 1/2 = 9 courses.
—150 (length in feet) × 3/4 = 112 1/2 blocks for each course.

Each course requires 110 stretcher blocks, 2 corner blocks, and 1 half block. The entire wall requires 990 stretcher blocks, 18 corner blocks, and 9 half blocks. The mortar necessary for laying up this number of block will require: 26 sacks of Type II masonry cement and 6800 pounds of sand.

Laying Concrete Block

For most jobs around the house stretcher, corner, and half blocks are needed. Common sizes are 8-×-8-×-16 inches, 8-×-4-×-16 inches, and 6-×-8-×-16 inches.

The mortar for block work consists of 1 part masonry cement and 1 1/4 to 3 parts clean sand. Enough mixing water is added to obtain a workable mortar.

Always lay block from the corners first. Each block is carefully leveled and plumbed because the corners are the guides for the rest of the wall. A line stretched between the corners serves as a guide for the intermediate block. If the wall is long, and the line sags at the center, lay block near the center to hold up the line.

Many techniques are used to place mortar for the joints. One way is to spread a strip of mortar along the face shells of the block. The only mortar placed on the block being laid is put along the end face shells.

A mason's rule of thumb is to use approximately 1/2 inch or mortar between the bricks horizontally and vertically. This rule is known as buttering a thin 1/4-inch layer, of mortar on the brick.

Chapter 5

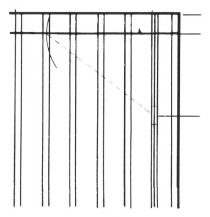

Ceilings

Lowering the ceiling in an older home. Covering unsightly water spots and imperfections in a bedroom. Finishing the ceiling in a remodeled basement while retaining access to pipes, ductwork, and wiring. All these options are available with ceiling tiles.

There are, of course, hundreds of varieties of tile and dozens of manufacturers; so you can easily find the tile of your choice.

Some patterns of ceiling tile have a washable latex finish and can be cleaned with a damp sponge and mild detergent. Some are coated with an acrylic overspray for superior cleaning ability. All offer high light reflectance to brighten dark areas when they are installed with the proper light fixtures.

The Celotex Company of Tampa, Florida, has an outstanding array of ceiling tiles which can fit every room in the house. They range from large 2-×-4 and 2-×-2 lay-in panels to 12-×-12 tiles. A 12-×-12 ceiling tile looks clean, uncluttered, and contemporary.

You can install Celotex 12-×-12 ceiling tile in less than a day. Be sure your measurements and calculations are correct. Don't use shortcuts since every step is important. You will save on the high cost of labor and in no time have a brand new ceiling.

You will need the following tools:

—staple gun,
—9/16-inch staples,
—utility knife,
—chalk line,
—hammer,
—carpenter's square or metal straight edge,
—stepladder, and
—tape measure.

If you are installing your ceiling by the adhesive method include:

—wire brush,
—putty knife, and
—tile adhesive.

CEILING TILES

There are three methods of installing Celotex 12-×-12 ceiling tiles:

103

—stapling to wood furring strips,
—stapling directly to the existing ceiling,
—the adhesive method.

The method you choose will depend on the condition of your ceiling. With any method, however, the tiles should be conditioned to room temperature and humidity. Leave them in the room in opened cartons for 24 hours before installation.

Stapling to Wood Furring Strips. The furring strip method is recommended for installing a new ceiling flush to open joists or onto any type of finished surface. It is ideal for remodeling or for new construction, and it is the easiest of the three recommended methods.

The furring strip method can be used to conceal cracks, warps, and other imperfections in an existing ceiling and, by shimming, can level an uneven ceiling.

Remember that different types of wood have different expansion, contraction, and distortion characteristics; so furring strips should be carefully chosen to adapt to the specific environment. They should also be kiln dried to avoid warping. For best results, store the furring strips in the installation area for 24 hours before you use them.

Stapling Directly to Existing Ceiling. By stapling the tiles directly to an existing ceiling, you save the step of installing furring strips. Only use this method over sound, level gypsum wallboard, however; it should not be used over plaster or over gypsum wall board that is uneven or structurally incapable of holding staples.

To anchor tiles, drive two 9/16-inch staples into a fastening point. Drive the second staple directly over the first one "piggy-back" style so the legs of the second staple flare out to provide the required holding strength.

The Adhesive Method. The adhesive method is designed for use directly over ceilings made of drywall or plaster. The surface must be clean, level, and free of cracks. Loose paint, wallpaper, or other coverings must be removed, and new plaster must be thoroughly dry and have a smooth finish. New gypsum needs no taping, priming, or finishing. After the ceiling is prepared, wire-brush it lightly to remove dust and to increase the "tooth" of the surface.

Although the adhesive method is not as easy to use as the other installation methods recom-

TABLE 5-1. HOW TO ESTIMATE LINEAR FOOTAGE OF FURRING STRIPS.

		8'	9'	10'	11'	12'	13'	14'	15'	16'	17'	18'	19'	20'
					Room dimension perpendicular to joist direction									
	8'	72	81	90	99	108	117	126	135	144	153	162	171	180
	9'	80	90	100	110	120	130	140	150	160	170	180	190	200
	10'	88	99	110	121	132	143	154	165	176	187	198	209	220
	11'	96	108	120	132	144	156	168	180	192	204	216	228	240
Room dimension parallel to joist direction	12'	104	117	130	143	156	169	182	195	208	221	234	247	260
	13'	112	126	140	154	168	182	196	210	224	238	252	266	280
	14'	120	135	150	165	180	195	210	225	240	255	270	285	300
	15'	128	144	160	176	192	208	224	240	256	272	288	304	320
	16'	136	153	170	187	204	221	238	255	272	289	306	323	340
	17'	144	162	180	198	216	234	252	270	288	306	324	342	360
	18'	152	171	190	209	228	247	266	285	304	323	342	361	380
	19'	160	180	200	220	240	260	280	300	320	340	360	380	400
	20'	168	189	210	231	252	273	294	315	336	357	378	399	420

mended, it has an advantage in that the existing ceiling height is maintained.

Estimating Needs

Use the room dimensions in Table 5-1 to estimate your furring strip needs. Because tiles measure 1 square foot, it is not too difficult to estimate how many tiles you will need.

First, measure your ceiling width and length. Round off inches to the next higher whole number of feet. Add one foot to width and one foot to length to allow for borders, special fittings, and spares. Multiply the new length by the new width to get the exact number of tiles you will need. For example:

Actual room size	11'5" × 12'4"
Round off inches	12 × 13
Add 1	13 × 14
Multiply length and width	13 × 14
Total	182 tiles

To be completely accurate, use a grid to draw a diagram of your ceiling before you make your purchase. If you have any questions at all, be sure to discuss them with your tile dealer before you begin.

Calculating Width of Border Tiles

For a balanced ceiling appearance, the border tiles on the opposite sides of the room should be the same width, preferably more than 1/2 the width of a 12-inch tile.

To determine the border tile widths, measure the short wall of the room first (Fig. 5-1). If the wall does not measure an exact number of feet, add 12 inches to the odd inches left over and complete the simple calculations shown in the following example:

Short wall:	12 feet 8 inches
Add:	12 inches
Total:	20
Divide by:	2
Total:	10-inch width for long wall border tiles

For short wall border tile width, measure the long wall and calculate as before:

Long wall:	14 feet 6 inches
Add:	12 inches
Total:	18
Divide by:	2
Total:	9-inch width for short wall border tiles

☐ If you are using the furring strip method, install furring strips. Locate the direction and spacing of joists. If the room has a gypsum or plaster ceiling, find the joists by tapping the ceiling with a hammer, drilling a small hole, or driving a finished nail. Any surface blemishes on the existing ceiling will be concealed by the new tile.

☐ Apply the first 1-×-3-inch wood furring strip flush against the wall at right angles to the ceiling joists with the 3-inch width flat against the ceiling.

☐ Install the second furring strip so that the center of strip is one border tile width from the wall. Snap a chalk line on the ceiling as a guide.

☐ Nail the remaining strips across the joists, measuring 12 inches from the center of one strip to the center of the next strip. Install the final strip flush against the opposite wall (Fig. 5-2).

Snapping Chalk Lines Along Long and Short Walls

Many rooms are not perfect rectangles, but you can create them by snapping chalk lines and marking the border tile widths from the long and short walls. This procedure will allow you to correct any room abnormalities by cutting individual border tiles to fit flush against the walls, giving you a balanced, symmetrical arrangement (Fig. 5-3).

☐ Measure the border tile width (established in the previous calculations) from the short wall. Snap a chalk line. If you are using furring strips, snap the chalk line down the center of the furring strip placed earlier at the border tile width.

☐ Measure the border tile width on the opposite wall and mark point A on the existing chalk line (Fig. 5-4).

☐ Measure exactly 3 feet from point A and mark point B along the same chalk line.

Fig. 5-1. Measure a short area first (courtesy Celotex Corporation).

□ From point A, strike an arc exactly 4 feet away from the chalk line. In the furring strip method, it will appear on the sixth strip.

□ Measure exactly 5 feet from point B and strike an arc intersecting with the first arc, to establish point C. (Fig. 5-5).

□ Snap a chalk line through points A and C, the entire length of the wall. This procedure will assure you of chalk lines at exact right angles to each other.

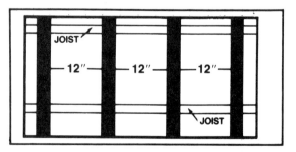

Fig. 5-2. Joist nailing (courtesy Celotex Corporation).

Fig. 5-3. Snap a chalk line (courtesy Celotex Corporation).

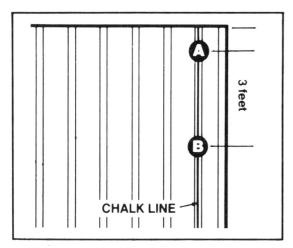

Fig. 5-4. Chalk line area (courtesy Celotex Corporation).

Cutting Corner Border Tiles

Cut border tiles one at a time so that they fit perfectly, correcting for walls that may not be square. Make sure flanges are facing into the room (Fig. 5-6).

One technique for closely fitting border tiles is to place the tile upside down in position so the outside corner is temporarily the inside corner. Mark the tile at the chalk lines and trim with a utility knife, using a carpenter's square or metal straight edge. Remember, always trim the tongue, never the flanges (Fig. 5-7).

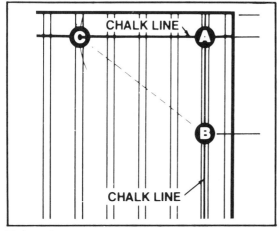

Fig. 5-5. Chalk line detail (courtesy Celotex Corporation).

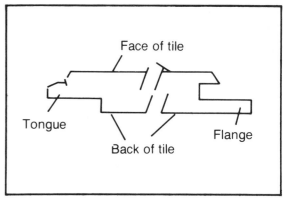

Fig. 5-6. Border tile detail (courtesy Celotex Corporation).

Installing Corner Border Tile

Adhesive Method. Using a putty knife, apply a walnut-sized dab of adhesive approximately 3 inches in from each corner. Keep the size of dabs consistent throughout, or the tiles will not be level.

Place the corner tile in position. Slide it back and forth to obtain good contact with your ceiling. Apply uniform pressure from tile to tile, or tiles will not align evenly.

Drive one or two staples along adhesive sets. Staple the first three rows to prevent sliding. Staple around fixtures if possible.

Furring Strip Method. Position the tile, aligning with chalk marks. Face nail edges of the tile against the wall to the furring strips. Staple the flanges to the furring strips.

Existing Ceiling Method. Position the tile, aligning with chalk marks. Face the nail edges of the tile against the wall to the ceiling. Staple the flanges to the ceiling (Fig. 5-8).

Other Border Tiles

Cut the next two border tiles to fit on either side of the corner tile. Using the upside-down method, accurately measure the border tiles adjacent to the corner tile and cut along the tongue. Install according to the instructions given in the "Installing Corner Border Tile," section.

Installing the 12-×-12 Tiles

The three border tiles form the area for the

Fig. 5-7. Cutting tile (courtesy Celotex Corporation).

first full tile. Install this tile by snugly fitting the interlocking joints and stapling the flanges to the ceiling or furring strips or by applying the adhesive and stapling.

Continue cutting and affixing border tiles according to the method you have selected. If tiles must be cut to fit around lighting fixtures or posts, use a coping or keyhole saw. Be sure to cut with the decorative side of the tile up to prevent damage to the tile surface.

Finishing

When all tiles are in place, apply prefinished border molding to all trim edges of the room to cover any spaces remaining between tiles and walls. Use matching finishing nails. You may wish to countersink finishing nails and cover them with matching putty for an attractive, professional look (Fig. 5-9).

CEILING PANELS

An inexpensive and highly attractive answer to many ceiling needs is the suspended ceiling system, such as designed by Celotex. Celotex's system consists of an easily installed suspended metal grid framework and a choice of attractive 2-×-4 and

109

Fig. 5-8. Staple tiles to furring strips (courtesy Celotex Corporation).

2-×-2 lay-in panels with the option of integrated lighting. They can be used in many ways.

Room Additions. A dramatic alternative to a conventional ceiling is a Celotex lay-in panel system, which can be quickly installed beneath exposed joists in an unfinished room.

Problem Ceilings. A too-high ceiling or an unsightly one can be replaced simply with a Celotex Suspended Ceiling System installed beneath and secured to the existing overhead.

Basement Recreation Rooms. Ordinary ceilings do not lend themselves well to basement

110

Fig. 5-9. Apply a prefabricated border (courtesy Celotex Corporation).

applications because they make overhead wiring, piping, and ducts inaccessible for inspection or repairs. In contrast, Celotex panels can be conveniently lifted out and replaced by hand.

Dark Rooms. A suspended ceiling permits the strategic positioning of fluorescent lighting throughout the room. Fixtures are positioned above the suspended ceiling framework, and translucent luminous panels are installed to provide pleasant, diffused lighting.

Kitchens. In kitchens, an especially modern and attractive effect can be achieved with a dropped ceiling consisting entirely of luminous panels, (also produced by Celotex), in the suspended framework with appropriate fluorescent lighting.

Acoustical Control. A family or recreation room is often a source of high noise levels. Lay-in panels are available which feature acoustical qualities, without sacrificing outstanding appearance, to abate the noise levels in rooms.

Cost. Economy and low budget: the key words in remodeling. You can save money when you in-

stall suspended ceilings yourself because material costs are low, and you eliminate high labor costs.

First Steps

Carefully measure your ceiling twice and draw an accurate dimensional outline on the graph (Fig. 5-10). Be sure to show all columns, lights, ducts, and alcoves. Each square on the graph equals 2 feet.

Next, decide the primary objectives of installing a new ceiling.

Decorative. Celotex 2-×-4-foot or 2-×-2-foot lay-in panels come in a wide choice of attractive patterns, textures, and subtle color tones. Consider the over all decorative effect you wish to achieve so you can make a proper selection of lay-in panel when you visit your tile dealer.

Lighting. If integrated lighting is to be part of your new ceiling, indicate on your graph where luminous panels will be installed.

Acoustical Control. Sound conditioning a room may be one of your objectives. Several styles

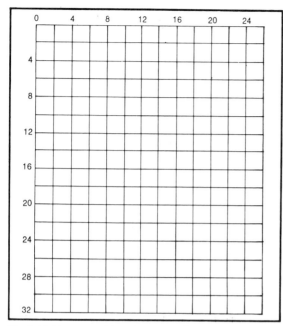

Fig. 5-10. Use a graph to get accurate dimensions (courtesy Celotex Corporation).

of lay-in panels offer acoustical control and also provide you with a selection of beautiful materials.

Determining Material Requirements

Figuring material needs for your new ceiling is not difficult, but it is still best to have your tile dealer check your calculations, especially if your ceiling does not measure an exact number of feet. In this case, a little extra arithmetic is necessary to determine the proper widths for border panels so your ceiling will have a well-balanced appearance.

For example, a room measuring 12 1/3 feet × 14 1/2 feet would require the following calculations to arrive at the approximate widths for border panels:

	Short Wall: 12'4"	
	2' × 4' Panels	2' × 2' Panels
Odd inches:	4"	4"
Add:	48"	24"
Total:	52"	28"

Fig. 5-11. Mark the ceiling height (courtesy Celotex Corporation).

112

Fig. 5-12. Snap a chalk line on your measurement (courtesy Celotex Corporation).

	2′ × 4′ Panels	2′ × 2 Panels
Divide by 2:	2	2
Total:	26″	14″

26 inches is the proper width for long wall border panels when using 2-×-4-foot panels, and 14 inches is the proper width for the long wall border panels when 2-×-2-foot panels are used.

Long Wall: 14′6″	
Odd inches:	6″
Add:	24″
Total:	30″
Divide by 2:	2
Total:	15″

15 inches is the proper width for short wall border panels.

A 48-inch factor is always added to the short wall odd inches when using 2-×-4-foot panels, and a 24-inch factor must be used when working with 2-×-2-foot panels. In both cases, the 24-inch factor is added to the long wall odd inches.

Installation

The simple tools needed to install a suspended panel system include:

—hammer,
—screwdriver,
—measuring tape,
—AWI,
—pliers,

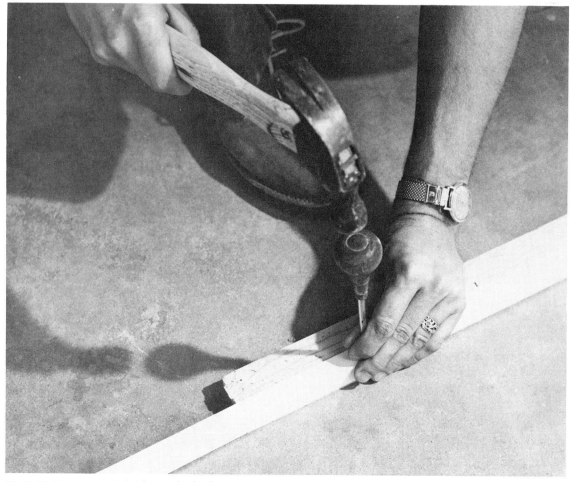

Fig. 5-13. Prepunch wall molding (courtesy Celotex Corporation).

—metal snips,
—chalk line,
—utility knife,
—straight edge, and
—carpenter's level to check the alignment of the suspended grid framework.

Establish the level for your ceiling between the highest window or door frame and the lowest hanging obstruction, such as a pipe or duct. Allow at least 3 inches between the new finished ceiling line and the existing overhead construction. For luminous lighting or ceilings which include recessed lighting the suspended ceiling should be at least 6 inches below the fluorescent lamps. Mark the desired height for your ceiling at each end of each wall (Fig. 5-11), then follow these steps:

☐ Using the ceiling height marks as reference points, snap a chalk line around the perimeter of the room to provide a guide for installing the metal wall angle molding, adjusting it as needed to ensure a perfectly level ceiling (Fig. 5-12).

☐ Prepunch the wall molding with an awl or other metal punch or drill to provide holes for nails or screws. Holes should be spaced for fastening to studs, which are usually 16 inches on center space them 24 inches apart for fastening to a masonry wall (Fig. 5-13).

☐ Keep the bottom of the molding aligned with the chalk line and nail or screw in place at each stud on framed walls. Use plastic anchors and screws spaced 24 inches apart on masonry walls (Fig. 5-14).

☐ As starting reference points, determine the centers of the opposite walls. From the center points mark 24-inch increments along the walls to the corners. Depending on the border tile width you desire, the center of the first main runner will either be on the center line of the marked wall or on the next 24-inch increment mark (Fig. 5-15).

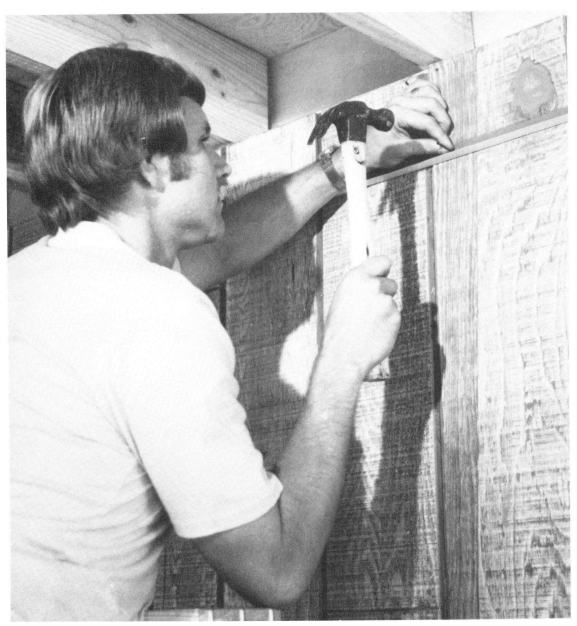

Fig. 5-14. Nail or screw molding in place (courtesy Celotex Corporation).

Fig. 5-15. Determine the center of the wall (courtesy Celotex Corporation).

Fig. 5-16. Hanger wires (courtesy Celotex Corporation).

116

Fig. 5-17. Attach the hanger wires to the cross tees (courtesy Celotex Corporation).

☐ Snap chalk lines from the selected increment mark between the opposite walls across the bottom of the joists to determine the center lines of the main runners—48 inches on center for 2-×-4-foot panels, and 24 inches on center for 2-×-2-foot panels.

☐ Install nails or screw eyes every 4 inches along the main runner chalk lines. Attach No. 14 gauge hanger wires to the nails. Over an existing ceiling, install screw eyes, being certain they penetrate the ceiling and enter the bottoms of joists a minimum of 1 inch.

☐ Grip the hanger wire 1 1/4 inches higher than the base of the wall angle molding and bond

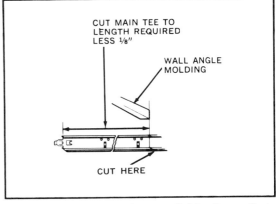

Fig. 5-18. Cut the main tee (courtesy Celotex Corporation).

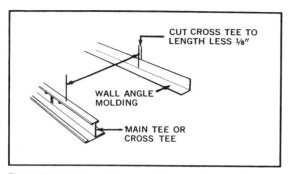

CUT CROSS TEE TO LENGTH LESS ⅛"

WALL ANGLE MOLDING

MAIN TEE OR CROSS TEE

Fig. 5-19. Join the main runners (courtesy Celotex Corporation).

each wire to a 90-degree angle (Figs. 5-16 and 5-17).

☐ To determine the width of the border tile along the walls parallel to the main runners repeat the sequence described for the main runners, but use 12-inch increments.

☐ All starting main runners must be cut 1/8 inch shorter than the desired length to allow for the thickness of the wall molding on which they rest. Cut them at a point to ensure the slots for engaging the cross tees are in the same vertical plane and in line with the selected increment marked on the

Fig. 5-20. Attach the cross tee for the border panels (courtesy Celotex Corporation).

118

Fig. 5-21. Insert ties into the slots (courtesy Celotex Corporation).

walls parallel to the main runners (Fig. 5-18).

☐ Main runners are joined end to end by engaging the end splice tabs, with the painted sides face to face. For added support, attach hanger wires at both sides of the splice (Fig. 5-19).

☐ Cross tees for border panels are cut to the necessary length, again less 1/8 inch to allow for the thickness of the wall angle molding (Fig. 5-20).

☐ The end connectors of the 4-foot cross tees are inserted into the slots of the main runners with the lock tabs to the outside of the slots. If it is necessary to disengage cross tees, use a coin or your thumb to depress the lock tab spring. For ceilings using 2-×-2-foot panels, 2-foot cross tees are inserted into the slots of the 4-foot cross tees at the mid-point (Fig. 5-21).

☐ If applicable, lighting fixtures, associated wiring, and fluorescent lamps should be installed next. Use 40-watt lamps located a minimum of 6 inches above the suspended grid system.

For *individual recessed units:* center 2-lamp fluorescent fixtures over the location of each luminous panel. Box the unit with foil or paint the wood a high light-reflecting white to direct light through the luminous panel.

For an *all-over luminous ceiling:* install single lamp fluorescent fixtures on the center line between grid members in parallel rows, 24 inches apart. The ends of fixtures should be butted to ensure a continuous area of light. For the most effective illumination, the entire area above the ceiling should be painted white.

☐ With the grid framework and any fixtures in place, cut border lay-in panels to the appropriate size with a sharp utility knife, using a straightedge as a guide (Fig. 5-22).

☐ If the room has a column, measure its shape and location within the module (Fig. 5-23).

☐ Mark the size and shape of the column on the panel in its exact location; then carefully cut the opening to the shape with a utility knife or a fine-toothed keyhole saw. Cut the panel from one short

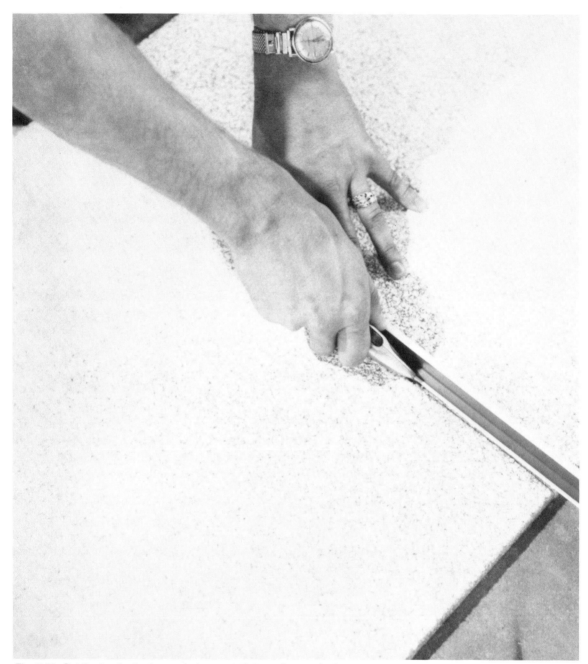

Fig. 5-22. Cut the border lay-in panels (courtesy Celotex Corporation).

edge to the opposite short edge through the centerline of the column opening (Fig. 5-24).

☐ Place the two parts of the panel in the grid system around the column (Fig. 5-25).

☐ Complete your new ceiling by tipping entire panels through the openings and lowering them to rest on the flanges of the main runners and cross tees (Fig. 5-26).

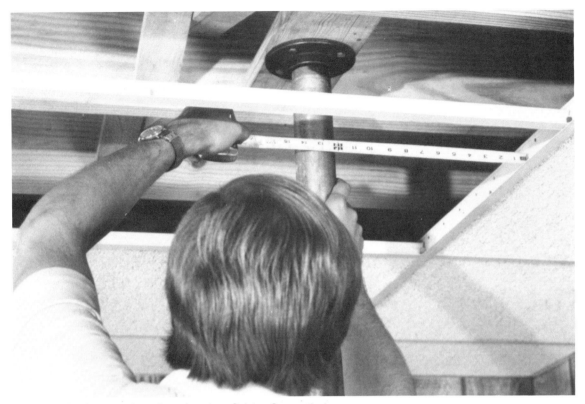

Fig. 5-23. Working around a column (courtesy Celotex Corporation).

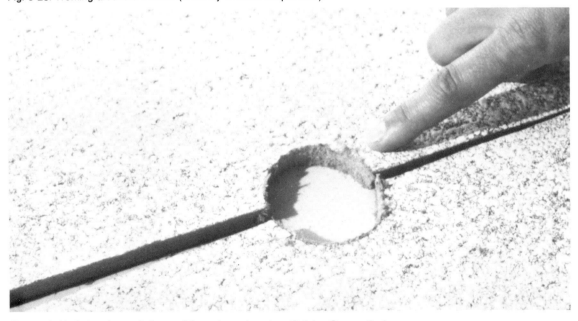

Fig. 5-24. Mark the size and shape of the column (courtesy Celotex Corporation).

Fig. 5-25. Panels are in place around the column (courtesy Celotex Corporation).

Fig. 5-26. Complete the ceiling by tapping in the panels (courtesy Celotex Corporation).

OTHER CEILING COVERINGS

There are, of course, other ceiling coverings, such as gypsum board or other sheet materials, which are installed in much the same manner as interior walls. Cracks in plaster can be repaired with plaster patching in the same manner as walls are patched; however, where cracks are extensive, a new ceiling is the only cure.

Gypsum board can be applied directly to ceiling joists by first removing existing ceiling material. It may also be applied directly over plaster or to furring strips nailed over the existing ceiling where plaster is uneven.

Use 2-×-2 or 2-×-3-inch furring strips ori-

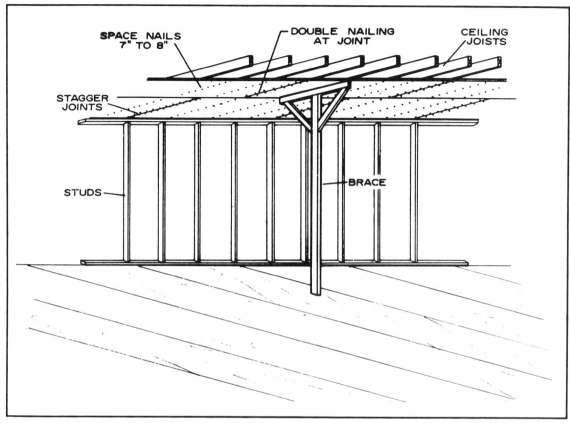

Fig. 5-27. Install gypsum board on the ceiling (courtesy USDA).

ented perpendicular to the joists and spaced 16 inches on centers for 3/8-inch gypsum board, or 24 inches on centers for 1/2-inch gypsum board. Nail the furring strips with 2d nails at each joist. Apply the gypsum boards with end joints staggered and centered on a joist or furring strip. Place the sheets so there is only light contact at the joints. One or two braces slightly longer than the ceiling height are useful (Fig. 5-27). (Nail the gypsum board to all supporting members with nails spaced 7 to 8 inches apart. Use 5d cooler-type nails for 1/2-inch gypsum board and 4d nails for 3/8-inch gypsum board. Nail heads should not penetrate the surface. Each nail-head location should be slightly dimpled with the head of a hammer, but be careful not to break the surface of the paper.

Gypsum board should be applied to the ceiling before wall finish is applied.

Chapter 6

Flooring

Plywood and plywood systems have virtually revolutionized construction practices, especially in renovation. And with good reasons. For low budget, in-place cost, versatility, good looks, and superior structural performance, plywood is simply hard to beat.

Plywood can be used many ways in remodeling, and what better place to start than with your flooring—to give a sound foundation to your renovation project.

Let us assume that the floors in your home will need total reworking, which means that the entire flooring of the house will require remodeling. First, however, let us discover a little about the construction panel products with which you will be dealing.

PRODUCT AND PERFORMANCE STANDARDS

Panels for construction applications can be manufactured in a variety of ways: as plywood (cross-laminated wood veneer), as composites (veneer faces bonded to reconstituted wood cores),

and as nonveneered panels (including waferboard, oriented strand board, and certain specific classes of particleboard).

Some grades of veneered panels are manufactured under the provisions of *U.S. Product Standards PS 1-74/ANSI A 199, 1 for Construction and Industrial Plywood*, a detailed manufacturing specification developed cooperatively by the plywood industry and the United States Department of Commerce. Other veneered panels, however, as well as an increasing number of performance-rated composite and nonveneered panels, are manufactured under the provisions of American Plywood Association Performance Standards, which establish performance criteria for specific construction applications. It is mostly with these standards that you, the homeowner, will be confronted.

These APA performance-rated panels are easy to use and specify because the recommended end use and maximum support spacings are clearly indicated in the APA trademark. APA performance-rated panels are also designed and manufactured to meet building code requirements.

A typical trademark for one of the new APA performance-rated panels, APA-Rated Sheathing, is explained in Fig. 6-1.

Grade

Panel grades are generally identified in terms of the grade of veneer used for face and back plies (i.e., A-B, B-C, etc.), or by a name suggesting the panel's intended end use (i.e., APA-Rated Sheathing, APA-Rated Sturdi-I-Floor, etc.).

Veneer grades define veneer appearance in terms of natural, unrepaired growth characteristics and the allowable number and size of repairs that can be made during manufacture. The highest quality of veneer grades are N and A. D-grade veneer is the lowest grade veneer, and it is used only for backs and inner plies of panels intended for interior use or for applications protected from exposure to permanent or severe moisture.

Panels with B-grade or better veneer faces are always sanded smooth in manufacture to fulfull the requirements of their intended end use, such as cabinets, shelving, furniture, and built-ins. APA-rated sheathing panels are unsanded because a smooth surface is not a requirement of their intended end use. Still other panels require only touch-sanding for "sizing" to make the panel thickness more uniform.

All unsanded and touch-sanded panels and panels sanded on one side only carry the APA trademark on the panel back. Panels that are sanded on both sides (panels with B-grade or better veneer on both sides) or that have special overlaid surfaces carry the APA trademark on the panel edge.

Exposure Durability

APA performance-rated panels can be manufactured in three exposure durability classifications: Exterior, Exposure 1, and Exposure 2. Panels marked *Exterior* are designed for applications subject to continuous exposure to the weather or moisture. Panels marked *Exposure 1* are intended for protected construction applications where the ability to resist moisture during long construction delays or where exposure to conditions of similar severity is required. Panels marked *Exposure 2* are intended for protected construction applications where moderate delays in providing protection from moisture may be expected or where conditions of high humidity or water leakage may exist.

Plywood manufactured under Product Standard PS 1 is designated either as exterior or interior

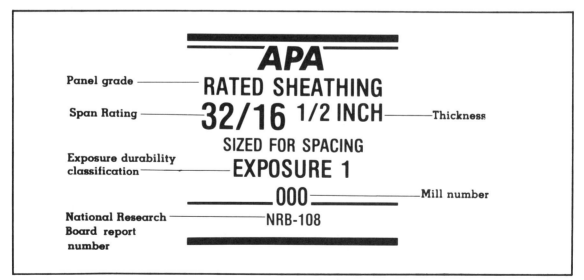

Fig. 6-1. APA performance rating code (courtesy American Plywood Association).

with exterior, intermediate, or interior glue. Most interior-type panels with exterior glue are comparable in exposure durability to performance-rated panels designated Exposure 1, and they are suitable for applications where the ability to resist moisture during long construction delays or where exposure to conditions of similar severity is required. Because the lower grade of veneer permitted for backs and inner plies of interior-type panels may affect glueline and performance, however, only exterior-type plywood should be used for permanent exposure to the weather or moisture.

Span Ratings

APA-rated sheathing, APA-rated Sturd-I-Floor, and APA 303 siding panels carry numbers in their trademarks called span ratings. These ratings denote the maximum recommended center-to-center spacing, in inches, of supports over which the panels should be placed.

The span rating in APA-rated sheathing trademarks appears as two numbers separated by a slash, such as 32/16 and 48/24. The first number denotes the maximum recommended spacing of supports when the panel is used for roof sheathing with the long dimension of the panel across three or more supports. The second number indicates the maximum recommended spacing of supports when the panel is used for subflooring with the long dimension of the panel across three or more supports. A panel marked 32/16 for example, may be used for roof decking over supports 32 inches on center or for subflooring over supports 16 inches on center.

The span ratings in the trademarks on APA-rated Sturd-I-Floor and 303 siding panels appear as a single number. APA-rated Sturd-I-Floor panels are designed specifically for single floor (combined subfloor-underlayment) applications and are manufactured with span ratings of 16, 20, 24, and 48 inches. The span ratings for APA-rated Sturd-I-Floor panels, like those for APA-rated sheathing, are based on the application of the panel with the long dimension across three or more supports.

APA 303 sidings are produced with span ratings of 16 and 24 inches and may be used directly over studs or nonstructural wall sheathing (Sturd-I-Wall construction), or over plywood which can be nailed or lumber sheathing (double-wall construction). Panels with a span rating of 16 inches can be applied vertically to studs spaced 16 inches on center. Panels bearing a span rating of 24 inches can be used vertically over studs 24 inches on center. APA 303 siding panels can be applied horizontally directly to studs 16 or 24 inches on center provided that horizontal joints are blocked. When used over nailable plywood or lumber sheathing, the 303 siding span rating refers to the maximum recommended spacing of vertical rows of nails rather than to stud spacing.

JOIST LAYOUT

Figure 6-2 shows an overall view of a typical floor framing. Joists are the main supporting members of the floor. They rest on the sill plate at the outer end and the girder at the inner end. Joists are generally 2- × -1 lumber placed on edge. When purchasing lumber for joists, order kiln-dried material if available to minimize shrinkage. Be sure to check for joist size and spacing and for any special lumber grade requirements. The most common spacing for joists is 16 inches on center.

In planning joist layout, remember that panels are 4 × 8 feet and that panel ends must be supported on joists to provide the necessary floor stiffness.

Any joists having a slight edgewise bow should be placed so that the bow, or *crown*, is on top. You can determine if a joist is crowned by sighting along the edge. A crowned joist will tend to straighten out when subfloor and normal floor loading are applied. With straight joists, place the edge having the largest edge knots on top so the joists are stronger.

The following directions call for joists 16 inches on center; however, a spacing of 24 inches or wider can be used.

☐ Lay out floor-joist positions. Mark joist locations on the sill plates using two marks, one for each side of the joist (Fig. 6-3). Mark the end joist location on the sills, even with the outside edge of the sill. Mark the location of the first interior joist, so that spacing between joists is 13 3/4 inches (16 inches from the outside of the sill to the centerline of the first interior joist). Mark the position of other

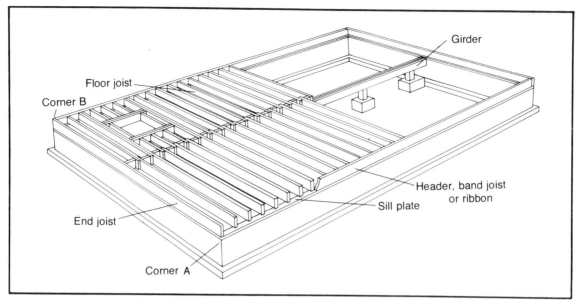

Fig. 6-2. View of typical floor framing (courtesy American Plywood Association).

joists, spacing them 16 inches on center, continuing to the end of the house. The location of the end joist at this end of the house should also be marked on the sill.

☐ Repeat this process on the opposite sill, but space 12 1/4 inches between the end and first interior joist (14 1/2 inches from the outside of the sill to the centerline of the first interior joist), to allow for joist overlap at the center of the house. You must start the joist layout from the same end wall as in the last step, so that all joists are parallel to the outside walls. Also, mark joist locations on

the girder to ensure alignment of joists between the sidewalls.

☐ Check the floor plan and mark on the sill plates the location of all partitions parallel to the joists. Generally, double joists are required under each partition, and the extra joists must be located and marked on the sill. A regular joist can serve as one of the "doubling" joists (Fig. 6-4).

☐ Mark the location of any openings for crawl-space access, chimney, etc. Regular joists on each side of these openings will be placed with other regular joists, but all special framing should

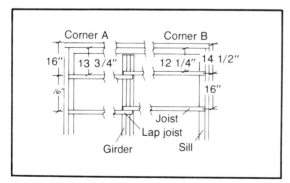

Fig. 6-3. Joist location layout (courtesy American Plywood Association).

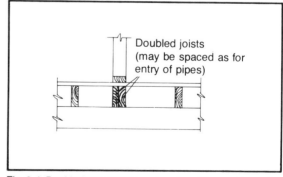

Fig. 6-4. Doubled joist (courtesy American Plywood Association).

be left out until these regular joists are in. When locating a floor opening, measure from its center in opposite directions to locate the inside edges. This procedure ensures that the opening is located properly according to the house plans.

□ Select straight pieces of joist material for headers and end joists. Cut and nail them in place. Use 8d common nails and toenail from the outside lower edge of the header and end joist into the sill, spacing nails about every 16 inches. Nail corner joists with three 16d common nails.

□ Using a steel square, mark the vertical alignment for each joist on the inside face of the header joists. Continue the horizontal lines on the sill to the inside face of the header.

□ Cut joists to length, if necessary. The lap of the joists over the center of the girder should be at least 4 inches and no more than 28 inches. Lay the joists across the sill and girder with all crown edges facing the same direction. This procedure eliminates the need for additional checking when joists are tipped up for installation. Floor joists can be butted over the center girder to form in-line joists instead of being lapped if joists are spliced with a 24-inch long piece of plywood or lumber nailed to each joist.

□ Place joists at the marks and drive two 16d common nails through the headers into the end of each floor joist. Toenail joists to the girder, using three 8d common nails for each joist. Nail lapped joists together over the girder with three 10d common nails.

□ Frame openings in the floor as shown in your house plans. One such opening is illustrated in Figs. 6-2 and 6-5. The order of placing members is critical if you are going to end-nail the members. The order of placement is given in Fig. 6-5 for the particular opening shown. If members are placed in the order shown, all but the "trimmers" can be end-nailed.

□ An alternative method involves the use of *framing anchors* specially made steel angles which will allow placement of members in a more logical, less critical order.

□ Install solid blocking between joists over the girder to help keep the joists parallel and to straighten any that tend to twist. Nail blocking on alternate sides of the girder centerline (Fig. 6-6). Drive two 16d nails into each end of each piece of blocking. Keep solid blocking flush with the top edges of the joists.

□ Check the level of the top of all joists, headers, and blocking. Shim up or trim down as needed to provide a firm, level base for structural wood panel subflooring.

INSTALLING SUBFLOORING

Subflooring is used over joists in two-layer construction to form a working platform and base for finish flooring. That is, the floor consists of

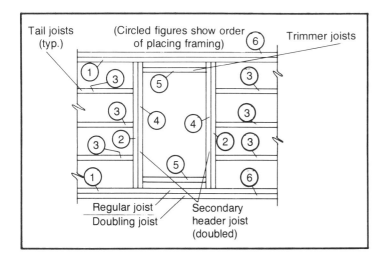

Fig. 6-5. Frame opening (courtesy American Plywood Association).

structural wood panel subflooring, a separate layer of underlayment, and finished floor covering, such as carpet or resilient tiles. The subflooring can also be covered with hardwood. Single-floor construction with APA-rated Sturd-I-Floor panels is also widely used.

Many grades and thicknesses of structural wood panel sheathing are suitable for use as subflooring, but APA Rated Sheathing Exposure 1 is most commonly used. Always cover and protect subflooring and other panels during construction if possible.

When applying subflooring, place and panel on the joists so that the face, or best side, is up. Space sheathing panels 1/8 inch at panel and joists and 1/4 inch at edge joints.

Subfloor Sheathing Layout

Begin at the corner of the house where you began the joist layout. A little time spent planning can save time and material in the long run.

☐ Review your plans and make trial measurements with your tape to estimate how the first row of panels will come out at the other end of the floor. To ensure proper alignment of the first row, strike a chalk line across the joists the length of the floor area 4 feet from the outside edge of the header.

☐ Start the first row with a full-sized 4- × -8 panel set flush with the outside edge of the end joist and the long panel dimension across the joists. Use the chalk marks as a guide to align the first row. Allow appropriate spacing between panel ends. Trim the end of the last panel in the first row flush

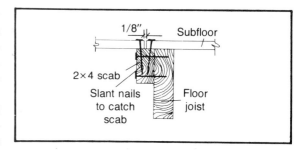

Fig. 6-7. A 2 × 4 scab (courtesy American Plywood Association).

with the end joist. Any odd-sized panel sections required to fill in at the end of a row should cover two or more spans. These fill-in panels must be placed with the face grain across supports.

If the last panel in the first row comes out 1 inch or more short of the inside edge of the end joist because of an odd building dimension, nail a 2-×-4 "scab," or block, to the end joist to support the panel end (Fig. 6-7). Then use a filler strip of scrap material as required. Remember that you can increase the panel end gaps slightly to gain length in a row. Always maintain appropriate spacing between panel ends.

☐ Lay out the remaining rows up to the place where the joists are lapped, usually at the center of the floor area. To stagger the panel joints, start the second row with a half panel (4 × 4 feet). Leave appropriate spacing at the panel edges between rows. Start the third row with a full panel once again, and so on. Trim an occasional panel end slightly, if required, as you go down the row to keep the end joists roughly centered over the joists. Usually only one panel per row must be trimmed.

☐ Since the floor joists are generally lapped side by side over the interior girder, you will need to "step back" your panel layout somewhere near this point. Usually, house dimensions and joists overlap work out so that a joint between rows of panels falls over the joist lap area. If so, you have no problem. You will simply cut the first panel of the next row 1 1/2 inches short to allow for the lap. If this joint does not fall over the lap, it will be necessary to "scab" a 2 × 4 on the side of a joist every 8 feet to support the end of one of the panels (Fig. 6-7).

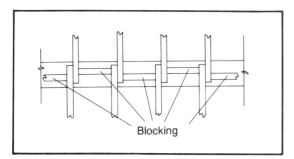

Fig. 6-6. Nailing blocking (courtesy American Plywood Association).

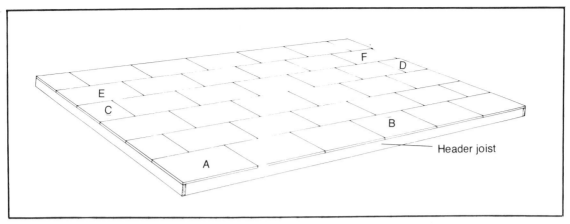

Fig. 6-8. Floor layout (courtesy American Plywood Association).

□ Begin the second half of the floor so that the panel joists are staggered as indicated in the first two steps.

Example

Some of the previous steps can be illustrated by the example subfloor layout in Fig. 6-8. If you simply started from corner A and laid the first row of panels with the recommended gap, you would probably need to trim the fourth panel (B), since it would force the fifth one too far off the centerline of the joist. By figuring carefully, or by laying the fifth and sixth panels in place and measuring, you can make just the right amount of cut on only one panel in the row. Some manufacturers size panels for proper spacing so that panel ends will remain on the joist centerline.

In the example house, the first row could start with 4-×-8-foot panel, the second row with a

4-×-6-foot panel, and the third with a 4-×-8-foot panel. The joint between this row and the next then falls very nearly over the centerline of the girder.

The first panel in the next row (C) would be 4 feet wide by 46 1/2 inches long. Cutting it 46 1/4 inches long will facilitate end spacing in that row. This row of panels can probably be spaced so that the panel at the other end of the row will be the only other one to be cut (D).

The fifth row will start with a 48-×-94 1/4-inch panel (E). The fourth panel in that row will probably need to be cut to achieve a bearing for the fifth, and a scab may be required under the end of the last panel (F).

Theoretically, there would be a 1 1/2-inch gap at the far end of this row, because of the loss at the near end from lapping joists, and because this house is a length that is a multiple of 8 feet. This 1 1/2-inch space could be filled with the trim cut from

Fig. 6-9. Nailing along joist (courtesy American Plywood Association).

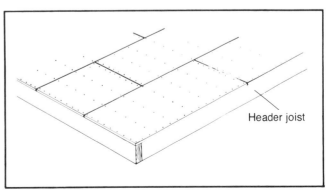

Panel E, or it could be ignored since it will be covered by the wall plate.

These small-dimensional trade-offs are best handled as they appear, and few rules can be laid down for handling them.

Subfloor Nailing and Placement

☐ Nail panels in place. Use 6d common nails for 1/2-inch panels or 8d for 5/8- or 3/4-inch panels. Place nails 3/8 inch from the edge of the panel and space them 6 inches apart along the outside perimeter of the house and along the panel end butt joint over the interior joists. Drive nails at a slight angle to penetrate floor joists. Space nails 10 inches apart when nailing into joists under the panel interior. With these spacings, 9 nails are required across each end of each panel, 17 nails along an 8-foot supported panel edge, and 6 nails along each interior joist (Fig. 6-9).

Drive subfloor nails accurately so that they all penetrate the joists. Nails that miss joists or angle out the side of joists can cause floor squeaks. Snap chalk lines on the panels showing joist locations to ensure that nails are driven correctly. Take special care where the joists lap at the girder, because rows of nails must jog at that point. Where scabs are required because of the offset at the overlapped joists over the girder, use 10d nails to attach a 2 × 4 scab to the side of the joist to support the panel ends. The scab should be of sufficient length to provide full support to the panel ends.

INSTALLING APA-RATED STURD-I-FLOOR

APA-rated Sturd-I-Floor panels are designed specifically for residential single-floor applications. They serve as both subflooring and underlayment.

Panels are manufactured with tongue-and-groove edges that eliminate the need for blocking. Panels may also be ordered with square edges however. All Sturd-I-Floor panels are moisture resistant, but if panels will be exposed permanently to the weather or moisture, use the exterior type.

The following steps pertain to APA-rated Sturd-I-Floor 16, 20, and 24 on center—the most commonly used grades for residential applications. For applications where wider spans are required,

panels 48 on center (2-4-1) are recommended. There are two basic support spacing arrangements for Sturd-I-Floor 48 on center—2 × lumber joists spaced 32 inches on center and 4 × girders spaced 48 inches on center. Layout and application for panels 48 on center are similar to that described for conventionally framed floors.

☐ Measure the area to be covered and estimate how the first row of panels will come out at the other end of the floor. Use the same plywood panel layout and trimming plan described in the first two steps for subflooring. Always place the long dimension of panels perpendicular to the joists and across two or more spans between joists.

☐ End joists of panels should be staggered between rows (Fig. 6-10). Starting from the outside edge of the one header, snap chalk lines across joists every 4 feet to serve as a guide for panel alignment and for gluing boundaries.

FLOOR COVERINGS

Traditionally, people have used linoleum in the kitchen, ceramic tile in the bathroom, and wood floors throughout the rest of the house. Today, with the wide variety of flooring materials available, — there is little reason to be bound by tradition.

The variety of materials include wood in various forms, asphalt, vinyl, vinyl asbestos, rubber and cork tile, ceramics, linoleum, sheet vinyl, carpeting, and liquid seamless flooring.

In making a choice, liveability, aesthetics, durability, maintenance, and cost must be considered. Remember, no one material is ideally suited to the requirements of every room in your home.

The principle kinds of floor coverings used as wearing, or *finished,* surfaces are: resilient, wood, ceramic tile, clay and carpet.

Resilient Flooring

Resilient surfaces refer to a number of different types of water-resistant materials. They range from the traditional linoleum available in rolls to thin sheets of asphalt, vinyl, vinyl asbestos, rubber, or cork tile.

Resilient surfaces are dense and have nonab-

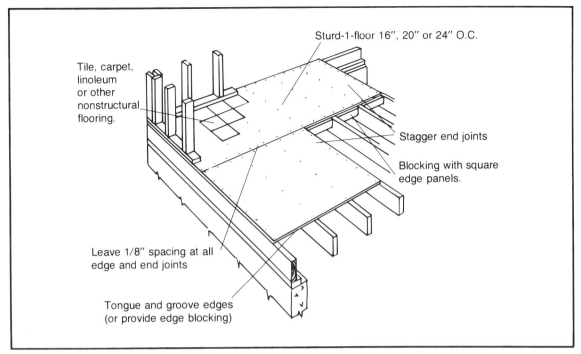

Tile, carpet, linoleum or other nonstructural flooring.

Sturd-1-floor 16″, 20″ or 24″ O.C.

Stagger end joints

Blocking with square edge panels.

Leave 1/8″ spacing at all edge and end joints

Tongue and groove edges (or provide edge blocking)

Fig. 6-10. Stagger the end joists of panels (courtesy American Plywood Association).

sorbent surfaces. Their resilience aids in sound control and provides resistance to indentation. The density of the material usually provides long life and ease of maintenance. The most expensive material will usually give the most beauty and highest wear resistance, thus making these materials especially desirable for the budget minded. The lowest cost materials give the least wear and should be used only as a short-term covering.

Sheet materials are more difficult to install than tile; however, in comparable materials, sheet usually costs less than tile. Most resilient surfaces are secured to the subfloor with an adhesive, such as linoleum paste, asphalt emulsion, latex, or epoxy. Use what the flooring manufacturer specifies.

Linoleum. Linoleum is a blend of linseed oil, pigments, fillers, and resin binders bonded to a backing of asphalt-saturated felt. It is available in solid colors or with inlaid, embossed, or textured patterns, simulating stone, wood, or tile. It is available in rolls 6 feet, 8 feet, or wider and in tiles either 9 × 9 inches or 12 × 12 inches with thicknesses of 1/16, .09, and 1/8 inch.

Linoleum should be laid according to the manufacturer's instructions and is usually rolled to ensure adhesion to the floor. Linoleum and resilient tile both require a smooth underlayment or a smooth concrete to which they are bonded with an adhesive. Linoleum should not be laid on concrete slabs on the ground or basement floors, but many of the other resilient tiles can be used in these areas.

Linoleum provides fair wear resistance, and its color extends completely through to the backing material. It has a hard, durable surface, is greaseproof, and is easy to clean; however, it will be damaged by cleaning products containing alkali solutions.

Asphalt Tile. Asphalt tile is a combination of asbestos fibers, ground limestone, and mineral pigments, with an asphalt binder. It is one of the lowest-priced resilient coverings. Some types are damaged by grease and soil; so they should not be used in kitchens. Its price depends on the color:

133

dark colors are the least expensive; light colors and special patterns are the most expensive.

Asphalt tiles are manufactured with the pattern through the total thickness. Some tile patterns simulate other materials but the pattern does not penetrate its thickness, and it will wear rapidly under heavy use.

This tile is about 1/8 inch thick and either 9 × 9 or 12 × 12 inches in size. Adhesive is spread using a notched trowel, with both size of notches and adhesive recommended.

Asphalt tile will stain and break down if it contacts animal fats and mineral oils; it is brittle and breaks easily, and its recovery from indentation is negligible. It can, however, be used on concrete slabs, on grade, and where there may be a moisture problem.

Rubber Tile. Rubber tile is based on natural or synthetic rubber. Mineral fillers and nonfading organic pigments are used to produce a narrow range of colors and patterns.

The standard sizes are 9 × 9 inches and 12 × 12 inches. Larger sizes are available at a higher cost. The thicknesses are .08, 1/8, and 3/16 inch.

Rubber tile is resilient and has high resistance to indentation. The material is softened by petroleum products, and its resistance to grease and kitchen oils depends on its methods of manufacture. Waxing and buffing are necessary to maintain a high gloss and the surface becomes slippery when wet. Use of a vapor barrier or epoxy adhesive for a slab on a grade installation is required.

Cork. Cork tile consists of granulated cork bark bound by a synthetic resin. The best tile has a clear film of vinyl applied to improve its durability, water resistance, and ease of maintenance. Tile sizes are 6 × 6 inches and 12 × 12 inches, with a range of thicknesses from 1/8 to 1/2 inch.

Cork floors are great for foot comfort and sound control. They wear rapidly and do not resist impact loads well, however. Maintenance is difficult since the material is broken down by grease and alkalies.

Vinyl Flooring. Vinyl floor covering's chief ingredient is polyvinyl chloride (PVC). It also contains resin binders, with mineral filters, stabilizers,

plasticizers, and pigments. The vinyl may be filled or clear.

Clear vinyl consists of a layer of opaque particles or pigments covered with a wearing surface of clear vinyl bonded to a vinyl or polyvinyl surface. It provides high resistance to wear.

Filled vinyl is made of chips of vinyl of varied color and shape immersed in a clear vinyl base and bonded by heat and pressure. When it is installed in a basement, a vapor barrier or an epoxy adhesive should be used.

Vinyl tile is the most costly, but also the most wear resistant and easily maintained of the various tiles. It is produced in standard size squares of 9 × 9 inches and 12 × 12 inches, and in standard thicknesses of 1/6 inch, .080 inch, 3/32 inch, and 1/8 inch.

Sheet Vinyl. Sheet vinyl may be produced with a layer of vinyl foam bonded to the backing or between the finished surface and the backing. The result is a resilient flooring with good walking comfort and effective sound-absorbancy.

Sheet vinyl with resilient backing smooths out minor surface imperfections. Most vinyl will lay flat; so no adhesive is required. Double-faced tape is used at joints and around the edge to keep the covering from moving. Most sheet vinyls are available in widths of 6, 9, 12, and 15 feet, so that complete rooms can be covered with a minimum of splicing, permitting a fast, easy installation. The material is cut to room size with scissors and then taped down.

Vinyl is produced in rolls 8 feet or more wide and can be installed over most subsurfaces. While the material has high resistance to grease, stains, and alkali, its surface is easily damaged by abrasion and indentation.

Vinyl-Asbestos. Vinyl-asbestos tile consists of blended compositions of asbestos fibers, vinyls, plasticizers, color pigments, and fillers. The tiles, without backing, are 9 × 9 inches, or 12 × 12 inches square, and 1/16, 3/32, or 1/8 inch thick. The tile is available in marbled patterns, or textured to simulate stone, marble, travertine, and wood.

Vinyl-asbestos tile is semiflexible and requires a rigid subfloor support. It has high resistance to grease, oils, alkaline substances, and some acids. It is quiet underfoot and many forms do not need frequent waxing. It can be used almost anywhere and can be obtained with a peel-and-stick backing.

Seamless Flooring

Seamless flooring consisting of resin chips combined with a urethane binder can be applied over any stable base, including old floor tile. It is applied as a liquid in several coats and allowed to dry between coats. Complete application may take from 1/2 to 2 days depending on the brand used. Manufacturers' instructions for application are quite complete. This floor covering is easily renewed by additional coatings, and damaged spots are easily patched by adding more chips and binder.

Carpeting

While carpeting was at one time one of the most expensive floor coverings, there are many good carpets which may be obtained even for those building or remodeling on a tight budget. Avoid low prices if they are too low to be real, and any questionable package deals unless you have thoroughly investigated them. Since furnishing styles are more mixed today than they were years ago you are not bound to an all-traditional or all-modern style, any more than you are bound to using just one type of flooring throughout your house.

Carpeting lends itself beautifully to the remodeling of an older home where only traditional linoleum has been previously used. It can be installed over almost any flooring that is level, relatively smooth, and free from major surface imperfections, and it is now available for all rooms, even the kitchen, where a very closely weaved carpet must be used.

Thought must be given to the cost, however. Usually carpeting is more expensive initially than are wood floors. The cost of carpeting may be two or three times that of a finished wood floor, and the life of the carpeting before replacement is much less than that of a wood floor. Carpeting requires less maintenance, however, and has the advantage of sound absorption and resistance to impact. For the most part, today many feel it is the ultimate in

decor and luxurious flooring.

Tweed and shag carpeting is usually more informal, while plush-cut pile, sculptured patterns, and formal designs are best for more formal rooms. Colors of medium intensity show oil the least and usually allow more freedom in the overall color scheme. Plush piles show footprints and traffic patterns more than dense piles of low to medium loops or twists.

Density in carpeting refers to the amount of pile per square inch of carpeting. To check density, roll the edge of the carpet back to back to see how close the rows and stitches of yarn are. If there are large spaces, and the backing is quite evident, the quality is low.

Fiber content is very important to carpet performance, maintenance, and appearance. Wool, the traditional carpet fiber, is resilient, luxurious, resistant to abrasion and soil, warm, and easy to maintain. It is, however generally higher in cost per square yard than the synthetic fibers, such as nylon, acrylic, and polyester.

Acrylic fibers are most nearly like wool. An acrylic carpet is a good choice if you want the look and feel of wool at a lower cost, and, because of its hypoalergenic properties, it should be highly considered.

Polyesters have the weight and luxury of wool but also have more shine and less resilience. They are in the same price range as acrylics.

Nylon is the best-wearing synthetic fiber, and for budget-saving it is the one that is suggested because it is tough, has great soil resistance and cleans easily.

Regardless of which you choose, padding, or underlay will lengthen the life of any carpeting and add luxury and warmth. Pads may be made of hair, sponge, foam rubber, foam rubber on hair, or jute and hair.

Wood Flooring

Many varieties of both hardwoods and softwoods are available for flooring. Certain hardwoods, because of their resistance to wear, are more often used than others. Two are oak and maple.

Wood flooring is finished with a combination of coatings, such as a sealer and varnish or a liquid plastic.

Wood flooring can be simply nailed to the subfloor or, when used over a concrete slab, nailed to wood "sleepers" fastened to the slab. In either case, the floor is sanded smooth and finished with stain and sealer. Damaged spots are easily patched by adding more chips and binders.

Hardwood. The most commonly used hardwood flooring is oak because of its beauty, warmth, and durability.

Maple flooring, produced from the sugar, or rock, maple, is smooth, strong, and hard. The grain of maple does not have as much contrast as oak; however, where a smooth, polished surface is necessary, maple makes a superior floor.

Beech, birch, hickory, and several other hardwoods are also used.

Hardwood flooring is graded on its appearance according to the number of defects, variations of color, and surface characteristics. Strength and wear are not dependent on grading because all grades are comparable in these respects.

Softwood. Softwood flooring is available in several sizes and thicknesses; the most common is 25/32 inch thick and 4 1/2 inches wide. The long edges of the flooring are tongue-and-grooved or side matched in order to give tight joints. Similar to hardwood flooring, the underside is hollowed or V-grooved to minimize worming.

Parquet. Parquet flooring is made from hardwood squares 9 × 9 inches or 12 × 12 inches by 5/16 or 1/2 inch thick. These squares are available in several types of wood, such as oak, maple, mahogany, cherry, and teak.

Nonresilient Flooring

Types of nonresilient flooring include brick "pavers," ceramic, and clay tile, stone, and terrazo. These materials are more difficult to install than other flooring materials, but today they are becoming very popular. They should not be overlooked because they have a long life and the availability of hand tools enable you to do it yourself.

Any of the tiles may be installed using a special "thin-set" cement or in the traditional 3/4-inch bed of mortar. They require a *grout,* or cement fill, between the tiles.

Glazed ceramic tile and terra-cotta are relatively nonporous; so they resist staining. These glazed tiles are, however, susceptible to scratching and *crazing,* the formation of minute cracks, with age. Ceramic tiles range in size from what is called "mosaic" tile 3/8-×-3/8 inches to a larger 16-×-18-inch size.

Mosaic tiles are commonly sold on a backing sheet, making possible the installation of larger areas at one time. It is necessary to grout the joints between each tile after they are set in place.

Unglazed ceramic tile, slate, and flagstone are porous unless they are treated with special stain-resistant sealants. Clay or quarry tile, usually unglazed, is produced from clays that result in a strong, long-wearing surface. It is relatively easy to maintain and withstands impact well.

There is a wide range of colors and designs from which to choose. They can literally be used anywhere; from the kitchen and hallway, to bathrooms and walls. They come in many different shapes; rectangular, square or geometric, providing you with many possibilities for original design.

Terrazo is made of marble chips combined with portland cement mortar and is ground and polished to a smooth finish. It is very resistant to moisture and therefore relatively easy to maintain. Terrazo is very noisy, however, and is a tiring walking and working surface.

INSTALLATION OF FLOOR COVERINGS

Wood flooring, sheet vinyl with resilient backing, seamless flooring, and carpeting can all be installed directly over old flooring, if you have only needed to sand it. Of course, for your new, smooth floor installation will be quite simple. These coverings can also be installed over old resilient tile that is still firmly cemented.

Wood Flooring Installation

Wood flooring may be hardwood or softwood. Grades and descriptions are listed in Table 6-1. Table 6-2 lists materials, characteristics, installa-

TABLE 6-1. GRADE AND DESCRIPTION OF STRIP FLOORING.

Species	Grain Orientation	Size		First Grade	Second Grade	Third Grade
		Thickness	Face Width			
		In.	In.			
			Softwoods			
Douglas-fir and hemlock	Edge grain	25/32	2 3/8—5 3/16	B and Better	C	D
	Flat grain	25/32	2 3/8—5 3/16	C and Better	D	—
Southern pine	Edge grain	5/16-	1 3/4—5 7/16	B and Better	C and Better	D (and No. 2)
	Flat grain	1 5/16				
			Hardwoods			
Oak	Edge grain	25/32	1 1/2—3 1/4	Clear	Select	
	Flat grain	3/8	1 1/2, 2	Clear	Select	No. 1 Common
		1/2	1 1/2, 2			
Beech, birch, maple, and pecan[1]		25/32	1 1/2—3 1/4			
		3/8	1 1/2, 2	First grade	Second grade	
		1/2	1 1/2, 2			

[1]Special grades are available in which uniformity of color is a requirement.

tion, and usages. Types are illustrated in Fig. 6-11.

Hardwood flooring is available in strip or block and is usually tongue-and-grooved and end matched, but it may be square edged in thinner patterns. The most widely used pattern of hardwood strip flooring is $25/32 \times 2\ 1/4$ inches with hollow back. Strips are random lengths varying from 2 to 16 feet. The face is slightly wider than the bottom, resulting in tight joints.

Softwood flooring is also available in strip or

TABLE 6-2. FLOORING MATERIALS.

Material	Characteristics	Difficulty of Installation	Where to Use	Cost Per Square Foot
Wood Strip Flooring	Long Wear Life Moderate Resiliency	Moderate	All areas except bath and utility	$ .70-$1.50
Wood Block Flooring	Moderate Long Wear Life Moderate Resiliency Moderate Care Required	Moderate	All areas except bath and utility	$ .75-$1.30
Linoleum	Moderate Wear Life Resilient Moderate Care Required	Moderate—Low	All areas	$ .40-$1.00
Sheet Vinyl	Long Wear Life High Resiliency Low Care Required	Moderate—Low	All areas	$ .35-$4.00
Vinyl Tile	Long Wear Life High Resiliency Low Care Required	Low	All areas	$ .40-$4.00
Vinyl Asbestos Tile	Long Wear Life Resilient Moderate Low Care Required	Low	All areas	$ .20-$ .70
Asphalt Tile	Moderate Wear Life Moderate Resiliency Moderate High Care	Low	Avoid areas where grease is used	$ .20-$ .30
Ceramic Tile	Long Wear Life No Resiliency Easy Care	Moderate—Difficult	Bathrooms, entrance areas, kitchens, halls	$ .60-$1.75
Clay Tile	Long Wear Life No Resiliency Easy Care	Moderate—Difficult	Bathrooms, entrance areas. kitchens, halls, utility rooms	$1.00-$1.50

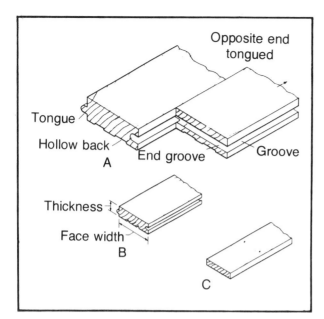

Fig. 6-11. Three types of strip flooring are shown (courtesy USDA).

block. Strip flooring has tongue-and-grooved edges, and some types are also end matched. Softwood flooring costs less than most hardwood types, but it is less wear-resistant and shows surface abrasions more readily. It can be used in light traffic areas, though.

Bundles of flooring should be broken and kept in a heated space until the moisture content of the locale is achieved.

Strip flooring is normally laid crosswise to the floor joists; or old strip flooring. Nail sizes and types vary with the thickness of the flooring. For 25/32-inch flooring use 8d flooring nails; use 6d flooring nails for 1/2-inch flooring, and use 4d cas-

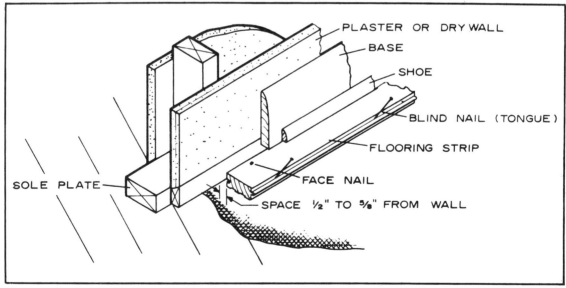

Fig. 6-12. Installation of the first strip of flooring (courtesy USDA).

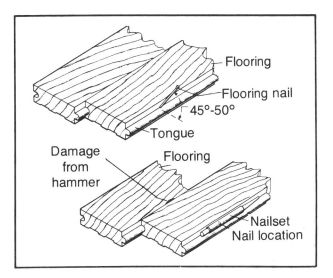

Fig. 6-13. Nailing of flooring: (A) angle of nailing and (B) setting the nail without damage to the flooring (courtesy USDA).

ing nails for 3/8-inch flooring. Other nails, such as the ring shank and screw shank, can be used, but it is well to check the following manufacturer's recommendations on size and diameter for specific uses. Flooring boards with blunted points which prevent splitting of the tongue are also available.

☐ Begin installing matched flooring by placing the first strip 1/2 to 5/8 inch away from the wall to allow for expansion when the moisture content increases.

☐ Nail straight down through the board near the grooved edge (Fig. 6-12). The nail should be close enough to the wall to be covered by the base or shoe molding and should be driven into a joist when the flooring is laid crosswise to the joists. The tongue should also be nailed. Consecutive flooring boards should be nailed through the tongue only.

☐ Drive nails into the tongue at an angle of 45 to 50 degrees. Do not drive them quite flush, or the edge may be damaged by the hammer head (Fig. 6-13).

☐ The nail is then set with the end of the large nail set or by laying the nail set flatwise against the flooring. Contractors use nailing devices designed especially for nailing flooring, which drive and set the nail in one operation. This device may be rented; however, most do-it-yourselfers do just as well with a regular hammer.

☐ Select lengths of flooring boards so that butts will be well separated in adjacent courses. Drive each board tightly against the one previously installed. Crooked boards should be forced into alignment or cut off and used at the ends of a course or in closets.

Leave the last course of flooring 1/2 to 5/8 inches from the wall, just as you did in the first course. Face-nail it near the edge where the base or shoe will cover the nail.

Square-edged strip flooring must be installed over a substantial subfloor and can only be face-nailed. The installation procedures relative to spacing at walls, spacing joints, and general at-

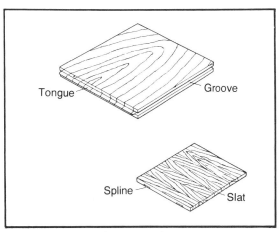

Fig. 6-14. Two types of wood block flooring (courtesy USDA).

139

tachment are the same as those for matched flooring.

Most wood or wood-base tile is applied with an adhesive to a smooth base, such as underlayment or a finished concrete, with a properly installed vapor barrier. Wood tile may be made up of a number of narrow slats held together by a membrane, cleats, or tape to form a square (Fig. 6-14). To install wood tile, an adhesive is spread on the concrete slab or underlayment with a notched trowel; then the tile is laid.

Wood flooring may have tongues on two edges and grooves in the other two edges. It is usually nailed through the tongue into a wood subfloor. It may be applied on concrete with an adhesive. Shrinking and swelling of wood block flooring are minimized by changing the grain direction of alternate blocks.

Particleboard tile is installed much like wood tile, except it should not be used over concrete. This tile is usually 9 × 9 × 3/8 inches in size, with tongue-and-grooved edges. The back is often marked with small saw kerfs to stabilize the tile and provide a better key for the adhesive.

Installation of Other Flooring

Keep in mind that a beautifully installed floor is the result of good preparation and thorough planning. With this in mind, the selection of the floor covering is the first important step. Ask yourself the following basic questions:

How much material will you need? To find the amount of material you will need, make a diagram of the room in which the floor is to be installed. The diagram should include all measurements including the length and width of the room and any island and cabinet cutouts that exist. Because the flooring material is measured by square yards, the amount of the floor covering can easily be calculated from the diagram. Always add at least 3 inches to all measurements to allow for uneven walls.

The calculations in Table 6-3 reflect material requirements for rooms where seams will not be needed. If you do need to put a seam in large rooms, these calculations should be used only to approximate the material you will need.

What type of flooring should you use? There are many different types of flooring. Visit your local dealer and get his expert advice. Biscayne Decorative Products, for instance, manufacturers several different types of floors; every type is recommended for installation on any 3/4-inch interior plywood or concrete subfloor on, above, or below grade level.

What tools are needed? These tools are always needed for installation:

—Utility knife,
—Tape measure,
—Metal straightedge,
—Multi-purpose flooring adhesive (available from a flooring dealer), and
—Notched trowel for spreading adhesive.

Tools which are not always needed, but are handy to have are:

—Pry bar,
—Hammer,
—Push broom,
—Putty knife, and
—Heavy scissors.

Because of seams, existing subfloor irregularities, or other conditions you will also need seam sealer and latex patching compound.

TABLE 6-3. MATERIAL REQUIREMENTS FOR ROOMS (NO SEAMS NEEDED).

	Actual Measurements		Recommended Measurements (uneven wall allowance)
Room Width	9'9"		10'
Room Length	13'3"		13'6"
Calculations	9'9"×13'3" - 9		10'×13'6" - 9
Room Size	14.4 square yards		15.0 square yards

140

After you have purchased the flooring material, but before you begin the installation, you should prepare the subfloor, lay out the material in another room, and have the tools handy.

When preparing the subfloor, keep in mind that any unevenness caused by cracks, nails, dirt, etc., may embed in the back of the floor and show through to the surface of the floor covering. The subfloor should, therefore, be thoroughly inspected and free of all indentations and protrusions.

Next, remove all furniture and appliances that are not stationary. Remove all floor moldings, such as quarter round or cove base. You will reuse them after the new floor is installed; so save them and handle with care.

Remove protruding nails or renail. Fill indentations, cracks, and irregularities with a hard-setting, nonshrinking latex compound. Remove all dust and dirt by cleaning thoroughly.

☐ Lay out the flooring material in a larger room with the design side up. Trace the outline of the room you will be covering from the diagram to the material, adding 3 inches to all measurements. Use a metal straightedge when cutting with a utility knife. Place the straightedge on the inside of the diagram or cut with the utility knife exposed to the extra material. Remember to provide protection from the utility knife against the floor or working area below. Transfer the material rolled pattern

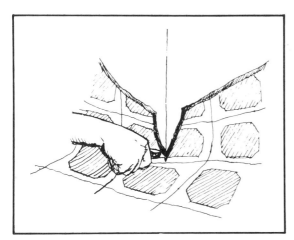

Fig. 6-15. Relief cuts for outside corners (courtesy Biscayne Decorative Products).

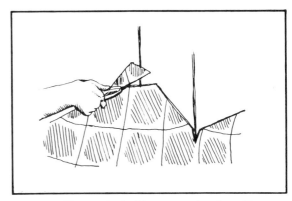

Fig. 6-16. Fit cuts for inside corners (courtesy Biscayne Decorative Products).

side into the room in which it will be installed.

In many rooms, you may be able to position the factory edge of the material against the longest wall. This positioning will save cutting along this wall and will help to align the design of the material. The factory edge does have matching marks; so be sure that the wall molding that will go on top of the installed floor covers all markings before you cut the material.

☐ Once the flooring material is in place with the additional 3 inches tapped up on the walls, make relief cuts on all outside corners made by appliances, cabinets, island partitions, etc. A relief cut relieves pressure on the flooring caused by protruding objects and allows the flooring material to lay flat. This cut is very important for an accurate fit along the walls, cabinets, etc. Figure 6-15 displays the procedure for relief cuts on an outside corner. The cutting begins from the top of the extra material down to the point where the floor and the sides meet.

☐ After all relief cuts are made and the material lies flat on the floor, cut the inside corners. Proceed a little at a time in a semicirclular form. The deepest point in the cut should not expose the subfloor. Test by shaping the flooring material to fit the angle of walls, so that the 3 additional inches along the walls form a "V" in the corner (Fig. 6-16).

☐ Once all corners are cut, the best method to fit a doorway is to make a series of little cuts (Fig. 6-17).

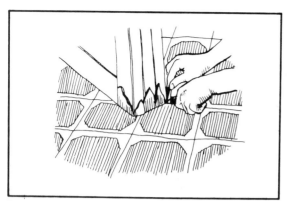

Fig. 6-17. Make a series of table cuts for fixed doorways (courtesy Biscayne Decorative Products).

Remember the doorway must be a neat fit; material must be flush to the doorway trim, because this area receives no molding. To avoid a gap between the flooring material and doorway, press a putty knife or any other flat metal object firmly into the right angle formed by the floor and the doorway. Cut the excess material with a knife blade angled 45 degrees to the trim (Fig. 6-18).

☐ In most cases you can finish the job by placing quarter round or cove base on the flooring material and nailing it to the wall. You can leave a permissible gap of 1/8 inch less than the molding that is to be used after the floor is installed; however, for those rooms which do not have any type of molding, a *neat fit*, a fit without a gap, must be made. Depending on the room, you can use the freehand or straightedge method.

For the freehand method, gradually trim down the flooring material that is lapped up against the wall until the material lays flat. A utility knife

should be placed as close to the wall as possible, so that the blade forms a 90-degree angle to the floor.

You can instead press a straightedge into the material where a right angle is formed by the wall and the subfloor. Using a utility knife, cut along the straightedge as close to the wall as possible (Fig. 6-19).

Neither of these methods is recommended for long distances unless molding is to be employed; however, a neat fit may be necessary against certain wall areas or under kitchen cabinets.

☐ For a neat fit, place the flooring material a few inches away from the area to be fitted and accurately measure from the wall the object that is being fitted (Fig. 6-20). The markings should be transferred to the face or the surface of the floor material, where a straightedge line can be traced. Cut using straightedge and utility knife.

☐ An *alcove* is a recessed opening commonly caused by refrigerators, stoves, etc. To fit a room alcove, measure to find the deepest point made by the recessed alcove (Fig. 6-21).

☐ Place the flooring material as close to that point as possible and transfer the diagram of the alcove to the flooring material (Fig. 6-22).

☐ Several measurements should be made so an accurate outline of the area can be drawn. The straightedge should be used to connect these measurements placed every 12 to 18 inches apart. The outline of the alcove should be complete and ready to be cut (Fig. 6-23).

☐ The last step is to glue and adhere the flooring material to the subfloor. All types of Biscayne flooring, for example, can be installed on any

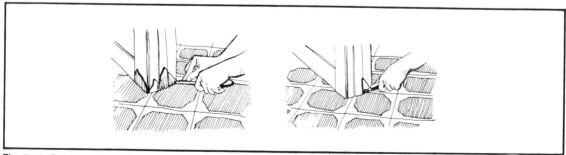

Fig. 6-18. Cut around the doorway (courtesy Biscayne Decorative Products).

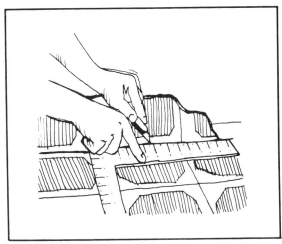

Fig. 6-19. Cut as close to the wall as possible (courtesy Biscayne Decorative Products).

subfloor grade levels with any latex multipurpose adhesive. Be sure to follow the manufacturer's directions and recommendations.

To use the full-sheet method, after the flooring is fitted, roll back approximately 1/2 of the material with the pattern side in. Apply white latex multipurpose adhesive with a trowel. Leave 2 inches from walls and apply the adhesive in a semicirclular approach. Figure 6-24 displays the best procedure.

Once the adhesive is applied, roll the flooring back and begin the other side. To ensure a lasting and adhered floor, sweep the top of the floor with a push broom to eliminate any air pockets.

When the perimeter method is used, only the outside areas, or the perimeter, of the room receives the adhesive. A 12- to 18-inch strip of adhesive should be made around the room. Remember to keep a 2-inch margin from the walls. Apply adhesive around any columns, pipes, etc.

☐ If a seam is necessary, by using the methods already described, fit half of the room and adhere the material to the subfloor. Place the material that is not yet fitted to the room on top of and overlapping the flooring material that is already adhered. Align the pattern of the overlapped material to the pattern of the adhered material.

☐ Cut little notches throughout the length of the material on top. The cuts should be no greater

than 1/2 inch deep and 3 to 4 inches long. The notches should not be deeper than where the seam is to go (Fig. 6-25), or gaps will appear in the seam. After the design is matched, fit the overlapped material and apply adhesive.

☐ For a tight seam if possible, place a scrap piece of material under the place the seam is to go and under the two overlapped sheets of material (Fig. 6-26). The seam should be cut with a utility knife and a metal straightedge. Once you begin to cut the seam, do not take the knife out of the material. Try to make one continuous cut with the blade of the knife at 90 degrees.

☐ Sealing a seam is an easy process. Your dealer will be able to advise you accordingly. Follow the directions and recommendations by all manufacturers, regardless of the flooring you use.

☐ Either one of the adhesion methods described may be used when seaming the floor. Since the seam divides the room in two, apply the adhesive to 1/2 of the room to within 8 to 9 inches of the seam.

☐ After the seam is matched and the other half of the flooring material is fitted to the room, apply adhesive to within 8 to 9 inches of the seam.

☐ Turn both edges of the flooring material and apply adhesive to the subfloor left exposed about 3 inches from the seam on both sheets.

☐ When using a push broom to press the air pockets out, sometimes the adhesive creeps into

Fig. 6-20. Measure to fit around cabinets (courtesy Biscayne Decorative Products).

Fig. 6-21. Measure around alcoves (courtesy Biscayne Decorative Products).

Fig. 6-22. Place flooring as close to the alcove as possible (courtesy Biscayne Decorative Products).

Fig. 6-23. Alcove measuring (courtesy Biscayne Decorative Products).

144

Fig. 6-24. Apply latex with a trowel (courtesy Biscayne Decorative Products).

the seam and on to the surface; so it might be necessary to clean the seam area with a damp sponge.

☐ Remember, no job is complete until everything is put back in its place, including molding, coverings, appliances, furniture, etc. To move heavy appliances, cut hardboard into four pieces 4 × 1 inches. Lay two strips under the object and slide it to the end of the strips. Place the other two strips at the ends of the first strips and slide the object to the end. Continue to move the object in this manner until it is in its desired location (Fig. 6-27).

☐ To protect your new floor, replace small metal dome glides with wide surfaced domes that have rounded edges. Place glass and plastic coasters under the legs of heavy furniture or appliances. All area rugs should be plastic or a woven material; rubber often stains floors.

FINISHES AND COVERINGS

We have seen that floors play an important role in the interior housing scene, and many treatments are available, but a final decision on what to use and why requires careful consideration of a number of factors. If you are concerned with finishes and maintenance for hardwood floors or with selection of carpets and rugs, the following will provide you with some facts and suggestions that can help.

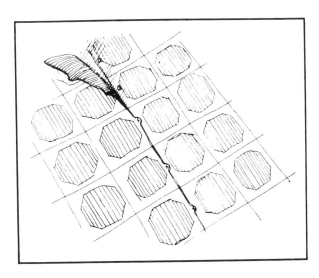

Fig. 6-25. Notch the length of material (courtesy Biscayne Decorative Products).

145

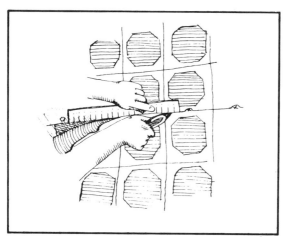

Fig. 6-26. Make a tight seam (courtesy Biscayne Decorative Products).

Types of Finishes

Hardwood floors have a natural beauty which should be emphasized and protected by the finish. There are two basic types of floor finishes from which to choose: penetrating seals and surface coatings.

Penetrating Seals. Penetrating seals with or without stain soak into the flooring material to form a strong bond with the wood. When you add a good paste or solvent base liquid wax and buff well, the result is a tough floor with a beautiful gloss. Both the wood and the sealer are worn away at the same time, leaving little evidence of wear. When necessary, heavy traffic areas can be repaired with sealer, and the floor will not appear spot finished.

Surface Coating. The surface coating group includes shellac, varnish, polyurethane, epoxy, and amino resin. Shellac is the oldest and cheapest of these finishes, but it does not wear as well as the others, especially under heavy traffic. If you do use shellac, buy a 4 or 5 pound "cut" and be sure the date on the label is not more than 6 months old.

Varnish will wear well under light use, but it will not withstand heavy abrasion or abuse. Varnish also scratches white, making it less nice in appearance.

Polyurethane, epoxy, and amino resin finishes, all plastic finishes, are tough, long wearing, resistant to chemicals, and quick drying. They are also resistant to the scratching and marring which are readily apparent with shellac and varnish.

Gum-finish varnish can be a very satisfactory choice for an area of low traffic or little wear, such as a bedroom with a room-sized rug, and they will cost much less than the newer plastic finishes. The extra money could, however, be spent on a tougher plastic finish, which may cost from two to three times as much as shellac or varnish.

Some epoxies are very good waterproofers, and when used in basements, which are prone to dampness, they are very effective.

Most finishes are available in high and low gloss and some in medium gloss.

Preparation of the Floor

Preparation of the floor to be finished is highly important for a satisfactory job. Whether you are refinishing an old floor or treating a new one, the floor must first be made smooth. If you must do some smoothing or sanding, although it can be done by hand, a power sander is generally used. Rental agencies, paint stores, hardware stores, and lumber and building supply dealers can recommend, and often have, the equipment you need.

Paint and varnish removers are sometimes used to remove old finishes, but power sanding is still considered more practical and effective. When finishing floors, all furnishings must be removed from the room, and all dust and debris from sanding should be vacuumed away before finish is applied. Pay particular attention to window ledges and baseboards.

Fig. 6-27. Strips for moving objects (courtesy Biscayne Decorative Products).

In some situations you may be able to apply new finish directly over an old one, particularly if the old finish is in good condition. Check finish labels carefully to determine over which finishes it can be applied.

Generally, penetrating seals are brushed, rolled, or swabbed on the floor and allowed to dry for 20 to 30 minutes. The excess is wiped off and the finish is allowed to dry according to the label instructions. Shellac and lacquer should be brushed on evenly and sanded with a fine sandpaper before additional coats are applied. Two or three coats are required.

Polyurethane may be applied with a brush or a roller and is also sanded before each additional coat. Clear polyurethane is used to give a high gloss or to build the finish, and a low gloss or satin finish is used only as the final coat.

Epoxy and amino resin finishes are brushed on and sanded between coats. Thinning is required before use in some instances. When the two parts of the amino resin are combined, the finish has a short "pot life," so only the quantity needed should be mixed.

MAINTENANCE OF FLOORS

Proper maintenance of floors is necessary for maximum service and enjoyment.

Wood Floors

In addition to regular vacuuming to remove dust and heavy grit, weekly cleaning of wood floors with a spray-treated dust mop is necessary to remove fine particles and dust and to get into corners that are difficult to vacuum.

Occasional damp mopping with a sponge mop will not harm the floor if the finish is in good condition and provides a good seal. Do not saturate the floor with water, however.

Periodic buffing will restore the gloss to the floor; if it does not, it is time to rewax.

The main function of a wax is to protect the floor finish. Three basic types available for wood floors are buffable paste, buffable liquid, and self-polishing liquid. Be sure you purchase a wax for wood floors and follow label directions.

Paste waxes are best applied on your hands and knees with a soft cloth. Work with small areas, spreading the wax evenly first across the wood grain and then with the grain. Next buff with the grain of the wood.

Liquid waxes are poured on the floor in small amounts and spread evenly with a long-handled applicator.

Research has shown that there is no appreciable difference in the wear of paste or self-polishing liquid wax. Further, finishes waxed with the liquid wax are consistently rated better in appearance than those waxed with a paste wax. Therefore, the self-polishing liquid wax might be a more convenient choice since time is important too.

If you switch from buffable wax to the self-polishing liquid type, however, all old buffable wax must be removed from the floor before applying the new liquid wax because the two types are not compatible. A solvent wood floor cleaner can be used for this purpose.

Carpet Maintenance

Not only should you select your carpeting with care, but you should plan to maintain it with care. Carpeting is easy to maintain with vacuum cleaners, which have fixtures for any type of carpet you might install. Most people also have a waxer-polisher, and shampooer, so you can clean your carpets yourself. There are many carpet cleaning liquids on the market, and manufacturer's directions should be followed carefully.

One of the biggest errors people make is thinking that they must soak their carpets in order to get them clean. Most carpet cleaning liquids are highly concentrated, and a 2-quart size will clean approximately 650 square feet of carpeting or six 9- x -12-inch rugs.

—Shake well before using.

—Mix 1 part rug shampoo to 12 parts water, or 1 cup to three quarts of water.

—Vacuum the carpet. Test for colorfastness. Clean 3- x -3-foot area at a time using overlapping strokes.

—Place aluminum foil under the legs of furniture if you don't plan to move all of the furniture from the room.

—While drying, brush the carpet in one direction with a clean brush or broom to get a uniform appearance.

—Vacuum when thoroughly dry.

Between cleanings and during your regular vacuuming, the use of carpet freshener provides a fresh aroma in any room. They do not, have any cleaning power; they are simply deodorizers.

Chapter 7

Windows and Doors

Whether you are adding on or remodeling, windows and doors will play a major role. For new construction, of course, you will have outlined on your plans the placement of doors, how you want them to appear, and all of the phases of building them into your house.

From the renovating aspect some doors will need repairs. In some instances, you will find it well within your low budget to replace them because doors made now have been much upgraded and play such an important function in the efficiency of the home's heating and cooling system, which in itself plays a major financial role in your budget.

SELECTION AND PURCHASE

When you select storm doors and windows, consider the following points:

—The strength of the main frames and frames for the glass or screen inserts is important. Also look for good design to ensure easy and efficient handling.

—Check that they are weathertight to prevent the entrance of water, cold air, dust, and insects. An opening or weep system is standard at the base of all storm windows to release excess moisture.

—You should be able to remove the glass and screen inserts from inside the house so that cleaning is easier and no outside climbing is required.

—Think ahead to possible repair problems. Does the dealer offer repair service, or can you get replacement parts and do the repairs yourself?

—When you buy new units, check to see that you have all the hardware: hinges, closers, wind chains, locking latches, vinyl base weather stripping, and screws. Check the parts for quality and sturdiness.

—What kind of viewing will windows give?

—Will the windows give good ventilation? Is it easy to open and close?

—Are materials, workmanship, finish, and assembly under warranty for an adequate period?

—Select the appropriate finish to match your exterior finish.

—When metal-framed storm panels are placed on metal storm windows, use a gasket to prevent metal-to-metal contact.

Windows should be constructed with wood frames and sash, and should be fitted with double-sealed glass in extremely cold climates. You can make your own insulated window by sealing in another layer of glass in the sash, with an air space between the two panes. To eliminate condensation problems along the edge of these double-insulated glass panes, you can install storm windows over the outside of the wood sash.

Ordinary storm windows fitted onto the window frames are not suitable for prolonged periods of subzero temperatures. Moisture will condense on the storm window and obscure the glass with heavy frost.

Windows should be chosen as much for the view they will provide and the light they let in as for the amount of ventilation they give, especially considering modern central heating and air conditioning systems.

There are many variations and designs of windows from which to choose. Tables 7-1 and 7-2 provide a handy reference guide to help you "window shop." Remember, the cheapest way isn't always the best way. While you want to keep as low a budget as possible you do not want to make the mistake of buying the cheapest, which may not wear as well and may need to be replaced or repaired too early. A little more outlay initially will ultimately provide a consistently low-cost remodeling project.

To get a true picture, be sure you are comparing total cost. Find the cost of the unit itself. Then add it to the extras, such as hardware and screens, and if you are not doing the entire job yourself, add installation and finishing costs.

WINDOWS

If you are renovating, you will not need to do much window planning unless you decide to move windows. This procedure should be kept to a

TABLE 7-1. GUIDE FOR WINDOW SHOPPERS.

Window Type	How Does It Operate?	Is It Easy to Clean?	How is It for Viewing?	How is It for Ventilation?
Fixed	Does not open, so requires no screens or hardware	Outside job for exterior of window	No obstruction to views or light	No ventilation Minimum air leakage
Sliding Double-Hung	Sash pushes up and down. Easy to operate except over sink or counter	Inside job if sash is removable	Horizontal divisions can cut view	Only half can be open
Horizontal-Sliding	Sash pushes sideways in metal or plastic tracks	Inside job if sash is removable	Vertical divisions cut view less than horizontal divisions	Only half can be open
Swinging Casement (Side Hinged)	Swings out with push-bar or crank Latch locks sash tightly	Inside job if there is arm space on hinged side	Vertical divisions cut view less than horizontal	Opens fully. Can scoop air into house
Awning (Top Hinged)	Usually swings out with push-bar or crank. May swing inward when used high in wall	Usually an inside job unless hinges prevent access to outside of glass	Single units offer clear view. Stacked units have horizontal divisions which cut view	Open fully. Upward airflow if open outward; downward flow when open inward
(Bottom Hinged)	Swings inward, operated by a lock handle at top of sash	Easily cleaned from inside	Not a viewing window, usually set low in wall	Airflow is directed upward
Jalousie	A series of horizontal glass slats open outward with crank	Inside job, but many small sections to clean	Multiple glass divisions cutting horizontally across view	Airflow can be adjusted in amount and direction

TABLE 7-2. GUIDE FOR WINDOW MATERIALS.

GLASS AREA	
Single-strength glass	Suitable for small glass panes. Longest dimension—about 40 inches
Double-strength glass	Thicker, stronger glass suitable for larger panes. Longest dimension—about 60 inches.
Plate glass	Thicker and stronger for still larger panes. Also more free of distortion. Longest dimension—about 10 feet
Insulating glass	Two layers of glass separated by a dead air space and sealed at edges. Desirable for all windows in cold climates to reduce heating costs. Noise transmission is also reduced
Safety glass	Acrylic or Plexiglas panels eliminate the hazard of accidental breakage. Panels scratch more easily than glass. Laminated glass as used in automobiles also reduces breakage hazard
FRAME	
Wood	Preferable in cold climates as there is less problem with moisture condensation. Should be treated to resist decay and moisture absorption. Painting needed on outside unless frame is covered with factory-applied vinyl shield or other good coating.
Aluminum	Painting not needed unless color change is desired. Condensation a problem in cold climates unless frame is specially constructed to reduce heat transfer. Often less tight than wood frames.
Steel	Painting necessary to prevent rusting unless it is *stainless* steel. Condensation a problem in cold climates
Plastic	Lightweight and corrosion-free. Painting not needed except to change color
HARDWARE	Best handles, hinges, latches, locks, etc. usually are steel or brass. Aluminum satisfactory for some items but often less durable. Some plastics and pot metal are often disappointing.

minimum, but where necessary it can be done—either by elimination, size change, or removal and addition.

Until recently, windows were not generally treated with a preservative; so moisture may have gotten into some joints and caused decay. Also, older windows may allow more air to infiltrate than newer types. It will often be desirable to replace the windows. This process is not difficult where the same size window can be used; however, where the window size is no longer produced, you will need to reframe the windows you replace.

The sequence of window replacement will depend on the type of siding you use. Where new panel siding is being applied, the window is installed after the siding. Where horizontal siding is used, the window must be installed before the siding.

Repairing of Existing Windows

If the wood in a window is showing some signs of deterioration, but the window is still in good operating condition, water-repellent preservative may arrest further decay. First, remove existing paint; then brush on the preservative, let it dry, and repaint the window. Paint cannot be used over some preservatives; so make sure you use a preservative that can be painted.

Double-hung sash may bind against stops, jambs, or the parting strip. Before doing any repair,

151

try waxing the parts in contact. If the problem still exists, try to determine where the sash is binding. Excessive paint buildup is a common cause of sticking and can be corrected by removing paint from stops and parting strips. Nailed stops (Fig. 7-1) can be moved away from the sash slightly; if stops are fastened by screws, it will probably be easier to remove the stop and plane it lightly on the face that contacts the sash. If you loosen the contact between sash and stop too much, however, excessive air will infiltrate at the window. If the sash is binding against the jamb, remove the sash and plane the vertical edges slightly.

You may want to add full-width weather-strip and spring-balance units so you have an airtight window that will not bind. These units are easily installed, requiring only the removal of the parting strip and stops. Install the units according to the manufacturer's instructions; then replace the stops.

Replacing Existing Windows

If windows require extensive repairs, it will probably be more economical to replace them. New windows are usually purchased as complete units, including sash, frame, and exterior trim. The units are easily installed where a window of the same size

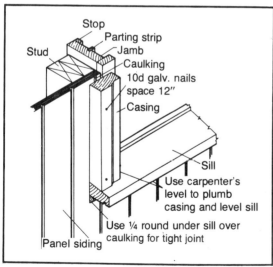

Fig. 7-1. Installation of a double-hung window frame (courtesy USDA).

and type is removed. Many older homes have tall, narrow windows of sizes that are no longer commercially produced, and in some cases you may want to change the size or type of window. Most window manufacturers list rough-opening sizes for each of their windows. Some general rules to follow to find these sizes are:

For a double-hung window (single unit):

—Rough-opening width = Glass width + 6 inches,

—Rough-opening height = Total glass height + 10 inches,

For a casement window (two sash):

—Rough-opening width = Total glass width + 11 1/2 inches,

—Rough-opening height = Total glass width + 11 1/4 inches.

After the existing window is taken out, remove the amount of interior wall covering required for the rough-opening width of the new window. If a larger window must be centered in the same location as the old one, 1/2 the necessary additional width can be cut from each side; otherwise, the entire additional width can be cut from one side.

For windows 3 1/2 feet or less in width, no temporary support of the ceiling and roof should be required. Where windows more than 3 1/2 feet wide are to be installed, however, provide some temporary support for the ceiling and roof before you remove the existing framing in the bearing walls.

Remove framing to the width of the new window and frame the window as shown in Fig. 7-2. The header must be supported at both ends by cripple studs. Headers are made up of two 2-inch-thick members, usually spaced with lath or wood strips to produce the same width as the 2-×-4 stud space. You can use the sizes in Table 7-3 as a guide for headers.

For wider openings, an independent design may be necessary. Do not oversize headers. Cross-grain shrinkage causes distortion and should be kept to a minimum.

Cut the sheathing, or panel siding used without sheathing, to the size of the rough opening. If bevel

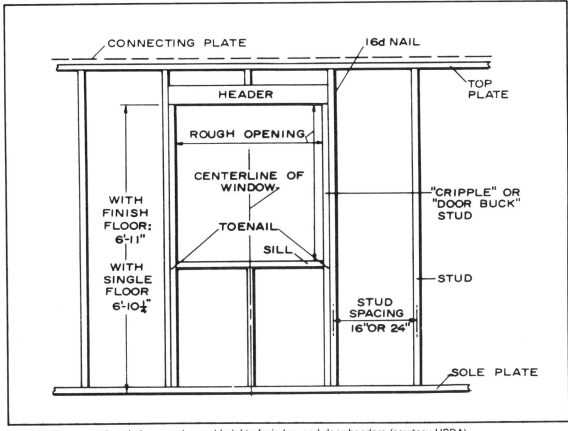

Fig. 7-2. Framing at the window opening and height of window and door headers (courtesy USDA).

siding is used, it must be cut to the size of the window trim so that it will butt against the window casing. To determine where to cut the siding, insert the preassembled window frame in the rough opening and mark the siding around the outside edge of the casing.

Before you install the window frame in the rough opening, precautions must be taken to ensure that water and wind do not come in around the finished window. Where panel siding is used, place a ribbon of caulking sealant of a rubber or similar base over the siding at the location of the side and head casing (Fig. 7-3). Where horizontal siding is used over sheathing, loosen the siding around the opening and slide strips of 15-pound asphalt felt between the sheathing and siding around the opening.

Place the frame in the rough opening, prefera-

bly with the sash in place to keep it square, and level the sill with a carpenter's level. Use shims under the sill on the inside if necessary. Check to be sure the side casing and jamb are level and square; then nail through the casing into the side studs and header, spacing the nails about 12 inches apart.

When double-hung windows are used, slide the sash up and down while nailing the frame to be sure that the sash works freely. For installation over panel siding, place a ribbon of caulking sealer

TABLE 7-3. HEADER SIZES.

Maximum Span Ft.	Header Size Inch
3 1/2	Two 2 by 6
5	Two 2 by 8
6 1/2	Two 2 by 10
8	Two 2 by 12

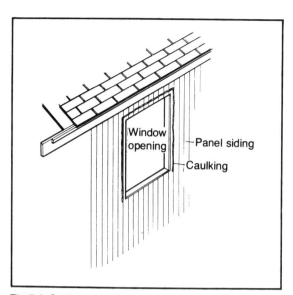

Fig. 7-3. Caulk around the window opening before you install the frame (courtesy USDA).

at the junction of the siding and the sill and install a small molding, such as a quarter round, over the caulking.

If you have decided to move a window to a different location use the method just outlined.

Where a window is removed, close the opening as follows:

☐ Add 2-×-4 vertical framing members spaced no more than 16 inches part.

☐ Keep the framing in line with existing studs under the window or in sequence with wall studs so covering materials can be nailed to them easily.

☐ Toenail new framing to the old window header and to the sill using three 8d or 10d nails at each joint.

☐ Install sheathing of the same thickness as that existing, add insulation, and apply a vapor barrier on the inner face of the framing. Make sure the vapor barrier covers the rough framing of the existing window and overlaps any vapor barrier in the remainder of the wall.

☐ Apply interior and exterior wall covering to match the existing coverings on the house.

Installing Storm Windows

Storm windows are necessary regardless of your locale, but they are very necessary in cold climates for comfort and economy of heating, and to avoid damage from excessive condensation on the inside face of the window. If old windows are not standard sizes, storm windows must be made by building a frame to fit the existing window and fitting glass to the frame. Storm windows are available commercially, and one of the most practical and low-budget types is the self-storing, or combination, storm and screen.

A simple and immediate method of providing storm windows which can later be removed so more permanent fixtures can be provided is to use plastic.

Plastic Storm Windows. Plastic storm windows can be installed as a quick do-it-yourself project. Tack plastic sheets over the outside of your windows or tape sheets over the inside.

To do this job you will need:

—4- or 6-mil polyethylene plastic in rolls,
—Shears to cut the trim plastic, and
—2-inch wide masking tape.

The width of plastic you need is determined by the width of your largest window. Measure the length of your windows to figure the total linear feet you must buy.

Attach the plastic to the inside or outside of the frame so that it will block air flow around the movable parts of the window. If you attach the plastic to the outside, use slats and tacks. If you attach it to the inside, use masking tape.

Inside installation is easier and will provide greater protection to the plastic. Outside installation is more difficult, and the plastic is also more likely to be damaged by the elements.

Be sure to install the plastic tightly and securely, and to remove all excess. The job will look better, and the plastic will be less susceptible to deterioration during the winter.

Jalousie Windows. Jalousie windows are particularly difficult to insulate against the cold; however, a homemade plastic covering can be slipped over the screen of a jalousie window to prevent the movement of air (Fig. 7-4).

Use lightweight plastic such as 2 to 4 mil. The width of the plastic covering is determined by the

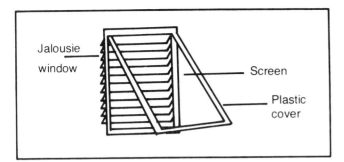

Fig. 7-4. Jalousie window installation (courtesy Extension Service, University of Florida).

width of the screen on the jalousie window. Measure the length of the screen; then double the measurement in order to determine the length of plastic needed. Fold the plastic in half; sew up the sides on your machine using the longest stitch. Pull the plastic covering over the screen like a large plastic pillowcase. Fold under the open end and replace the screen. The plastic covering can be put on and removed easily, and it does an effective job of insulating against the cold.

Single-Pane Storm Windows. So that you can give some forethought to this phase of your project, note that single-pane storm windows are not as expensive as the double- or triple-track combination windows. The major disadvantage of single-pane windows is that you cannot open them easily after they are installed.

Select glass windows with a frame finish; a mill finish (plain aluminum) will oxidize quickly and degrade appearance. Windows with an anodized or baked enamel finish look better.

Rigid plastic windows are always installed on the inside.

Glass windows can be installed either on the inside, if the window is built to permit it, or on the outside. If you install them on the inside, you will not be able to open the existing window. If you install them on the outside, they only cover the moving part of the window, and you will save energy, but they will be permanently installed.

Exterior installation of single-pane storm windows on metal casement windows is usually a job for a contractor (Fig. 7-5).

Determine how you want the windows to sit in the frame. Your measurements will be the outside measurements of the storm window. Be as accurate as possible, then allow 1/8 inch along each edge for clearance. You will be responsible for any errors in measurement if you do contract them; so measure carefully.

When your windows are delivered, check the actual measurements carefully against your order prior to installation.

Install the windows and fix them in place with movable clips so you can take them down for cleaning.

Remember that, while plastic storm covers should be snug, they need not be completely airtight. Weep vents in aluminum storm windows allow a small circulation of air, thus preventing condensation. You will have less condensation on the inside surfaces of glass panes when you install storm doors and windows. There might be some condensation if you draw drapes or shades at night or if the inside air is especially moist.

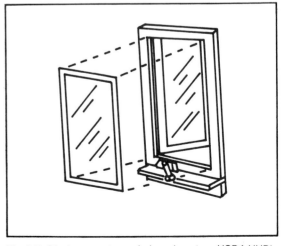

Fig. 7-5. Single pane storm windows (courtesy USDA HUD).

Weather Stripping

The side of the storm window frame which touches the existing window frame should have a permanently installed weather strip or gasket to make the joint as airtight as possible. Weather stripping on sashes of the house windows can prevent moisture condensation inside the storm windows.

A minimum of tools and materials are required to weather-strip your windows. They include:

—Hammer and nails,

—Screwdriver,

—Tin snips,

—Tape measure,

—Thin spring metal installed in the channel of the window so it is virtually invisible. It is somewhat difficult to install but very durable.

—Rolled vinyl with or without metal backing. It is easy to install and durable, and is also visible when installed.

—Foam rubber with adhesive backing. It is easy to install, but it breaks down and wears rather quickly. It is not as effective a sealer as metal strips or rolled vinyl. Never use it where friction occurs.

Upper story windows can be a safety hazard. You should be able to do all the work from the inside, but try not to lean out of windows when you are tacking weather stripping into place.

Weather stripping is purchased either by the running foot or in kit form for each window. In either case you will need to make a list of your windows and measure them to find the total length of weather stripping you will need. Measure the total distance around the edges of the moving parts of each window type you have, and complete the list in Fig. 7-6.

☐ Install weather stripping by moving the sash to the open position and sliding the strip in between the sash and the channel. Tack in place into the casing. Do not cover the pulleys in the

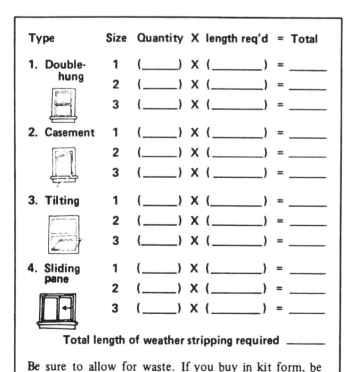

Type	Size	Quantity	X	length req'd	=	Total
1. Double-hung	1	(_____)	X	(_____)	=	_____
	2	(_____)	X	(_____)	=	_____
	3	(_____)	X	(_____)	=	_____
2. Casement	1	(_____)	X	(_____)	=	_____
	2	(_____)	X	(_____)	=	_____
	3	(_____)	X	(_____)	=	_____
3. Tilting	1	(_____)	X	(_____)	=	_____
	2	(_____)	X	(_____)	=	_____
	3	(_____)	X	(_____)	=	_____
4. Sliding pane	1	(_____)	X	(_____)	=	_____
	2	(_____)	X	(_____)	=	_____
	3	(_____)	X	(_____)	=	_____

Total length of weather stripping required _____

Be sure to allow for waste. If you buy in kit form, be sure the kit is intended for your window type and size.

Fig. 7-6. Figure how much weather stripping you need (courtesy USDA HUD).

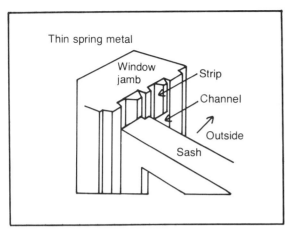

Fig. 7-7. Strip channel (courtesy USDA HUD).

upper channels (Fig. 7-7).

☐ Install strips the full width of the sash on the bottom of the lower sash bottom rail and the top of the upper sash top rail (Fig. 7-8).

☐ Attach a strip the full width of the window to the upper sash bottom rail. Countersink the nails slightly so they will not catch on the lower sash top rail (Fig. 7-9).

Rolled Vinyl. Nail on vinyl strips on double-hung windows as shown in Fig. 7-10. A sliding window is much the same and can be treated as a double-hung window turned on its side.

A casement and tilting window should be weather-stripped with the vinyl nailed to the win-dow casing so that the window will compress the roll as it shuts (Fig. 7-11).

Adhesive-Backed Foam Strip. Install adhesive-backed foam on all types of windows, but only there is no friction. On double-hung windows, the bottom and top rails have no friction. Other types of windows can use foam strips in many places (Fig. 7-12).

DOORS

Installing doors is much the same as installing windows, except that there are many different styles, and, of course, the major consideration is whether or not you should select steel or wood doors. For the do-it-yourself remodeling job, it is highly recommended that you use the door you think is right for your particular needs. What will suit one individual or family will not suit another. Both solid wood and steel doors are durable.

Selection

Basically, if you are looking at wood doors, the solid door has the highest quality and the highest price. The solid-core door is next and consists of a wood-filled core between two slabs of high quality wood veneer, such as birch, oak, or mahogany. They work very well for inner doors. Solid wood is recommended for exterior doors, although many contractors do use doors which are not solid wood.

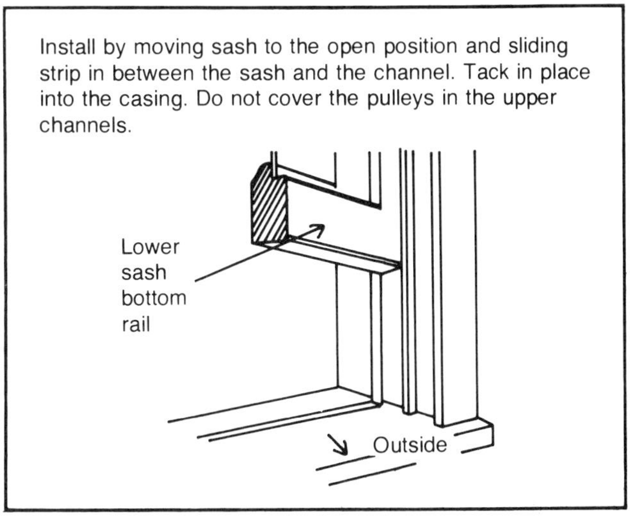

Install by moving sash to the open position and sliding strip in between the sash and the channel. Tack in place into the casing. Do not cover the pulleys in the upper channels.

Lower sash bottom rail

Outside

Fig. 7-8. Install strips the full width of the sash (courtesy USDA HUD).

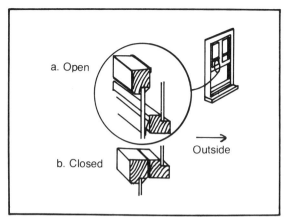

Fig. 7-9. Attach the strip the full width of the window (courtesy USDA HUD).

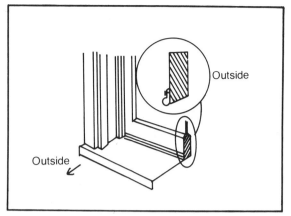

Fig. 7-11. Weather strip with vinyl (courtesy USDA HUD).

Hollow-core doors may have high quality veneer faces, but the lower-priced ones are covered with less durable wood or composition board.

Modern insulated steel doors are gaining favor for exterior use. Regardless of your location, they are especially good for keeping cold air in and hot air out; they also are a tremendous asset in burglar safety. They do not warp, shrink, or swell with weather changes, and they need to be painted less often.

Whether you buy wood, steel, or glass, carefully consider the width of the doorway. To move major pieces of furniture in and out, at least one door in the house must be a minimum of 36 inches wide, generally the front door. Width may also be a

factor in interior doorways as well, however.

Interior doors are usually either wood or metal, but some plastic is now being used (Table 7-4). In wood doors used inside, hollow-core construction is most commonly used; however, solid wood is also available. Thickness of interior doors is less than that of doors made for exterior use; this thinner construction is not meant to stand outside use.

Most wood doors are sold unfinished; however, factory-finished doors are available. Metal doors, on the other hand, are usually factory primed. Most are made of steel. Finish painting on these doors can be done either before or after you have hung your door.

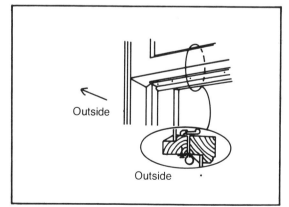

Fig. 7-10. Nail on vinyl strips (courtesy USDA HUD).

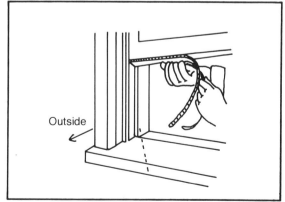

Fig. 7-12. Install adhesive-backed foam strip (courtesy USDA HUD).

158

TABLE 7-4. GUIDE FOR INTERIOR DOORS.

Type of Door	
Hinged	The most common type for openings 18 to 36 inches wide. Use wherever there is no objection to a swinging door.
Bifold	A special type of hinged door. Panels fold against each other to reduce swing-out space. Gives access to full width of closets. Use in openings 3 to 8 feet wide.
Glide-by	Two or more door panels slide by each other. Main use is on closets where door projection is not permissible. Gives access to only half the opening at once.
Pocket	Door which slides into wall. Use where a hinged door would interfere with traffic or other doors.
Folding	A special type of sliding door with *accordion-fold* sections. It can substitute for the other types, but door width is reduced unless a stacking pocket is provided.

Whether they are of metal or wood, interior doors are found in five basic styles. The style you select generally depends on the intended purpose and the conflicts involved with both traffic patterns and construction details.

Before you choose doors, ask yourself if the doors:

—Won't interfere with each other.
—Insulate well against colds.
—Won't interfere with traffic.
—Are wide enough to meet needs.

Like wood doors, steel doors come in designed styles and can be fitted with glass openings for viewing. Those with magnetic gaskets that grip like refrigerator doors give the tightest seal against the weather. They are usually prehung; so the frame and hinges are included. Steel is comparable in price to commonly used wood doors.

Glass is used in exterior doors primarily where a view is desired, such as of a landscaped backyard.

Minor Problems

Doors in houses of all ages frequently cause problems by sticking and by failing to latch. To remedy the sticking problem, if the frame is not critically out of square, some minor adjustments may remedy the situation. The top of the door could be planed without removing the door. If the side of the door is sticking near the top or bottom, the excess width can also be planed off without removing the door; however, the edge will need to be refinished or repainted. If the side of the door sticks near the latch or over the entire height of the door, remove the hinges and plane the hinge edge. Additional routing is then required before the hinges are replaced. Where the door is binding on the hinge edge, the hinges may be routed too deeply. You can correct this problem by loosening the hinge leaf and adding a filler under it to bring it out slightly.

If the latch does not close, remove the strike plate and shin it out slightly. Replace the strike plate by first placing a filler, such as a matchstick, in the screw hole and reinserting the screw so that the strike plate is relocated slightly away from the stop.

Exterior Doors

If exterior doors are badly weathered, they should be replaced. Doors can be purchased separately or with frames, including exterior side and head casing with a rabbeted jamb and a sill (Fig. 7-13).

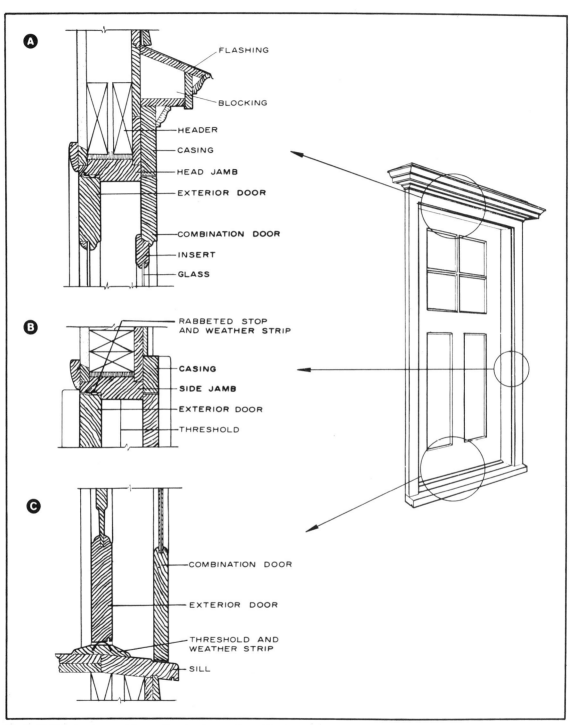

Fig. 7-13. Exterior door and frame. Exterior door and combination-door (screen and storm) cross sections: (A) head jamb, (B) side jamb, (C) sill (courtesy USDA).

160

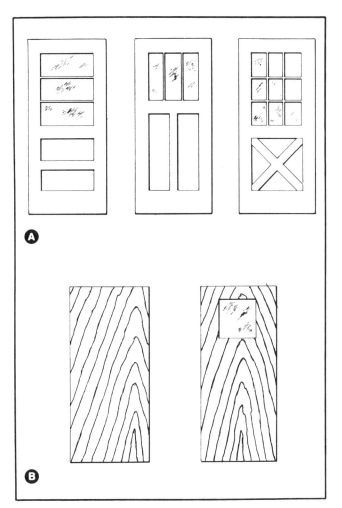

Fig. 7-14. Exterior doors: (A) panel type, (B) flush type (courtesy USDA).

Exterior doors should be either panel or solid-core flush type (Fig. 7-14). Several styles are available, most of them featuring some type of glazing. Hollow-core flush doors should only be used for interior use, except in warm climates, because they warm excessively during the heating season when used as exterior doors. The standard height for exterior doors is 6 feet 8 inches; the standard thickness is 1 3/4 inches. The main door should be 3 feet wide, and the service or rear door should be at least 2 feet 6 inches, and preferably up to 3 feet wide.

Where rough framing is required either for a new door location or because old framing is not square, provide header and cripple studs. Rough-

opening height should be the height of the door plus 2 1/4 inches above the finished floor; width should be the width of the door plus 2 1/2 inches. Use doubled 2 × 6s for headers and fasten them in place with 6d nails through the stud into each member. If the stud spare on each side of the door is not accessible, toenail the header to the studs. Nail cripple, or door buck, studs, supporting the header, on each side of the opening to the full stud with 12d nails staggered and spaced about 16 inches apart.

After sheathing or panel siding is placed over the framing, leaving only the rough opening, the door frame can be installed. Apply a ribbon of caulking sealer on each side and above the opening where the casing will fit right over it. Place the door

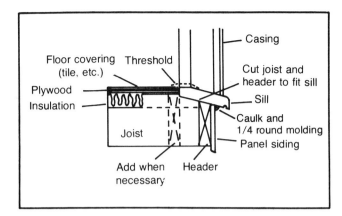

Fig. 7-15. Door installation at the sill (courtesy USDA).

frame in the opening and secure it by nailing through the side and head casing. Nail the hinge side first.

In a new installation the floor joists and header must be trimmed to receive the sill before the frame can be installed (Fig. 7-15). The top of the sill should be the same height as the finished floor so that the threshold can be installed over the joint. Shim the sill when necessary so that it will have full bearing on the floor framing. When joists are parallel to the sill, headers and short support members are necessary at the edge of the sill. Use a quarter-round molding in combination with caulking under the doorsill when a panel siding or other single exterior covering is used. Install the threshold over the junction with the finished floor by nailing it to the floor and sill with finishing nails.

Exterior doors are usually purchased with an entry lock set which is easily installed. Any trimming to reduce the width of the door is done on the hinge edge. Hinges are routed or mortised into one edge of the door with about 3/16- or 1/4-inch back spacing (Fig. 7-16). Exterior doors that swing in require 3 1/2-inch loose-pin hinges. Nonremovable pins are used on outswinging doors. Use three hinges to minimize warping. Bevel edges slightly toward the side that will fit against the stops. Clearances are shown in Fig. 7-17. Carefully measure the opening and plane the edge for the proper side clearances. Next, square and trim the top of the door for proper fit; then saw off the bottom for the proper floor clearance. All edges should then be sealed to minimize the entrance of moisture.

In cold climates, weather-strip all exterior doors. Check weather stripping on old doors, and replace it where there is an indication of wear. Also consider adding storm doors in hot as well as cold climates. Storm doors will not only save on heat, and air-conditioning, but they protect the surface of the exterior door from the weather and help prevent warping in cold climates.

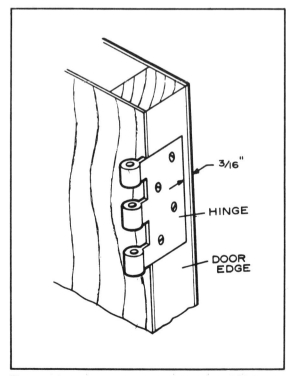

Fig. 7-16. Installation of door hinges (courtesy USDA).

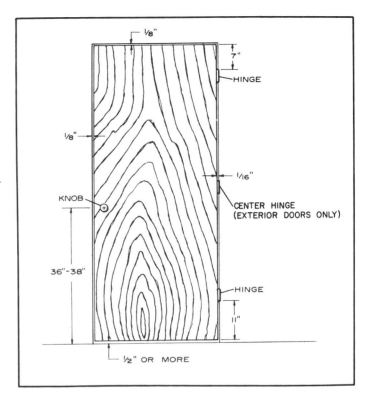

Fig. 7-17. Door clearances (courtesy USDA).

Labels in figure: 1/8", 7", HINGE, 1/8", 1/16", KNOB, CENTER HINGE (EXTERIOR DOORS ONLY), 36"-38", HINGE, 11", 1/2" OR MORE

Interior Doors

If a new interior door is being added or replaced, or the framing is replaced, the opening should be rough framed in the manner outlined for exterior doors. Rough-framing width is 2 1/2 inches plus the door width; height is 2 inches plus the door height above the finished floor. The head jamb and two side jambs are the same width as the overall wall thickness where wood casing is used. Where metal casing is used with drywall (Fig. 7-18), the jamb width is the same as the stud depth.

Jambs are often purchased in precut sets, and can even be purchased complete with stops and with the door prehung in the frame. Jambs can also easily be made with a table or radial-arm saw (Fig. 7-19).

Prehung Door. The prehung door is by far the simplest to install, and is usually the most economical because it saves labor. Even if the door and jambs are purchased separately, installation is simplified by prehanging the door in the frame at the building site. The door then serves as a jig to set the frame in place quite easily.

Before installing the door, temporarily put in place the narrow wood strips used as stops. Stops are usually 7/16-inch thick and may be 1 1/2 to 2 1/4

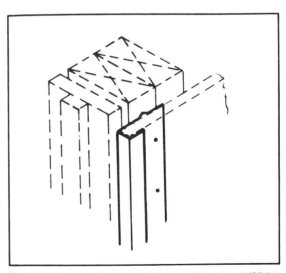

Fig. 7-18. Metal casing used with drywall (courtesy USDA).

163

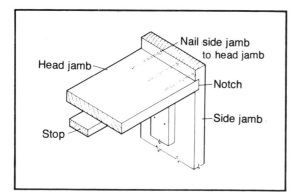

Fig. 7-19. Door jamb assembly (courtesy USDA).

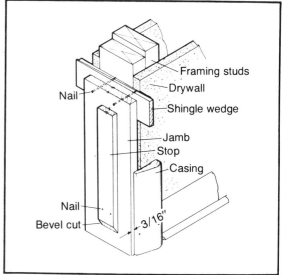

Fig. 7-20. Installation of door trim (courtesy USDA).

inches wide. Install them with a mitered joint at the junction of the head and side jambs. A 45-degree bevel cut 1 to 1 1/2 inches above the finished floor will eliminate a dirt pocket and make cleaning easier (Fig. 7-20). This bevel is known as a *sanitary stop*.

Fit the door to the frame, using the clearances shown in Fig. 7-17. Bevel edges slightly toward the side that will fit against the stops. Route or mortise the hinges into the edge of the door with about 3/16- or 1/4-inch back spacing. Make adjustments, if necessary, to provide sufficient edge distance so that the screws have good penetration in the wood. For interior doors, use two 3-×-3-inch loose-pin hinges.

If a router is not available, mark the hinge outline and depth of cut, and remove the wood with a wood chisel. The surface of the hinge should be flush with the wood surface.

After attaching the hinge to the door with screws, place the door in the opening, block it for proper clearance, and mark the location of door hinges on the jamb. Remove the door and route the jamb the thickness of the hinge half. Install the hinge halves on the jamb, place the door in the opening, and insert the pins.

Locksets are classed as:

—entry locksets (decorative keyed lock),
— privacy lockset (inside lock control with a safety slot for opening from outside),
—lockset (keyed lock),
—lath set (without lock).

The lockset is usually purchased with the door and can be installed with the door. If not installed, directions are usually provided by the door manufacturer, including paper templates, which provide for the exact location of holes. After the latch is installed, mark the location of the latch on the jamb when the door is almost closed. Mark the outline of the strike plate for this position and route the jamb so the strike plate will be flush with the face of the jamb (Fig. 7-21).

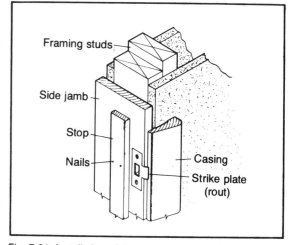

Fig. 7-21. Installation of door strike plate (courtesy USDA).

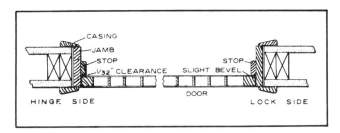

Fig. 7-22. Door stop clearances (plan view) (courtesy USDA).

The stops that were temporarily nailed in place can now be permanently installed. Nail the stop on the lock side first, setting it against the door face when the door is latched. Nail the stops with finishing nails or brads 1 1/2 inches long and spaced in pairs about 16 inches apart. The stop at the hinge side of the door should allow a clearance of 1/32 inch (Fig. 7-22).

Door Frame. To install a new door frame, place the frame in the opening and plumb and fasten the hinge side of the frame first. Use shingle wedges between the side jamb and the rough door buck to plumb the jamb. Place wedge sets at hinge and latch locations, and intermediate locations along the height, and nail the jamb with pairs of 8d nails at each wedge area. Fasten the opposite jamb in the same manner. After the door jambs are installed, cut off the shingle wedges flush with the wall.

Casing. The *casing* is the trim around the door opening. Shapes are available in thicknesses from 1/2 to 3/4 inch and widths varying from 2 1/2 to 3 1/2 inches. A number of styles are available (Fig. 7-23). Metal casing used at the edge of drywall eliminates the need for wood casing.

Nail the casing about 3/16-inch edge distance from the face of the jamb (Fig. 7-20), with 6d or 7d nails. Casing with one thin edge should be nailed with 1 1/2-inch brads along the edge. Space nails in pairs about 16 inches apart. Casings with molded forms must have a mitered joint where the head and side casings join, but rectangular casings are butt joined (Fig. 7-24).

Metal casings can be installed by either of two methods. The casing can be nailed to the door buck around the opening. The dry wall is then inserted into the groove and nailed to the studs in the usual fashion.

The second method, first fit the casing over the edge of the drywall, positioning the sheet properly. Nail through the drywall and casing into the stud behind. Use the same type of nails and spacing as for drywall alone.

Types of Doors. Interior doors are either panel or flush type. Flush doors (Fig. 7-25) are usually hollow cored. Moldings are sometimes included on one or both faces. Such moldings can also be applied to existing doors where added decoration is desired. The panel-type doors are available in a variety of patterns.

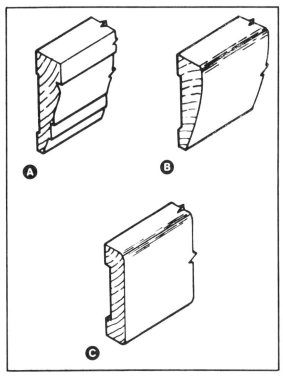

Fig. 7-23. Styles of door casings: (A) colonial, (B) ranch, (C) plain (courtesy USDA).

165

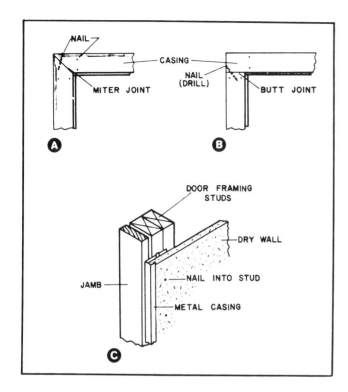

Fig. 7-24. Installation of door trim: (A) molded casing, (B) rectangular casing, (C) metal casing (courtesy USDA).

Door Sizes. Standard door height is 6 feet 8 inches; however, a height of 6 feet 6 inches is sometimes used with low ceilings, such as in the upstairs of a 1 1/2-story house or in a basement. Framing is limited in hollow-core doors; so, framing that is removed in major cutting to length must be replaced. Door widths vary, depending on use and personal taste; however, minimum widths may be governed by building regulations.

Usual widths are:

—Bedroom and other rooms: 2 feet 6 inches.
—Bathroom: 2 feet 4 inches.
—Small closet and linen closet: 2 feet.

Metal Doors

There are, of course, many manufacturers of metal and wood prehung doors. One of the finest metal doors is manufactured by the General Products Company of Fredericksburg, Virginia, and is called the Benchmark door. This door is engineered to block heat flow across an entrance sill and has an energy-efficient aluminum threshold which cuts energy loss through its insulated steel entrance system.

This frost-break feature has a rigid polyurethane polymer connector built into the extruded aluminum threshold. It is designed to form a thermal barrier while preserving the strength of the metal (Fig. 7-26).

The Benchmark door's energy-saving threshold group features a 6-inch wide, one-piece aluminum threshold for the 2-×-6-inch stud wall energy construction method and also offers inswing and out-swing standard width versions.

There are many benefits to the homeowner of this unique aluminum threshold: in additon to saving energy, it has exceptional durability, ease of cleaning, no maintenance, and absence of rotting or splitting problems.

Thresholds are integrated into the Benchmark entrance systems with completely weathersealed frames and a wide choice of styles for insulated steel doors. The Benchmark line includes single- and double-door units, sidelights, and the Vista two- and three-panel insulated patio door systems.

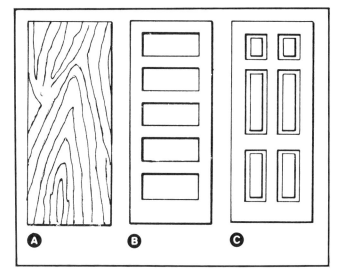

Fig. 7-25. Interior doors: (A) flush, (B) five-cross-panel, (C) colonial panel (courtesy USDA).

The new Benchmark Steel Insulated Remodeling Door is a prehung unit specially designed for quick, easy installation. There are only a few basic steps to the job because the new remodeling unit simply fits inside your existing wood frame.

Energy Efficiency

The energy-saving factors of this type of door fit right in with low budgets. The amount of energy a homeowner can save depends on the efficiency of the insulating materials used to block heat flow in or out. Various rating systems are used to compare the energy-saving abilities of these materials. It is easy, however, to become confused because there is a "numbers game" which is played with letters. A simplied explanation of the most common letters that represent the values being compared follows.

"R-value" stands for resistance—how well a material resists the flow of heat. The higher the R-rating the stronger the resistance to thermal movement. This value is the most commonly used yardstick, and it gives a total picture of the efficiency of the component.

The R-value for a typical Benchmark Insulated Entry Door with its dense core of polyurethane foam is 14.58. For comparison, a solid wood door is rated at 2.75; blanket or batt insulation is rated at 11 for 3 1/2 inches and 19 for 6 inches.

To give you an easier way to compare the insulating efficiency of various door systems available, a new rating method is now being used. This is the Door Insulating Systems Index (DISI) developed by the Insulated Steel Door Systems Institute.

The DISI rating gives a single number that includes heat flow through the door/frame system and from the inflow and outflow of air. This heat loss or gain is calculated in Btus per day and divided by 1,000 to give the rating number.

With a DISI rating of 1.5 a typical Benchmark door would lose only 1,500 Btus daily. The maximum allowable loss set by the Institute for the doors of its member companies is 8,600 Btu per day. A typical solid core wood door with storm door is rated at 19,000 Btu loss per day under the DISI standards.

"U-value" stands for a unit factor used to calculate how much heat is transmitted through a material in a given amount of time, generally an hour. Lower U-ratings signify that less heat is moving in or out of a space.

A typical Benchmark door 36 × 68 inches has a U-value of 1069. The typical solid wood door has a U-factor of .64 which is roughly six times less efficient.

A fourth rating value sometimes used is the "K-factor," which is a measure of the heat flow through

Fig. 7-26. Cutaway of the Benchmark steel insulated door (courtesy General Products Company).

168

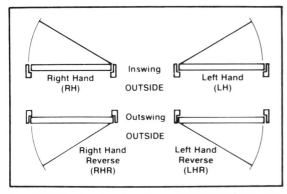

Fig. 7-27. Handing (courtesy General Products Company).

a material 1-inch thick. Benchmark doors have a K-factor of .122.

With the Benchmark Remodeling Door, you can qualify for an energy Credit Tax deduction since these doors meet the 1.5-inch insulation thickness required under the Residential Energy Credit regulation. This saving is an added incentive to use this highly versatile door system.

Installing Doors

By using your existing wood frame and interior trim, any right- or left-handed in-swing remodeling door can be installed.

□ Before you begin be sure that you have the correct "handing"—an in-swing or out-swing. The handing chart in Fig. 7-27 will be helpful in your determination. Handing is always taken from the outside. Astragal is handed by the inactive door it mounts to.

□ First measure your doorway for size by measuring the width and height of the wood frame. Remodeling doors accommodate the measurements shown in the chart (Fig. 7-28). Determine the distance between jambs and determine the distance from the top of the finished floor to the bottom of the header. Allow space for extra-thick carpet.

□ Remove the old door system. Remove the existing interior trim, avoiding damage if you plan to reuse it. Remove the old door hinges, strike, and other old weather stripping.

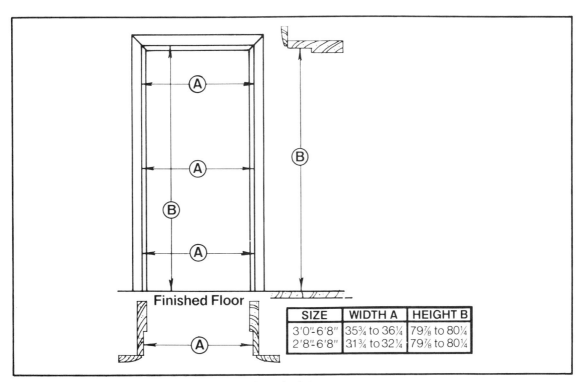

SIZE	WIDTH A	HEIGHT B
3'0"-6'8"	35¾ to 36¼	79⅞ to 80¼
2'8"-6'8"	31¾ to 32¼	79⅞ to 80¼

Fig. 7-28. How to measure a door (courtesy General Products Company).

□ Unpack your remodeling door. Remove the screws through the strike and header that hold the door from swinging in the frame. Loosen the screws in the white vinyl sweep and remove the aluminum threshold. Save the wooden shims to use as shim material.

□ Prepare the sill and hinge jamb. In order to ensure ease of installation, the sill area must be solid and level with the interior flooring. The hinge jamb must be square with the sill. Use the wood shims provided to fill the old hinge route and to level the jamb and sill as necessary. Shim thickness should be a maximum of 1/4 inch (Fig. 7-29).

□ Notch the existing wood frame for clearance of the new vinyl threshold. Slide the aluminum threshold lengthwise into the slot provided on the vinyl threshold and center (Fig. 7-30).

□ Open the door and install the lockset and strike to hold the door in place while installing the frame (Fig. 7-31). Do not screw the strike screws tightly, to allow clearance when installing the door. After installation it may be necessary to provide a clearance for the strike bolt and deadbolt (if used) by drilling or chiseling away the old wood frame.

□ Place the door assembly in the opening, making sure the hinge jamb is tight against the framed opening. You may need to remove layers of cardboard spacers or add wood shims to the jambs to make sure the frame is centered in the opening. Check at the header and strike jamb to be sure the frame is square. If not, remove it and check again that the sill and hinge jamb are level. Replace the frame and temporarily nail through several holes provided on the interior faces of the hinge, header, and strike jambs. Open and close the door several times and check for proper operation. Complete the final nailing of the frame (Fig. 7-32).

□ Secure the frame with six #10 by 2-inch wood screws through holes provided at the hinges. Screw four #10 by 2-inch wood screws through the four holes provided on the strike jamb, being careful not to overtighten them. Secure the dead-bolt cover plate with two #8 by 1/2-inch brass screws (Fig. 7-33).

□ Install weather-strip stops, replace the interior trim, and caulk the threshold. Cut the fac-

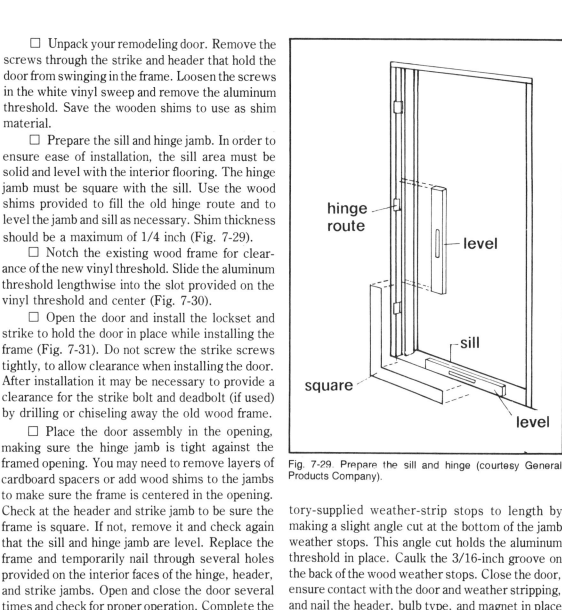

Fig. 7-29. Prepare the sill and hinge (courtesy General Products Company).

tory-supplied weather-strip stops to length by making a slight angle cut at the bottom of the jamb weather stops. This angle cut holds the aluminum threshold in place. Caulk the 3/16-inch groove on the back of the wood weather stops. Close the door, ensure contact with the door and weather stripping, and nail the header, bulb type, and magnet in place (Fig. 7-34).

□ Replace the interior trim, nailing through large slots on the interior face of the door frame. Remove the backing from the pile pads and place them at the bottom of each jamb at the threshold. Caulk as indicated.

□ The door is supplied with standard latch drilling provisions for conversion to deadbolt locations at 3 5/8 inches above the latch. To prepare for a deadbolt, locate a crossbore at 3 5/8-inch space;

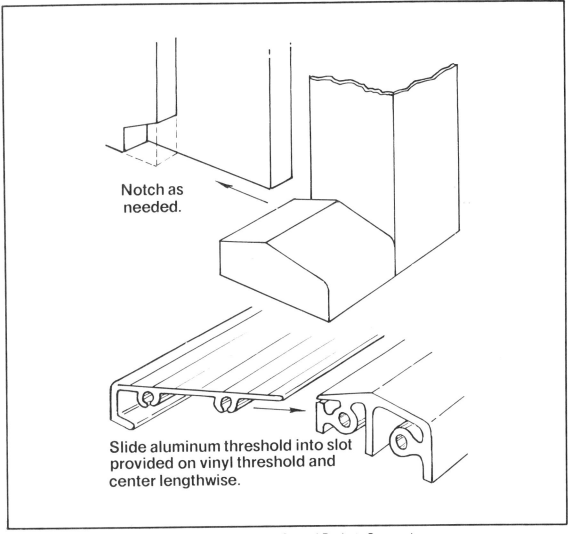

Notch as needed.

Slide aluminum threshold into slot provided on vinyl threshold and center lengthwise.

Fig. 7-30. Clearance notching for vinyl threshold (courtesy General Products Company).

remove the 2 1/4 and 2 3/8-inch covers, snap apart, and discard the 2 1/4-inch cover. Locate the 2 3/8-inch cover over position A in Fig. 7-35. Snap out the knockout hole at B and drill a 1-inch diameter edge bore hole through the rigid foam at point B.

Where the "U" dimension is 1 inch leave the filler in. Attach the bolt cover to the door edge with screws provided at the covers. Remove the circular crossbore support from the lock housing and insert into the deadbolt crossbore, to prevent crushing when the deadbolt is tightened.

☐ If the "U" dimension is 1 1/8 inch, remove the filler. Shim as necessary. Install the bolt and secure with screws.

Note: 1- and 1 1/8-inch latch plates at screw eyelets are manufactured to a standard size of 5/32 inch (.156 inch) thick. Variations may occur and final shimming behind the latch may be required.

Patio Doors

Patios play a big part in today's lifestyle, and

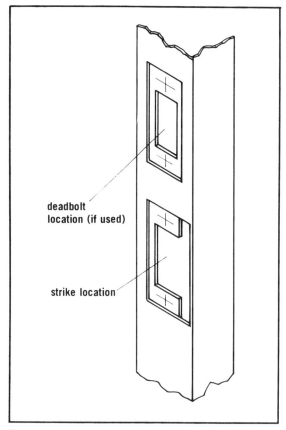

Fig. 7-31. Install the lockset (courtesy General Products Company).

Benchmark's Vista is a revolutionary center-hinged patio door for more convenience. Vista patio doors also give you decorating freedom because the active door swings in against an inactive panel, freeing adjacent walls and interior space for furniture. There are no maintenance problems, such as rollers wearing out, leaking, track jumping, sticking or warping. They are fully insulated and ready to install. Vista's sturdy center jambs are firmly anchored into the frame, top, and bottom for more resistance to forced entry than sliding doors or double doors with astragals (Fig. 7-36).

To remove old patio doors you will need a saw and a trim-stripping tool.

☐ Remove the old metal sliding doors from the tracks and the metal from the inside jamb. This frame is usually screwed to the jamb.

☐ Remove any remaining sill or threshold and fill the void to the level of the finished floor (Fig. 7-37).

☐ Strip off the old brickmold from the outside and the trim from the inside. Remove the inside trim carefully so you can reuse it to trim your new door.

☐ Take out the old jamb to expose the rough opening (Fig. 7-38). Saw through the side jambs for easier removal.

To install new patio doors you will need:

—Carpenters level,
—Shim materials,
—16d galvanized finish nails,
—Screwdriver,
—Caulking gun, and
—Exterior caulk.

Caution: you must make an allowance for thick carpets. There will be only about 1-inch clearance between the door bottom and finished floor. Higher shims and rough openings must be used to allow for extra high carpets.

Hand is always taken from the outside. See the handing chart in Fig. 7-39.

☐ To install the new doors, first check the rough-opening dimensions and be sure the sill is level. Raise the sill to the finished floor level if necessary. Now remove the bottom brace from under the threshold. Apply continuous beds of construction adhesive to the bottom of the aluminum threshold on all contact surfaces. Do not remove other braces. The active door must not be opened until the unit is in place, plumbed, and shimmed.

☐ Center the unit in the rough opening. Allow at least 3/8 inch between the jambs and rough studs on each side to accommodate the shims. From the outside, plumb both sides of the door unit. Nail through the brickmold for temporary support at two points on each side. Do not drive the nails completely until the unit is thoroughly plumbed and shimmed.

☐ Go inside the house through another entry. On the inactive side of the unit, insert shims between the jamb and stud. On the three-door Vista

172

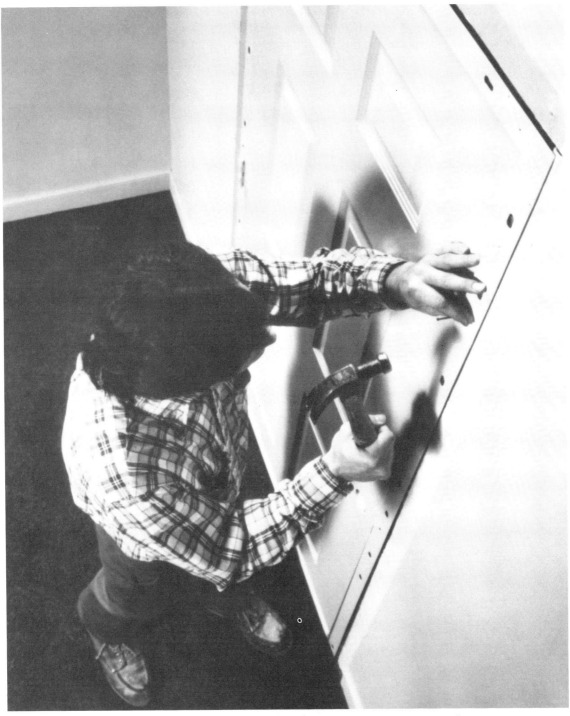

Fig. 7-32. Position the remodeling unit into the opening and nail the steel frame to the existing wood frame (courtesy General Products Company).

unit, both sides are inactive since only the middle door opens. Shim at four points, evenly spaced from top to bottom. Constantly check to be sure the jamb remains plumb in both directions.

Also, level and shim between the header jamb and rough opening at both ends and center, constantly checking to be sure it is level.

☐ Shim behind the strike jamb. In the three-door Vista installation, this is an inactive door jamb. Shim at the top, bottom, and at the strike locations. Again, check constantly to be sure the jamb is plumb in both directions.

☐ Now carefully remove the remaining bracing. At this point your unit should be plumb, level, and securely held with the shims and temporary nailing outside. Open the active door and remove the spacers stuck to the jamb and the spacer on the strike end of the sweep. Step outside and carefully close the door. Check to be sure the active door

makes even contact, top to bottom, with the magnetic weather seal on the strike jamb and header. If the contact is not complete, adjust the strike jamb in or out at the top or bottom until even contact is achieved, but do not use a level.

☐ Use 16d finish nails to nail the side and head jambs. Nail through the jambs and into the studs at all shim locations except the shim behind the strike plate. This area should be nailed securely only after the lockset is installed to allow for final strike adjustment. Frequently check weather-seal contact by carefully opening and closing the door while nailing. Complete the brickmold on the sides and header. Caulk the nail holes.

☐ Open the active Vista door and install a lockset.

☐ Pack insulating material between the side jambs, header, and studs.

☐ Loosen the screws on the bottom sweep

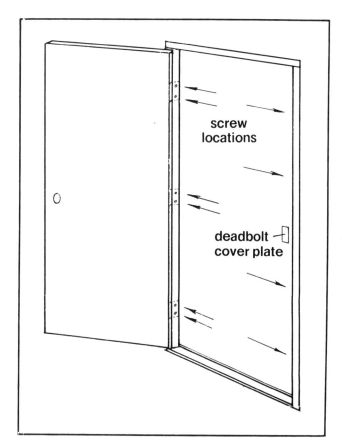

screw locations

deadbolt cover plate

Fig. 7-33. Secure the remodeling unit (courtesy General Products Company).

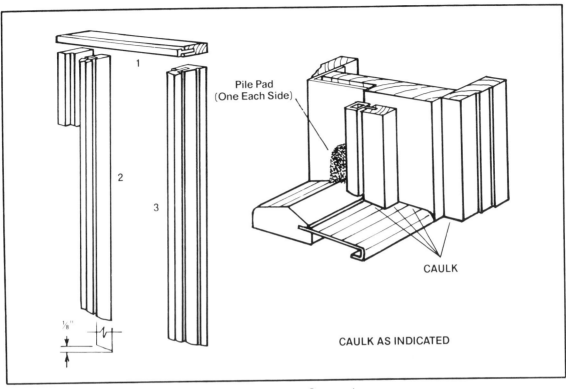

Fig. 7-34. Install weather-strip stops (courtesy General Products Company).

just enough to adjust the sweep up or down on the active door. Compress the "fingers" by 1/16 inch on the threshold and tighten the screws.

Vista patio doors also have their own packaged screens, making them easy to hang. The package includes top and bottom track, self-tapping screws, and latch. You will need a Phillips screwdriver.

☐ Before installing the screens remove the mullion strip from one Vista jamb in order to clear space for the track and door.

☐ Center the top track right to left on the header brickmold. Position the horizontal leg of the track back against the frame so that the vertical leg of the track is out 5/8 inch from the frame. Secure the track with self-tapping screws (Fig. 7-40). Do the same for the bottom track (Fig. 7-41).

☐ Remove the bag from the door handle to find the instructions for adjusting the rollers. Fit the upper roller onto the flange of the top track. Pushing up on the door, place the bottom rollers over their track (Fig. 7-42).

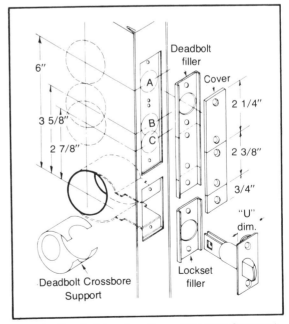

Fig. 7-35. Deadbolt (courtesy General Products Company).

☐ Use a Phillips screwdriver to adjust both the top and bottom roller assemblies for correct tension to ensure smooth action (Fig. 7-43).

☐ Close the screen and mark the correct position for the latch on the jamb brickmold. Then secure the latch with screws (Fig. 7-44).

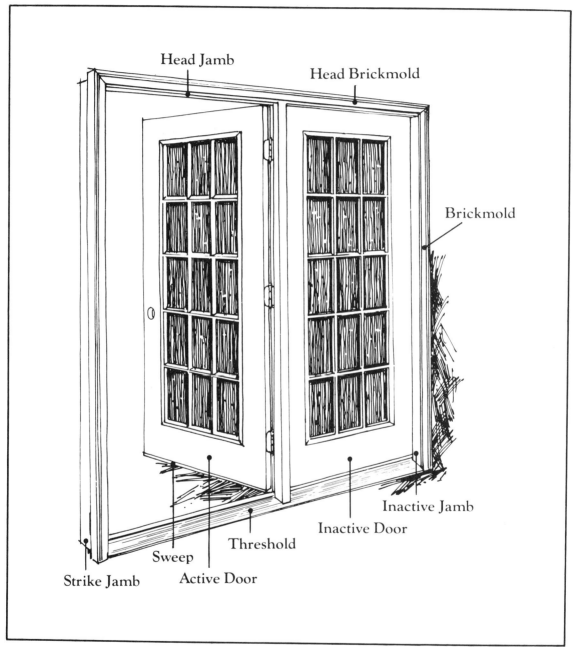

Head Jamb

Head Brickmold

Brickmold

Inactive Jamb

Inactive Door

Threshold

Sweep

Active Door

Strike Jamb

Fig. 7-36. Vista double hinge patio door (courtesy General Products Company).

Fig. 7-37. Remove any remaining sill or threshold and fill void to the level of the finished floor (courtesy General Products Company).

Fig. 7-38. Take out the old jamb to expose the rough opening. Saw through the side jambs for easier removal (courtesy General Products Company).

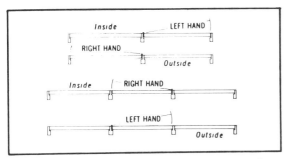

Fig. 7-39. Handing chart (courtesy General Product Company).

Sidelights

A decorative and interesting feature which can be used with your door is a sidelight. Sidelights can dress up any dull doorway since they come in a variety of shapes and colors (Fig. 7-45).

You will need, for the wood sill Benchmark model:

—1 sidelight (14″ × 79 1/2″ × 1 3/8″) or (12″ × 79″ × 1 3/8″),
—2 sidelight jambs (1RH, 1LH),

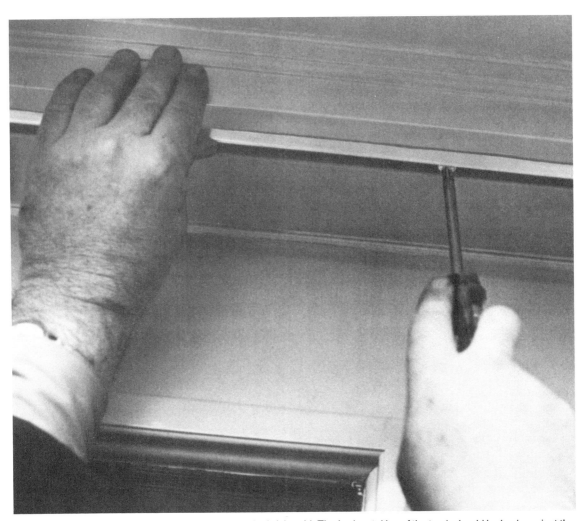

Fig. 7-40. Center the top track right to left on the header brickmold. The horizontal leg of the track should be back against the frame to space the vertical leg of the track out 5/8″ from the frame. Secure the track with self-tapping screws (courtesy General Products Company).

Fig. 7-41. Center the bottom track right to left on the threshold. The horizontal leg of the track should be back against the frame to space the vertical leg of the track out 5/8″ from the frame. Secure the track with self-tapping screws (courtesy General Products Company).

Fig. 7-42. Fit the upper rollers onto the flange of the top track. Pushing up the door, place the bottom rollers over their track (courtesy General Products Company).

Fig. 7-43. Use a Phillips screwdriver to adjust both the top and bottom roller assemblies (total of four) for correct tension to ensure smooth action (courtesy General Products Company).

Fig. 7-44. Close the screen and mark the correct position for the latch on the jamb brickmold. Then secure the latch with screws (courtesy General Products Company).

Fig. 7-45. Sidelights (courtesy General Products Company).

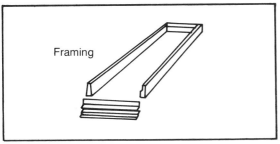

Fig. 7-46. Assemble the frame (courtesy General Products Company).

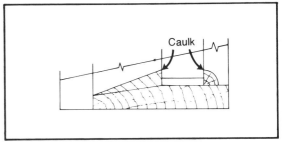

Fig. 7-48. Alternate caulking for wood sill (courtesy General Products Company).

— 1 12- or 14-inch wood sill w/1/4/" spacer moldings, miter cut,

— 2 79 3/4-inch quarter-round stop moldings, miter cut,

— 2 79 3/4-inch quarter-round stop molding, miter cut.

For Aluminum Threshold model, you will need:

—1 sidelight (14″ × 79 1/4 × 1 3/8″ or 12″ × 79 1/4″ × 1 3/8″),

—2 sidelight jambs (1RH, 1LH),

—1 12- or 14-inch header,

—1 12- or 14-inch quarter-round stop molding,

—2 79 3/4-inch quarter-round stop molding,

—1 12- or 14-inch threshold, aluminum thermal break (FBI),

— 1 rubber gasket (sidelight bottom seal),

— 6 screws for attaching the threshold.

☐ Staple through the two side jambs on the Aluminum Threshold model into the header. Secure the threshold to the jambs with screws. Lay the completed frame with the exterior side down (Fig. 7-46).

☐ Place the sidelight. Put a rubber gasket on

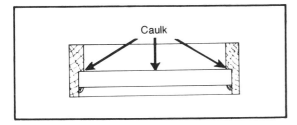

Fig. 7-47. Outside weather stripping (courtesy General Products Company).

the bottom of the sidelight so that the contour of the gasket matches the threshold. Lay the sidelight in the frame with the gasket pressed firmly against the threshold.

☐ Anchor the sidelight by laying a bead of caulk around the sidelight edges at the jambs and header. Place the stop molding firmly against the sidelight and caulk the bead. Making sure the sidelight is tight in the frame, staple the molding to the jambs and header.

☐ To weather seal, turn the frame over so that the exterior side is up. Caulk around the entire sidelight to ensure a weathertight seal. The unit is ready for installation (Fig. 7-47).

☐ For the wood sill model, attach the sill to the jambs with staples. Turn the frame exterior down. Place the sidelight, making sure it presses firmly against the sill and spacer. Caulk and staple all four stop moldings. Caulk the exterior (Fig. 7-48).

Prehanging Instructions. To assemble the door and sidelights as a unit, place them on a prehanging table, exterior side up. Remove the brickmold from the prehung door if necessary, and replace as required later.

☐ Place a 2-×-4-inch stud 81 3/4 inches long between the sidelight jamb and the door jamb. The 2-×-4-inch stud should be flush with the bottom of the thresholds and flush with the tops of both frames. Secure the sidelight and door to the stud with four screws through each jamb into the stud (Fig. 7-49).

Sidelight/Door Assembly Instructions.
Prepare the rough opening. Make sure it is square and level to the dimensions shown in Table 7-5.

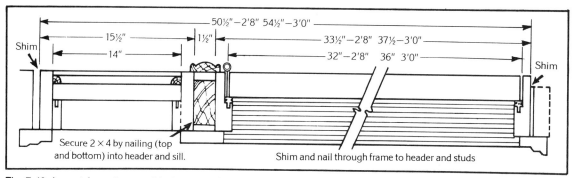

Fig. 7-49. Layout for unit assembly (courtesy General Products Company).

Shim and nail through frame to header
and studs at points marked by arrows.

Secure 2 × 4 by nailing (top and bottom) into header and sill.

Fig. 7-50. Shim through the header (courtesy General Products Company).

TABLE 7-5. ROUGH OPENING DIMENSIONS FOR SIDELIGHTS.

Single Sidelight		Double Sidelight	
Door Size	Rough Opening	Door Size	Rough Opening
2'8"	51 1/4" × 6'0 3/4"	2'8"	68 1/4" × 6'0 3/4"
3'0"	55 1/4" × 6'9 3/4"	3'0"	72 1/4" × 6'9 3/4"

Note: These tables allow 17" rough opening for each 14" sidelight, in addition to door width.

For 12" sidelights, subtract 2" for each sidelight.

☐ Install the door/sidelight unit. The 2-×-4-inch stud between the door and sidelight should be nailed to the sill and header. Use shims as shown in Fig. 7-50 to avoid problems with bowing, etc.

☐ To cover the 2-×-4-inch stud on the outside, use a 1 1/18-×-3-inch piece of finished lumber 80 1/2 inches long. For the inside trim, select a 1 1/2-inch side milled piece.

Chapter 8

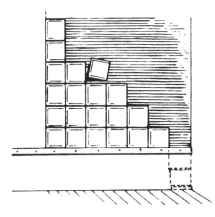

Interior Wall Finishings

The interior wall finish of your home is the final touch in remodeling a room. You can choose from a variety of materials, from the most commonly used and very practical wall sheet metal to gypsum, plywood, hardboard, fiberboard, ceramic tile, and wallpaper to extremely versatile wood paneling in an array of colors and designs to fit any room, any decor that you desire. An entire house of wood-paneled walls often becomes boring to the decor, however, and it is better to break it up, using it in the areas where it works best: family room, dining room, and basement. Because it is easy to cut and fit, it can be used on parts of walls working in with regular wallboard. No matter what materials you choose, ideas are only limited by your designs and imagination.

DRYWALL

Drywall is usually applied to framing or to furring strips over the framing. If the existing wall finish is smooth, new wall finish can sometimes be glued or nailed directly to it. If directly applied

there is no thickness requirement for the new covering because it is continuously supported. For application over framing or furring strips, however, thicknesses for 16- and 24-inch spacing of fasting members are needed. See the list in Table 8-1.

To prepare a room for new wall finish, first locate each stud. They are usually spaced 16 inches apart and at doors and windows. The simplest way to find them is to look for nailheads in drywall or baseboards. These nails have been driven into studs. Where there is no evidence of nailheads, tap the wall finish with a hammer. When you hit a stud, the sound will be hollow. If you are not sure you can locate the stud in this manner, you can rent a stud finder from your local rent-it or hardware dealer. Stud finders use a magnet that points to nailheads. Mark the stud locations so you can attach horizontal furring strips or nail on paneling.

Check the wall for flatness by holding a straight 2 × 4 against the surface. Mark locations that are very uneven. Also, check for vertical alignment by holding a large carpenter's level on the straight 2 × 4 against the wall. As furring is

Finish	Minimum materials thickness (in.) when framing is spaced	
	16 inch	24 inch
Gypsum board	3/8	1/2
Plywood	1/4	3/8
Hardboard	1/4	-
Fiberboard	1/2	3/4
Wood paneling	3/8	1/2

TABLE 8-1. THICKNESS REQUIREMENTS FOR DRYWALL.

applied, use shingles as shims behind the furring where needed to produce a smooth vertical surface (Fig. 8-1).

Apply 1-×-2-inch furring horizontally at 16- or 24-inch spacing, depending on the cover material to be used (Fig. 8-2). Nail the furring at each stud.

Remove existing base trim and window and door casings and apply furring around all openings. Also use vertical furring at each stud where vertical joints will occur in the drywall.

After this preparation, any of the usual drywall materials can be applied.

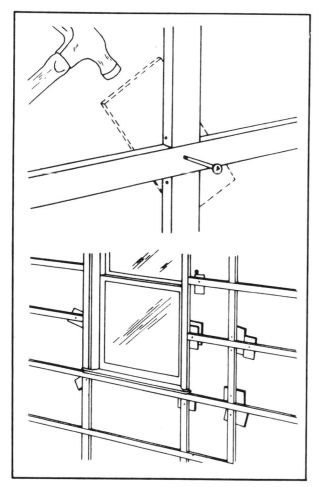

Fig. 8-1. Shingle the shims behind the furring to produce a smooth, vertical surface.

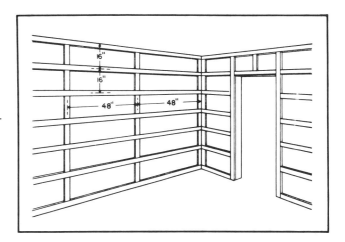

Fig. 8-2. Application of horizontal furring to an interior wall (courtesy USDA).

FINISHING MATERIAL

Gypsum Board. Gypsum board is one of the lowest-priced materials for interior finish; however, the labor required to finish joints may offset the lower material cost (if you do not do the work yourself). This sheet metal is composed of a gypsum filler faced with paper. Recessed edges accommodate tape for joints. Sheets are 4-feet wide and 8-feet or more long. They can be applied vertically or horizontally. Room-length sheets can be applied horizontally, leaving only one joint at the middle of the wall height.

For both horizontal and vertical application, nail completely around the perimeter of the sheet and at each furring strip. For direct application to framing, nail at each stud. Use 4d cooler-type nails for 3/8-inch thick gypsum board and 5d cooler-type nails for 1/2-inch thick gypsum board (Fig. 8-3).

Lightly dimple the nail location with a hammerhead, being careful not to break the surface of the paper. Minimum edge nailing distance is 3/8 inch.

Gypsum board generally is finished, or prepared, for painting using a joint cement and perforated joint tape. Some gypsum board is supplied with a strip of joint paper along one edge, which is used in place of the tape.

After the gypsum board has been installed and each nail is driven in a "dimple" fashion, the walls are ready for treatment. Joint cement, also called "spackle" compound, in powder or ready-mix form,

should have a soft putty consistency so that it can be easily spread with a trowel or wide putty knife. The gypsum board edges are usually tapered so that, where two sheets are joined, there is a recessed strip to receive the joint cement and tape. If a sheet has been cut, the edge will not be tapered. A square edge is taped in much the same way as the beveled edge, except the joint cement will raise the surface slightly at the seam, and edges must be feathered out further for a smooth finish.

To tape, use a 5-inch wide spackling knife. Spread the cement over the tapered and other butt edges, starting at the top of the wall. Press the tape into the recess with the knife until the joint cement is forced through the small perforation. Cover the tape with additional cement to a level surface, feathering the outer edges; allow to dry. Sand lightly and apply a thin second coat, feathering the edges again. A third coat may be required after the second coat has dried. After the cement is dry, sand smooth. To hide nail indentations at members between edges, fill with joint cement. A second coat is usually required. Again sand when dry.

Treat interior and exterior corners with perforated tape. Fold the tape down the center to a right angle. Apply cement on each side of the corner. Press with joint cement and sand when dry (Fig. 8-4).

Wallboard corner beads of metal or plastic can be added to improve strength. They should be nailed to the outside corners and treated with joint

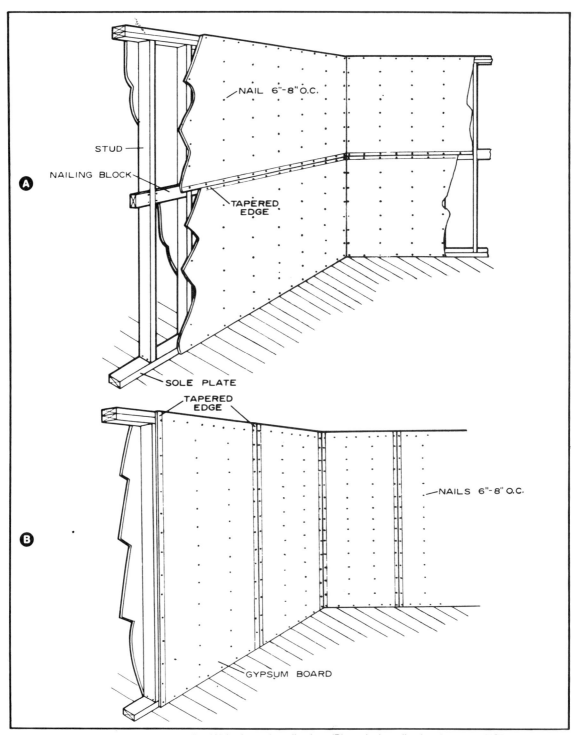

Fig. 8-3. Installing gypsum board on walls: (A) horizontal application, (B) vertical application (courtesy USDA).

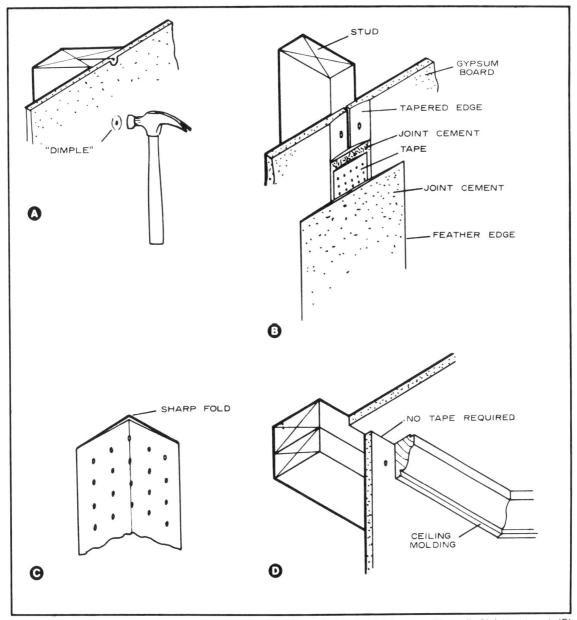

Fig. 8-4. Preparing gypsum drywall sheets for painting: (A) drive nails in "dimple" fashion, (B) detail of joint treatment, (C) corner tape, (D) ceiling molding (courtesy USDA).

cement. The junction of the wall and ceiling can also be finished with a wood molding in any desired shape, which will eliminate the need for joint treatment. Nail 8d finishing nails spread 12 to 16 inches apart into the top wallplate.

Plywood and Hardboard. Plywood is stable. Because it comes from the mill as a very dry material, and because of the way it is made, plywood swells, shrinks, and warps very little, even with repeated wetting and drying.

Plywood is also durable; it will not rust or corrode. Both plywood and hardboard come in 4-×-8-foot sheets for vertical application; however, 7-foot-long panels can sometimes be purchased for use in basements or other areas with low ceilings.

Interior plywood is made with highly moisture-resistant or waterproof glue. Veneers used in interior plywood can be of lower quality than those used in exterior types.

Plywood can be purchased in a number of species—over 70 are used in its manufacture. Strength and stiffness of wood varies somewhat among species in each group; they are numbered from 1 through 5, and the woods in species group 1 are the strongest and stiffest.

The better hardboard paneling uses a photograph of wood to provide the wood-grain effect and produce a very realistic pattern. Both plywood and hardboard can be purchased with a hard, plastic finish that can easily be wiped clean. Hardboard is also available with vinyl coatings in many patterns and colors.

Be sure the plywood or hardboard interior finish material is delivered well before it is to be applied so the panels can acquire the moisture and temperature conditions of the room. Stack the panels, separating them with full-length furring strips to allow air to get to all panel faces and backs. Panels should remain in the room at least two days before application.

Wood and Fiberboard Paneling. Wood and fiberboard paneling are tongued-and-grooved and are available in various widths. Wood is usually limited to no more than 8 inches in nominal width. Fiberboard paneling is often 12 or 16 inches wide. Paneling should be stacked as recommended for plywood and hardboard so they can stabilize at the temperature and moisture conditions of the room. Paneling is usually applied vertically, but it can be applied horizontally for special effects.

Vertically applied paneling is nailed to horizontal furring strips or to nailing blocks between studs. Nail with 1 1/2- to 2-inch finishing or casing nails. Blind-nail through the tongue, and, for 8-inch boards, face-nail near the opposite edge. Where 12-

or 16-inch wide fiberboard is used, two face nails may be necessary. Color-matched nails are sometimes supplied with the fiberboard. Staples can be used in the tongue of fiberboard instead of nails. Where adhesive is used, the only nailing required is the blind nailing in the tongue.

INTERIOR TRIM

Interior trim consists of window and door casings and various moldings. The type of trim used in houses varies considerably, depending on the age, style, and quality of the house. Trim found in many older houses is probably no longer available; so matching it requires expensive custom fabrication. If you plan to use existing trim, remove pieces carefully where windows, doors, or partitions are changed so it can be reused where needed.

Where new trim is to be used, the type of finish you desire is the basis for selecting the species of wood to be used. For a paint finish, the material should be smooth, close-grained, and free from pitch streaks. Some species that meet these requirements are ponderosa pine, northern white pine, redwood, mahogony, and spruce. The additional qualities of hardness and durability are provided by such species as birch, gum, and yellow poplar. For a natural finish, the wood should have a pleasing appearance, hardness, and uniform color. These requirements are satisfied by such species as ash, birch, cherry, maple, oak, and walnut.

Casing. Casing is the interior edge trim for door and window openings. New casing patterns vary in width from 2 1/4 to 3 1/2 inches and in thicknesses from 1/2 to 3/4 inch. Place the casing with about 3/16-inch edge distance from door and window jambs. Nail with 6d nails or 7d casing or finishing nails, depending on the thickness of the casing. Space nails in pairs about 16 inches apart, nailing to both jambs and framing. Rectangular casings can be butt-jointed at corners, but molded forms must have a mitered joint.

Baseboard. *Baseboard*, the finish between the finished wall and floor, is also available in several sizes and forms (Fig. 8-5). It may be either one or two pieces. The two-piece base consists of a baseboard topped with a small base cap which con-

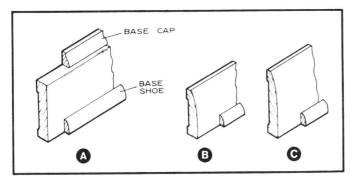

Fig. 8-5. Baseboard: (A) two-piece, (B) narrow, (C) medium width (courtesy USDA).

forms to any irregularities in the wall finish. Most baseboards are finished with a base shoe, except where carpet is installed. The base shoe is nailed into the subfloor, so it conforms to irregularities in the finished floor.

Install square-edged baseboard with a butt joint at inside corners and a mitered joint at outside corners. Nail at each stud with two 8d finishing nails. Molded base, base cap, and base shoe require a coped joint at inside corners and a mitered joint at outside corners (Fig. 8-6).

INSTALLING GYPSUM BOARD

A little thought and planning before you start your project can result in a better appearance and a saving in materials and time. Make a sketch of the areas to be surfaced with gypsum wallboard and lay out the board panels. Install the boards perpendicular to the joists or studs. Use the longest board you can handle to eliminate or reduce end joints. For example, in a 12-×-13-foot room where the ceiling joists run parallel to the 13-foot dimension, you should use 12-foot-long boards. If they were 8 feet long, an end joint would be necessary in each course. Where end joints cannot be avoided, be sure to stagger them.

The adhesive/nail-on method of application is easy to use and results in a higher-quality installation.

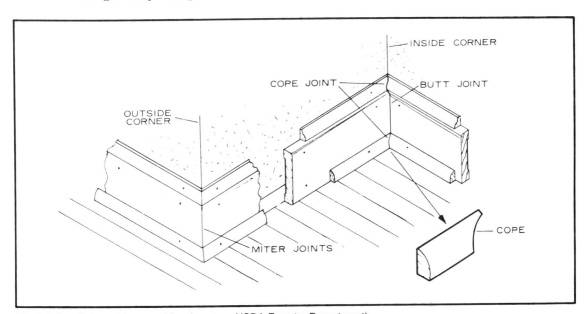

Fig. 8-6. Installation of base molding (courtesy USDA Forestry Department).

TABLE 8-2. ESTIMATING NAILS.

Wallboard Thickness	Nail Type	Approx. Lbs. Per 1000 Sq. Ft. of Gypsum Wallboard
1/2"	1 5/8 coated type gypsum board nail	5 1/2 lbs.
5/8"	1 7/8 coated type gypsum board nail	5 1/4 lbs.

Materials

Using your sketch of the area, determine the lengths and number of boards required. Nails can be estimated as outlined in Table 8-2.

After the wallboard is installed, reinforce the flat joints and inside corners with paper tape and joint compound. Reinforce the outside corners with a gypsum board metal corner bead and joint compound. Georgia-Pacific's Ready Mix is premixed, *and* ready to use for the complete job of tapering, filling, spotting, covering nailheads, and finishing. Table 8-3 indicates the approximate amount of joint compound to buy.

In the adhesive nail-on method, Georgia-Pacific gypsum board adhesive is applied to the joists and studs before each piece of wallboard is positioned and nailed. The adhesive is applied to the framing member from a caulking gun in about a 3/8-inch diameter bead. For each 1,000 square feet of wallboard use eight 1-quart tubes of adhesive.

Tools required include:

—wallboard cutting knife and heavy-duty knive blade,
—wallboard hammer or regular crown head carpenter's claw hammer,
—4-foot T-square or steel straightedge,
—steel tape measure,
—utility saw or keyhole saw,
—joint finishing knives—4" and 10" blades,
—plastic pan for joint compound,
—sandpaper (medium texture) for joint finishing,
—caulking gun.

Installation

☐ Use a T-square or straightedge and wallboard knife for scoring. With the knife at right

TABLE 8-3. MATERIALS NEEDED.

Gypsum Wallboard Square Feet	Estimated Amount of Ready Mix Compound	Estimated Amount of Wallboard Tape
100-200 sq. ft.	1 gal.	2 - 60' rolls
300-400 sq. ft.	2 gals.	3 - 60' rolls
500-600 sq. ft.	3 gals.	1 - 250' roll
700-800 sq. ft.	4 gals.	1 - 250' roll 1 - 60' roll
900-1000 sq. ft.	1-5 gal. Pail	1 - 250' roll 2 - 60' rolls or 1- 500' roll

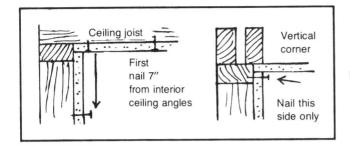

Fig. 8-7. Wall application (courtesy Georgia-Pacific).

angles to the board, score completely through the face paper; then apply firm, even pressure to snap the board. Fold back the partially separated portion of the board and use the knife again to cut the back paper. Rough edges should be smoothed. Panels can be cut with a saw if desired.

☐ It will be necessary to cut holes in the wallboard for electrical outlets, light receptacles, etc. The distance of the opening from the end and edge of the board should be carefully measured and marked on the face of the wallboard. The opening should then be outlined in pencil and cut out with a keyhole saw. The cutout must be accurate, or the cover plate will not conceal the hole.

☐ "Dimple" all nails with a hammer blow firm enough to indent the board's face paper but not to break the paper.

☐ For horizontal application on side walls, install the top board first. Push the board up firmly against the ceiling and nail, placing nails 7 inches apart. Keep all nails back 7 inches from interior

ceiling angles, however, since nails in the interior angles are apt to pop. If the adhesive/nail-on method is used, all of the field nailing can be eliminated. Nailing is done around the edges of the board. If the board is bowed out in the center, you may want to secure it with a temporary nail until the adhesive sets.

☐ For a vertical application, place the long edges of the wallboard parallel to the framing members. This method is more desirable if the ceiling height of your wall is greater than 8 feet 2 inches or the wall is 4 feet wide or less. Nailing recommendations are the same as for the horizontal application (Fig. 8-7).

☐ To protect outside corners from edge damage, install metal corner bead every 5 inches through the gypsum board into the wood framing (Fig. 8-8).

☐ A premixed material, such as Georgia-Pacific Ready Mix Joint Compound, is the easiest to use to finish joints, corners, and nailheads. A

Fig. 8-8. Metal corner bead (courtesy Georgia- Pacific).

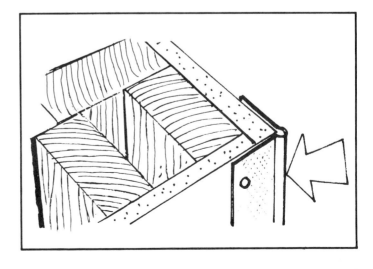

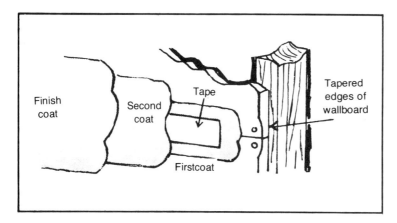

minimum of three coats of mix is recommended for all taped joints, including an embedding coat to bond the tape and two finishing coats over the tape (Fig. 8-9). Each coat should dry thoroughly, usually for 24 hours, so that the surface can be easily sanded. Wrap sandpaper around a wood sanding block so that you sand the surface evenly. Do not oversand or sand the paper surface. If you do, it may outline the joint or nailhead through the paint.

☐ Take your 4-inch joint finishing knife and apply the bedding compound fully and evenly into the slight recess created by the adjoining tapered edges of the board (Fig. 8-10).

☐ Next, take your wallboard tape, center it over the joint and press the tape firmly into the bedding compound with your wallboard knife held at a 45-degree angle. The pressure should squeeze some compound from under the tape, but enough must be left for a good bond (Fig. 8-11).

☐ When thoroughly dry, at least 24 hours, apply a fill coat extending a few inches beyond the edge of the tape and feather the edges of the compound. When the first finishing coat is thoroughly dry, use your 10-inch joint finishing knife and apply a second coat, feathering the edges about 1 1/2 inches beyond the first coat. When this coat is dry, sand lightly to a smooth, even surface. Wipe off the dust in preparation for the final decoration. Total width of the application should be 12 to 14 inches (Fig. 8-12).

☐ To finish nailheads, draw your 4-inch joint finishing knife across nails to be sure they are below

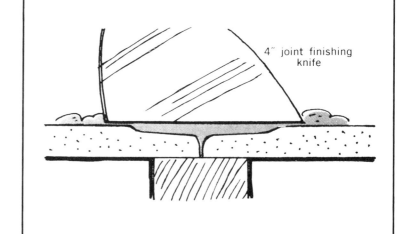

Fig. 8-10. Applying bedding compound (courtesy Georgia-Pacific).

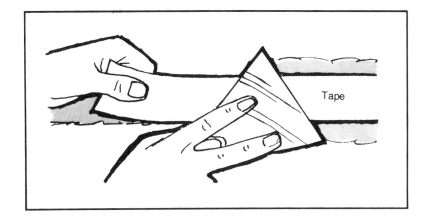

Fig. 8-11. Applying wallboard tape (courtesy Georgia-Pacific).

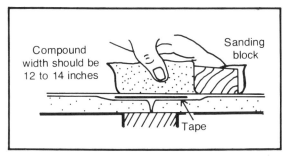

Compound width should be 12 to 14 inches

Sanding block

Tape

Fig. 8-12. Applying finishing coats (courtesy Georgia-Pacific).

the surface of the board. Apply the first coat of mix with even pressure to smooth the compound level with the surface of the board. Do not bow the knife blade with excessive pressure since it will tend to scoop compound from the dimpled area. When dry, apply the second coat, let dry, sand lightly, and

apply the third coat. Sand lightly before applying your decoration. An additional coat may be needed depending on temperature and humidity (Fig. 8-13).

☐ You use basically the same steps with end or butt joints as you do with tapered edges. The two long edges are tapered slightly to aid in joint finishing. The two short or cut edges require more feathering with a larger putty knife or trowel. The end joints are not tapered; care must be taken not to build up the compound in the center of the joint. This build-up encourages ridging and shadowed areas. Feather the compound well out on each side of the joint. The final application of joint compound should be 14 to 18 inches wide (Fig. 8-14).

☐ To finish inside corners, cut tape the length of the corner angle you are going to finish. Apply the compound with a 4-inch knife evenly about 1 1/2

Fig. 8-13. Finishing nailheads (courtesy Georgia-Pacific).

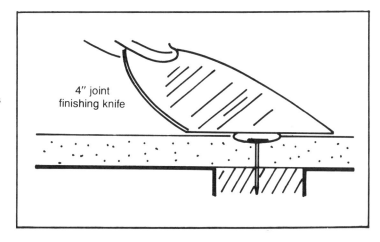

4″ joint finishing knife

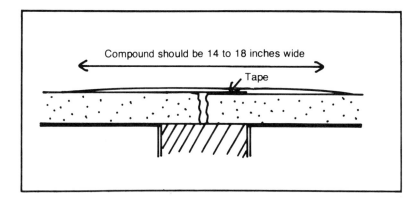

Compound should be 14 to 18 inches wide

Tape

Fig. 8-14. Finishing end joints (courtesy Georgia-Pacific).

inches on each side of the angle. Use sufficient compound to embed the tape. Fold the tape along the center crease and firmly press it into the corner. Use enough pressure to squeeze some compound under the edges. Feather the compound 2 inches from the edge of the tape.

When the first coat is dry, apply a second coat. Feather the edges of the compound 1 1/2 inches beyond the first coat. Apply a third coat if necessary, let dry, and sand to a smooth surface. Use as little compound as possible at the apex of the angle to prevent hairline cracking (Fig. 8-15).

☐ To finish metal corner bead, be sure the metal corner is attached firmly. Use a 4-inch finishing knife to spread the compound 3 to 4 inches wide from the nose of the bead, covering the metal edges.

When completely dry, sand lightly and apply a second coat, feathering edges 2 to 3 inches beyond the first coat. A third coat may be needed depending on your coverage. Feather the edges of each coat 2 to 3 inches beyond the preceding coat (Fig. 8-16).

Ceiling Installation

It is more difficult to install the ceiling boards because of the overhead positioning. Use T-braces to hold the board in place while it is being nailed. A satisfactory T-brace consists of a 2-foot piece of 1 × 4 nailed onto the end of a 2 × 4. The length should be about an inch longer than the floor-to-ceiling height.

When the adhesive/nail-on method is used, the edges should be nailed. All edges should be supported on framing. The nails should be driven to bring the board tight to the framing; then another blow struck to dimple the nail, being careful not to break the face paper (Fig. 8-17).

For ceilings with joists 16 inches on center, use 1/2-inch gypsum board. If your ceiling has joists 24 inches on center, use 5/8-inch gypsum board (Fig. 8-18).

PANELING

There is no mystery to installing wall panel-

Fig. 8-15. Finishing inside corners (courtesy Georgia-Pacific).

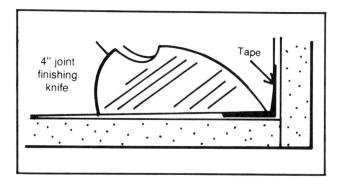

4″ joint finishing knife

Tape

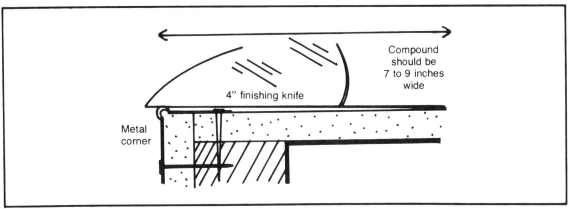

Fig. 8-16. Finishing metal corner bead (courtesy Georgia-Pacific).

Fig. 8-17. Gypsum board ceiling installation (courtesy Georgia-Pacific).

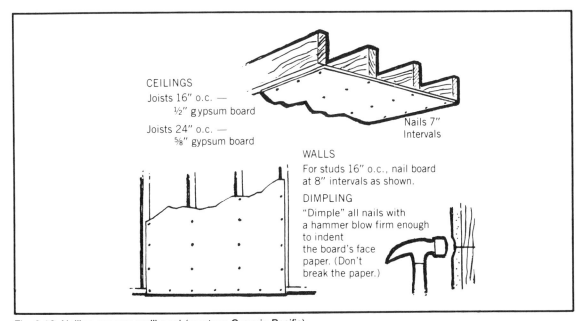

Fig. 8-18. Nailing gypsum wallboard (courtesy Georgia-Pacific).

ing. It is an easy do-it-yourself project that almost any homeowner can tackle. If your walls are 8 feet high and in good repair, simply follow the standard procedures for installing wall paneling just outlined. If you have problems like uneven walls, if your room has unusual architectural features, or if you are just looking for novel solutions to old decorating dilemmas, with the help of the following instructions, you should be able to panel any room. Remember, wall paneling is made for a low budget. It is not only priced low, but it is almost maintenance free and so easy to install that there is no need to even think of contracting outside help, unless time is a factor.

Paneling is available in 4-×-8-foot sheets which literally add dimension to any room interior. Grooving patterns accent the three-dimensional qualities of paneled surfaces and add decorating excitement to the plainest wall. Unlike paint and wallpaper, paneling can correct or cover problem walls.

Decorating Tips

Before making your paneling selection, it is wise to review some basic decorating principles. Depending on your room's shape and size, paneling can highlight architectural features or minimize awkward dimensions.

Professional decorators recognize that a pleasing room has the proper relationship of color and lines within the space. For instance, a light-colored ceiling appears higher, while a darker color can visually lower an extra high ceiling. The same color rules apply to walls. Light-colored walls appear farther away, while darker walls optically shrink the size of a room.

Lines, such as the V-grooves in wall paneling, create similar effects. Applied with grooves running vertically, paneling makes a wall appear taller but narrower in width. Used horizontally, the grooves create the effect of a wider but lower wall. Paneling also offers an additional dimension—a wood-grain pattern. A bold, pronounced grain attracts the eye and accents the surface, while the more subtle, refined grain provides a muted backdrop to complement furniture and art objects within a room.

With a careful analysis of your room's dimensions and an understanding of how color, line, and pattern interact, you can achieve a professional looking job with decorative wall paneling.

Selection of Wall Paneling

Like pieces of furniture, paneling brings the natural beauty of real wood into your home. Paneling is available in an almost limitless variety of styles, colors, and textures. Knowledge of the various types of paneling will help you make a selection that is best for your room.

Prefinished interior paneling may be plywood or processed wood fiber products. Paneling faces may be real hardwood or softwood veneers finished to enhance their natural texture, grain, and color. Other faces may be printed, paper overlaid, or treated in other ways to simulate wood grain. Finishing techniques on both real wood and simulated wood-grain surfaces provide a durable and easily maintained wall.

Hardwood and Softwood Plywood. Some plywood wall panelings are manufactured with a face, core, and back veneer of softwood and/or hardwood. The face and back veneer wood grains run vertically, and the core runs horizontally to give strength and stability (Fig. 8-19). Hardwood and softwood plywood wall paneling is normally 1/4-inch thick, but some varieties range up to 7/16-inch thick.

The most elegant plywood paneling has real hardwood or softwood face veneers of walnut, birch, elm, oak, cherry, cedar, pine, or fir. The subtle variety of texture and grain in real wood paneling makes each one distinctive. These panels create the rich variety of pattern and warm wood tones only real wood can offer.

Tropical Hardwood Plywood. Other plywood paneling may have a face veneer of tropical hardwood. Finishing techniques include embossing, antiquing, or color-toning to achieve a wood grain or decorative look. Panels may also have a paper overlay with wood-grain or patterned paper laminated to the face. The panel is then grooved and finished. Most of these panelings are 5/32-inch thick.

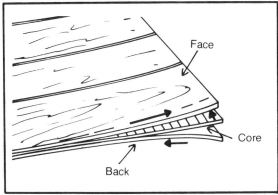

Fig. 8-19. Face and back veneer wood grains run vertically; core runs horizontally (courtesy Georgia-Pacific).

Wood Fiber Substrates. Processed wood fiber (particleboard or hardboard) wall paneling is also available with grain-printed paper overlays or printed surfaces. These prefinished panels are economical yet attractive. Thicknesses available are 5/32 inch, 3/16 inch, and 1/4 inch.

Economical wood fiber substrate paneling requires special installation techniques. Instructions are on the back of each panel; follow them carefully for cutting, spacing, placing, and applying with nails or adhesives.

Groove Treatment. Most vertical wall paneling is "random grooved." Grooves fall on 16-inch centers so that nailing over studs will be consistent. A typical random-groove pattern may look like the one in Fig. 8-20.

Other groove treatments include uniform spacing of 4 inches, 8 inches, 12 inches, or 16 inches and cross-scored grooves randomly spaced to give a "planked" effect. Grooves are usually striped darker than the panel surface and are cut or embossed into the panel in V or channel grooves. Less expensive paneling sometimes has a groove "striped" on the surface.

How to Buy Paneling

Paneling, like most products for the home, is available in a wide range of prices, from as little as $5 per panel to over $30 per panel. Real wood surface-veneered plywood paneling is considered the best. Its price, from about $16 to $35 per 4-×-8-foot sheet, reflects the quality and beauty of natural hardwood and softwood veneers. Real wood paneling is an investment that will last a lifetime. Its warmth and character adds both value and enjoyment to your home.

Generally, paneling with a simulated wood-grain finish is less expensive than real wood surfaced panels. Printed or plywood overlaid paneling is an excellent choice for many decorating needs and is available from $9 to $15 per panel. Paneling with wood fiber substrate is $5 to $8 per sheet and is a good-looking choice for the decorator on a low budget.

Your selection of paneling should take many things into consideration: type of furnishings, room size, number of walls, quantity needed, price, and other preferences. Whatever your final decision, paneling will provide years of beauty and easily maintained walls for any room in the home.

Paneling Preliminaries

Some preliminary steps which will help assure you of a quality installation in a trouble-free manner.

How to Measure Your Room. Every successful project begins with a plan. It does not need to be a complicated blueprint, but it must be accurate and complete. The plan will be a big help in

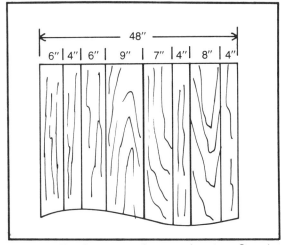

Fig. 8-20. Random grooved veneer (courtesy Georgia-Pacific).

figuring the amount of material needed and the steps for application. It will also help you visualize the completed project so you can coordinate the entire room, including carpeting, furniture, and other decorating accessories.

Start your plan with graph paper, perhaps with 1/4-inch squares. Then measure your room width carefully, making note of window and door openings as you proceed. Now translate your measurements to the graph paper.

Let us assume that you have a 14-×-16-foot room. If you let each 1/4-inch square represent 6 inches, your scale is 1 inch = 1 foot, so you end up with a 7-×-8-inch rectangle. Indicate window positions, doors (and the direction in which they open), fireplaces, and other structural elements.

Now you can begin figuring your paneling requirements. Total all four wall measurements.

Example: 14 feet + 16 feet + 16 feet = 60 feet

Then divide your total perimeter footage by the 4-foot panel width:

60 feet ÷ 4 feet = 15 panels

To allow for door, window, and fireplace cutouts, use the following deductions: (approximate) door: 1/2 panel, window: 1/4 panel, fireplace: 1/2 panel.

For the total panels needed, deduct the cutout panels from your original figure:

15 panels − 2 panels = 13 panels

If the perimeter of the room falls between the numbers in Fig. 8-21, use the next higher number. These figures are for rooms with walls not more than 8 feet high. For higher walls, add in the additional materials needed above the 8-foot level.

Conditioning Panels. Once purchased, your paneling should be stored in a dry location. Freshly plastered walls must be allowed to thoroughly dry before panels are installed. Prefinished paneling is highly moisture resistant, but, like all wood products, it is not waterproof and should not be stored or installed in areas subject to excessive moisture. Ideally the paneling should be stacked between sheets to allow air circulation or propped on the 8-foot edge. The panels should remain in the room 48 hours prior to installation to permit them to acclimatize to the surrounding temperatures and humidity conditions.

Perimeter	No. of 4' x 8' panels needed (without deductions)
36'	9
40'	10
44'	11
48'	12
52'	13
56'	14
60'	15
64'	16
68'	17
72'	18
92'	23

Fig. 8-21. Measuring guide (courtesy Georgia-Pacific).

Fig. 8-22. Place paneling around the room (courtesy Georgia-Pacific).

Tools for Paneling. Paneling does not require a lot of expensive tools. In fact, you probably already have most of the tools you need if you have been remodeling. For accurate measurements, you will only need a retractable tape 8 feet or longer, a large square, and a level. To trim the paneling, you will need a power or hand saw with a sharp, fine-toothed blade, a drill, and a keyhole or saber saw to make cutouts for electrical and wall switches. For actual installation, a nail set and hammer are necessary, and an adhesive caulking gun and padded wooden block if you are gluing the panels in place. Finally, you should have an inexpensive miter box to make professional-looking molding joints, and a pair of saw horses to elevate the paneling to a comfortable work height.

The Final Step. The beauty of real wood paneling is found in the natural variety of grain and color inherent in each panel. Before you begin application, place the panels around the room on each wall. Rearrange to achieve the most pleasing balance of color and grain pattern; then number the back of each panel in sequence (Fig. 8-22).

How to Install Paneling

Installation of paneling over existing true walls requires no preliminary preparation. The basic procedure will be covered step by step.

Locating Studs. *Studs*, the vertical solid wood members, make up the skeleton of most frame walls. Since you want to nail directly into this solid wall, locating each stud is important. In most homes, studs are usually spaced 16 inches on center, but 24-inch centers or other spacing may be found (Fig. 8-23).

If you plan to replace the present molding, remove it carefully. As you remove it, you may reveal the nailheads used to secure the plaster lath or drywall to the studs. These nails mark the stud locations. If you cannot locate the studs, start probing into the wall surface you plan to panel with a nail or small drill until you hit solid wood. Start 16 inches from one corner of the room with your first try and make the test holes at 3/4-inch intervals on each side of the initial hole until you locate the stud (Fig. 8-24).

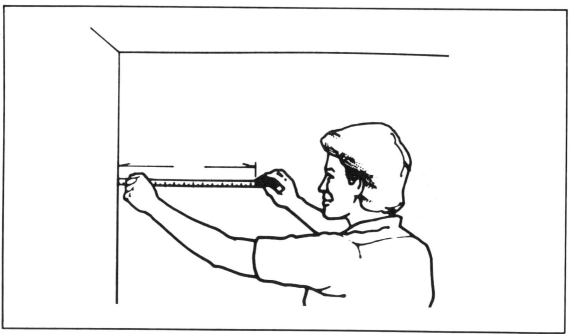

Fig. 8-23. Locate the stud (courtesy Georgia-Pacific).

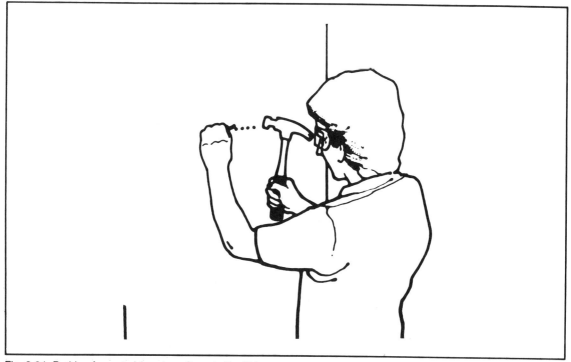

Fig. 8-24. Probing for a stud (courtesy Georgia-Pacific).

Since studs are not always straight, it is a good idea to probe at several heights. Once located, make a light pencil mark at the floor and ceiling to position all studs, and then snap a chalk line at 4-foot intervals (the standard panel width).

Measuring and Cutting. Start in one corner of the room and measure the floor-to-ceiling height for the first panel. Subtract 1/2 inch for top and bottom clearance. Moldings will later cover this gap. Transfer the measurements to the first panel and mark the dimensions in pencil, using a straightedge to provide a clean line.

All cutting should be done with a sharp saw with a minimum set to the teeth to reduce splintering. Use a crosscut hand saw with 10 or more teeth to the inch, or a plywood blade in a table saw, cutting with the panel face up. If you are using a portable circular saw or saber saw, mark and cut the panels from the back.

Cutouts for door and window sections, electrical switches and outlets, and heat registers require careful measurements. Take your dimensions from the edge of the last applied panel for width and from the floor and ceiling line for height. Transfer the measurements to the panel, checking as you go. Unless you plan to add molding, door and window cutouts should fit against the surrounding casing. If possible, cutout panels should meet close to the middle over doors and windows.

For electrical boxes, shut off the power and unscrew the protective plate to expose the box. Then paint or run chalk around the box area, transferring the outline to the back of the panel (Fig. 8-25). To replace the switch plate, a 1/4-inch spacer or washer may be needed between the box screw hole and the switch or receptacle.

Drive small nails in each corner through the panel until they protrude through the face. Turn the panel over, drill two 3/4-inch holes just inside the corners, and use a keyhole or saber saw to make the cutout (Fig. 8-26). The hole can be up to 1/4 inch oversize and still be covered when the protective switch plate is replaced.

Applying Panels. The first panel is the im-

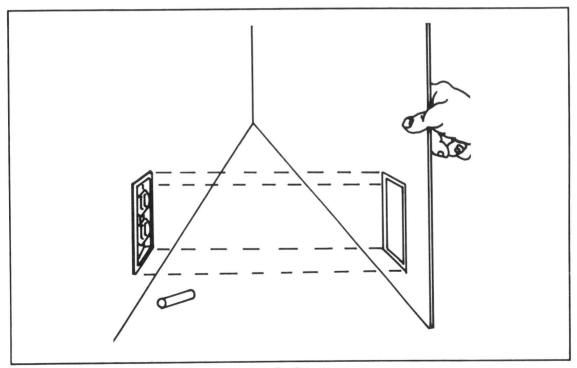

Fig. 8-25. Expose the electrical outlet (courtesy Georgia-Pacific).

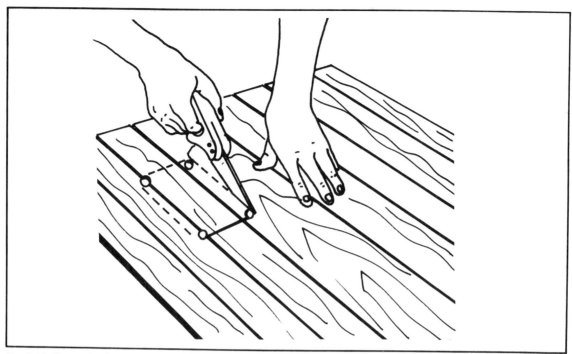

Fig. 8-26. Cutout for the electrical outlet (courtesy Georgia-Pacific).

Fig. 8-27. Plumb the first panel (courtesy Georgia-Pacific).

portant one. Put the first panel in place and butt on the adjacent wall in the corner. Make sure it is completely plumb and both left and right panel edges fall on solid stud backing (Fig. 8-27). Most corners are not perfectly true, however; so you will probably need to trim the panel to fit into the corner properly. Fit the panel into the corner, checking with a level to be sure the panel is plumb vertically. Draw a mark along the panel edge, parallel to the corner.

On rough walls like masonry, or that adjoining a fireplace wall, scribe or mark the panel with a compass on the inner panel edge; then cut on the scribe line to fit (Fig. 8-28). Scribing and cutting the inner panel edge may also be necessary if the outer edge of the panel does not fit directly on a stud. The outer edge must fall on the center of a stud to allow room for nailing your next panel.

Before installing the next panel, paint a strip of color to match the paneling groove color on the wall location where the panels will meet. The appearance of any slight gap between the panel edges will be minimized in this way.

Nailing Paneling. Most panels are random grooved to create a solid lumber panel effect. If you check carefully, however, you will notice that there is usually a groove located every 16 inches so most nails can be placed in the grooves, falling directly on the 16-inch stud spacing. Regular small-headed finishing nails or colored paneling nails can be used.

For paneling directly to studs, 3d (1 1/4-inch) nails are recommended, but if you must penetrate backing board, plaster, or drywall, 6d (2-inch) nails are needed to give a solid bite into the stud. Space nails 6 inches apart on the panel edges and 12 inches apart in the panel field (Fig. 8-29). Nails should be countersunk slightly below the panel surface with a nail set, then hidden with a matching putty stick. Colored nails eliminate the need to countersink and putty. Use 1-inch colored nails to apply paneling to studs, and 1 5/8-inch nails to apply paneling through gypsum board or plaster.

Applying Adhesive. Using adhesive to install paneling is a simple method which eliminates

Fig. 8-28. Scribe the panel with a compass (courtesy Georgia-Pacific).

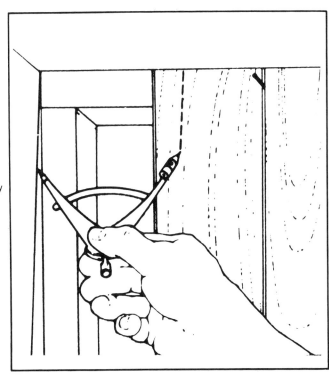

Fig. 8-29. Space nails 6″ on edge and 12″ in the panel field (courtesy Georgia-Pacific).

the chore of countersinking and hiding nailheads. Adhesive may be used to apply paneling directly to studs or over existing walls as long as the surface is sound and clean.

Paneling must be properly cut and fitted prior to installation. Make sure the panels and walls are clean and free from dirt and particles before you start. Once applied, the adhesive makes adjustments difficult; however, used properly, adhesive gives a more professional appearance.

A caulking gun is the simplest method of application. Trim the tube end so that a 1/8-inch wide adhesive bead can be squeezed out. Once the paneling is fitted, apply beads of adhesive in a continuous strip along the top, bottom, and both edges of the panel. On intermediate studs, apply beads of adhesive 3 inches long and 6 inches apart (Fig. 8-30).

With scrap plywood or shingles used as a spacer at the floor level, set the panel carefully in place and press firmly along the stud lines, spreading the adhesive into the wall. Using a hammer with a padded wooden block or a rubber mallet, next tap over the glue lines to ensure a sound bond between the panel and backing.

Be sure to read the adhesive manufacturer's instructions carefully prior to installation. Some

require the panel to be placed against the adhesive, then gently pulled away from the wall for a few minutes until the solvent "flashes off" and the adhesive sets up. The panel is then repositioned and tapped home.

PROBLEM WALLS

As we have seen, when you start with a sound, level surface, paneling is quick and easy. Not every wall is perfect, however. In fact, some can be a downright disaster, with chipped, broken, and crumbly plaster, peeling wallpaper, punctured gypsum board, or roughly poured concrete or cinderblock walls.

Uneven Surfaces

Your paneling installation is only as good as the surface to which the panels are applied. Walls in disrepair must be improved before you attempt to cover them with prefinished paneling.

Most problem walls are either plaster or gypsum board applied to a conventional wood wall or to a stud wall, such as brick, stone, cement, or cinderblock. The solution to both types is the same, but getting there calls for slightly different approaches.

On conventional walls, clean off the obviously damaged areas. Remove torn wallpaper and scrape

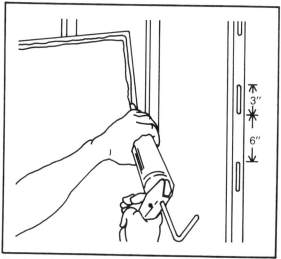

Fig. 8-30. Bead with adhesive (courtesy Georgia-Pacific).

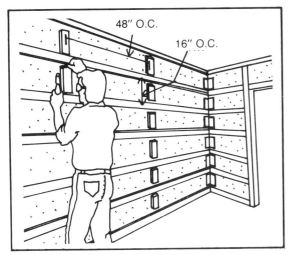

Fig. 8-31. Vertical and horizontal stripping (courtesy Georgia-Pacific).

Construct a lightweight wood frame system of furring strips to which you will apply your paneling. Furring strips are either 1-×-2-inch lumber of 3/8-×-1/2-inch plywood strips cut 1 1/4 inches wide. The bottom strip is placed 1/2 inch from the floor. The furring strips shown in Fig. 8-31 are applied horizontally 16 inches apart on center on the wall (based on an 8-foot ceiling) with vertical members at 48-inch centers where the panels butt together. Leave a 1/4-inch space between the horizontal and vertical strips to allow for ventilation.

Begin by locating the *high spot* on the wall—the area that protrudes farthest into the room. To determine the high spot, drop a plumb line. Fasten your first furring strip, making sure that the thickness of the furring strips compensates for the protrusion of the wall surface. Check with a level to make sure each furring strip is flush with the first strip. Use wood shingles or wedges between the wall and strips to ensure a uniformly flat surface (Figs. 8-32 and 8-33). Remember to put furring strips around doors, windows, and other openings.

off flaking plaster and any broken gypsum board sections. On masonry walls, chip off any protruding mortar. Don't bother making repairs; there is an easier solution.

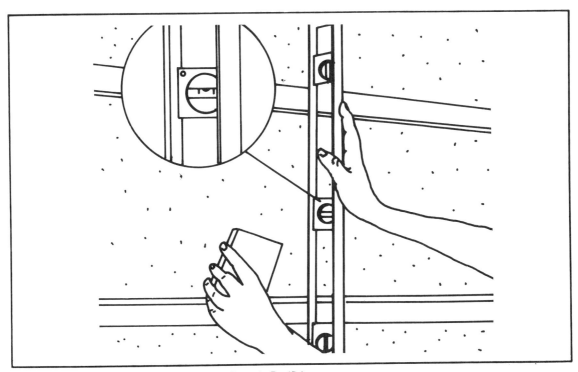

Fig. 8-32. Wood furring construction (courtesy Georgia-Pacific).

Fig. 8-33. Use wooden edges for uniformity (courtesy Georgia-Pacific).

On stud walls, the furring strips can be nailed directly through the shimming wedge and the gypsum board or plaster into the stud. Depending on the thickness of the furring strip and the wall covering, you will need 6d (2-inch) or 8d (2 1/2-inch) common nails.

Masonry walls are a little tougher to handle. Specially hardened masonry nails can be used, or you can drill a hole with a carbide-tipped bit, insert wood plugs or expansion shields, and nail or bolt the shimmed frame into place.

If the masonry wall is badly damaged, construct a 2-×-3-inch stud wall before you apply paneling. See the Troublesome Construction section in this chapter.

Damp Surfaces

Masonry walls, besides being uneven, often present a more serious problem: dampness. Usually these surfaces are found partially or fully below ground level. Damp basement walls may result from seepage of water from outside sources or *condensation*, moist warm air within the home which condenses or beads up when it comes in contact with the cooler outside walls. Whatever the cause, the moisture must be eliminated before you begin to panel.

Seepage may be caused by a variety of problems. Check your gutter and downspouts to see if they are dumping excessive rain run-off around foundation walls. See if the slope of your yard is channeling water toward the foundation rather than away from the house (Fig. 8-34).

You should also inspect the foundation to locate any holes or cracks. They should be repaired with concrete patching compound or special hydraulic cement designed to plug active leaks (Fig. 8-35). Consult your masonry supply house for the recommended material and instructions on preparing the wall and applying the cement.

Weeping or porous walls can often be cured with an application of masonry waterproofing paints. Formulas for wet and drywalls are available, but the paint must be scrubbed onto the surface to

Fig. 8-34. Check the downspouts (courtesy Georgia-Pacific).

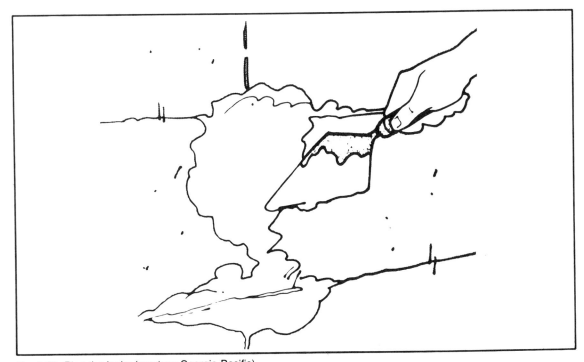

Fig. 8-35. Plug the leaks (courtesy Georgia-Pacific).

213

penetrate the pores, hairline cracks, and crevices (Fig. 8-36).

Condensation problems require a different attack. Here, the answer is to dry out the basement air. The basement should be provided with heat in the winter and cross ventilation in the summer. Wrap cold water pipes with insulation to reduce sweating. If you have a washer, dryer, or shower in the basement, vent them directly to the outside. Consider installing a dehumidifying system to control the condensation.

Once you have the dampness problem under control, construct a plumb-level furring strip wall framework. Apply insulation if desired. See the Thermal and Sound Control Insulation section in this chapter.

Next, line the walls with a polyvinyl vapor/moisture barrier film, installing it over the furring strips (Fig. 8-37). Rolls of this inexpensive material can be obtained from your dealer. Installation is easy, but be sure to provide at least a 6-inch lap

where one section of the film meets a second. Now apply paneling in the conventional method. If your dampness is so serious that you cannot effectively correct it, then get a professional to help. Prefinished hardwood paneling is manufactured with interior glue and must be installed in a dry setting for satisfactory performance.

Troublesome Construction

Sometimes the problem is out-of-square walls, uneven floors, or studs placed out of sequence. You may need to trim around a stone or brick fireplace, make cutouts for wall pipes or handle beams and columns in a basement. Hopefully, you will never face all of these problems in the same room, but each has a solution.

If the plaster, masonry, or other type of wall is so uneven that it can't be trued by using furring strips and shimming them out where the wall bellows, 2- × -3 inch studs may be needed. You can use studs flat against the wall in order to conserve

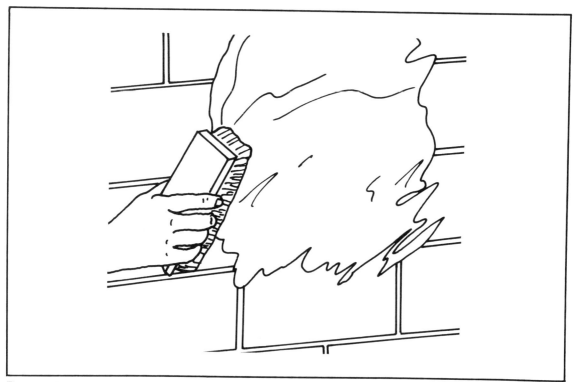

Fig. 8-36. Scrub the paint into the surface for deep penetration (courtesy Georgia-Pacific).

214

Fig. 8-37. Install a moisture barrier (courtesy Georgia-Pacific).

space. Use studs for top and bottom plates and space vertical studs 16 inches on center. Apply paneling directly to studs or over gypsum insulation or plywood backing board.

Out-of-sequence studs require a little planning, but they are usually not a serious problem. Probe to find the exact stud locations as described earlier, snap chalk lines, and examine the situation. Usually you will find a normal stud sequence starting at one corner, then perhaps where the carpenter framed for a mid-wall doorway, the spacing abruptly changes to a new pattern. Start paneling in the normal manner using adhesive and nails. When you reach the point where the pattern changes, cut a filler strip of paneling to bridge the odd stud spacing and then pick up the new pattern with full-sized panels.

Occasionally you will find one or two slanted studs. The combination of panel adhesive with the holding power of the ceiling and baseboard moldings usually solves this problem.

Uneven floors can usually be handled with shoe molding. Shoe 1/2 × 3/4 inch is flexible enough to conform to moderate deviations. If the gap is greater than 3/4 inch, the base molding or panel should be scribed with a compass to conform to the floor line. Spread the points slightly greater than the gap, hold the compass vertically, and draw the point along the floor scribing a pencil line on the base molding (Fig. 8-38). Remove the molding, trim to the line with a copy or saber saw, and replace. If you have a real washboard of a floor, then you have a floor problem, not a wall problem. Either renail the floor flat or cover with plywood or particleboard underlayment before paneling.

The same compass trick is used to scribe a line where paneling butts into a stone or brick fireplace. Tack the panel temporarily in place, scribe a line parallel to the fireplace edge, and trim for a snug, professional-looking fit. Check to be sure the opposite panel edge falls on a stud before you apply the panel permanently.

Older homes may have heating pipes, usually near the ceiling, protruding through the wall. To

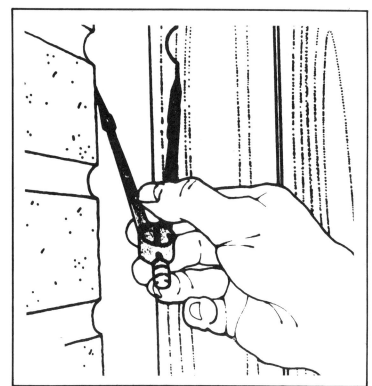

Fig. 8-38. Compass-scribe (courtesy Georgia-Pacific).

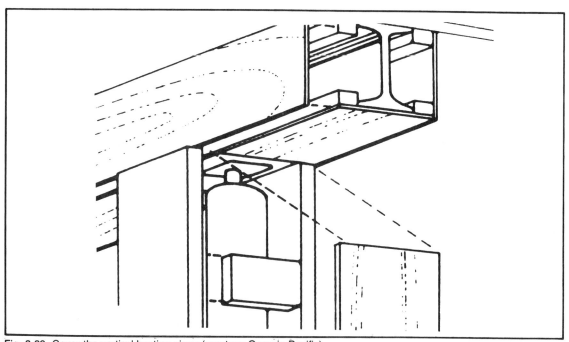

Fig. 8-39. Cover the vertical heating pipes (courtesy Georgia-Pacific).

panel around pipes or heating ducts, make a double cut the width of the hole diameter, install the panel, and nail the cutout section above the pipe. Colored putty sticks will blend out edges, and metal collars are available to snap around the pipes in the corner.

Vertical heating pipes in the corner, overhead beams, and support columns in a basement are unattractive elements that are best hidden from sight. Construct a simple 1-×-2-inch lumber framework, tying it to the adjacent wall or ceiling. Apply your paneling and cover the joints with outside corner molding for a neat job (Fig. 8-39).

Thermal and Sound Control Insulation

Few home improvement projects are undertaken without giving thought to increasing the amount of insulation to save energy. An additional benefit of proper insulation is improved sound control. Since you are continually assaulted by waves of noise from both inside and outside the home—traffic, lawnmowers, appliances, power tools—you may want to include adequate sound barriers when you plan your paneling project.

While hardwood paneling itself offers only modest sound reduction properties, the correct wall system can definitely reduce annoying noise levels. In addition, many of the steps taken to improve home heating insulation can also reduce noise. For instance, well-placed shrubs, trees, and hedges act as both a wind and sound barrier outside the home. Fully weather-stripped windows and doors, twin-glazing, and storm windows and doors can all aid dramatically in sealing out outside noise.

Rolls of fiberglass or mineral wood insulation stapled between the wall studs add insulation and reduce sound transmission. For additional control within the stud wall system, you can nail gypsum sound-deadening board to the studs.

On masonry walls the easiest way to achieve both heat and sound insulation is to apply 1-×-3-inch furring strips, then a 3/4-inch expanded polystyrene foam board between the strips. Finish with gypsum wallboard or sound-deadening board (Fig. 8-40). Other products combine the rigid foam and wallboard in one panel for easier installation.

The finishing touch is the installation of a decorative, prefinished hardwood paneling. Now you have a package that provides excellent heat and noise insulation, the fire safety of gypsum, and the beauty of paneling.

If you have a severe sound control problem, you could also add resilient metal furring channels to attach the gypsum wallboard to studs, or use two layers of 1/2-inch gypsum wallboard (Fig. 8-41). Double wall construction can also be considered.

For maximum sound reduction, stagger the joints between the gypsum sound-deadening panels and the prefinished hardwood paneling. Start in a

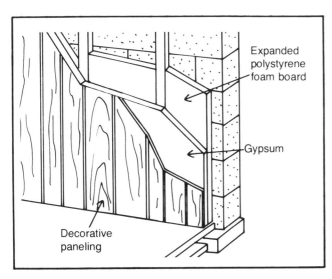

Expanded polystyrene foam board

Gypsum

Decorative paneling

Fig. 8-40. Gypsum and polystyrene board (courtesy Georgia-Pacific).

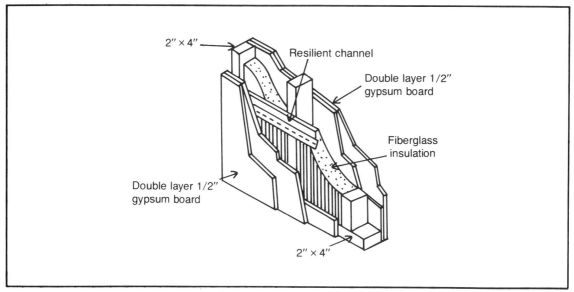

Fig. 8-41. Resilient channel for sound control (courtesy Georgia-Pacific).

corner with a 16-inch wide gypsum panel and then continue with the standard 48-inch wide sheets. Begin paneling at the same corner with a full-width sheet. The gypsum panel joints will fall 5 feet 4 inches, 8 feet 4 inches, etc., from the corner, while the hardwood paneling joints will fall 4 feet 8 inches, 12 feet, etc.

If you are constructing a paneled wall between a recreation room and a noisy laundry, shop, or furnace room, a thicker, 2-×-6-inch wall is recommended. Here use 2-×-4 1/4-inch studs, but offset the alignment so that studs don't meet back to back. This staggered spacing allows you to weave blanket insulation horizontally between the studs, or apply two layers of insulation (Fig. 8-42). Then apply gypsum sound-deadening board and prefinished hardwood panels.

When wiring a sound-control interior wall, do not position your electric boxes back to back. The box cutouts, if placed in direct line with each other, transmit the sound from one room to another.

A few extra dollars spent to install a solid core door frame will pay big dividends in sound control. To reduce noise within a room, include sound-absorbing surfaces such as acoustical ceiling tile, deep pile carpets, and heavy drapes.

Unusual Architecture

While a square room with straight, plumb walls is easy to panel, it is often architecturally plain and uninteresting. The boxlike space can be enlivened with "supergraphic" paneling or mirror strips applied between the panels to create a feeling of depth to the wall. Panels applied in horizontal or herringbone patterns give dramatic interest to a room.

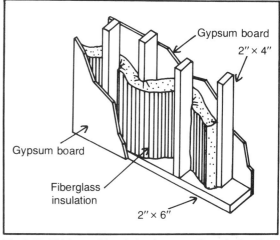

Fig. 8-42. Thicker wall insulation (courtesy Georgia-Pacific).

218

What about the opposite problem—a room with almost too many architectural features? How do you panel when faced with alcoves, arches, low knee walls in an attic, or intricate stair sides in a basement room? As difficult as these features may seem, there is a solution for each, and the unusual architecture often ends up as the highlight of the room.

Alcoves. Alcoves are probably the simplest to handle if you look at the space as a miniature three-sided room. Although it is smaller in scale, regular paneling procedures are used. Then you work the inside and outside corners and ceiling and baseboard moldings as in any full-size room.

Before you begin paneling an alcove, however, investigate the possibility of building additional features into the space, such as a window seat or a desk in a small area; perhaps a daybed or full-size bed in its own private setting, if space permits.

Arches. Arches present an exciting challenge. Paneling the outside of an arch is not really any different from paneling a standard wall. Care-fully probe to locate the supporting framing members; then measure the paneling from the nearest full-size panel.

The underside of the arch and application of curved cove molding may be a problem, however. If the arch falls between two rooms where the second room will remain painted or wallpapered, you can duplicate this treatment on the other side of the arch. Where paneling will be carried through both rooms for a coordinated look, the paneling may be flexible enough to bend in strip form to line a large-radius, walk-through arch. If the radius is too small to flex the strip of paneling to fit, you can increase the panel's flexibility with saw kerfs on the back of the panel strip (Fig. 8-43).

A caution before you begin: remember that you are working with a natural material. Every piece of paneling has a different degree of resilience, based on wood species and panel construction. Use only plywood paneling since arch wood-fiber substrate panelings can break.

☐ To start, measure the required length of

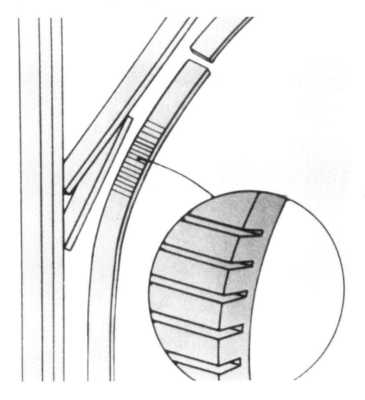

Fig. 8-43. Saw kerfs for an arch (courtesy Georgia-Pacific).

paneling along 8-foot edge of the wall. The width of most arches is 4 to 8 inches. You should be able to select a strip without a groove of this width from your paneling. The reason for using an ungrooved section is to avoid cutting through a groove with the saw kerf, which would weaken or break the panel strip.

☐ Experiment on sample paneling strips before you cut the final arch strips. Before cutting the strip, flex the panel. If the paneling will not bend enough to fit the arch, carefully make saw kerfs on the back of the panel strip along the length of the strip at right angles to the long edge of the paneling. A 1/8-inch blade can be used for cutting kerfs. The distance between the saw cuts should be no less than needed to conform to the radius of the arch.

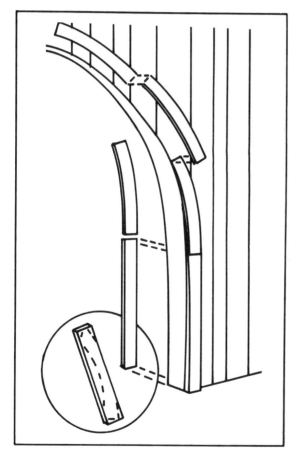

Fig. 8-44. Carved sections for arch (courtesy Georgia-Pacific).

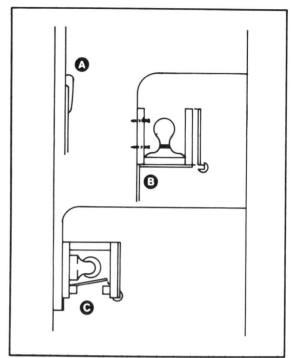

Fig. 8-45. Box in cove area (courtesy Georgia-Pacific).

☐ Decide where you want the end joints of the strips to meet: at the top of the arch or at wainscot level. Apply the paneling strips to the arch with adhesive, following the adhesive manufacturer's instructions. Use enough nails to hold the strip in place while the adhesive dries.

Standard 3/4-inch outside corner molding is usually flexible enough to conform to arches, but this narrow molding often looks skimpy and out of proportion when used to frame large arch openings. A better solution is to cut carved sections 2 1/2 to 3 inches wide from 1-×-6-foot pine board with a saber saw (Fig. 8-44). Then stain or paint.

An even easier and sometimes more dramatic solution is to eliminate the curved arch, and instead angle your trim boards in short, straight sections.

The curved, plaster cove ceilings often found in older homes present both a challenge and an opportunity. Since they are usually found in rooms with walls higher than 8 feet, the quickest solution is to panel to the 8-foot height and finish off the panel top line with cap molding. See Fig. 8-45(A).

Then paint the wall above to match the ceiling color.

A more creative answer takes advantage of the situation and allows for a dramatic lighting installation. Run your paneling up the wall; then box in the cove area at the ceiling line with a simple, paneled lumber framework. See Fig. 8-45(B) and (C). Now you have the option of installing indirect perimeter lighting, bouncing soft illumination off the ceiling back into the room, or wiring the box for built-in spotlights to wash down the walls, accenting artwork and furnishings.

Attic. With the help of paneling an unfinished attic can yield several extra rooms. Short side walls may already be in place, or they may need to be built with a stud framework tied to the roof rafters and floor. To avoid bumping your head in the finished room, most professionals recommend walls that are a minimum of 5 or 6 feet high. Because of the angle where the side wall meets the angled roofline, architects refer to this area as a *knee wall*.

Before you panel, take the opportunity to install sufficient insulation in the walls and ceiling to ensure comfortable living. You can recapture lost space behind the short knee wall by building in low closets or sets of storage drawers. If you are fortunate enough to have a dormer window in the roof, plan an alcove with a window seat for this area.

Knee walls are not difficult to panel, but you may find that existing walls have studs spaced 16 inches on center, while the roof rafters are 24 inches apart. Check carefully before you proceed. Begin by paneling the ceiling. Place the bottom edge of the panels where the roof meets the side wall. Now panel the walls, making sure the wall panel grooves line up exactly with the ceiling grooves. Use moldings to cover the joints where the wall and ceiling panels meet.

Since attic end walls are usually over 8 feet in height, refer to the section on High Ceilings for ideas on treating them.

High Ceilings. Paneling on the ceiling? Why not? The warm wood tones of paneling can "lower" a high ceiling and add drama to any room. Lay out the room on graph paper before you panel so that panel joints are spaced symmetrically on the ceiling. A center joint could be covered with stained batten molding in a 14- to 16-foot wide room. You could also install false ceiling beams made of 1-inch stained lumber, 3/4-inch plywood, or "handhewn" Styrofoam beams positioned 4 inches on center to mask the panel joints.

Before you panel the ceiling, locate the floor joist so that the paneling can be nailed into the solid wood framing. When applying the paneling, make sure to butt each panel so that the V grooves match up from one sheet to the next. Use panel adhesive both between and at the floor joist locations to provide the best installation, preventing any sag.

To make your ceiling paneling job even easier, construct a T-shaped prop of 2- × -4-inch lumber a few inches longer than the wall height, with foam rubber to pad the top. Wedge it between the floor and ceiling to hold the panel in place while you nail it home (Fig. 8-46).

Basement Stairs. Figure 8-47 illustrates the trick job of cutting paneling to fit accurately in remodeling projects around a basement stairwell. Here the vertical risers are usually flush to the stringer side, but the horizontal stair treads overhang by several inches. Paneling this area is a difficult job, since a slight error in measuring on one step is magnified on all the succeeding lines.

Rather than using a compass to scribe these lines, you can easily make a paper pattern. Tape a section of the protective paneling slip sheets or pieces of newspaper over the stair area. With a sharp knife or razor, trim the paper to an accurate pattern. Remove the pattern from the wall and transfer the measurements to your paneling. Then carefully trim to size with a saber saw. Test your cutout for accuracy, and then apply with nails and adhesive.

High Ceilings. Since most prefinished paneling is supplied in a standard 4- × -8-foot panel size, how do you best handle extra high ceilings, peaked end walls, and tall stairwells? Answers range from the simple to the spectacular, but there is a solution for every situation, from the end wall in a remodeled attic to the sweeping three-story-high great hall in a country manor.

It all starts with planning. Choose one of the

Fig. 8-46. T-shaped prop (courtesy Georgia-Pacific).

Fig. 8-47. Paneling a basement stair (courtesy Georgia-Pacific).

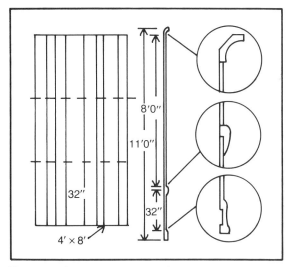

Fig. 8-48. Cut the panels into three sections (courtesy Georgia-Pacific).

following approaches, then sketch it out on graph paper. Tal' walls tend to dominate a room, so pay particular attention to the overall impact of line and scale before you make your final choice.

☐ Stack the panels one above the other with matching grooves. This is an easy answer to both high, square walls, and slanted-roof end walls. Finished battern molding is used to cover the panel joints.

☐ For walls up to 11 feet high, a wainscoting makes good decorating sense. For best panel efficiency, cut your 8-foot panel into three 32-inch high sections (Fig. 8-48). Apply to the lower section of the wall; then install full-size panels above it. By varying the size of your baseboard and ceiling moldings, and using a batten strip or other decorative molding at the joint, you can achieve a well-balanced, high wall.

☐ For walls up to 14 feet high, you can use the approach just mentioned, but use a plate rail rather than the smaller wainscoting. Here, apply a 5 1/2- to 6-foot paneling section at the floor line. Top it with a wider plate rail and continue the paneling to the ceiling. A high, narrow plate rail provides a perfect opportunity to display pewter, antique chinaware, or other collectibles in a safe, but highly visible manner (Fig. 8-49).

For a less conventional, more dramatic solution, you can choose one of these suggestions:

Fig. 8-49. Plate rails (courtesy Georgia-Pacific).

223

□ Apply your paneling horizontally. Cover the panel end joints with matching moldings at either 4- or 8-foot centers.

□ Combine several previous ideas, such as using vertical wainscoting sections at the floor line with horizontally applied paneling above the molding break.

□ To accent your high wall areas, try paneling in a herringbone pattern. Cut your paneling at a 45-degree angle, then apply in facing pairs for a striking wall effect. Before attempting this approach, carefully measure your wall width and determine on graph paper the best balance of herringbone patterns (Fig. 8-50). Your finished wall should either have a vertical batten strip at the exact midpoint, or one full 4-foot herringbone section should be positioned in the wall center (Fig. 8-51).

□ If paneling in a 45-degree angle is striking, then you can increase the angle to 60 degrees for an even more impressive wall. Because of the sharper angle, the eye is attracted upward to further em-phasize the extra wall height.

When cutting panels at 45- and 60-degree diagonals, a certain amount of paneling scrap is generated with proper preplanning, many of these extra pieces can be used above windows and doors and other sections of the room.

□ You can also panel in a checkerboard design. Cut your panels into 16- or 24-inch squares and apply them so that the grooves run vertically in one section and horizontally in the next (Fig. 8-52). Remember to use a plane or wood rasp to bevel-cut the edges. Then stain the raw edges to duplicate the look of factory grooves.

□ For an even more dramatic checkerboard effect, select two different, but complementary, panels for square applications—perhaps a strong and a subtle grain pattern, or a light- and a dark-colored species.

□ A checkerboard design is effective in small areas, such as stairwells, but the repetitive pattern can begin to look busy over large wall surfaces. Try sketching out paneling sections cut in a 1:2 ratio on

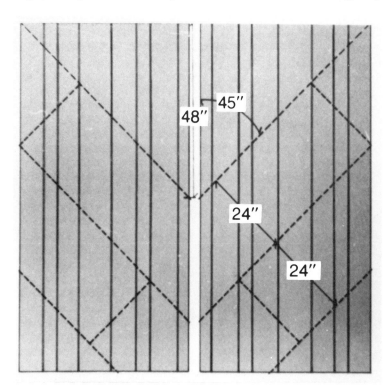

Fig. 8-50. Pattern paneling in her-ringbone design (courtesy Georgia-Pacific).

Fig. 8-51. Position a full herringbone section (courtesy Georgia-Pacific).

your graph paper and see if these large rectangular sizes create a more interesting wall design. Trim panels to 16-×-32- or 24-×-48-inch sections for optimum economy from a standard 4-×-8-foot panel.

☐ For supergraphics on a high wall, all you need is planning and a dash of decorating courage. Lay out bold paneling patterns, then accent with colored touches of paint, metallic wallpaper, mirror sections, or shag carpeting on the wall. Your room will take on a whole new personality.

REPANELING

If you can repaint and repaper, why not repanel? In most cases, repaneling is considerably quicker and less expensive than starting from scratch; however, there are several differences in repaneling an existing wall.

Usually the original paneling is left in place rather than removed. It provides a solid nailing surface, and the extra layer of wood increases heat and sound insulation properties. Begin your repaneling project with a careful examination of the

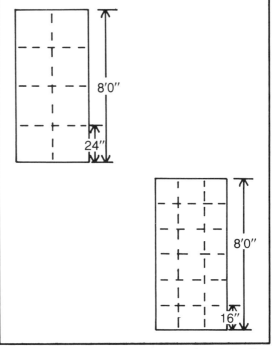

Fig. 8-52. Panel in checkerboard (courtesy Georgia-Pacific).

existing surface. All loose joints should be renailed. Cupped or warped sections of solid lumber paneling must be nailed flat. If the original paneling was installed properly, the wall should be flat and plumb; so it will require no shimming.

Locating studs is usually a simple task. Carefully check the old plywood paneling surface to detect the puttied nailheads, and determine if the studs behind are on 16- or 24-inch centers. On an old, solid-lumber paneled wall, you don't need to locate the studs. Instead, you can nail directly into the lumber surface itself.

Preparation begins with the removal of old moldings. If they are to be replaced with new material, simply pull off the old and throw them away; however, if you want to retain the original moldings, there are several salvage tips that will be helpful.

Salvaging old molding without destroying it takes a gentle touch. The old wood may be dry and brittle. If the moldings have been painted, start by breaking the paint seal at all joints with a sharp razor or knife blade. Then insert a broad-bladed putty knife or shim between the molding and paneling and gently pry them apart (Fig. 8-53). As the joint begins to open, leave the putty knife or shim in place and insert a chisel or pry bar for greater leverage (Fig. 8-54). The blade or shim protects the existing wall from being damaged by the pry bar. As you remove the base and ceiling moldings and the trim around doors and windows, write the location on the back of each piece to simplify the replacement job.

Don't pound out the molding nails from the back through the face; it will inevitably split out the face side, and you will need to reglue splinters and fill large holes. Instead, pull out the nails from the back of the molding (Fig. 8-55). The small finishing nailheads can usually be extracted with a claw hammer. Stubborn nails may require a plier to grip the tip, with a hammer claw beneath to gain the needed holding power.

The final preparation is the removal of the protective light switch and outlet surface plates. Then proceed with normal paneling installation techniques; replace new or original moldings, putty

Fig. 8-53. Remove molding (courtesy Georgia-Pacific).

Fig. 8-54. Leave the chisel for leverage (courtesy Georgia-Pacific).

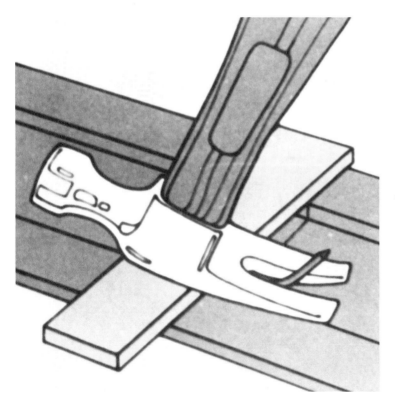

Fig. 8-55. Pull nails from the back of the molding (courtesy Georgia-Pacific).

or repaint nail holes, and you are almost finished.

The final step is to replace the electrical outlets. Since you have added 1/4 inch thickness to the wall, a little modification is usually necessary. First, shut off the power at the fuse or breaker box. Then unscrew the switch or outlet receptacle and pull the element from the box. Now is the time to put in a dimmer switch control, or three-prong grounded outlets.

Because of the additional 1/4-inch wall depth, the fixture screws may now be too short; however, longer screws are readily available. In most cases, the electrical box can be left in the original position on the studs, but a 1/4-inch spacer or washer is needed between the box's screw hole and the switch or receptacle.

Replace the electrical element and protective wall plate, and your repaneling wall project is completed (Fig. 8-56).

FINISHING TOUCHES

Just as a fine painting requires the right frame, paneling needs decorative moldings for a profes-sional appearance. Moldings frame the doors and windows, cover the seams and joints at the ceiling and floor line, and finish off and protect the corners.

Any good molding installation starts with accurate measurements. Do not assume ceiling and floor lengths are the same. Measure each area separately. The diagram in Fig. 8-57 indicates where various types of moldings are used in the average room.

Moldings should be cut with a fine-toothed saw. To splice lengths of moldings along a wall, 45-degree cuts are made at the same angle on both pieces. Where moldings meet at right angles, such as at corners and around windows and doors, use a miter box for accuracy (Fig. 8-58). Trim both pieces at opposite 45-degree angles so that together they form a tight right angle (Fig. 8-59). Finish moldings with stain or paint. Install with 3d finish nails countersunk and covered with matching putty stick, or you can use colored nails instead.

Some people use prefinished moldings to harmonize with their paneling colors. Others prefer to start with unfinished wood moldings and stain them

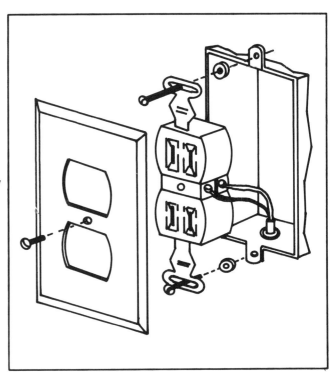

Fig. 8-56. Replacing the electrical element (courtesy Georgia-Pacific).

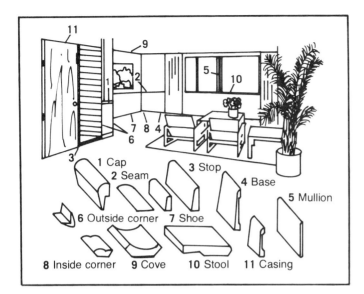

Fig. 8-57. Moldings (courtesy Georgia-Pacific).

1 Cap
2 Seam
3 Stop
4 Base
5 Mullion
6 Outside corner
7 Shoe
8 Inside corner
9 Cove
10 Stool
11 Casing

to either harmonize or contrast with their paneling. For instance, darker molding can be used as an accent to highlight the lighter colors of birch and elm paneling.

PANELING MAINTENANCE

Minimum maintenance is all that is needed to keep your paneling looking its best. The tough finish on most panels can be cleaned with a damp cloth to remove most normal household stains and fingerprints. A quality liquid wax cleaner can be used. For tougher problems, such as heavily soiled areas and pencil or crayon marks, mild soap or detergent on a damp cloth will do the trick. When clean, rinse, dry, and apply a clear liquid wax.

Avoid cleaners which contain coarse abrasives or those that leave a deposit in the pores of the wood. Light scratches that penetrate the finish, but

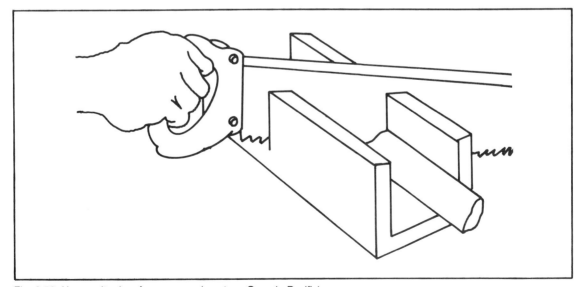

Fig. 8-58. Use a miter box for accuracy (courtesy Georgia-Pacific).

229

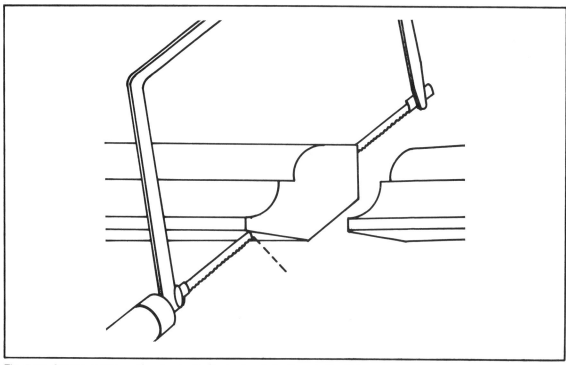

Fig. 8-59. Cut the molding with a fine-toothed saw (courtesy Georgia-Pacific).

not the wood, can usually be waxed out. Deeper scratches must be filled with a matching putty stick. Textured panelings should be cleaned with a vacuum cleaner's wall brush.

A few well-chosen pictures can highlight any room decor. Rearranging your art collection on a paneled wall can sometimes leave nail holes and faded sections, however. To minimize redecorating efforts, try placing nail holes in the panel grooves where they are easily repaired. Pushpins or small rubber bumpers will allow light to seep behind the picture, eliminating the possibility of sharp color contrast.

TILE

Ceramic tile has found its place in interior wall coverings along with paneling and wallpapering, and yet, you can really do it yourself.

Today ceramic tile comes in an infinite range of colors, shapes, decorative motifs, textures, and sizes. You will have no trouble, then, finding just the look you have been seeking. Since tile is such a permanent product, however, it pays to choose fairly conservatively. Avoid faddish colors that will tire you quickly, and limit bright colors to accents.

Visit the showrooms of manufacturers, contractors, distributors, and dealers, and buy the right product for the job. Some tiles are not suitable for floors, for example. Also buy enough to finish your project, so all the tile is from the same production run, and therefore, uniform in color.

Be picky about quality. Making allowances for varying thicknesses and other imperfections is best left to professionals. Don't you try it; cracked tiles aren't what you worked so hard for.

Ask questions. Find out about the latest easy installation methods and aids. It is a good idea to bring along a snapshot or sketch of the area to be tiled, with dimensions clearly indicated. Be prepared to answer questions about the surface you will be tiling. Seek the dealer's help in laying out the job. Above all, follow the manufacturer's instructions.

The bath that nobody has done anything with

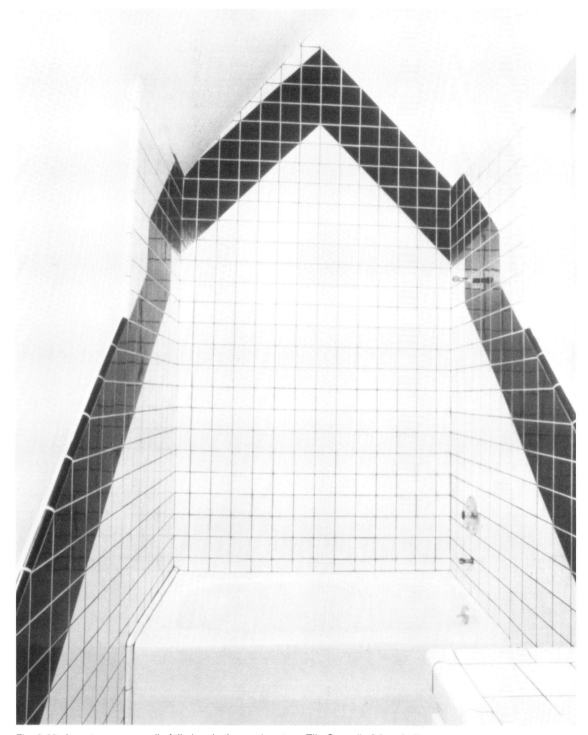

Fig. 8-60. A contemporary wall of tile in a bathroom (courtesy Tile Council of America).

since the days before you found your home to re-model is one of America's most common remodeling headaches. For creative penny pinchers, however, ceramic tile can transform an old bath from bedraggled to beautiful.

First, consider the implications of newly developed technology, which makes it possible to install new ceramic tile right over the old tile work. It is your chance to rid your life of those lavender or chartreuse tile walls, without enduring a messy and costly rip-out process.

Install the tile yourself and that spruced-up tub area will probably cost no more than a set of new towels and one of those novelty shower curtains. It is so affordable, in fact, that it should be a "must" in your remodeling plan.

You must, however, be sure that the surface that will be tiled is structurally sound and well bonded. Many older bathrooms feature tile work that ends 3/4 the way up the wall. If you would rather have floor-to-ceiling sleekness, install wallboard on the upper part of the wall to make up for the thickness of the tile below it and tile over the entire area.

Think of tiling a one-of-a-kind wall. It could be as simple as a broad ribbon of red on a gleaming white background, a Navajo motif, or the contemporary black and white shown in Fig. 8-60. Geometric designs adapt most easily to tile work.

How to Tile It Yourself

Quick-setting adhesives, special trim pieces, and premixed grouts are just a few of the improved materials that speed up tiling and help amateurs achieve professional results. Of course you should not be overconfident. Start small. First tackle a kitchen backsplash or a modestly sized floor. Then you can go on to bigger and better things. Big or small, your ceramic tile project will provide an excellent investment with a guaranteed yield of long-lasting, carefree beauty.

The Tools. Do-it-yourselfers probably already have most of the basic tools needed for tiling, such as a straightedge, tape rule, chalk/line, carpenter's level, square, carborundum stone, scraper, sponge, and cleaning rags. Special tiling tools,

including a tile cutter, notched trowel, rubber trowel or squeegee, and tile nippers, can be rented or purchased from ceramic tile dealers.

Basic Tile Setting. Tile setting is a simple four-step process, which does not differ whether your project is a floor, wall, counter, tabletop, or other item.

☐ Apply the adhesive with a notched trowel. See Fig. 8-61(A). Only do a small area at a time so you will have time to correct any mistakes before the adhesive dries. If you are installing extra-thick tile with a deep pattern, spread the adhesive on each tile also.

☐ Set each tile with a slight twisting motion, as in Fig. 8-61(B). Press firmly into place. Align tiles so that all joints are uniform and straight. Many products come with built-in spacers to ensure uniform joints. Don't panic if your tile doesn't line up straight the first time, though. Just wiggle the tiles till they are in line. Clean excessive adhesive off the face of the tile immediately.

☐ Few projects end with a full row of tiles at the edges. Mark the cutting location, place the tile in position, score with a tile cutter, and break off. See Fig. 8-61(C). Since few corners are perfectly plumb, do not cut a whole row of tile at a time. Cut each one as you get to the end. Tile nippers are used to shape cuts to fit around pipes and other edges. See Fig. 8-61(D).

☐ Wait about 24 hours to grout. Mix the grout according to the manufacturer's instructions. Apply with a rubber trowel or squeegee, spreading the grout diagonally across the joints as in Fig. 8-61(E). Wash the excess grout from the face of the tiles. When the joints are firm, wipe the tiles clean with a damp sponge; then polish with a dry, clean cloth.

Tiling Walls

It's fun, easy, *and* economical to install ceramic wall tile. You can do it yourself and turn out a successful ceramic tile installation. Follow the step-by-step instructions, and you will have a durable ceramic tile surface that will add value and beauty to your home. Careful planning and preparation will result in a satisfactory installation.

Tools and Accessories. You may have most

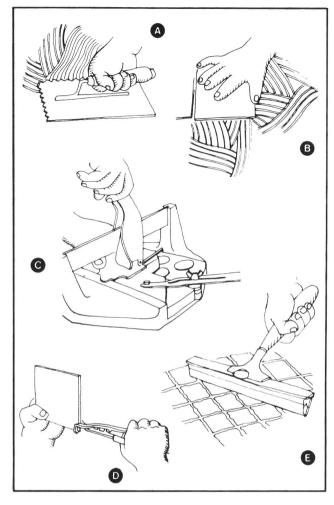

Fig. 8-61. Basic tile setting (courtesy Tile Council of America).

tools, but if not your dealer has them for sale or rent. They are:

—saw tooth trowel,
—1- to 3-inch putty knife,
—3-foot level,
—tile cutter or glass cutter,
—tile nippers,
—sponge, joint striking tool with a toothbrush handle,
—abrasive stone or paper,
—rags for cleaning,
—shims, wood, cardboard, or toothpicks,
—adhesive and grout,
—1-×-2-inch furring strips,
—rule and pencil,

—squeegee.

Ceramic Wall Tile and Trim. Your dealer can provide you with the proper amount of wall tile and trim for your installation. Take *careful* measurements for whatever room you plan to tile (Fig. 8-62).

Suitable Base Surfaces. Almost any clean, dry, structurally sound surface that is firmly anchored to the wall, is a suitable base surface. They include: finish coat plaster, painted plaster (oil and enamel base only), gypsum wallboard, plywood (exterior grade), mortar, concrete, and old ceramic tile firmly anchored to the wall.

Unsuitable base surfaces include: linoleum

233

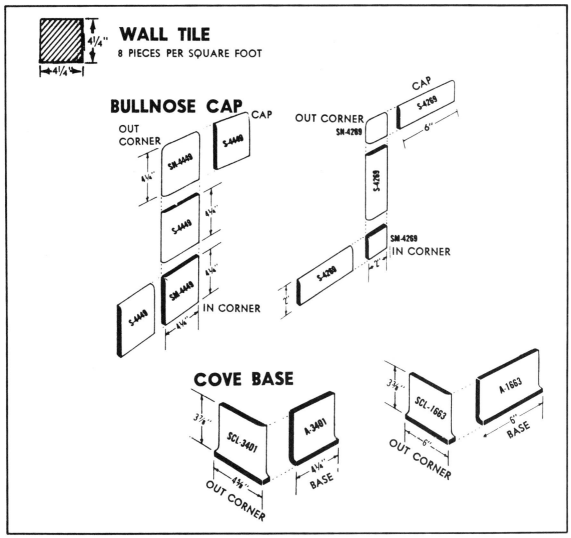

WALL TILE
8 PIECES PER SQUARE FOOT

BULLNOSE CAP

Fig. 8-62. Ceramic wall tile and trim (courtesy Tile Council of America).

paste, water-based paint, uncured plaster, fiberboard, particleboard, unclean surfaces of any type including dirty or flaking surfaces, and painted surfaces where paint is peeling or not firmly anchored.

Surface Preparation. The surface of the wall must be clean, with no grease, dust, loose or flaky paint, or plaster. It must also be dry, with no moisture or condensation, and have a plumb, even surface, and be square at the corners (Fig. 8-63).

Laying Out or Measuring the Wall. The walls in a room are usually covered with ceramic tile to a height of 4 feet 6 inches to 5 feet. Tub areas or alcoves usually have at least one row of tile above the shower head. Shower stalls are tiled to ceiling height, and the ceiling also may be covered.

The layout of the area to be tiled begins by finding the horizontal baseline and the vertical centerline of the wall areas (Fig. 8-64).

To find the baseline for a room without a tub, set the level on the floor at various locations against the walls. Find the lowest point in the room and place a cove base tile on the floor (Fig. 8-65), and a

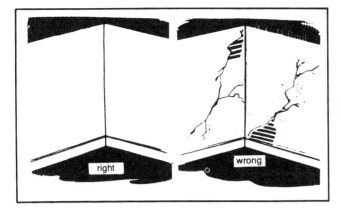

Fig. 8-63. Surface preparation (courtesy Tile Council of America).

Fig. 8-64. Finding baseline and centerline for the wall (courtesy Tile Council of America).

piece of wall tile. If a cove base is not required, then just place a piece of wall tile on the floor and mark the wall above it. Using the level and the mark you made as a guide, draw a line on the wall. Mark the other walls in the room using the ends of this line as a starting point. Nail a wood strip along this line to serve as the baseline and to support the wall tile.

In a room with a bathtub, the tub line will serve as the starting point. Find the lowest point on the tub ledge using the level. Place one piece of wall tile at this point and shim up 1/8 inch to allow for caulking. Draw a mark on the wall above the tile. Using the level, extend the line around the tub walls. Drop the line to the floor and measure the courses of tile to the floor line, to establish the baseline for the walls and allow a full tile course at the tub ledge (Fig. 8-66).

To find the centerline of each wall, measure each wall from corner to corner at the floor line and at the tile wainscot line. Mark the exact center of

each line and draw the vertical centerline. Lay out a row of tile from the centerline to the corner. If you have half a tile or more left at the corner, that is fine. If you have less than half a tile at the corner,

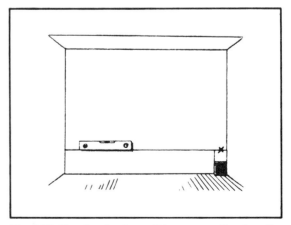

Fig. 8-65. Baseline for the wall in a room other than the bathroom (courtesy Tile Council of America).

235

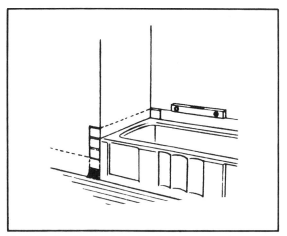

Fig. 8-66. Baseline for the wall in the bathroom (courtesy Tile Council of America).

then shift your centerline until you have at least 1/2 of a tile for a cut in each corner. Draw the new centerline being sure it is vertical. Set the tile from this new centerline to the corners on each wall. The last row of the tile will be cut to fit at each corner. Find the center and layout for all walls in the room in this manner (Fig. 8-67).

Adhesive Application. With the putty knife, put some adhesive on the wall at the centerline. Hold the notched trowel at a 45-degree angle and spread the adhesive from the centerline toward the corners of the wall. Spread only what you can cover in about 30 minutes or in an area about 4 × 4 feet.

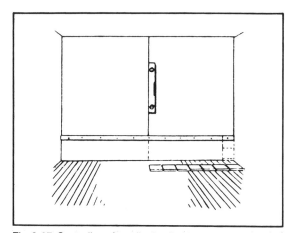

Fig. 8-67. Centerline of a wall to be tiled (courtesy Tile Council of America).

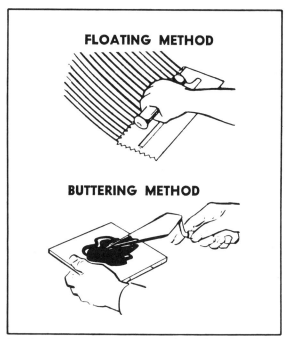

Fig. 8-68. Floating and buttering methods for wall tiling (courtesy Tile Council of America).

Hold the notches on the trowel firmly against the wall so the adhesive forms ridges.

A tub or shower area should have a very thin coat of adhesive spread over the walls with the flat side of the trowel for waterproofing. Allow it to set for one hour; then apply the trowel coat and set the tile. Pack adhesive into the openings around the tub and pipes with a putty knife to seal and waterproof. The cove base and cuts can be set by using a buttering method (Fig. 8-68). Do not smoke in areas where adhesive is being used and provide adequate ventilation.

Setting Tile. Start setting tile on the baseline with the edge of the first tile at the vertical centerline. Press the tile firmly into place with a slight twisting motion. Do not slide or press too hard or you will push the adhesive onto the edges of the file. Set the tile in rows, being careful to keep the joints lined up and the rows level. Check frequently with the level to make sure the tiles are even and smooth. Spread the adhesive and set the tile until you reach the corners. Make the cuts and set into the corners. Allow the walls to set at least 5 hours

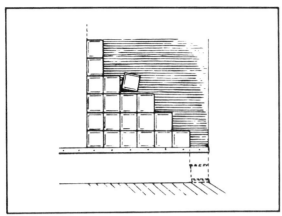

Fig. 8-69. Vertical starting line (courtesy Tile Council of America).

or overnight. Remove the wood strips and set the cove base or cut in the bottom row of the wall tile.

If only a tub alcove is tiled, center the walls and lay out as previously described. Set the tile on the back wall from the center to the corners. Set the tile on the end walls starting with the bullnose or cap at the outside edge of the tub and working to the center. This method will allow all cuts in the corners and full tile at the tub line (Fig. 8-69).

Cutting Tile. Straight cuts on tile are easily made with a glass cutter. Mark the tile where it is to be cut. Using a straightedge as a guide, scribe a line with the cutting wheel on the glazed side of the tile. Press down firmly for a good, clean score in the glaze on the tile. Place the scored line on the tile over a piece of wire about 1/8-inch thick. A coat hanger will do fine. Press firmly on each side of the tile and break it.

Cuts for round or irregularly shaped openings are made with tile nippers. Mark the outline of the opening on the tile. Take small bites or nibbles to avoid cracking or breaking the tile. To score and break the tile with a tile cutter, set the gauge to the desired size of the cut. Insert the tile and hold it with your left hand. Set the cutting wheel on the edge of the tile. Pull the cutting wheel slowly on the lower edge of the tile and press down gently on the handle to break the tile (Fig. 8-70). Cut edges of tile should be smoothed with abrasive stone or paper.

Grouting. Allow the tile to set at least 6 hours or overnight before grouting. Clean all adhesive smears from the face of the tile and from the joints. Use Naphtha or white gasoline to clean off adhesive, or you can follow the manufacturer's direc-

Fig. 8-70. Cutting tile (courtesy Tile Council of America).

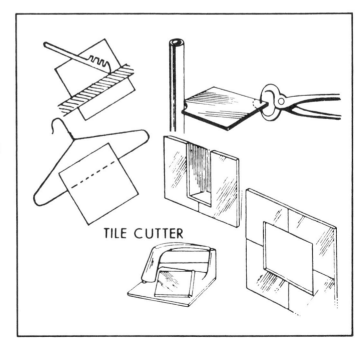

TILE CUTTER

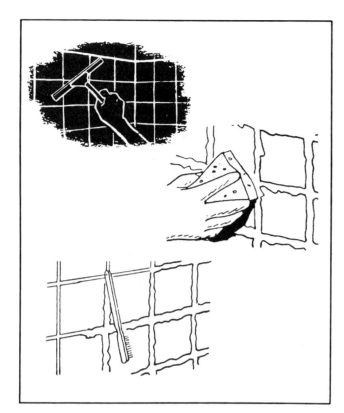

Fig. 8-71. Grouting tile (courtesy Tile Council of America).

tions. Tile should be cleaned of all dirt and dust. Rubber gloves should be worn to protect against skin irritation.

In a clean bucket, mix grout, according to the manufacturer's instructions until you get a thick, creamy paste. Completely fill the joints by forcing the grout in with a squeegee or sponge. Wipe off surplus grout by drawing the sponge or squeegee blade diagonally across the face of the tile to a 45-degree angle. Remove excess grout from the face of the tile with a damp sponge.

Let the grout set for 10 to 15 minutes. Strike or smooth the grout joints with the handle of a toothbrush or wooden dowel to compact the grout and leave a uniform line between the tile. Now clean the tile with clean water and a damp rag or sponge, being careful not to rake out or damage the grout joint (Fig. 8-71). Let it dry until a haze forms on the tile, then polish with a dry cloth. Setting will require several days, and it will harden completely in two weeks. Do not use for at least 72 hours.

Bath Accessories

Your dealer can supply you with bath accessories especially designed to fit in the wall tile without cutting into the wall surface. Before you lay the wall tile, plan where you want the fixture to be

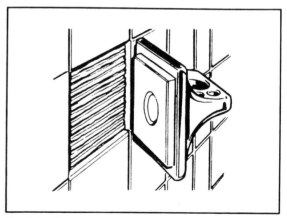

Fig. 8-72. Bath accessories to fit tiled wall (courtesy Tile Council of America).

in the wall. Leave out the piece of wall tile that would fit there.

Spread a thin coat of adhesive on the wall and on the back of the accessory. Let it dry and spread a second coat of adhesive on the wall and on the fixture. Let it set until it becomes tacky, then set the accessory in the wall (Fig. 8-72). Use masking tape to hold the tile until the adhesive has set, which will take at least 72 hours.

WALLPAPER

Besides paneling and ceramic tile finishes, wallpaper is still popular. Today there are unlimited designs, colors, and materials which provide versatility, beauty, durability, and ease of care. All of these varieties work well on a low budget since they are easy to use.

Hanging wall coverings really is not a complicated process. The only prerequisites are the ability to follow directions, the knowledge of how to use scissors, the ability to draw a straight line (aided by a ruler), and no fear when you get up on the first rung of a stepladder.

It is very rewarding, too. Just imagine the satisfaction you will get watching the mood of your room change with every strip of wallpapering you put up, and the admiration you will receive when your friends and family walk into your stylishly decorated room.

A large room is just as easy to cover as a small one. Bedrooms are great for starters, because the wall covering can really reflect the individual's personality.

Avoid foils the first time out; they require a bit more expertise. Enlist the help of a friend if you intend to paper a ceiling.

You don't need to estimate the amount of wall covering you will need. Bring the measurements and rough layout of the room to your wall covering retailer and he will be glad to figure it out for you. If you want to estimate the amount yourself, note that single rolls of wallpaper contain approximately 36 square feet. Plan on 30 square feet per roll to allow for trimming and pattern match. Rolls are usually packed in 2-roll bolts.

Measure the distance in feet around the room,

as well as the height of the walls to be covered. Using these measurements, refer to Table 8-4 to determine the number of rolls you will need. Subtract 1/2 roll for every window and door in the room.

Once you have selected your pattern, look at the information on the back of the swatch in the sample book. You will find the pattern's name and style number and the pattern repeat, which gives you a proper scale for hanging. The type of pattern match will also affect how you cut your wall-covering strips for hanging.

Three types of pattern matches are:

—Straight across. The pattern will match up on a horizontal line from strip to strip.

—Drop match. The design will line up on a diagonal from strip to strip.

—Pro trip. When working with a large pattern repeat, save material by cutting strips from alternate rolls.

General Information

Glue. Buy glue in powder or premixed form. If you are mixing it yourself, just follow the directions on the package. The whisk from your kitchen works well to remove any lumps. Ask your dealer what adhesive to use with your particular wall covering, because the weight and type of wall covering chosen is a determining factor.

Preparing Your Walls. Wall preparation is the least fun part of the paper hanging process, but it is important and not difficult. The key is clean, smooth walls. If your walls are covered with flat paint, you can paper right over it. Just be sure they are free of grease, loose paint, etc. Surfaces covered with gloss paint, such as enamel, should be sanded dull with sandpaper and then washed.

Newly plastered walls should be thoroughly dry before sizing. Sometimes newly plastered walls have "hot spots" or alkaline deposits. If yours do, you should use an "indicating wall size." To determine this size, brush on a thin coat of "indicating wall size;" any areas which turn pink should be neutralized with a mixture of one pound zinc sulfate and one gallon of warm water.

TABLE 8-4. ESTIMATED MATERIALS.

Distance around room in feet	Single Rolls of Sidewall Ceiling Height				Single rolls of ceiling	Single yards of border
	8 ft. high	9 ft. high	10 ft. high	12 ft. high		
28	8	8	10	12	2	11
32	8	10	10	13	2	12
36	10	12	12	16	4	13
40	12	12	14	16	4	14
44	12	14	16	18	4	16
48	12	14	16	20	6	17
52	14	16	18	22	6	18
56	16	18	20	24	8	20
60	16	18	20	24	8	21
64	18	20	22	26	10	23
68	18	22	24	28	10	24
72	20	22	24	30	12	25

If you are faced with old wallpaper, remove what you can either by wetting it down and scraping with a putty knife, or by renting a steamer. Then roll on a coat of shellac.

Some Special Hints. Turn off the current of electrical outlets. Remove switch plates, thermostat covers, etc. Hang the wall covering over these spots, trim around them, and replace the plates or covers.

If the wall covering comes loose, pull it away enough to get a thin coat of white household glue underneath. Press down firmly for a minute or two, then wipe off the excess glue. If the edges seem reluctant to stick, put masking tape over the newly glued area until it is dry.

Dry bubbles may develop in the middle of a strip. Slit the bubble with a razor blade, put glue underneath, and press down with a wet sponge.

If you must patch the wall covering, tear off a piece from your leftovers and match the pattern to the damaged surface. By tearing you get a "feathered" edge, which blends a lot better than a straight edge.

A sponge and a mild detergent solution will keep your wall covering beautiful for years. Add a bit of bleach if you have a really tough trouble spot. Rinse it with clean water and towel it to avoid streaking.

How To Wallpaper

Follow these simple step by step directions for an easy and professional job.

Fig. 8-73. Run a plumb line (courtesy National Gypsum Company, Decorative Products Division).

□ You probably already have most of the tools you will need. You can buy the water tray in any wallpaper store.

□ A plumb line gives you the perfect starting point (Fig. 8-73).

□ Cut a wall-covering strip the height of the wall plus 8 to 9 inches for overlap top and bottom (Fig. 8-74). Roll on adhesive (Fig. 8-75).

□ Put your water tray by the wall and fill it to the marked level mark with lukewarm water. Rolling the prepasted wall fashion strip into the water activates the adhesive (Fig. 8-76).

□ Line up the first strip with the plumbline (Fig. 8-77).

□ Roll over the edges with a seam roller (Fig. 8-78).

□ Use a razor blade to trim the strips at the ceiling and baseboard (Fig. 8-79).

□ At doors and windows paper over the edges. Then make diagonal cuts to the corners to get a neat fit (Fig. 8-80).

□ At the corner, measure the width from the last strip to the corner plus 1 inch. Cut a strip that width and hang. Hang the remaining strip on the next wall after you have dropped another plumbline, and slide it right into the corner (Fig. 8-81).

□ Now that you are an accomplished do-it-yourselfer, put the wall covering's companion fabric to work. Making draperies and window shades to

Fig. 8-74. Fold the ends of pasted paper in half (courtesy National Gypsum Company, Decorative Products Division).

Fig. 8-75. Brush roll adhesive (courtesy National Gypsum Company, Decorative Products Division).

Fig. 8-76. Placing of water tray (courtesy National Gypsum Company, Decorative Products Division).

match the walls brings uniformity to any room (Fig. 8-82).

NEW WALL CONSTRUCTION

Part of the excitement and satisfaction of re-modeling your home is the creation of new living space by finishing a basement or attic, converting a garage into a family room, or dividing one large room into several more efficient spaces. All these projects call for building and framing non-bearing partitioned walls. Because non-bearing partitions don't support the floor load above them, they are simpler to construct then load-bearing walls.

Non-Load-Bearing Walls

Typical non-bearing wall construction consists of 2-×-4-inch studs placed either 16 or 24 inches on center and nailed to a 2-×-4 sole plate at the floor line and a similar 2-×-4-inch top plate at the ceiling. First lay out the wall position on the floor with a chalk line, carefully measuring at right angles from the existing wall. Indicate any openings for door-ways and the locations for electrical boxes. Your floor becomes a full-size working blueprint.

Cut your 2-×-4-inch sole and top plate sections to the exact length, place them side by side, and use a carpenter's square to mark off the exact stud spacing locations (Fig. 8-83). By marking stud locations in this manner, you make sure that both the top and bottom plates are identical.

Begin actual construction by nailing the sole plate to the floor. Specially hardened concrete nails are available for this job. Where your new wall butts perpendicularly to an existing wall, measure from

Fig. 8-79. Use a razor-blade knife to trim (courtesy National Gypsum Company, Decorative Products Division).

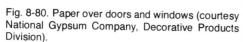

Fig. 8-80. Paper over doors and windows (courtesy National Gypsum Company, Decorative Products Division).

Fig. 8-81. Measure strips at corners (courtesy National Gypsum Company, Decorative Products Division).

Fig. 8-82. Use companion draperies (courtesy National Gypsum Company, Decorative Products Division).

Fig. 8-83. Cut sole and top plate (courtesy Georgia-Pacific).

the top of the sole plate to the ceiling line and subtract 1 1/2 inches, the thickness of the top plate.

Cut your first stud to this length. Position it on top of the sole plate and toenail into the 2 × 4 on the floor (Fig. 8-84). With a level, adjust the stud until it is perfectly plumb and nail to the adjoining existing wall. Now slip your top plate into position and nail to the above ceiling joist; then toenail the stud top to the plate.

Toenailing, driving the nails at an angle, is not nearly as tough as it looks. To construct partitions, use 8d (2 1/2-inch) common nails, two on each side of the stud at all joints. Place the nails approximately 1 inch above the sole plate on the outer side of the stud, angled at about 60 degrees from the horizontal. Drive the nail at this angle through the side of the stud into the plate below it. Drive a second nail on this side and repeat the process on the other side of the stud. A single nail on each side

will inevitably twist the stud out of line as you hammer (Fig. 8-85).

To ensure proper stud spacing as you continue

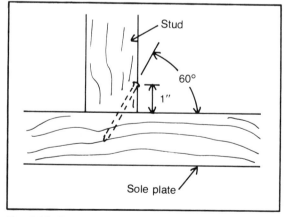

Fig. 8-84. Cut stud and position on sole plate (courtesy Georgia-Pacific).

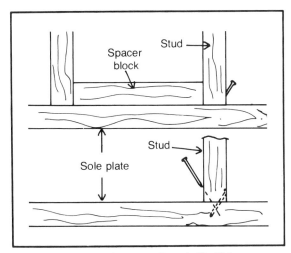

Fig. 8-85. Toenailing (courtesy Georgia-Pacific).

constructing your frame wall, cut a scrap piece of 2 × 4 to use as a spacer block. For studs 16 inches on center, cut a spacer 14 1/2 inches; for 24-inch stud spacing use a 22 1/2-inch block. Place the space block on the sole plate against the positioned stud, place a new stud at the end of the block, and pound two nails from the outside. Knock the spacer block

out of position and toenail two nails in the stud from the inside. Sound construction practices call for double studs at the sides and tops of all wall openings.

Once your wall is completely framed, attach the electrical boxes to the studs, setting them out into the room slightly to allow for the thickness of your paneling and/or wallboard. For both sound control and fire protection, I recommend that Georgia-Pacific gypsum wallboard panels be applied directly to the studs and covered with decorative, prefinished wall paneling.

If all this toenailing and locating of ceiling joists seems a bit beyond your carpentry skills, there is a simpler system for constructing non-load-bearing partition walls. Once you have determined the position for the new wall and marked the location on the floor, the total wall is built flat on the floor, raised into position, and wedged into place. This method of construction allows you to nail directly through the sole and top plates into the stud ends. Use two 10d (3-inch) common nails for each stud.

In order to provide ceiling clearance when you

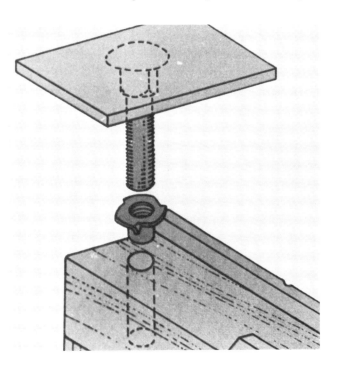

Fig. 8-86. Insert t-nuts (courtesy Georgia-Pacific).

Fig. 8-87. Raise the wall into position (courtesy Georgia-Pacific).

raise this wall into place, the total wall height must be 1 inch less than the floor-to-ceiling measurement. Once the upright wall is in position, use small wooden wedges to hold the wall firmly in place. Fasten to the floor and ceiling joists as previously outlined. Then apply your paneling and cover the

gap in the floor with baseboard molding.

Temporary Walls

Occasionally, you want to divide room space and still be able to, at some time, change the area back to its original size. In these instances, you want a temporary non-load-bearing wall.

For a lightweight, temporary wall, 2-×-2-inch framing is used, rather than heavier lumber. Construct the framework on the floor with your 2-×-2 inch studs spaced 16 inches on center. This temporary wall system must be 1 inch less than the floor-to-ceiling measurement. A simple levering system is used to pressure-fit the wall frame into position. Drill 3/8-inch holes about every 4 feet in the top plate and insert *t-nuts*, small fasteners with internal screw threads, into the holes (Fig. 8-86). Screw 1/4-inch carriage-head bolts 2 inches long, into the t-nuts. These bolts have a square shank beneath a smooth, round head.

Raise the wall, aligning it with the desired position on the floor (Fig. 8-87). Use a small wrench to unscrew the carriage-head bolts against the ceiling, which will push the framework down against the floor and hold it in place. Paneling scraps above the bolt heads will protect the ceiling from damage.

If you plan to dismantle this lightweight wall in the future, construct individual 4-foot-wide frame sections, apply the paneling, raise it into position, and install one section at a time. Matching cover crown molding at the ceiling line will cover the 1-inch space that remains at panel tops. Once the upright wall is in position, use small wooden wedges to hold the wall firmly in place; then fasten to the floor and ceiling joists as previously outlined. Apply your paneling and cover the gap in the floor with baseboard molding.

Chapter 9

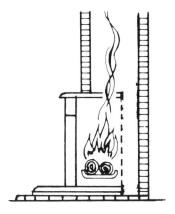

Fireplaces

All over America, people are rediscovering the joys, both practical and economical, of heating with wood. With the cost of heating rising higher and higher, it is easy to understand why fireplaces are becoming even more popular than in the past, even in areas of the country where the winters are relatively mild.

There once was a time when fireplaces were deemed uneconomical; it was considered that they let the warm air out and the cold air in, even though they provided that cozy feeling that only a burning fire can.

As with all other phases of construction, manufacturers of fireplaces have had 15 to 20 or more years in which to develop newer and better in-place and free-standing models. During new construction and renovation, there is no better time to put in the fireplace of your choice.

BUILT-IN MODELS

Most companies manufacture both built-in and free-stand models. The built-in model is more contemporary and usually requires some additional brick work for its surrounding, as well as any accessories you may wish, such as a mantelpiece. It is also more expensive than the free-standing model, but the cost is more than offset by its appearance and ease of care.

Two companies which produce a variety of designs, all within the budget price range, are the Birmingham Stove and Range Company and the Majestic Company.

The Majestic Company has introduced its newest and most advanced fireplace: the Warm Majic, which has been rated 41 to 43 percent efficient by the Wood Heating Alliance Testing Center at Auburn University, Alabama (Fig. 9-1). The Warm Majic rating falls within the range of typical woodstove efficiency ratings.

The Warm Majic is Majestic's top-of-the-line system, designed to meet the needs of the new home and remodeling markets.

Recent tests conducted at Majestic's calorimeter room in Huntington, Indiana, show that the Warm Majic exhausts the volume of air con-

Fig. 9-1. Built-in fireplace: The Majestic Warm Magic (courtesy The Majestic Company, An American Standard Company).

tained in an 1800 square foot home with ceilings 8 feet high only every 6 hours, while a masonry fireplace will dispose the air every 36 minutes. This study shows that the Warm Majic fireplace system is not an influential factor in excess home air infiltration as a result of the fireplace's higher efficiency capabilities. It is also easy to install.

Location of Your Majestic Fireplace

There are several things you must consider when determining where to install a Majestic fireplace. This fireplace can be installed against a wall, through an outside wall, in a corner, or out in a room as a room divider (Fig. 9-2).

If you install it in a room with carpeting or vinyl flooring, you will need to cut away the covering so it sets flat on a hard surface. Other than that, no surface preparation or insulation is required.

You should think about how you plan to finish the front of your fireplace. Will you use face brick, man-made stone, hardboard, etc? Will there be bookcases or other built-in features? Will you design a place to store wood?

It is very useful, in fact, to have a rough sketch of how you think the finished installation should look before you ever start. This sketch will help you decide whether you want to elevate the fireplace to get a better look at the fire, how much hearth extension you will want in front, and

whether or not the extension should be a raised hearth.

Also consider that if you install an energy-efficient heat-circulating fireplace, the best heating performance occurs when it is in a room that has fairly open access to other parts of the house and/or hallways. Such a location, in combination with your furnace's cold air returns, will help the fireplace heat a major portion of your house.

When used to help heat your home, the room that contains the fireplace will usually average only 6 to 8 degrees warmer than the rest of the house.

Location of Outside Air
Supply and Electrical Connections

Once you have decided the best location for your fireplace, you need to determine where you want to vent your optional outside air supply. You must also decide whether or not you will add a fan and where you will get the electricity to run it.

Outside air combustion means the fireplace will use less heated inside air to burn, and the fan will greatly improve the fireplace heat output.

Depending on the fireplace you buy, the outside air supply system consists of one or two duct terminations, one or two connecting collars, plus enough flexible duct to vent through an outside well or crawl space (Fig. 9-3). You may need more vent pipe to completely install your system; if you do,

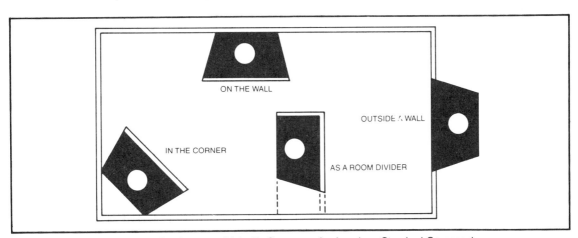

Fig. 9-2. Planning fireplace location (courtesy Majestic Company, An American Standard Company).

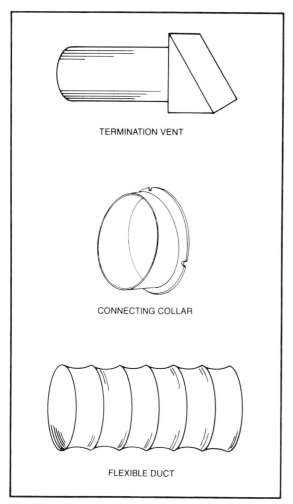

TERMINATION VENT

CONNECTING COLLAR

FLEXIBLE DUCT

Fig. 9-3. Outside air system (courtesy Majestic Company, An American Standard Company).

cycle electricity connected to the fireplace junction box. If you don't want to hire a licensed electrician, check your local wiring codes before you wire your system.

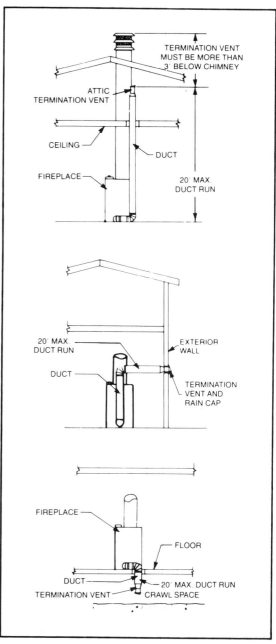

Fig. 9-4. Termination system (courtesy Majestic Company, An American Standard Company).

just use the same diameter flexible or rigid duct and elbows.

The duct terminations may be vented through an outside wall, into a crawl space, or into the attic (Fig. 9-4). Total duct length is limited to 20 feet, and vertical height must be at least 3 feet below the flue termination. In a crawl space or attic, there must be at least 100 square inches of unobstructed ventilation opening around the termination. For outdoor venting, rain guards are provided. Caution: Never install the outside air duct termination in a garage, which can have flammable liquids or gases.

To power the fan you will need 110 volt 60

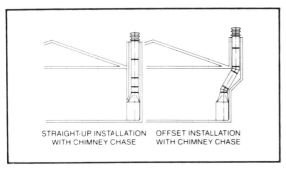

STRAIGHT-UP INSTALLATION WITH CHIMNEY CHASE   OFFSET INSTALLATION WITH CHIMNEY CHASE

Fig. 9-5. Straight and offset installation (courtesy Majestic Company, An American Standard Company).

You should connect the electricity prior to finishing the fireplace if you ever intend to install or use the fan. There is a junction box built into the fireplace that is easy to get to so you can permanently wire your fireplace.

Your Chimney System

The most complicated part of the entire installation planning process, is probably deciding where and how to run your chimney system. It is because accurately figuring out where you want your chimney to penetrate the roof will determine whether you need a chimney installation that is straight up or one that is offset using elbows. Straight-up installations are usually the most economical. It is also important because you must figure out the total run of your chimney pipe in order to buy the right length and number of materials.

You cannot use an existing chimney to install your Majestic fireplace. All components of the installation must be made and approved by Majestic. The Majestic fireplace and chimney components work as one unit.

Your chimney, depending on where the fireplace is installed, can be installed through the ceiling and roof. It can also be installed in a chimney chase that runs up the outside of the house (Fig. 9-5). A chimney chase is a vertical boxlike structure built to enclose the fireplace and/or its chimney.

If you install up through the ceiling and roof, you must decide where you want the chimney to come through the roof—on the front roof pitch, back roof pitch, or side roof pitch. Once you know, you

must plan the run of your chimney pipe to see if you can accomplish what you desire.

You must also determine if your chimney run will meet with any obstructions, such as ceiling joists or rafters. You can handle such obstructions one of two ways; you can either use the offset elbows to go around them, or you can cut and reframe the joists. Either way is acceptable and perfectly safe. Cutting and reframing will not weaken your home's structure.

To install a chimney and chimney chase, you can set the entire fireplace outside in the chase in a through-the-wall installation and run the pipe straight up. Measure the total height of the chase and purchase the required number of chimney sections. You can also install the fireplace against an inside wall and use elbows to offset the chimney out through the wall, and then up. Here you will need to

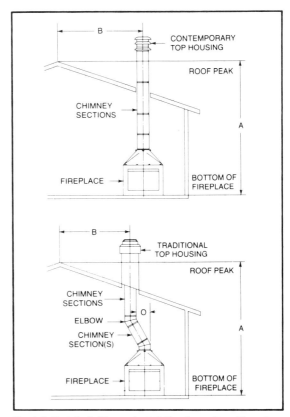

Fig. 9-6. Detail of chimney installation through roof (courtesy Majestic Company, An American Standard Company).

253

determine your offset distance, to get total height. Where you locate the fireplace will pretty much determine which option is more convenient and attractive.

Figures 9-6 and 9-7 show you how to determine your chimney run and the materials you need. Make the following four determinations and take them to your dealer. He can use them to figure your materials.

First you must determine how high your roof peak is above the bottom of the fireplace. See Fig. 9-6(A). Remember to consider if you plan to raise the unit for your installation. You must also know how far out from the roof peak your chimney will penetrate the roof. See Fig. 9-6(B). You must know your *roof pitch,* which is the number of inches your roof rises per one foot of horizontal run (Fig. 9-7).

If your installation is straight up, you are ready to take your figures to your dealer, but if you must offset your installation, either to avoid obstructions, or to penetrate the roof at a certain place, you must also figure out how far you need to offset from vertical to run the chimney pipe to the right location. See Fig. 9-7. The planning and determination of the chimney run are a little complicated, but once you have these 3 or 4 simple dimensions, you know enough to buy the right amount of components.

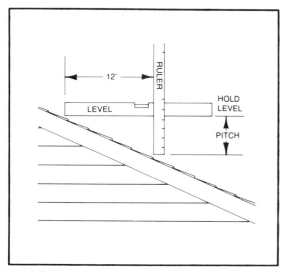

Fig. 9-7. Chimney pitch (courtesy Majestic Company, An Amercan Standard Company).

To Install the Fireplace and Chimney System

Actual installation of the fireplace and chimney can be done by most reasonably handy individuals. Not including the finishing, you will need the following tools:

—hammer,
—power saw,
—carpenter's level,
—plumb line,
—tin snips,
—screwdriver, and
—measuring tape.

These instructions can be applied to any fireplace you choose. Figure 9-8 identifies the parts of a Majestic Warm Majic fireplace.

☐ Check how accessories are installed. Determine where selected accessories fit into the fireplace installation by checking the instructions provided with each accessory.

☐ Determine the fireplace location. The Majestic Warm Majic fireplace can be mounted on a flat, hard, combustible surface that must also have sufficient area to support the entire base of the fireplace at just a few points. The surface may be a raised wooden platform (Fig. 9-9).

The fireplace may be placed against a combustible wall without any clearance between the two. Nearby combustible floors and walls must be protected as detailed in Fig. 9-10.

Refer to the Reference Data Section to be sure that the location you have selected for your fireplace provides for clearance and framing restrictions.

At this point you should have decided what components to include in your installation, where the fireplace will be located, and how the chimney will be routed to the roof. If you have not decided how the chimney will be routed to the roof, whether straight-up, offset, or chase, consult your dealer. Note that the installed length of any chimney section except the last one is less than its total length because of its overlap at joints (Fig. 9-11).

☐ Install metal safety strips under the fire-

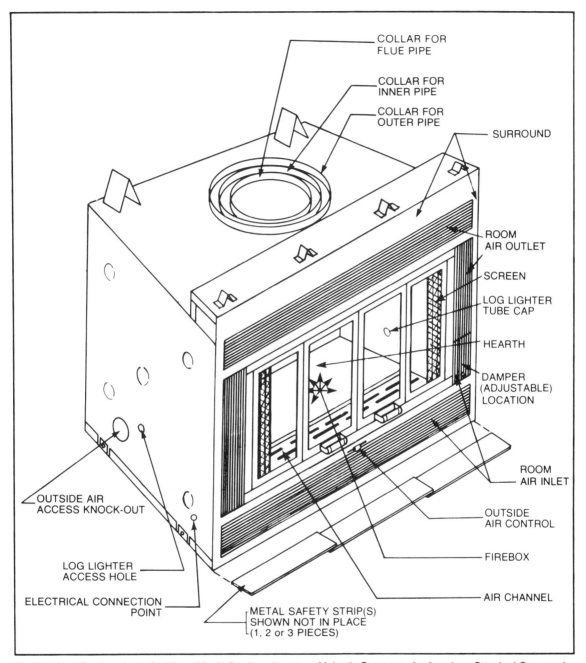

COLLAR FOR
FLUE PIPE

COLLAR FOR
INNER PIPE

COLLAR FOR
OUTER PIPE

SURROUND

ROOM
AIR OUTLET

SCREEN

LOG LIGHTER
TUBE CAP

HEARTH

DAMPER
(ADJUSTABLE)
LOCATION

ROOM
AIR INLET

OUTSIDE
AIR CONTROL

FIREBOX

AIR CHANNEL

OUTSIDE AIR
ACCESS KNOCK-OUT

LOG LIGHTER
ACCESS HOLE

ELECTRICAL CONNECTION
POINT

METAL SAFETY STRIP(S)
SHOWN NOT IN PLACE
(1, 2 or 3 PIECES)

Fig. 9-8. Identification chart of a Warm Magic fireplace (courtesy Majestic Company, An American Standard Company).

place. Thoroughly clean the intended fireplace location. Move the fireplace to the exact location where it will be installed. Lift the fireplace front slightly to slide the furnished metal safety strips under the front bottom edge about 1 1/2 notches, allowing the remainder to extend out in front of the fireplace. Overlap the strips at least 1/2 inch to provide a positive joint (Fig. 9-12).

Fig. 9-9. Raised wooden platform (courtesy Majestic Company, An American Standard Company).

☐ Anchor the fireplace in position to prevent the fireplace from shifting and to maintain sealing (Fig. 9-13). Turn down the four fastening tabs located along the sides of the base pan and nail them to the floor (Fig. 9-14).

☐ To install the chimney, first locate the centerpoint of the chimney. For straight-up installation (Fig. 9-15), if the fireplace is positioned against the wall behind it, measure out 12 1/2 inches from the wall and make a mark on the ceiling above the fireplace. Draw a line through this mark parallel to the back wall, defining the centerline of the chimney. Then, position a plumb bob directly over the imaginary centerpoint of the fireplace flue collar and mark the ceiling to establish the chimney center point (Figs. 9-16 and 9-17).

☐ In order to clear an obstruction you may need to offset the chimney from the vertical plane using Majestic Chimney Elbows Models 815 (15

degrees) and 830 (30 degrees). Each offset requires a pair of elbows. Use Table 9-1 and Fig. 9-10 to determine the offset.

The following safety rules apply to offset installations. The letters below match the letters in Fig. 9-10.

—Maximum height of the chimney measured from the hearth to the chimney exit at top (A) is 90 feet.

Minimum Warm Majic Range is 36 feet.
  12 feet 6 inches without elbows
  14 feet 6 inches with two elbows

Minimum Warm Majic Range is 36 feet.
  10 feet 6 inches without elbow
  12 feet 6 inches with two elbows
  28 feet 0 inches with four elbows

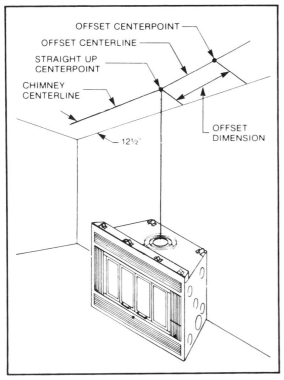

Fig. 9-10. Measure first ceiling offset distance from straight up center point (courtesy Majestic Company, An American Standard Company).

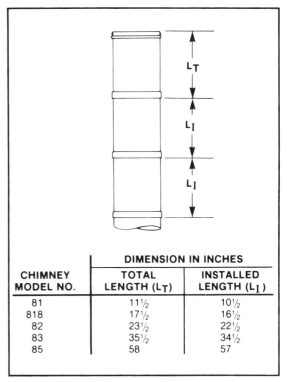

CHIMNEY MODEL NO.	DIMENSION IN INCHES	
	TOTAL LENGTH (L_T)	INSTALLED LENGTH (L_I)
81	$11\frac{1}{2}$	$10\frac{1}{2}$
818	$17\frac{1}{2}$	$16\frac{1}{2}$
82	$23\frac{1}{2}$	$22\frac{1}{2}$
83	$35\frac{1}{2}$	$34\frac{1}{2}$
85	58	57

Fig. 9-11. Installed lengths of chimney sections (courtesy Majestic Company, An American Standard Company).

—Do not use more than four elbows per chimney for WM 36. Attach the strps of all elbows to a structural framing member except the first elbow installed on the fireplace. If four elbows are used, the first pair of elbows must be separated from the second pair of elbows by a minimum of 1 vertical foot.

—The chimney cannot be more than 30 degrees from the vertical plane.

—The maximum length of the angled run of the total chimney system (G plus H) is 20 feet.

—A chimney support is required every 6 feet of angled run of chimney. Chimney supports are also required at 45 feet and 75 feet of chimney height above the hearth.

Determine the offset distance of your chimney arrangement from the centerline of the fireplace to the centerline of the chimney where it is to pass through the first ceiling. Note: This offset distance may not be your full offset distance (T).

Locate on the ceiling the center point of the chimney, as though a straight-up chimney arrange-

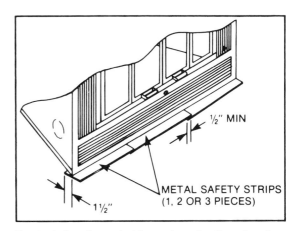

Fig. 9-12. Install metal strips and overlap them (courtesy Majestic Company, An American Standard Company).

257

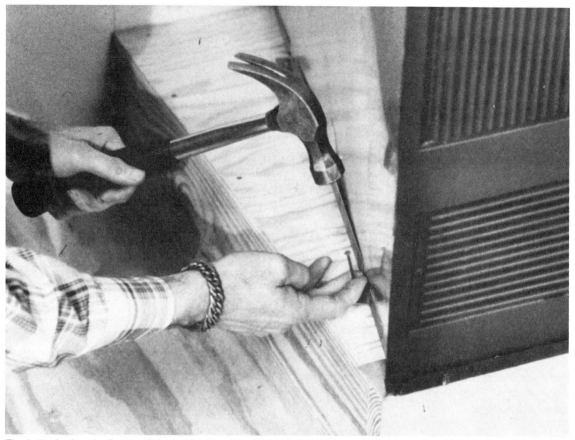

Fig. 9-13. Anchor the fireplace into position (courtesy Majestic Company, An American Standard Company).

ment will be used. Then measure your offset dimension from the straight-up chimney center point on the ceiling (Fig. 9-18).

☐ Mark the area of the ceiling chimney hole. The size will vary with the angle at which the chimney passes through the ceiling. Refer to Table 9-2.

Drive a nail up through the ceiling at the marked chimney center point. Go to the floor above and check where the hole will be cut, relative to the ceiling joists and any obstructions, such as wiring or plumbing runs. If necessary, reposition the chimney and/or the fireplace to better accommodate these joists and/or renumber obstructions. If you must cut a ceiling joist and frame it to allow for a pipe, Fig. 9-19 shows you how. It will not affect the structural integrity of your ceiling construction.

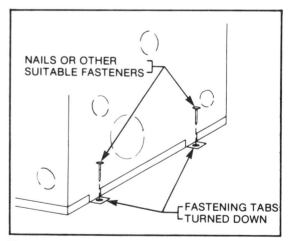

Fig. 9-14. Fasten the fireplace in position using four fastening tabs (courtesy Majestic Company, An American Standard Company).

258

TABLE 9-1. OFFSET DIMENSIONS.

	Dimensions			
	T		S	
	815	830	815	830
No Intermediate Section	0'2 1/2"	0'5"	1'4 3/4"	1'7 1/2"
One 1' Section	0'5 1/4"	0'10 3/4"	2'2 3/4"	2'2 3/4"
One 1 1/2' Section	0'6 3/4"	1' 1/4"	2'8 3/4"	2'9 3/4"
One 2' Section	0'8 1/2"	1'4 1/4"	3'2 1/2"	3'3"
One 1' and One 1 1/2' Section	0'9 1/2"	1'6 1/2"	3'6 3/4"	3"6 3/4"
One 3' Section	0'11 1/2"	1'10 1/4"	4'2"	4'1 1/4"
One 2' and One 1 1/2' Section	1' 3/4"	2' 1/2"	4'6 1/2"	4'5 1/4"
Two 2' Sections	1'2 1/2"	2'3 1/2"	5' 1/4"	4'10 1/2"
One 3' and One 1 1/2' Section	1'3 3/4"	2'6 1/2"	5'6"	5'3 1/2"
One 3' and One 2" Section	1'5 1/4"	2'9 1/2"	5'11 3/4"	5'8 3/4"
Two 2' and One 1 1/2' Section	1'6 1/2"	2'11 3/4"	6'4 1/4"	6' 3/4"
Two 3' Sections	1'8 1/2"	3'3 1/2"	6'11 1/2"	6'7 1/4"

☐ After covering the opening of the fireplace collar, cut the chimney hole through the ceiling. Recheck the hole to be sure that it measures the hole size selected from Table 9-2.

☐ Frame the ceiling chimney hole, using framing lumber that is the same size as the ceiling joists. This practice is a requirement at the attic level.

TABLE 9-2. SIZES OF CEILING CHIMNEY HOLE.

	Angle of Chimney at Ceiling		
Size of Chimney	Vertical	15"	20"
8" flue	17 1/2 × 17 1/2	18 7/8 × 22 1/2	17 1/8 × 29 5/8

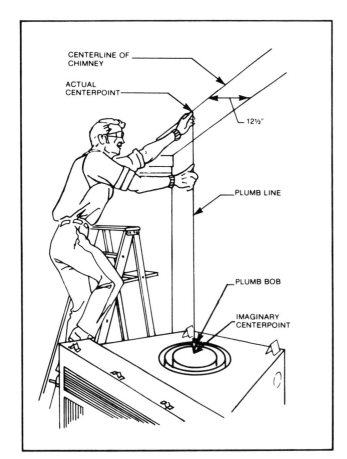

Fig. 9-15. Measure 12 1/2" from the back wall (courtesy Majestic Company, An American Standard Company).

Fig. 9-16. Locate the center point of the chimney (courtesy Majestic Company, An American Standard Company).

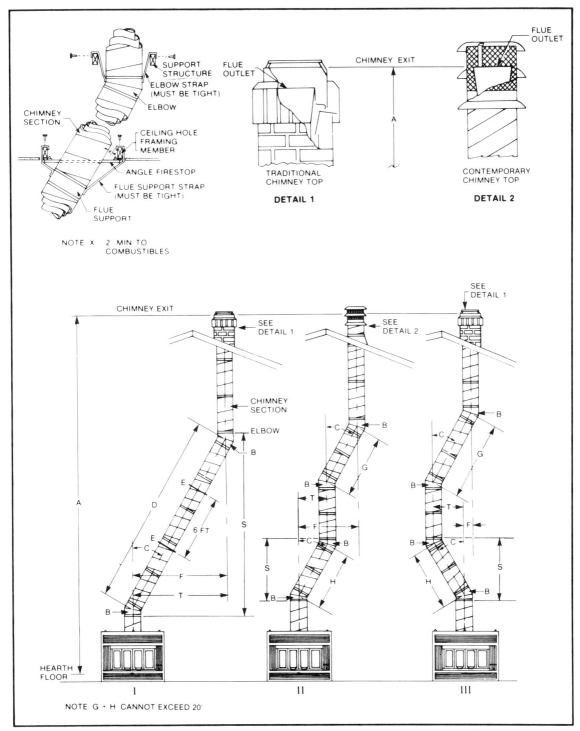

Fig. 9-17. Establish the chimney center point (courtesy Majestic Company, An American Standard Company).

261

Fig. 9-18. Mark the area of the chimney hole (courtesy Majestic Company, An American Standard Company).

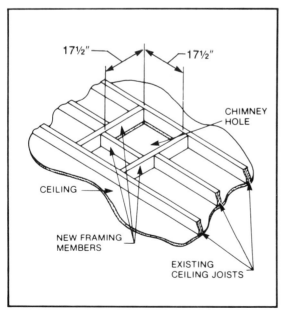

Fig. 9-19. Typical frame for a ceiling chimney hole (courtesy Majestic Company, An American Standard Company).

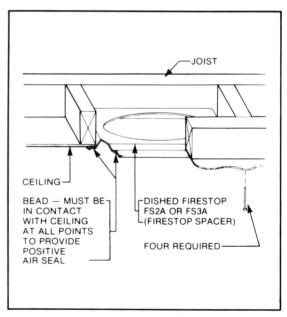

Fig. 9-20. Position of the firestop when the area above the ceiling is not an attic (courtesy Majestic Company, an American Standard Company).

TABLE 9-3. FIRESTOP MODEL NUMBERS.

Type Flue	Model No.	Type of Spacer
8″ Straight	FS2A	Dished
8″ 15° inclined	FS9A	Angled
8″ 30° inclined	FS6A	Angled

The inside dimensions of the frame must be the same as the hole size selected from Table 9-2 in order to provide the required 2-inch clearance between the outside diameter of the chimney and the edges of the framed ceiling hole.

☐ Firestop spacers are required for safety. The hole sizes listed in Table 9-3 for angled firestop spacers provide the minimum required clearance to the chimney pipe for ceiling thicknesses up to 8 inches. When the combined thickness of the ceiling materials, ceiling joists, and flooring material exceeds 8 inches, adjustments must be made in the framing to ensure that the minimum clearance to the chimney are maintained.

If the area above the ceiling is not an attic, position the firestop spacer with the flange on the ceiling side and the dished or angled portion extending up into the hole. If the area above the ceiling is an attic, position the firestop spacer with

Fig. 9-22. Use built-in, snap-lock fasteners to attach chimney pipe sections (courtesy Majestic Company, An American Standard Company).

the flange on the top of the framed hole and the dished or angled portion extending down into the hole (Figs. 9-20 and 9-21).

Nail each corner of the firestop spacer to the framing members of the ceiling hole. A firestop spacer is not required at the roof.

☐ Attach the first straight chimney section to the fireplace collar. Mount the flue pipe first, using the built-up snap-lock fasteners (Fig. 9-22). Then mount the inner pipe and finally the outer pipe. Position each pipe section so the direction arrow is pointed up. Make sure each pipe is firmly snapped and locked together as it is mounted. Continue installing chimney sections until one section (all

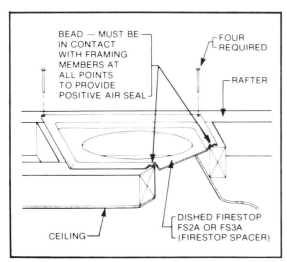

Fig. 9-21. Position of the firestop when the area above the ceiling is an attic (courtesy Majestic Company, An American Standard Company).

263

Fig. 9-23. Installation of chimney sections. Locate the center point of the ceiling hole (courtesy Majestic Company, An American Standard Company).

three pipes) extends up through the ceiling hole (Fig. 9-23). To extend through the ceiling, it may be necessary to assemble all three pipes, push them up through the ceiling hole and then slide them down one at a time to connect them.

☐ For an offset installation attach the first elbow where required. Note that only the outer pipe snap-locks. The flue and inner pipe telescope (Fig. 9-24). The strips for an elbow installed directly on the fireplace collar do not have to be attached however.

☐ Determine how many chimney supports are needed. The chimney system is supported by the fireplace for chimney heights less than 45 feet. Additional supports must be provided again at 75 feet of vertical chimney height. Locate chimney

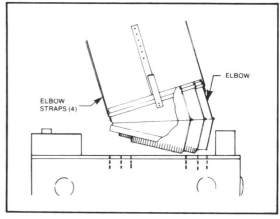

Fig. 9-24. Attach a one-piece elbow to the fireplace collar or chimney section (courtesy Majestic Company, An American Standard Company).

supports at the ceiling holes or other structural framing at the 45- and 75-foot heights. Spacing between chimney supports must not exceed 30 feet. Elbow straps fulfill the required support requirement only if they are spaced as just noted.

Angled chimney runs require support every 6 feet in addition to the elbow straps. Majestic chimney supports are used for this function.

Refer to the safety rules discussed earlier in this section to determine how many chimney supports are needed and where they will be placed in the chimney run. Note: A chimney support is 3 inches long when installed. This dimension must be

considered when determining how many straight chimney sections are needed to provide the desired offset.

☐ Chimney supports are attached to chimney sections in the same way as elbows are attached. Nail the chimney support straps to adjacent structural framing, as shown in Fig. 9-25. Bend the straps as necessary and make sure they are tight so they will be able to support the weight of the chimney.

☐ In a manner similar to that used to locate the chimney center point, mark the center point of the next ceiling hole (Fig. 9-26). If there is no other

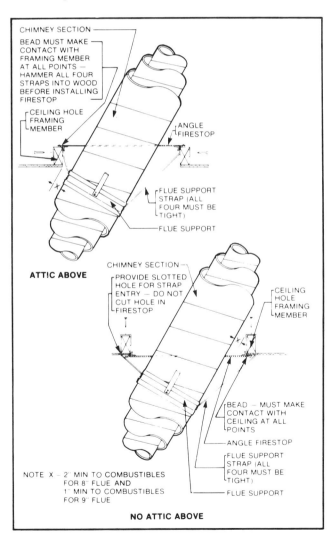

CHIMNEY SECTION
BEAD MUST MAKE CONTACT WITH FRAMING MEMBER AT ALL POINTS — HAMMER ALL FOUR STRAPS INTO WOOD BEFORE INSTALLING FIRESTOP

CEILING HOLE FRAMING MEMBER

ANGLE FIRESTOP

FLUE SUPPORT STRAP (ALL FOUR MUST BE TIGHT)

FLUE SUPPORT

ATTIC ABOVE

CHIMNEY SECTION

PROVIDE SLOTTED HOLE FOR STRAP ENTRY — DO NOT CUT HOLE IN FIRESTOP

CEILING HOLE FRAMING MEMBER

BEAD — MUST MAKE CONTACT WITH CEILING AT ALL POINTS

ANGLE FIRESTOP

FLUE SUPPORT STRAP (ALL FOUR MUST BE TIGHT)

FLUE SUPPORT

NOTE X — 2" MIN TO COMBUSTIBLES FOR 8" FLUE AND 1" MIN TO COMBUSTIBLES FOR 9" FLUE

NO ATTIC ABOVE

Fig. 9-25. Mount flue supports at ceiling hole frames or other structural framing (courtesy Majestic Company, An American Standard Company).

Fig. 9-26. Locate the center point of the ceiling hole (courtesy Majestic Company, An American Standard Company).

ceiling, you can begin roof penetration.

☐ Prepare the second ceiling hole, in the same way as you did for the first hole.

☐ Continue installing the chimney sections and chimney supports, as required, until the chimney passes through the second ceiling hole. Note: Repeat these steps as many times as necessary to pass through all the ceilings in the building and bring the chimney just short of the roof.

☐ If you are using a chase, skip the next five steps. The chimney system must be vented outdoors and must be determined in an approved Majestic Top Housing or Termination.

☐ To locate the chimney center point at the

roof, use the same procedure you did to locate the chimney center point. Drill a nail up through the roof at the marked center point to mark the center point on the outside of the roof.

☐ Cut and frame the roof hole. The size of the roof hole varies with the type of chimney top that will be installed. Refer to the installation instructions provided with your Majestic chimney top housing or termination to find the correct size of roof hole for this installation. There must be at least a 2-inch clearance between the outermost portion of the chimney section and any adjacent combustible surfaces. (Combustible surfaces include such things as ceiling members, joists, flooring, combustible insulation, and roof structures.) Mark the outline of the roof hole round the center point nail. The hole dimensions given in the chimney top installation instructions are horizontal dimensions; therefore, the hole size must be marked on the roof accordingly.

Cover the opening of the installed chimney. Cut and frame the hole. Use framing lumber that is the same size as the rafters. Install the frame securely since chimney top and flashing anchored to the frame must withstand heavy winds (Fig. 9-27).

☐ Major United States building codes specifying minimum chimney height above the roof top are summarized in the Ten Foot Rule (Fig. 9-28). The key points of this rule are:

—If the horizontal distance from the center of the chimney to the peak of the roof is 10 feet or less, the top of the chimney must be at least 2-feet above the peak of the roof but never less than 3 feet in height above the highest point where it passes through the roof.

—If a horizontal distance from the center of the chimney to the peak of the roof is more than 10 feet, a chimney height reference point is established on the surface of the roof 10 feet from the center of the chimney in a horizontal plane. The top of the chim-

Fig. 9-27. Cut and frame the roof hole (courtesy Majestic Company, An American Standard Company).

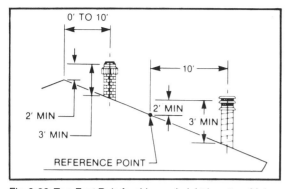

Fig. 9-28. Ten-Foot Rule for chimney height (courtesy Majestic Company, An American Standard Company).

ney must be at least 2 feet above this reference point, but never less than 3 feet in height above the highest point where it passes through the roof (Fig. 9-29). These chimney heights are necessary in the interest of safety. They do not ensure a smoke-free operation.

☐ Continue installing chimney sections up through the roof hole. Check your installation instructions to find how high above the rooftop the chimney sections should go.

☐ Install the chimney top housing or termination, following the installation instructions pro-

Fig. 9-29. Top of chimney clearance must be at least two feet (courtesy Majestic Company, An American Standard Company).

268

Fig. 9-30. Install the chimney housing (courtesy Majestic Company, An American Standard Company).

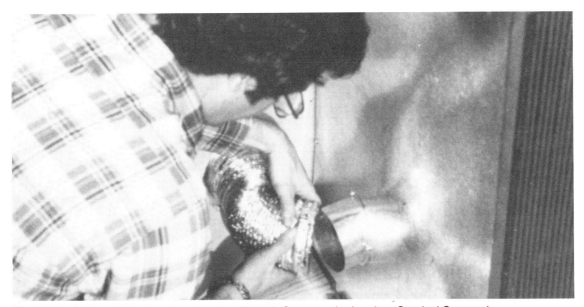

Fig. 9-31. Installing outside air system (courtesy Majestic Company, An American Standard Company).

vided with the Majestic chimney top you have selected (Fig. 9-30). Then proceed to the framing and finishing steps.

☐ Installing the chimney in a chase. Treatment of firestop spacers and construction of the chase may vary with the type of building. Your local building codes must be checked to determine the requirements for these steps. Other material may be required in addition to Majestic Firestop Spacers.

When installing a Majestic Warm Majic fireplace in a chase, it is always a good practice to insulate the chimney chase as you would an outside wall of your home. This practice will greatly reduce the amount of outside air that enters the room in which the fireplace is located and will also prevent a cold fire surround. (See the framing and finishing step.) When you have completed your chase frame, install the chimney system. Follow the instructions given for installing the chimney.

☐ To install the flashing and chimney top, follow the instructions provided with the chimney top you have selected. Then proceed to the framing and finishing step.

☐ Through the outside air system, outside air is drawn into the fireplace where it supplies the necessary air for combustion, virtually eliminating the need for room air for combustion purposes (Fig. 9-31). If the outside air system will not be used, skip the next three steps.

☐ Plan the location of the two duct terminations of the outside air system, and plan the path of the interconnecting duct. Two 16-inch sections of flexible duct are included with the fireplace. They will assist in easy installation of the duct. If additional duct is required, 4-inch diameter straight duct and elbow can be added, or additional flexible duct can be purchased to complete the installation.

Duct length is limited to a total of 20 feet, with vertical height limited to 3 feet less than the flue termination height. For typical duct installation, see Fig. 9-32.

The duct termination may be installed in an outside wall, in an attic space, or in a crawl space. If the termination is in an attic or crawl space, the area must allow a minimum of 100 square inches of

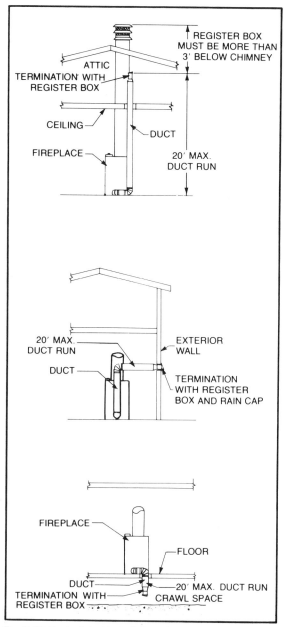

Fig. 9-32. Typical duct installations (courtesy Majestic Company, An American Standard Company).

unrestricted ventilation opening. The termination must be installed to avoid blockage from dirt or insulation. If installed on an outside wall, the termination should be located so it will not become blocked by shrubs or drifting snow.

270

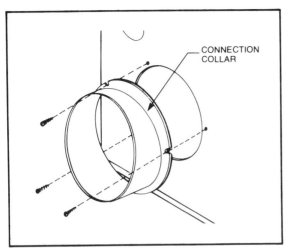

Fig. 9-33. Install connection collars (courtesy Majestic Company, An American Standard Company).

□ Install the terminations. The termination for attic installation should be supported in convenient manner and in a position where it cannot become clogged with dirt or insulation.

For an outside wall installation, locate the center point of the penetration and draw a circle approximately 4 1/2 inches in diameter for each penetration. Cut the marked hole. Put a bead of caulking around the hole, install the termination

through the wall, and attach it with small screws or nails.

□ Remove the two outside air access knock-outs and install the duct connection collar to the fireplace with the three screws provided (Fig. 9-3).

□ Install the duct to connect the fireplace connection collars and the terminations. Flexible duct, straight smooth duct and elbows, or a combination of the two may be used. Secure each duct joint with equally spaced sheet-metal screws.

□ If the outside air system is not going to be used, the room air panel must be removed.

Remove the bottom grille and take out the panels on the left and right sides of the fireplace (Fig. 9-34). These panels may be discarded. Do not reinstall the grille yet.

□ Electrical connections must be made by a licensed electrical technician or electrician. Run 115-volt power to the fireplace. 115-volt electrical power must be connected to the fireplace at the time of installation. Remove the lower front grille of the fireplace by removing the six screws retaining it.

Run electrical wiring to the electrical junction box on the left side of the fireplace. The cover plate can be removed from inside the lower grille area by taking out the two Phillips-head screws. Wiring

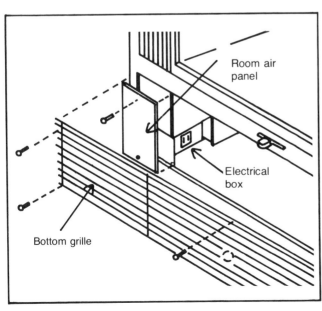

Fig. 9-34. Remove the bottom grille (courtesy Majestic Company, An American Standard Company).

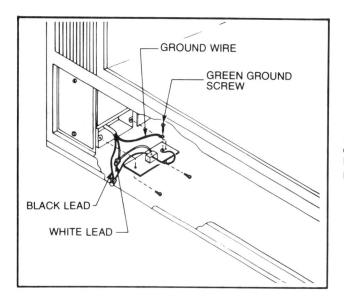

GROUND WIRE

GREEN GROUND
SCREW

BLACK LEAD

WHITE LEAD

Fig. 9-35. Run wiring through the hole in the outer casing and connect to the receptacle (courtesy Majestic Company, An American Standard Company).

Fig. 9-36. Framing and finishing (courtesy Majestic Company, An American Standard Company).

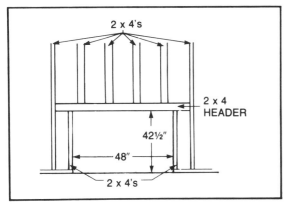

Fig. 9-37. Dimensions of fireplace opening (courtesy Majestic Company, An American Standard Company).

should be #14 gauge copper wire or heavier and must comply with all local electrical codes. Wiring not run in conduit must be connected to the electrical box with a cable connector.

□ Connect the incoming power leads to the white and black leads of the receptacle. The ground wire must be attached under the green grounding screw on the corner plate. See Fig. 9-35 for details. Reinstall the electrical box cover plate and receptacle.

□ Reinstall the lower front grille of the fireplace at this time, unless the fan kit is to be installed. Refer to the instructions provided if you will install the fan.

□ Determine when to install framing (Fig. 9-36). Fireplace framing can be built before or after the fireplace is set in place. Figure 9-37 shows the minimum framing dimensions.

□ The fireplace framing should be constructed of 2 × 4 or heavier lumber (Fig. 9-38). Refer to the framing data for basic fireplace dimensions that will affect the framing dimensions. The header may rest on the fireplace *standoffs,* which

Fig. 9-38. Framing the fireplace with lumber (courtesy Majestic Company, An American Standard Company).

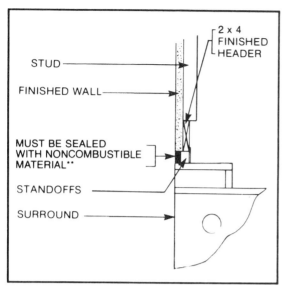

Fig. 9-39. Fireplace surround flush with finished wall (courtesy Majestic Company, An American Standard Company).

are angles on the front ledge of the fireplace, but it must not be notched to fit around them. Framing should be positioned to accommodate wall covering and fireplace facing material. See Figs. 9-39 and 9-40 for typical arrangements. All joints between the finished wall and the fireplace surround (top and sides) must be sealed with noncombustible material. Only noncombustible material can be applied as facing to the fireplace surround.

☐ Finish the wall with the material of your choice (Fig. 9-41). Do not install a combustible mantel or other combustible projection less than 12 inches above the outlet grille. If a combustible material is used, consult your local building codes for the minimum clearance from the top of the fireplace opening to the bottom of the mantel.

When finishing the fireplace, never obstruct or modify the air inlet/outlet grilles in any manner. Do not install decorative facing in a manner which would prevent grille removal. the grilles must remain fastened to the fireplace surround as they are shipped from Majestic except when you need to remove them for maintenance or the installation of accessories.

☐ Adjacent combustible side walls that are

within 24 inches of the fireplace opening must be protected with Majestic Wall Shield Model SP 40 or Majestic specifications 74-10-102A (Fig. 9-42). For fireplaces installed at 45 degrees to two side walls (corner installation), no protection of side walls is required.

☐ A hearth extension is required to protect combustible floor construction in front of the fireplace and may be of 3/8-inch asbestos millboard, covered with a rigid decorative noncombustible material or the equivalent. Secure the hearth extension to the floor to prevent shifting. Seal the crack between the fireplace hearth and the hearth extension with a noncombustible material. See Fig. 9-43. The finished height of the hearth extension cannot be higher than 21 1/16 inches above the bottom of the fireplace.

☐ The Majestic Warm Magic fireplace is designed to accept a 1/2-inch gas line for a gas log lighter. Get a qualified plumber log to install the gas log lighter in accordance with all building codes.

Find the log light tube cap located on the side of the fireplace and remove it. Then push out the internal metal plug on the firebox side, using a probe or a piece of iron pipe. Insert the 1/2-inch gas line pipe from outside the fireplace through the log lighter tube. The inner-wall fireplace insulation is designed to self-seal the space around the gas line (Fig. 9-44).

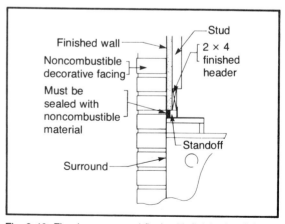

Fig. 9-40. Fireplace surround flush with finished wall (courtesy Majestic Company, An American Standard Company).

274

Fig. 9-41. Finish wall (courtesy Majestic Company, An American Standard Company).

Reference Data

Clearance Data. Any Majestic Warm Majic 36 Series fireplace can be located directly on a flat, hard-surfaced combustible floor, against a combustible wall or on a wooden platform without clearance from combustible construction. Some protection, however, is required for these surfaces as detailed.

Framing members can be placed directly against the side and back of the fireplace. The minimum clearance to combustibles requirements for chimney sections and dome are detailed in Fig. 9-45.

Framing Data. Framing data is shown in Fig. 9-46.

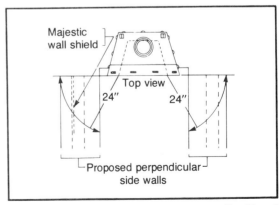

Fig. 9-42. Protect adjacent combustible side walls with wall shield(s) (courtesy Majestic Company, An American Standard Company).

275

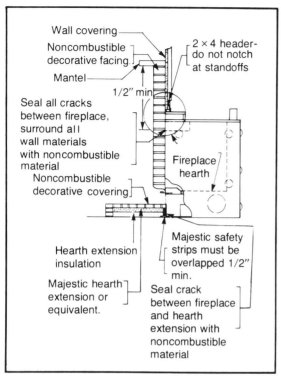

Fig. 9-43. Sealing details (courtesy Majestic Company, An American Standard Company).

FREE-STANDING FIREPLACE

Free-standing stoves were most commonly known as "Ben Franklin" wood-burning stoves since they originated with the old Ben Franklin stove. It was designed originally to replace the fireplace, and early models were actually nothing more than cast-iron fireplaces. They made their appearance during the middle of the 18th century and consisted of a cast-iron liner stuck in the fireplace opening with the front projecting a short distance into the room. The upper part was closed in, but beneath it the fire burned on an open cast-iron hearth. The smoke entered the fireplace through a flue. The first models were soon redesigned into free-standing, cast-iron stoves with doors. They were connected to the chimneys by stovepipes. Many variations of this stove were built in succeeding years.

The use of cast-iron liners and stoves, of course, was intended to improve the efficiency of the fireplace, the predominant means of heating American homes until after 1800. Cast iron projecting from a fireplace or free-standing stove provided a large heated surface to transfer warmth into the air circulation through the room. The traditional

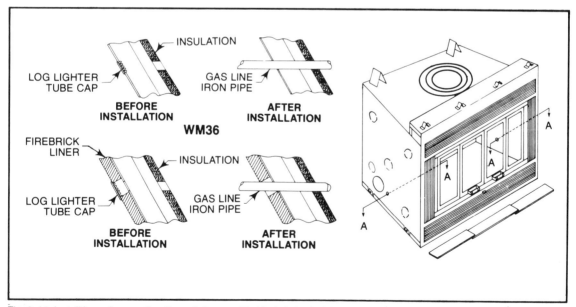

Fig. 9-44. Install iron pipe gas line through the provided hole in both sides of the fireplace (courtesy Majestic Company, An American Standard Company).

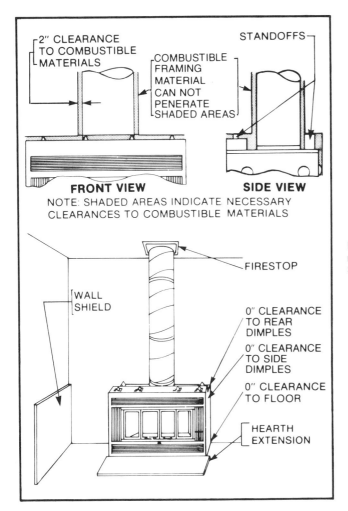

2" CLEARANCE
TO COMBUSTIBLE
MATERIALS

COMBUSTIBLE
FRAMING
MATERIAL
CAN NOT
PENERATE
SHADED AREAS

STANDOFFS

FRONT VIEW　　　**SIDE VIEW**

NOTE: SHADED AREAS INDICATE NECESSARY
CLEARANCES TO COMBUSTIBLE MATERIALS

FIRESTOP

WALL
SHIELD

0" CLEARANCE
TO REAR
DIMPLES

0" CLEARANCE
TO SIDE
DIMPLES

0" CLEARANCE
TO FLOOR

HEARTH
EXTENSION

Fig. 9-45. Minimum clearance to combustible materials (courtesy Majestic Company, An American Standard Company).

open fireplace heated only the area around the fire . . . toasting people in front and leaving them chilled behind. What Ben Franklin began as a fireplace became a functioning heating stove in a matter of 50 years.

The cast iron wood-or coal-burning stove in many forms has stayed with us. The Birmingham Stove and Range Company has manufactured the traditional coal and wood cast-iron stoves for over 75 years and is now one of the leading manufacturers of the rediscovered Ben Franklin fireplace (Fig. 9-47).

Rules for Safe Installation and Operation

Read these rules and the instructions care-fully. Failure to follow them could cause a malfunction of the fireplace which could result in death, serious bodily injury, and/or property damage.

—Check your local codes. The installation must comply with them.

—Do not install this fireplace in a mobile home or trailer.

—Always connect this fireplace to a chimney and vent to the outside. Never vent to another room or inside a building.

—Make sure the chimney is high enough to give a good draft. Keep the chimney and pipe clean inside to avoid blockage, or smoking will result.

—Always open the damper before lighting a fire.

—Keep the ash pit free of excess ashes. Failure to do so will cause the grate to warp and burn out.

☐ To hold a fire for a long period, place logs on the fire and close the front doors tightly. Leave the bottom draft slides closed. Ashes may also be heaped on top of the fire for better holding. The damper should be opened. When there is a poor draft, it may be necessary to open the door draft slides.

☐ Do not burn more than one *imitation log,* a log made of paraffin and compressed wood chips, at a time. Follow the directions on the logs closely.

☐ When the fire is out, always close the front doors, flue damper, and draft slides. A warm flue will remove heat from the living space. This step is especially important for homes with central heating systems.

☐ Cast-iron parts must be "seasoned" to avoid cracking. Build only small fires for the first two or three fires. Never build extremely large fires in your Franklin stove.

☐ To prevent injury, do not allow anyone who is unfamiliar with the operating instructions to use the fireplace.

☐ Do not touch the fireplace until it has cooled.

Assembly

Uncrate the fireplace and remove the parts inside it. Carefully remove the glass panels from

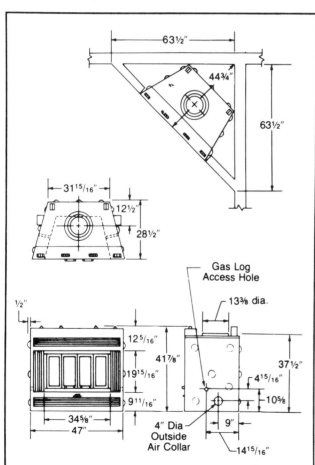

Fig. 9-46. Dimensions of framing data (courtesy Majestic Company, An American Standard Company).

278

Fig. 9-47. Ben Franklin stove (courtesy Birmingham Stove Works).

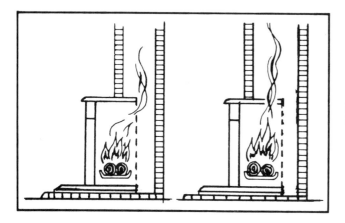

Fig. 9-48. Placement in existing fireplace (courtesy Birmingham Stove Works).

behind the slated baffle inside the fireplace. Put the glass in a safe place until the fireplace is installed. Tilt the stove toward the back and slide the front legs into the locking lugs. Then tilt the stove toward the front and install the rear leg with the nuts and bolts provided.

Selecting a Location

For a unique and very attractive installation, your Franklin can be placed in an existing fireplace opening (Fig. 9-48). It can be done either with or without the legs. Check the dimensions of your fireplace against the dimensions of your Franklin stove. If the opening is too large, you can fill it in with matching brick. If your fireplace has a good draft, it will have a good draft with the Franklin stove in place. Simply slide the stove into the opening. As a location is selected keep the following in mind:

—The flue connection should be as short as possible. The fireplace should have its own chimney. No other appliance should be connected to the chimney. If there is no chimney near where you wish to place the Franklin stove, you can use a metal prefabricated All-Fuel Chimney.

—The floor should be level and fireproof. If your floor is not fireproof, you can make a fireproof base. I suggest 2-inch thick concrete patio blocks or common bricks available from your local building supply dealer. The base must extend 36 inches from the rear of the Franklin stove to each side and 18 inches to the front (Fig. 9-49).

—Provide the following clearance to nonfireproof walls (Fig. 9-50): 36 inches from the rear of the Franklin stove and 24 inches from each side of it. The 36-inch clearance to the backwall can be reduced to 18-inches if you use a special heat shield kit (Fig. 9-51). If you have a solid brick or stone wall

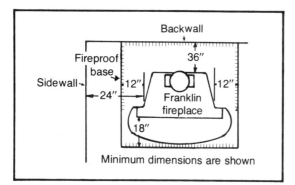

Fig. 9-49. Required clearances (courtesy Birmingham Stove Works).

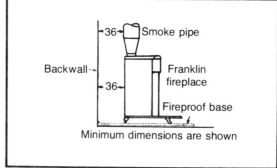

Fig. 9-50. Required clearances (courtesy Birmingham Stove Works).

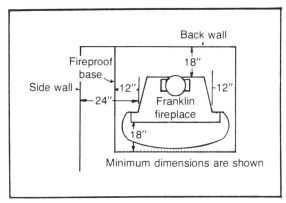

Fig. 9-51. Required clearances with heat shield kit (courtesy Birmingham Stove Works).

behind your stove, you can place the stove as close to the wall as you wish. If the wall is only faced with brick or stone, check your local code for the correct clearance.

Installation

Connect your Franklin stove to a masonry chimney having a flue liner at least 8 × 8 inches. If a chimney is not near the Franklin location, you can install a Type "A" All-Fuel Chimney (Figs. 9-52 and 9-53). This chimney is especially made for fire-

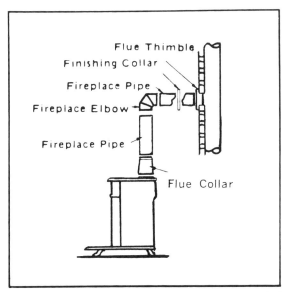

Fig. 9-52. Smoke pipe and fittings to connect the all-fuel chimney (courtesy General Products Company).

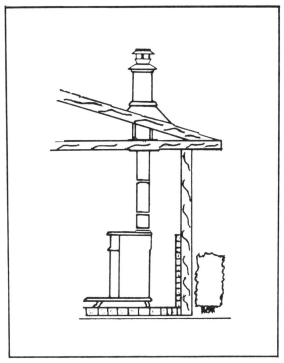

Fig. 9-53. All fuel chimney installation (courtesy General Products Company).

places. It has a stainless steel liner 8 inches in diameter, which is the same size as the Franklin stove's smoke pipe.

The smoke pipe and fittings you will need to connect to a masonry chimney or an All-Fuel chimney on the outside wall are shown in Fig. 9-54.

If your All-Fuel chimney starts at the ceiling, you will need the pipe reducer, enough pipe to reach the ceiling, a finishing collar, and a connector adapter. If you use the All-Fuel tee kit for outside venting, be sure that you have at least 18 inches of clearance between the horizontal piping and the ceiling.

To install glass panels in doors, remove the paper glass retainer angle. Place the glass in the door opening on the screen and slide under the lower glass retainer angle. Replace the upper glass retainer angle and tighten the screw. The glass should fit loosely in the retainers. If the glass is tight, bend the long leg of the angle upward to give more clearance (Fig. 9-55).

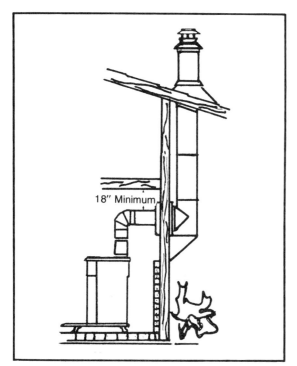

Fig. 9-54. Recommended clearance for all fuel chimney (courtesy General Products Company).

Treat glass doors with care and common sense; all glass breaks. This fireplace was built with a 1/8-inch thick, rolled tempered glass, but it will break if burning wood or flames consistently reach the glass, or you build fires that are too large.

Be sure the stainless screen is always in place. It serves as a spark guard in the event the glass is broken.

CONDENSATION NOTE

In cold climates, warm, moist, house air escaping through the fireplace damper can cause condensation to form on the cold, inside walls of a metal chimney. This condensation, which occurs when the fireplace is not in use, can cause water to drip into the fireplace.

Metal prefabricated chimneys perform well if they are properly installed. The following precautions must be observed however:

— Make all chimney sections absolutely verti-

cal. Do not allow any pipe or chimney sections to be cocked.

— The installation shown in Fig. 9-53 will avoid the problem of condensation. The elbow to the outside of the insulated tee offsets the chimney. Any condensation stays outside the house.

OPERATION OF A FIREPLACE

Never use gasoline or a lighting fluid. Open the damper and place paper and/or kindling in the grate basket.

You can get a better chimney draft with a warm flue. Hold a lighted roll of paper in the opening as near as you can to the flue opening inside the fireplace. Light the fuel in the grate. Add fuel, carefully at first to avoid smothering the fire. When the fire is going well, fuel may be added in the desired amount.

You can control the rate of burning by moving the damper knob or closing the front doors. Never close the doors when a large fire is burning. Use a fire screen to prevent sparks from entering the room.

A Smoking Fireplace

If the fireplace smokes, check the following:
Incorrect Chimney. The chimney should extend at least 3 feet above the highest point where

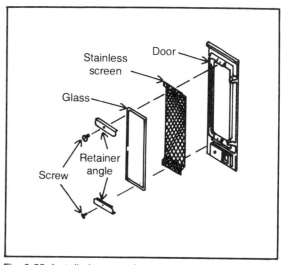

Fig. 9-55. Install glass panels (courtesy General Products Company).

it passes through the roof. It should also be at least 2 feet higher than any portion of the building within 10 feet.

The fireplace chimney should have no other appliances attached to it. All unused openings and the clean-out door at the chimney base should be sealed.

The draft, or drawing of the fireplace is fully dependent on the chimney. A chimney must be high enough and warm enough to provide draft. Adding chimney height should improve draft.

Air Supply. A tightly constructed home with well-fitting windows, weather stripping, and storm sashes has little air infiltration. No air will move up a chimney unless air enters the room containing the fireplace. A tight house should have a fresh air intake at least as large as the fireplace flue area. If there is no air intake in the room with the fireplace, air must be provided through open windows and doors when the fireplace is operating.

Ventilating fans move large volumes of air. If normal air infiltration is not great enough to satisfy the needs of a fireplace and ventilating fan, air will be drawn down the chimney, creating a smoking condition. The fresh air intake must provide enough for both.

A furnace or boiler also requires an air supply for proper burning. This air must be provided in addition to the fireplace and other needs.

Helpful Hints. Starting a fire in a cold room tends to produce smoke while the chimney is cold. When the chimney warms up, the smoking should stop.

Fires should be built to the rear of the unit. When adding fuel make sure that the damper is open. The use of the grate basket promotes a better fire and minimizes smoke.

Other Conditions. Pipe inserted too far into the chimney opening will result in smoke. Pipe obstructed with soot will also cause smoke.

Warnings

Never connect a wood-burning fireplace to an aluminum Type B gas vent. It is not safe and is prohibited by the National Fire Protection Association code. If you are connecting to a prefabricated chimney be sure it is a Type "A" All-Fuel Chimney having a stainless steel liner. The all-fuel chimney must be used even if gas logs are used.

When wood is burned slowly, such as under low fire conditions, tars are formed in the flue products. These tars are deposited gradually on the inside of the flue and chimney pipe. With enough build-up, these tars can ignite and cause a fire inside the chimney until the burnout is complete. A class "A" U. L. listed chimney is sufficient to contain the fire, but distortion can result. If a burnout occurs, your chimney should be inspected immediately, and any deformed, warped, or otherwise distorted parts should be replaced before you use your chimney again.

Because of high temperatures when in operation, the fireplace should be located out of traffic and away from furniture and draperies.

Children and adults should be alerted to the hazard of high surface temperatures and should be kept away to avoid burns or clothing ignition. Young children should be carefully supervised when they are in the same room with the fireplace.

Installation and service should be done by a qualified person. The fireplace should be inspected before use and at least annually by a qualified person.

Combustible materials must be kept away from the fireplace to avoid the possibility of ignition of such materials. This includes combustible walls, ceilings, furniture, rugs, draperies, and fuel. Clothing or other flamable material should not be placed on the fireplace.

There are dozens of manufacturers who can provide you the fireplace which suits you best, aesthetically and functionally. Nevertheless, overall, any fireplace will function as outlined in the previous paragraphs.

Remember always to adhere to the manufacturer's instructions and treat any fireplace, inserted or free-standing, with care and caution for years of good service and enjoyment.

Chapter 10

Fences and Decks

Leisure time is becoming more and more abundant, thus making your home not only your castle, but your playground, as well. To gain more enjoyment from your open space, give careful thought to developing recreational facilities when you remodel.

If you have the space and inclination you can build fencing and a deck. These areas do not have to be addressed at the onset of building and remodeling, but they are well worth keeping in mind for the future.

The construction of a fence, patio, or deck is a significant investment, therefore as a homeowner, you must do a competent job of planning.

During the thinking stages of the improvement, make a plot plan of your property to scale. You do not have to be an architect or an artist to make this plan; some simple graph paper is all you need. Write and/or draw out the dimensions and locations of the house and other permanent objects. After accurately measuring and plotting existing structures, trees, plants, etc., you have probably found that there is not as much space available as you had anticipated. With tracing paper over your plot graph, you can now try out your ideas.

FENCES

For the urban and city dweller, the most common types of fencing are chain link and wood. The basic considerations in selecting fencing are its purpose, cost, and your preference.

Preparatory Work

Before erecting a fence, you may need to lay out the fence line, clear it, or both.

Laying Out the Fence Line. Figure 10-1 shows how to lay out a fence line on level ground. Set a stake at each end of the proposed fence line and station another person at one of the ends. Starting from that end set a stake every 100 feet, with the other person verifying the alignment of the stakes with the two end stakes.

Figure 10-2 shows how to lay out a fence line over hills where you cannot see the other end stakes. Set two stakes on top of the hill where both can be seen from both end stakes. Line up the two

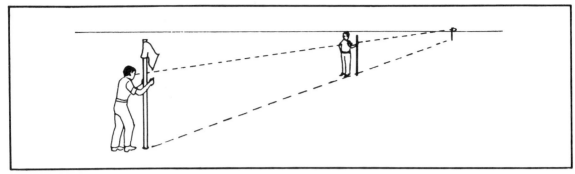

Fig. 10-1. Lay out the fence line on level ground (courtesy USDA).

stakes, first with one end stake, then with the other. You may have to move one or both of the stakes several times to obtain satisfactory alignment.

Clear a Fence Line. Fence lines should be cleared of trees, brush, stumps, rocks, old fencing, and other obstructions that might interfere with the construction of the fence or detract from its appearance.

The easiest and quickest way to clear a fence line is to use a bulldozer or a bulldozer blade mounted on a small home tractor for the city/urban dweller. Always wear leather gloves to protect your hands.

Large trees can be cut down or pulled down with a tractor. If you pull them down, use a heavy rope, cable, or log chain, long enough for you to be safe from the falling tree. Be careful of the dangerous recoil if the rope, cable, or chain should break.

After you have removed trees, larger brush, and old fencing, if any, plow down or turn under small brush and grass with a disc harrow or shovel. If you are clearing a heavily wooded strip make it

wide enough to allow you to unroll the fence, or place the wood in an area where there is enough room to allow you to distribute the posts and unroll the fence. A wide strip can later serve as a road or fire lane if you live on an acre or less.

Fence Posts

Fence posts may be made of wood, steel, or concrete. To determine the kind, size, and number of posts to use consider the availability and cost of the different kinds, the kind of fence you plan to erect, how strong it needs to be, and how long you want it to last.

Wood Posts. Wood posts are comparatively low in cost. For permanent fencing, use the most durable kind of wood posts available, or, better still, use pressure-preservative treated posts. If, however, you choose to use untreated wood posts, even of the more decay-resistant kinds, the durability depends largely on the heartwood content. Whether bought or cut, untreated wood posts should be mostly heartwood. Untreated sapwood of any wood species will usually rot in 1 to 3 years.

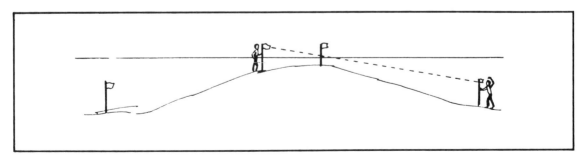

Fig. 10-2. Laying out a fence line, top, on level ground, and, bottom, over a hill (courtesy USDA).

TABLE 10-1. DURABILITY OF WOOD TYPES.

Kind	# of Years
Osage Orange	25 to 30 years
Red Cedar and Black Locust	15 to 25 years
Sassafras	10 to 15 years
White Oak, Blackjack Oak, and Cypress	5 to 10 years
Southern Pine, Sweetgum, Hickory, Red Oak, Sycamore, Yellow Poplar, Cottonwood, and Willow	2 to 7 years

The probable life expectancy of different kinds of untreated posts of mostly heartwood is shown in Table 10-1.

Wood posts can usually be purchased in lengths of 5 to 8 feet and in diameters of 2 1/2 to 6 or more inches.

Posts 5 inches or larger in diameter are used for *anchor posts,* gate, corner, end, and braced-line posts. The height of the fence and the depth of the post setting determine the length of posts required. Anchor posts are usually set 3 to 3 1/2 feet in the ground, and line posts are usually set 2 to 2 1/2 feet.

Steel Posts. Steel posts offer a number of advantages. They are lightweight, fireproof, extremely durable, and easily driven into most soils. They will also ground the fence against lightning when in contact with wet or moist soil.

Figure 10-3 shows the more common types of steel posts. The first three from the left are line posts and the fourth is a corner post. Steel posts are usually sold in lengths of 5, 5 1/2, 6, 6 1/2, 7, 7 1/2, and 8 feet.

Corner and End-Post Assemblies

Corner and end-post assemblies are the foundation of a fence. If one fails, the whole fence or a section may fail. Figure 10-4 shows different types of wood assemblies. The double-span assemblies have more than twice the strength of the single-span assemblies and only half the horizontal and vertical movement under heavy loads. Type C is superior to A and B, and B is superior to A.

Single-span assemblies may be used for fence lengths up to 10 rods. For fence lengths of 10 to 40 rods, use double-span construction. Over 40 rods, use double-span construction and braced-line posts.

Sizes. Minimum sizes for the components of single-span assemblies are:

—corner post: 6 in.,
—each brace post: 5 in. diameter,
—each brace: 4 in. diameter,
—each tie: 2 double strands of No. 9-gauge wire.

For *Double-Span* assemblies, sizes are as follows:

—corner post: 5 in. diameter,
—each brace post: 4 in. diameter,
—each brace: 4 in. diameter,
—each tie: 2 double strands of No. 9 gauge wire.

The height of the fence and the depth of the post setting determine the length of post needed. The posts should be set at least 2 1/2 feet into the ground.

Construction. Following are construction steps in single-span assemblies. Repeat as necessary for double-span assemblies.

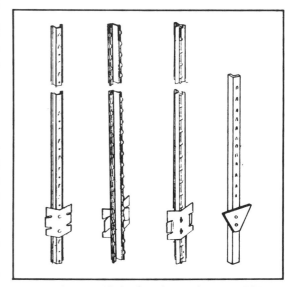

Fig. 10-3. Common kinds of steel posts (courtesy USDA).

287

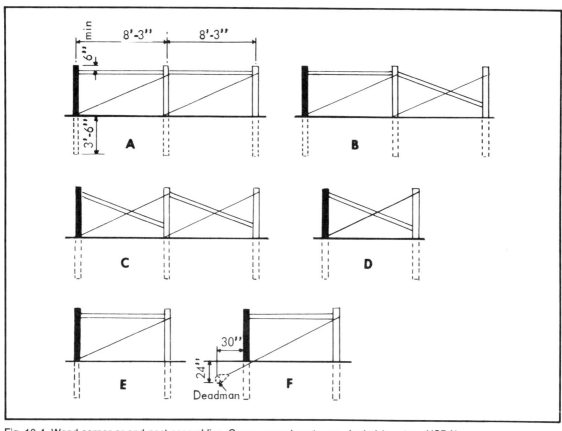

Fig. 10-4. Wood corner or end-post assemblies. Corner or end posts are shaded (courtesy USDA).

☐ Dig the holes for the anchor and brace posts, spacing them 8 feet apart.

☐ Set the anchor post, but not the brace post. Tamp the soil firmly as you replace it around the post. Lean the top of the post 1 inch away from the direction of the fence pull so that it will straighten to a plumb position when the fence is stretched.

☐ Stand the brace post in its hole and fasten the wood brace to both posts. Use dowel construction for a strong assembly (Fig. 10-5).

☐ Set the brace posts, tamping the soil firmly as you replace it around the post.

☐ Attach the brace wire as shown in Fig. 10-6 and splice the ends together. Tighten the wire by twisting it with a strong stick or rod. Leave the stick or rod in place so that you can adjust the tension when necessary.

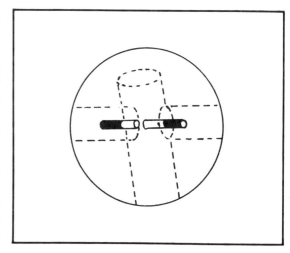

Fig. 10-5. Use dowel pins to connect wood brace to wood corner or end post or brace post (courtesy USDA).

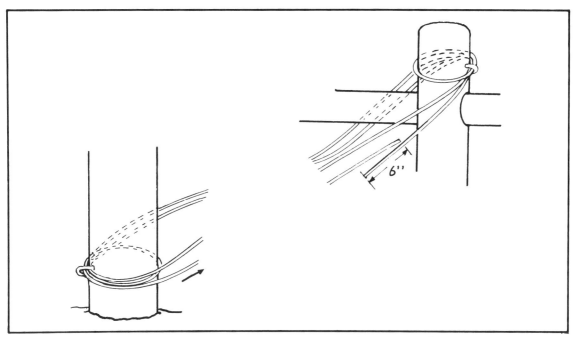

Fig. 10-6. Fastening of wire brace or tie in wood corner or end-post assembly (courtesy USDA).

Fig. 10-7. Basketweave design (courtesy John Wahlfeldt).

289

Fig. 10-8. Slanted slat design (courtesy Western Wood Products).

Board Fences

Board fences are very popular for home lots since they provide privacy. Installation of wood fencing not only enhances the liveability of a home, literally extending the dimensions of the living space to the outdoors, but it gives positive assurance that the fence will be useful and maintenance free for a long time.

A straight, vertical fence, the popular basketweave (Fig. 10-7), or slanted slates (Fig. 10-8) are three of the more popular styles which suit any location and are easily constructed by the do-it-yourselfer.

Preparation. Keep in mind the following helpful hints regardless of the design you intend to construct.

☐ Saw the tops of the posts slightly toward the side to which the boards will be fastened so that the top fascia boards will slope toward that side.

☐ At the beginning of the fence and at corners, set the first line post 7 feet 10 inches from the gate or corner post, center to center. Space the

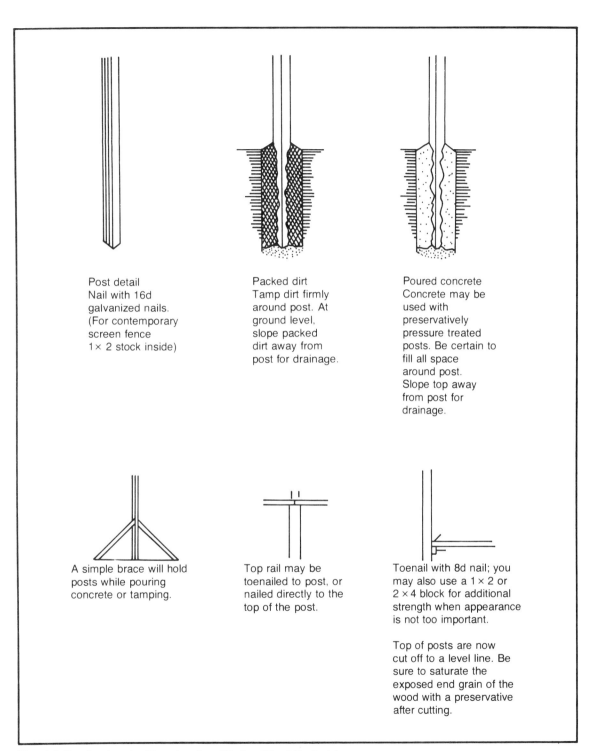

Post detail
Nail with 16d galvanized nails. (For contemporary screen fence 1 × 2 stock inside)

Packed dirt
Tamp dirt firmly around post. At ground level, slope packed dirt away from post for drainage.

Poured concrete
Concrete may be used with preservatively pressure treated posts. Be certain to fill all space around post. Slope top away from post for drainage.

A simple brace will hold posts while pouring concrete or tamping.

Top rail may be toenailed to post, or nailed directly to the top of the post.

Toenail with 8d nail; you may also use a 1 × 2 or 2 × 4 block for additional strength when appearance is not too important.

Top of posts are now cut off to a level line. Be sure to saturate the exposed end grain of the wood with a preservative after cutting.

Fig. 10-9. Details of post settings (courtesy Western Wood Products).

other line posts 8 feet apart, center to center. The first boards should extend across the face of the anchor post to the center of the first or second line posts. Subsequent boards are nailed center to center on the posts.

☐ Near corners or the end of the fence, you may need to shorten the spacing between posts to make it come out even. For the best appearance, however, make the last panel as nearly full length as possible.

☐ In the first or first two panels at the start of the fence and at corners, use 16-foot boards for the top and third rails and 8-foot boards for the second and fourth rails. With this arrangement, only two joints will fall on any one post, and you will have a stronger fence.

☐ For the best appearance, fasten the boards to the outside of the posts; however, if the fence will be subject to pressure, such as from livestock, attach the boards to the inside of the posts.

☐ Nail the boards to the posts with three ring-shank or screw-shank nails, staggered to avoid any splitting of the board. For a stronger fence, hold the boards in place with cleats bolted to the posts. This method makes it easier to remove the boards quickly if necessary.

☐ If you saw, trim, or bore preservative-treated boards, you may expose untreated or inadequately treated wood.

☐ To begin, use string to outline your area.

Locate the holes 4 or 8 feet apart, depending on which design you are using.

☐ Dig each hole 3 feet deep, then place 2 inches of gravel on the bottom to ensure good drainage. Set the post and hold or brace it while you plumb it with a level. Figure 10-9 shows the various ways in which to set posts.

Vertical Board Fence. The quickest, easiest fence to build is the traditional board fence. The surface material can be any width of 1-inch boards, spaced 1 inch apart. The standard height is 5 feet, but this fence easily adapts to any height. See Table 10-2 for various standard heights. Use 2-×-4 stringers nailed to the 4-×-4 posts.

The alternate panel fence offers a bolder pattern. Boards of the same size or of random widths may be used. Spaced board design, 6 inches apart, permits you to locate the fence near a house and eliminates the closed-in feeling (Fig. 10-10).

Horizontal Siding Fence. A horizontal siding fence offers a number of practical uses. You can use a 3/4-inch beveled siding to match your house, creating a long, luxurious look. An optional top cap of 1 × 5 adds to the appearance. Use 1-inch lap to overlap standard or beveled boards.

A doubled-beveled fence is more of a team project for you and your neighbor, if it is used to divide property. This fence is also attractive as a connector between the garage and house, as an exterior space divider, or as a visual screen to hide

TABLE 10-2. MATERIALS NEEDED.

Board Fence Alternating Board or Panel	4×4 posts	2×4 rails	1×4	1×6	1×8	1×10	1×12
Number of pieces	2	2	21	16	11	9	8

Horizontal Siding Fence	4×4 posts	2×4 rails	Pieces 8' long — using 1" overlap				
			1×4	1×6	1×8	1×10	1×12
Number of pieces	2	2	22	13	9	7	6

Contemporary Screen Fence	2×4 posts	2×4 post blocks	1×2 blocks 9⅝"	1×2 blocks 15⅝"	1×2 boards 8'0"	2×2 rail 8'0"	
Number of pieces	4	2	17	18	36	1	

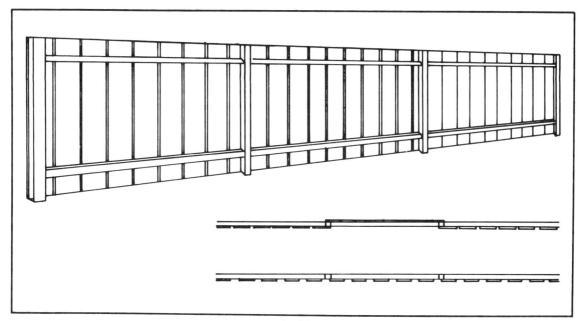

Fig. 10-10. Vertical board fence (courtesy Western Wood Products).

garbage cans or garden tools (Fig. 10-11).

Contemporary Screen Fence. Use 1 × 2s or rip pieces 1 5/8 inches wide from larger boards. Set posts 4 feet apart. Preserve and stain the 1-×-2 boards before installation; it will make your job much easier.

1 × 2s can be nailed as they are placed, then nailed occasionally to the 2-×-4 posts (Fig. 10-12).

Start by nailing 2-×-2 lumber to the post pieces. Next begin stacking and nailing the alter-

nating boards and spacers (Fig. 10-13).

Higher Fences. To build 8-foot panels for fences 5 feet high see Table 10-2. To make fences taller than 5 feet, order boards to the desired length. When increasing the height of posts, be sure to increase the depth for stability. It is advisable to add another 2-×-4 rail in the middle of taller fences.

Trim Idea. A basic structure can be visually improved through the innovative use of wood trim. A trellis for shade and pattern, a decorative see-

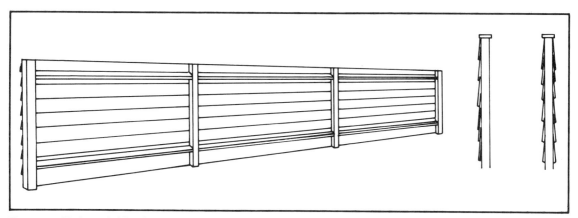

Fig. 10-11. Horizontal siding fence (courtesy Western Wood Products).

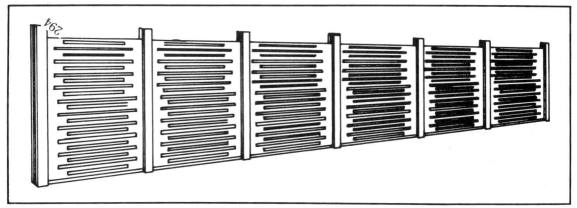

Fig. 10-12. Contemporary screen fence (courtesy Western Wood Products).

through gate (Fig. 10-14) to act as a divider, as well as a design element, all contribute to the overall appearance.

DECKS

Bring the indoors outdoors with an attractive deck. There are many varieties of lumber from which to choose, and the many species and grades of western lumber assure a wide selection, adequate local supply, and the greatest possible economy for a wide range of exterior uses.

Western Wood Products company offers materials of great durability and long life when properly installed. Wood is versatile and economical and is the most natural material of all for decks, fencing, railing, storage, garden structures, and other landscaping elements.

Greater serviceability can be attained if the bark side of the wood is placed to the outside when it is nailed in place, especially if the wood is to be exposed to the weather. Grain separation and the resultant tendency to splinter is prevented. Also this installation technique for boards and dimension retards paint checking and cracking. The outside, or bark side, is easily determined by the curvature of the growth rings, as observed on the end of the plank (Fig. 10-15).

Specification

Grades. In specifying grades and sizes, consideration should be given to visual appearance and the durability of the wood, as well as to strength factors. Western Wood products meet this test. Specific grade information is available from the Western Wood Products Company (see Sources).

Species. Western Wood species work well for exterior uses. Color, grain, durability, and strength factors all provide special mechanical or visual requirements for the natural setting. The range of species available makes it easy to specify a Western Wood regardless of the region in which you live.

Selection. Correct specification and selection of Western Wood lumber is easy. Follow these basic guidelines.

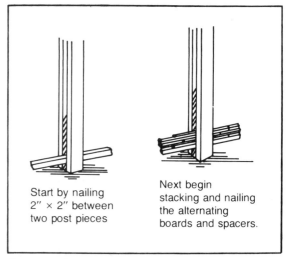

Start by nailing 2″ × 2″ between two post pieces

Next begin stacking and nailing the alternating boards and spacers.

Fig. 10-13. Setting boards and spacers (courtesy Western Wood Products).

Fig. 10-14. Trellis type fencing (courtesy Western Wood Products).

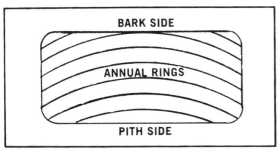

BARK SIDE

ANNUAL RINGS

PITH SIDE

Fig. 10-15. Ground rings on lumber (courtesy Western Wood Products).

—Identify the product by name, i.e., joists, stud, beams, etc.

—Include all species suited to the job to broaden the availability, and reduce cost.

—Specify standard grades as listed in the official Western Wood Products Association (WWPA) Grading Rules book.

—Specify WWPA grade-stamped framing lumber and other construction items.

—Nominal size by thickness and width in full inches are specified for standard products, such as boards and framing, i.e., 1×6, 2×4, 2×10.

—Where applicable, indicate whether lumber is to be smooth surface, called *surfaced*, or rough surfaced called *rough*. Surfaced material may be desirable to extend the character of the home into the garden area, but for a more "natural state" look, specify rough lumber.

—Specify "seasoned," or dry, lumber for long-range product quality and stability, increased

TABLE 10-3. HOW TO USE MATERIALS.

General Product	Finish to Use	Instructions	Comments
Paints	Alkyd paints	Apply alkyd primer and 2 finish coats.	Alkyds are quick drying, blister resistant and can be applied self-primed. Oil-base paints are not blister resistant unless applied over a zinc-free primer. Seal back of siding with water repellent.
	Oil-base paints	Use a zinc-free primer plus 2 finish coats.	
	Latex paints	Same as above.	Product development in this field rapid. Follow manufacturer's instructions.
Stains *Solid, but somewhat soft color. Shows wood texture, but little grain.*	Heavy-body, oil-base stain	1 or 2 coats. Brush, dip or spray.	Particularly suited for rough and saw-textured products.
	Semi-transparent oil base stain	2 brush applications. May be sprayed and smoothed with brush.	A natural for rough or saw-textured sidings. Gives transparent color which is durable and long lasting.
	Creosote stains	1 or 2 brush applications.	A durable type finish. Some brands suitable for subsequent painting after several years of weathering, if desired. Allows grain show-through.
Light coloring, emphasis on wood grain show-through.	Semi transparent resin stains	2 brush applications.	Fast drying with good penetration and durability.
Weathering Agents	Commercial Bleaches	Brush 1 or 2 coats. Renew in 3 or 5 years if necessary.	Will give natural wood a weather appearance.
Repellents	Water repellent	2 coats. Dip before installation, brush after.	Excellent for retaining the natural wood look. Pigmented or dye stain may be added.

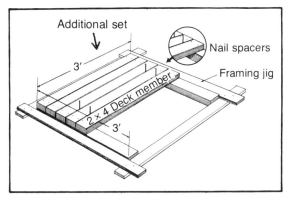

Fig. 10-16. Framed nailing jig (courtesy Western Wood Products).

nail-holding ability, and improved painting ability.

Finishes. A wide variety of finishes are available to enhance the design potential of Western Wood products. Bleaches are used to gain a weathered appearance quickly. Paints and stains are used for overall effect or for accent in combination with natural wood. Water-repellent treatment is used to retain the natural wood appearance.

Table 10-3 shows the different finishes and their uses.

Do-It-Yourself Wood Decks

Following are plans and building instructions for two inexpensive Western Wood decks which you can build and which fit in beautifully for low-budget remodeling. Each deck can be built with Western Woods products available in standard sizes from your local retail lumber dealer.

When building your deck next to a house, garage, or other structure, anchor the deck to the building to provide rigidity. Construction of this type often falls under local building codes; so check the building code requirements in your area.

To ensure long service from your deck, treat all wood with a preservative and use galvanized or nonferrous metal fastenings throughout.

12-×-12 Parquet Deck. Frame a nailing jig from scrap lumber with an inside dimension of 36 × 36 inches. Precut 176 pieces of 2-×-4 lumber each 3 feet long. Lightly ease the raw edges of each piece. When in direct contact with the ground, the lumber should be pressure treated with a preservative, or be untreated heart cedar. See Table 10-4 and Fig. 10-16.

☐ Using a jig, assemble 16 parquet blocks. Allow a 7/16-inch space between the parallel deck members. Nail each end of the deck member with two countersunk 10d nails.

☐ Lay out the deck site with stakes and line (Fig. 10-17). Excavate to a depth of 6 inches, maintaining a perpendicular edge and level bottom. Fill with 3 inches of gravel. Level the gravel with a hand rake and cover with 3 inches of sand. Level the sand and tamp firmly (Fig. 10-18).

☐ Lay parquet firmly in place. Alternate the direction of decking. When all parquets have been laid in place, fill the outside edge of the excavation with sand to ground level and tamp firmly to prevent the parquets from shifting. Should you wish, you may toe-nail the parquets together for rigidity (Figs. 10-19 and 10-20).

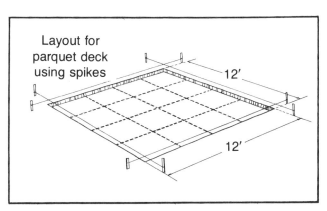

Fig. 10-17. Layout for deck site (courtesy Western Wood Products).

**TABLE 10-4. MATERIALS
LIST FOR DECK 1 1/2 × 12 PARQUET DECK.**

32- 2×4 nailing cleats 3′ long
144 - 2×4 decking 3′ long
38 cu. ft. sand
3 gallons Penta or alternate wood preservative

12-×-12 Raised Deck. Follow the dimensions in Fig. 10-21 to locate the position of pier blocks (Table 10-5). Install pier blocks by digging down to solid ground. Level the bottom of the hole, drop in the block, and surround with gravel.

☐ Locate 2-×-4 framing studs beneath the

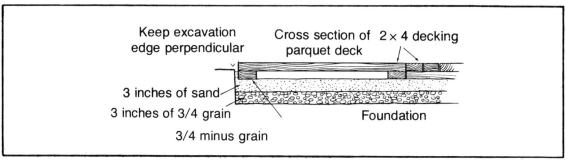

Fig. 10-18. Cover gravel with sand (courtesy Western Wood Products).

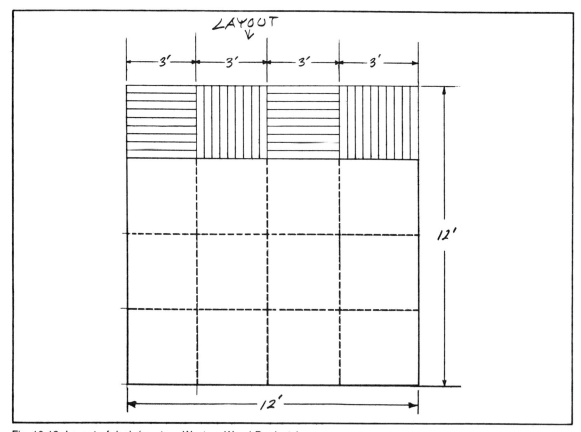

Fig. 10-19. Layout of deck (courtesy Western Wood Products).

298

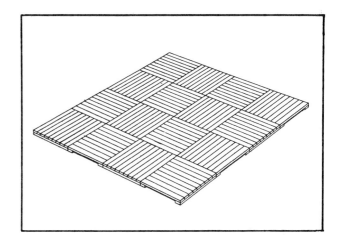

Fig. 10-20. General view of parquet deck (courtesy Western Wood Products).

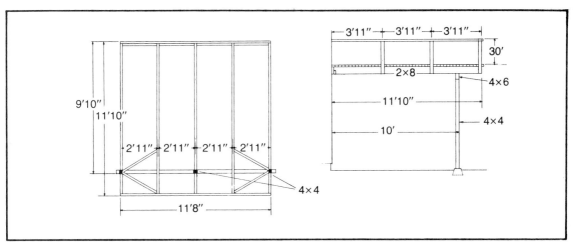

Fig. 10-21. Layout of raised deck (courtesy Western Wood Products).

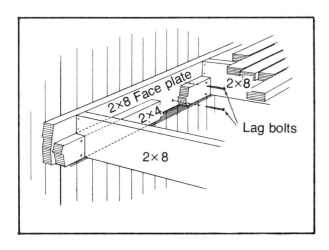

Fig. 10-22. Framing studs beneath house and notched stringers (courtesy Western Wood Products).

house siding. Drill through the faceplate and into the studs at one end of the faceplate and then into every fourth stud. Attach nailing ribbon to the faceplate with 16d galvanized nails, two at a time at 16-inch intervals (Fig. 10-22).

☐ Raise three posts and brace them in position. Install the beam and toe-nail to posts. See Step 7 for Optional beam.

☐ Notch stringers and attach to the nailing ribbon and beam. Check plumb, level, and measurements before nailing. Measure, cut, and nail four diagonal beam braces in position.

☐ Install decking. Use 10d nails for spacing guide between deck members. Nail a deck member to each stringer with two 10d nails. Countersink nails. Check the alignment every five or six boards. Adjust the alignment by increasing or decreasing the width between deck members.

☐ Notch railing posts and decking as shown in Fig. 10-23. Predrill railing posts, stringers, and fascia and attach posts with two 3/8-×-3-inch lag bolts per post. Install the railing cap with two 10d nails per post (Fig. 10-21). Figure 10-24 shows a general view of the finished deck.

A Larger Deck

Both decks just described can be enlarged using the same basic construction techniques and

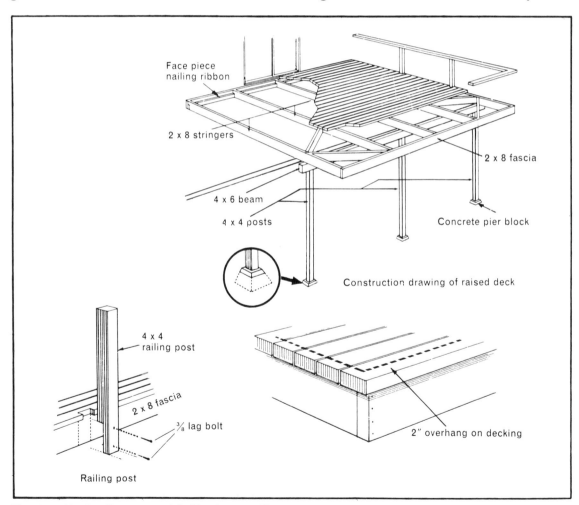

Fig. 10-23. Notch railing posts and decking (courtesy Western Wood Products).

TABLE 10-5. MATERIALS LIST FOR 12 × 12 RAISED DECK.

```
 1 2 × 8 faceplate 12' long
 1 2 × 8 fascia 12' long
 5 2 × 8 springers 12' long
 4 2 × 8 diagonal braces 3'3" long
 1 4 × 6 beam 14' long
 3 4 × 4 posts - undetermined length
 1 2 × 4 nailing ribbon 12' long
39 2 × 4 decking 12' long
 8 4 × 4 railing posts 4' long
 3 2 × 4 railing cap 14' long
 3 concrete pier blocks
 5 gallons Penta or alternate wood preservative
```

materials. For professional help, consult an architect or your retail lumber dealer. Choose one or more of the woods with the Western Wood Products patent on them. You have a variety from which to choose; all are durable and ideal for decks.

For those who do not wish to install an all-wood deck, a patio from concrete is the next choice. This option, of course, requires the pouring of concrete in either section or slab form and can be done without too much trouble (see Chapter 4). For a simple, inexpensive, and attractive patio/deck, other materials are easily applicable and work beautifully into remodeling plans. Flagstones, concrete slab stones, and bricks provide an easy, quick, do-it-yourself patio and can be installed with little effort. First, however, you will need to make sure that the area you wish to use is level.

Preparing the Site. Good drainage is essential. Grading may be necessary, too, and will depend on the materials you use. Grading is accomplished by digging out or adding soil. Section off areas with wooden stakes, string lines between the stakes, and use a level to determine the high and low points. Where areas are low, add dirt; where areas are high, dig out excess dirt. Soak the ground and tamp it down well.

Flagstones. Flagstones are available in a variety of shapes, sizes, and colors. When they are intermixed, they produce a pleasing and effective design. In addition, they are durable. Approximately 2 inches thick, flagstones can be laid on soil or sand with mortar or gravel set between each slab.

To lay flagstones with sand, rake a bed of sand 2 to 3 inches deep. Place the slabs firmly into the bed and fill with gravel or soil.

To lay flagstones with soil, dig the soil slightly

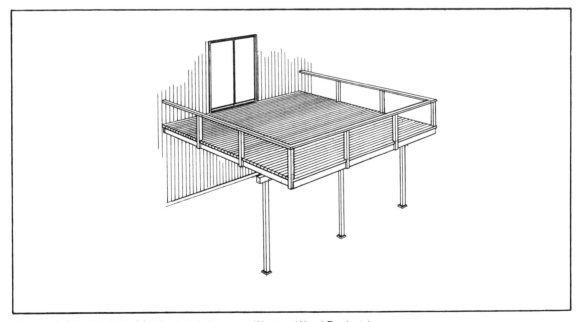

Fig. 10-24. General view of finished deck (courtesy Western Wood Products).

Fig. 10-25. Slabs, blocks, and poured concrete (courtesy John Wahlfeldt).

spaces with dirt, gravel, or soil. The finished area will be as solid as if layed in concrete. Wash down the area immediately after filling the cracks until the sand remains level with the set slabs. You can repeat this process over a period of several days until the finished slabs are smooth, firm, and solid.

For some variation, sections of concrete can be poured between the layed slabs, and decorative concrete blocks can be placed around the patio perimeter for added design (Fig. 10-25).

Bricks. Bricks come in varied sizes which makes it easy for you to vary your patio designs. They also come in many colors; however, dyes change from batch to batch; so purchase sufficient bricks at one time to do the entire job. If you are laying the patio floor in a particular pattern, discoloration of a new batch would show.

Table 10-6 provides you with a breakdown of sizes for ease in measuring and ordering the correct number of bricks for your particular size of patio.

The two basic types of bricks most commonly used for laying patio floors are slick-surfaced face brick and rough-textured common brick. Rough-textured common brick is the most popular because it is readily equated to old-fashioned paving; so it fits in beautifully to old homes being remodeled. Since it is irregular in size and color it is also less expensive.

Shop around to get the best price. Take into

deeper than the thickness of the slab and place the flagstones. Fill the joints with gravel or soil.

Blocks/Slab Stones and Bricks. Available in round, oblong, and square shapes, and in many colors, concrete slabs provide a quick and easy means of laying a patio floor. After the initial site preparation, the slabs can be layed in a variety of designs. Firm each slab into place and fill the open

Fig. 10-26. Running bond (courtesy John Wahlfeldt).

TABLE 10-6. FINDING THE NUMBER OF BRICKS YOU NEED.

Brick Sizes (in.)	Number Square Feet
2 2/3 × 4 × 8	742
2 × 4 × 12	660
3 1/5 × 4 × 8	495
4 × 4 × 8	618
4 × 4 × 12	495
4 × 4 × 12	330
2 2/3 × 6 × 12	495
2 1/4 × 3 3/4 × 8	715

account that delivery charges and the cost of delivering bricks on a pallet are added to the price. A pallet is well worth the minimum additional cost because it prevents breakage in unloading, and the bricks are not arbitrarily dumped around the site.

There are some basic and very pleasing bricklaying designs. The most popular are the running bond (Fig. 10-26), the basketweave (Fig. 10-27), and the diagonal herringbone (Fig. 10-28). All of these designs can be used separately or together, and they can be laid with or without mortar with open or closed joints.

The running bond design can be made with either regular 4-×-8 common or modular size brick and can be laid on masonry or sand. Tap the bricks down with a rubber hammer. Don't use a metal hammer; it will cause the brick to crack. Make sure

Fig. 10-27. Basketweave (courtesy John Wahlfeldt).

Fig. 10-28. Diagonal herringbone pattern (courtesy John Wahlfeldt).

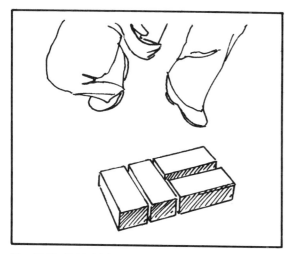

Fig. 10-29. Set brick in mortar (courtesy John Wahlfeldt).

that the bricks are level. Once the brick is laid, dump the sand onto the area, sweep it off, and then wet it down to allow the sand to pack tightly into the cracks. Repeat this procedure until all of the cracks are tightly packed with sand. All of the openings should be completely filled.

If you want to use regular 4-×-8 paving bricks for the basketweave design, you must set them in mortar, since the length of the brick is twice its width, producing an opening (Fig. 10-29). Modular

sized bricks, therefore, are recommended for this pattern, if you want only to lay them in sand.

The herringbone zigzag is most attractive and not difficult to lay. The hammer and chisel are used in this design because when the area is completed you will have protruding edges. The professional mason uses his trowel to cut off the extension of the brick; however, the beginner should use the hammer and chisel to get a better cut. Score it lightly all the way around, go over the same line, and break the brick.

Edging the patio after the bricks are laid provides a "finished" look. Dig a trench along the edge and turn the brick on its side (Fig. 10-30). Sink the brick until it is level with the edge of the brick laid. Do not allow it to stick up or it will form a ditch that will hold water. Another means of edging is to use a piece of 2-×-4 or 2-×-6 redwood or other treated wood to make a stable border.

These procedures can be used for either brick or concrete slabs. They will not move, and the permanency is more than adequate.

In freezing temperature zones, the ground will move. When it does, bricks laid in mortar will be susceptible to cracking. In that case, should you use mortar or sand? If there is any cracking after a freeze, then all, or sections, of the brick-laid patio

Fig. 10-30. Edging (courtesy John Wahlfeldt).

Mortar Mix			
4 parts plastering sand			
1 part cement			

Bricks Laid in Mortar per 100 Square Feet			
Laid in 2″ sand	Amount of Bricks	Sand Cubic Feet	Sacrete (Bags)
1/2″ closed joints	450	17	1

Bricks Laid in Sand per 100 Square Feet		
	Amount of Bricks	Amount of Bricks Amount of Sand (cubic feet)
Laid in 1″ sand		
Closed joints	500	9
1/2″ open joints	450	13

TABLE 10-7. BRICKS AND MORTAR.

on concrete would need to be redone—the concrete slab relaid, and the brick reset. Even though brick laid in sand will move, in a deep freeze, the brick and the sand would only become unlevel, which would be easy to repair. You choose. The use of slabs and bricks in sand is far more economical.

Laying the bricks on sand is the simplest way to lay bricks for the do-it-yourselfer. Bricks can be set in sand in areas where the ground does not freeze. Set bricks in the design of your choice. Till open joints with sand, dirt, or gravel to make the deck as solid as if layed in masonry concrete.

In freezing temperature zones, mortar is recommended. First pour a concrete foundation. Spread a layer of mortar 1/2 inch deep and leave a 1/2-inch joint between each brick and each row, or course, of bricks. Let things set until you are able to joint them with a trowel. Using the edge of the trowel, push the mortar into the joints. See Table 10-7.

Chapter 11

Easy Changes Large and Small

Once the outside is relumbered or bricked, and the inside walls are replaced, moved around, and refinished, in some cases your remodeling project will be complete. Usually, however, remodeling is never complete, since you always need more space for storage, or you may want to turn around, or relocate walls in some rooms. One of the most common occurrences in remodeling is the moving of partitions for a more convenient room layout.

BUILDING HINTS

These basic hints will help you build the projects discussed as well as undertakings that include APA-trademarked plywood. Since building methods and interpretations of suggestions may vary, the American Plywood Association, whose products are discussed extensively throughout this book, assumes no responsibility for the results of an individual's efforts.

Planning. Measure the area and plan the project. Rough sketches will help you determine the material needed. Room additions must meet

local requirements for setback from the property line.

Layout. Before cutting plywood, draw the cuts on the panel using a straightedge or carpenter's square. A compass can be used to draw corner radii. Allow for the width of the saw blade when planning the cuts.

Cutting. Use a 10- to 15-point crosscut saw for hand sawing. Support the panel firmly, face up. A fine-toothed coping saw can be used for curves. A coping or keyhole saw can be used for inside cuts, starting from a drilled hole.

A plywood blade is best for power sawing but a combination blade can be used. The panel face should be up for table saws and down for power hand saws. A scrap of lumber tacked or clamped underneath the panel will prevent it from splintering. Matching parts should be cut using the same saw setting. A jigsaw, bandsaw, or saber saw can be used for curved cuts.

Drilling. Support the plywood firmly when drilling. Use a brace and bit for larger holes. When the point appears through the panel, reverse and complete the hole from the back.

Planing. The edge grain of plywood runs in alternate directions; so plane from the ends toward the center. Use a shallow set blade.

Sanding. Most sanding should be confined to the edges with a fine sandpaper before sealer or primer is applied. It may be easier to sand the cut edges before assembling the unit. Plywood is sanded smooth when it is manufactured; so only minimum surface preparation is necessary. Use 3-0 sandpaper in the direction of the grain after sealing.

Assembly. Assemble by sections, such as drawers or cabinet shells. A combination of glue and nails, or screws give the strongest possible joints. Pieces should contact at all points for lasting strength. You may wish to predrill, using a drill bit slightly smaller than the nail if nails are to be close to the edge. Always predrill for screws.

REMOVING A PARTITION

A nonbearing partition can easily be removed because none of the structure depends on it. If the covering material is plaster or gypsum board, it cannot be salvaged; so you can remove it from the framing in any manner. The framing can probably be reused if it is removed carefully.

The main problem presented by removing nonbearing partitions is the unfinished strip left in the ceiling, wall, and floor. This unfinished strip in the ceiling and wall is easily finished by plastering to the same thickness as the existing plaster. You could also cut strips of gypsum board to fit snugly

into the unfinished strip and finish the joints with joint compound and tape.

Flooring can also be patched by inserting a wood strip of the same thickness and species as the existing floor. If existing flooring runs parallel to the wall, patching is fairly effective; but where the flooring runs perpendicular to the wall, the patch will always be obvious unless a new floor covering is added. In making the patch, cut the flooring to fit as snugly as possible. Even where the flooring is well fitted and of the same species, it may not be exactly the same color as the existing flooring.

Removing a load-bearing partition involves the same patching of walls, ceiling, and floor as the nonbearing partition, but some other means of supporting the ceiling joists must also be provided.

If attic space above the partition is available, a supporting beam can be placed above the ceiling joists in the attic, so that the joists can hang from the beam. The ends of the beam must be supported on an exterior wall, a bearing partition, or a post that will transfer the load to the foundation. Wood hanger brackets are installed at the intersection of the beam with each joist (Fig. 11-1). This type of support can be installed before the wall is removed, and it eliminates the need for temporary support.

Where an exposed beam is not objectionable, it can be installed after the partition is removed. A series of jacks with adequate blocking or some other type of support is required on each side of the partition while the transition between the partition and a beam is being made. The bottom of the beam should be at least 6 3/4 feet above the floor.

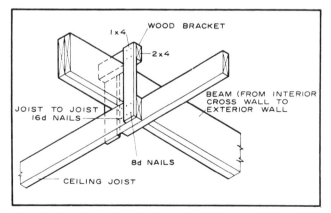

Fig. 11-1. Framing for flush ceiling with wood brackets (courtesy USDA).

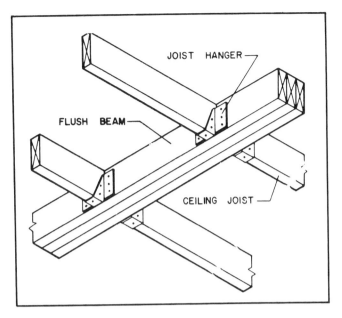

Fig. 11-2. Flush beam with joist hangers (courtesy USDA).

If an exposed beam is undesirable and no attic space is available, such as in the ground floor of a two-story house, a beam can be provided in the ceiling with joists framing into the sides of it. Temporary support for the joists is required similar to that used for installing an exposed beam. The joists must be cut to make room for the beam. Install joist hangers on the beam where each will frame into it (Fig. 11-2). Put the beam in place and repair the damaged ceiling.

The size of the beam required will vary greatly, depending on beam span, the span of joists framing into it, and material used for the beam. The determination of beam size should be made by someone experienced in construction if you are new to do-it-yourself remodeling.

ADDING A PARTITION

A partition is added by simply framing it in, much as in new construction. Framing is usually

Fig. 11-3. Blocking between joists to which the top plate of a new partition is nailed (courtesy USDA).

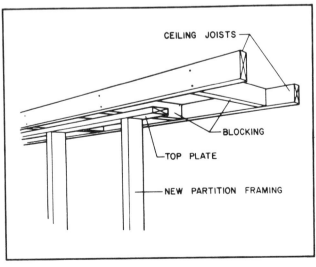

done with 2-×-4s although 2-×-3-inch framing is also considered adequate for partitions.

If ceiling joists are perpendicular to the partition, nail the top plate to each joist using 6d nails. If nailing joists are parallel to the partition, and the partition is not directly under a joist, install solid blocking between joists at no more than a 2-foot spacing (Fig. 11-3) and nail the top plate to the blocking. To ensure a plumb partition, hold a plumb bob along the side of the top plate at several points and mark these points on the floor. Nail the sole plate to the floor joists or to solid blocking between joists in the same manner as the top plate was nailed to the ceiling joists.

Next install studs to fit firmly between the plates at a spacing of 16 inches. Check the required stud length at several points. There may be some variation. Toenail the studs to the plate, using 8d nails.

If conditions permit, it may be easiest to partially assemble the wall on the floor and tilt it into place. First, the top plate is nailed to the studs and frame tilted into place, after which studs are toenailed to the bottom plate. Frame in doors where desired. The partition is then ready for wall finish and trim.

ROOM ADDITIONS

The following "ideas" will help you do further remodeling if the need arises. Although the plans illustrated are not drawn to scale, they can assist you in deciding on the feasibility of adding or, in some cases, deleting rooms.

Dining Room Addition

Many homes lack dining space. A single room adjoining the kitchen eases the entertaining load of the hostess, and gives the family a relaxing place to dine, and the existing dining room becomes extra family space.

A pass through from the kitchen makes serving in the new dining room convenient, and a built-in buffet consolidates the storage of table linens and serving pieces (Fig. 11-4). The outer end of the dining room incorporates a glass-ceiling corner that could be a minigreenhouse or bar. Patio privacy is increased with a wing wall that terminates in a shed.

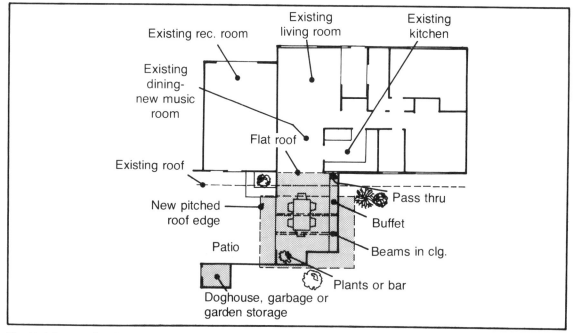

Fig. 11-4. Layout of a dining room addition (not to scale) (courtesy American Plywood Association).

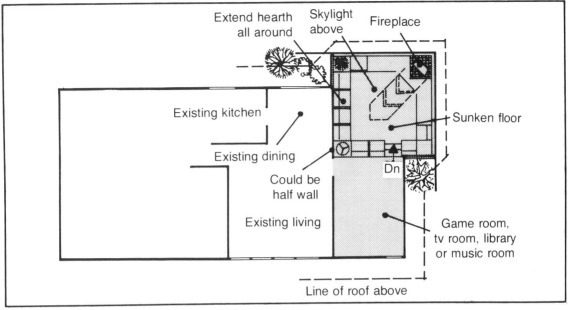

Fig. 11-5. Family room extension, not to scale (courtesy American Plywood Association).

All exterior walls have plywood-textured siding, which may be applied either horizontally or vertically. Because the room over the dining room entry is flat, the structural tie-in to the existing house is simplified, thus less costly.

Family Room Extension

The family room extension separates the conversation area from the game room. It can be adapted to suit your family's interests, such as a studio, music or TV room, or play area.

The lower level in this particular house (Fig. 11-5) has a raised contemporary fireplace with a metal flue enclosed in a plywood chimney. The hearth extends around the room for seating, and under-bench cupboards provide much needed storage space. Visual spaciousness is achieved by converting the dining room wall to a low railing wall. Outside, new plywood siding for the entire house keeps the addition from looking tacked on.

Plywood cost cutters are used throughout the extension. The American Plywood Association Glued Floor System, using a single layer of plywood for subfloor and underlayment glued and nailed to joists, provides a stiffer, stronger, no-squeak floor. Exterior load-bearing walls incorporate Texture 1-11 siding used as a combination sheathing and siding over 2-×-4 studs 24 inches on center.

The beamed ceiling deck is textured plywood that doubles as roof sheathing below rigid insulation and roofing. The textured plywood also finishes exposed soffits formed by the roof overhang.

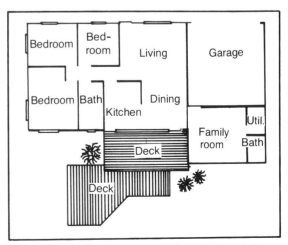

Fig. 11-6. Utility/family room expansion, not to scale (courtesy American Plywood Association).

Utility Family Room Expander

You can gain much needed elbow room without extensive structural change, and without basic design alteration. In Fig. 11-6, space was borrowed from the back of the garage, and the outside garage wall was lengthened. An extension of the roof line and a new back wall enclosure of the space results in a spacious family room that features a half bath and room to relocate laundry facilities into one compact utility room. A large, two-level wood deck off the existing dining room and the new family room invites greater indoor-outdoor living during warm summer months.

The family room's open-beam ceiling can be finished with textured plywood, which doubles as roof sheathing. It could also be closed to normal ceiling height, and the space between the roof and ceiling can then furnish extra storage space. Siding could be either stained textured plywood applied horizontally or vertically or smooth-surface medium density overlaid plywood painted to contrast or match the existing building textured and grooved plywood siding. It can also be applied as fencing and deck skirting.

Attic

The attic can easily be made into a hideaway for a teenager, a sewing nook for mother, or a fun place for the whole family.

From seemingly unusable, attic space can become the family's favorite room, doubling as an attic-study or even guest room.

In Fig. 11-7 you can see that it was truly an attic, and not an unfinished second floor. There are several large, but not insurmountable, problems. First, of course, was the problem of how to get there. Even in a small house, this problem can be easily solved with a spiral staircase, which occupies almost no floor space but adds a permanent point of interest. Basic steps in the remodeling process were the installation of subflooring, flooring, insulation, wiring, and paneling.

First, make sure the floor joists are spaced no more than 16 inches from center to center. If they are wider apart, you will need to install more before

a subfloor goes down. Insulation batts are then stapled between the roof rafters, and 2-×-4 blocking's nailed horizontally in 24-inch widths.

In this particular model, the only structural change was to open up one gable for the bay window, which was constructed by putting together three stock casements. This type of installation provides visual enlargement to a very small room and, by use of many-paned windows, encourages any vagrant breeze to enter.

The window seat in Fig. 11-8 conceals storage and a room-size heating system. Framing for this unit was built before the paneling was put up. Later, a plywood top and short panel doors were added.

The desktop was made by gluing and nailing sheets of 1/2-inch plywood to either side of 1-×-2-inch lumber frame. The top and edges were finished with laminated plastic. For the ceiling box above it 1 × 4s were used and the recess was paneled with 1-×-4-inch rough-sawn red cedar.

Wood panel doors make a simple yet handsome treatment for the short vertical wall sections. Doors can be hinged to provide access to storage space under the eaves. Custom trim, where ceiling and walls meet, was made up of 1-×-2-inch lumber and stock moldings.

STAIRWAY DRESS-UP

Most older homes have stairways that, for the most part, offer no light or attractive design. Often you will find staircases, like the one in Fig. 11-9, that were completely closed off behind one wall of a living room. Opening this staircase extended the open space by the width of the stairs, at one corner of the room at least. The stairway itself became a handsome focal point.

Before cutting away the wall of the stairway on the room's side, make sure that it is nonload bearing. This staircase was opened by removing the standard door at the foot of the stairs, then cutting down the wall on the room side to railing height. It was then capped down the remaining half wall with fir vertical grain 2 × 6s, which formed a railing.

The newly revealed back wall then became a lively accent area. Western cedar 1-×-5-inch tongued-and-grooved boards were applied diago-

Fig. 11-7. An unfinished attic (courtesy Western Wood Products).

nally, at right angles to the stair rail. To play up color and grain contrasts, boards were handpicked from mixed grain clears, then mixed for the fullest effect before nailing to the studs. No furring strips were needed.

WALLS THAT WORK

Walls need not just enclose a room or a house.

Open or closed, they can serve a multitude of purposes, such as reducing clutter and often providing dramatic highlights to an otherwise uninteresting room.

Dividers can take any form your ingenuity and requirements dictate. They can be half or full height, long or narrow, or square peninsulas. They can be completely closed or completely open, or

313

Fig. 11-8. Remodeled attic with concealed storage (courtesy Western Wood Products).

Fig. 11-9. Paneled, opened staircase (courtesy Western Wood Products).

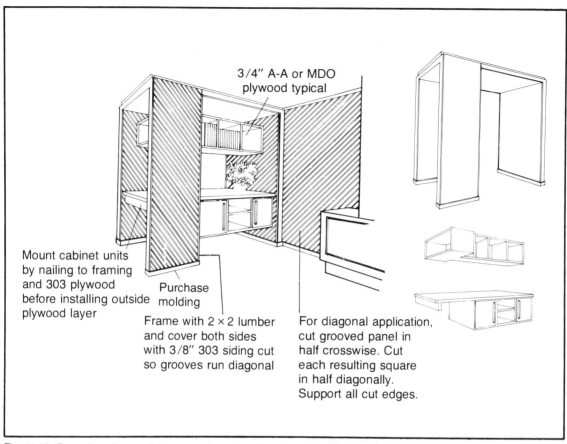

3/4″ A-A or MDO
plywood typical

Mount cabinet units
by nailing to framing
and 303 plywood
before installing outside
plywood layer

Purchase
molding

Frame with 2 × 2 lumber
and cover both sides
with 3/8″ 303 siding cut
so grooves run diagonal

For diagonal application,
cut grooved panel in
half crosswise. Cut
each resulting square
in half diagonally.
Support all cut edges.

Fig. 11-10. Examples of room dividers are shown (courtesy American Plywood Association).

use doors and shelf compartments in intriguing visual combinations. Strategically placed, they not only stretch your storage capacity, they also direct traffic flow and provide privacy (Fig. 11-10).

Planning

For walls, you need as little as 15 inches of floor space along the side of a room to gain a surprising volume of display and storage area. Odd locations, such as hallway ends, take on character and lose their drab, blank look with a new storage face.

Planning a storage wall or divider is much like customizing a closet. Analyzing what you need to store, then looking at the wasted dead space you have available are the first steps. APA 303 textured sidings provide you with another option in materials

choice. These panels, available in a wide variety of surface textures and patterns, impart beauty and character, as well as the strength and durability you need in storage walls.

Finishes

Plywood, both textured and smooth, accepts finishes that complement your decor. Textured plywoods accept stains—semitransparent or opaque (heavy bodied) oil and latex emulsion—as well as acrylic-latex paints. In interior application, transparent interior stains or clear sealers may also be used if you desire the grain or natural color of the wood to show through a lot. For very smooth paint finishes use MDO plywood. Standard grades may be finished either with acrylic-latex paints or light stains. Unusual effects may be obtained with stip-

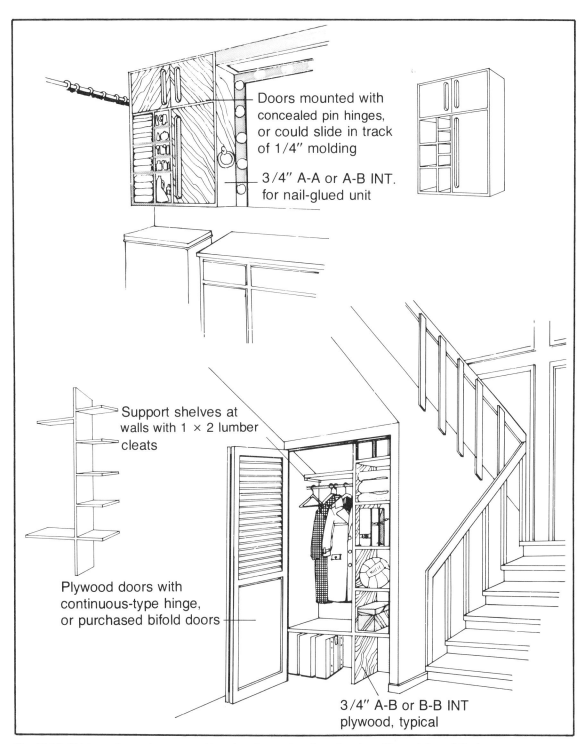

Doors mounted with concealed pin hinges, or could slide in track of 1/4″ molding

3/4″ A-A or A-B INT. for nail-glued unit

Support shelves at walls with 1 × 2 lumber cleats

Plywood doors with continuous-type hinge, or purchased bifold doors

3/4″ A-B or B-B INT plywood, typical

Fig. 11-11. Nooks and crannies can provide extra storage (courtesy American Plywood Association).

pling, and decorative vinyl wallpaper adds imaginative touches.

STORAGE

Someone once calculated that the average American family must find room to store more than 10,000 individual items; and it's a rare home that has enough room for it all. Even the smallest home though, has much "useless" space that you can capture and put to work.

Nooks and Crannies

Forgotten areas in the basement, ignored places under staircases or beds, and overlooked corners in the attic can be turned into storage extras.

The suggestions shown in Figs. 11-11 and 11-12 show you some of the unlikely spots in your home that can be put to efficient use. They take a minimal amount of money, keeping your "low budget" in line, and can be done in your spare time.

Convenient Closets

Many older homes are lacking in closet space. Often closets are not well arranged for good usage. Remodeling may involve altering existing closets, adding new ones, or using closet space to the fullest advantage.

Existing closets offer great potential for solving storage headaches. Ordinarily, closets with only a clothes pole and narrow shelf for organizers promote haphazard stacking on the shelf and a jumble on the floor. Closets, however, are easy to build into handsome, practical units.

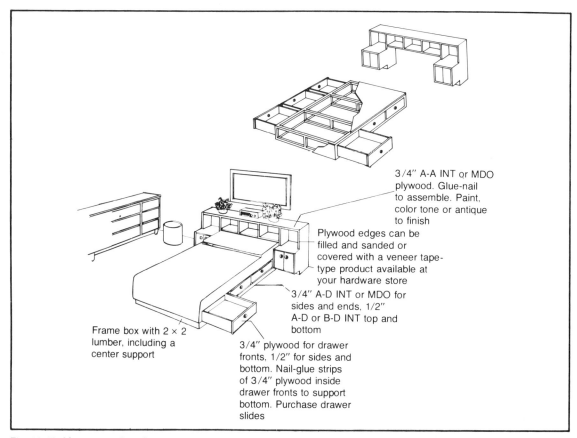

3/4″ A-A INT or MDO plywood. Glue-nail to assemble. Paint, color tone or antique to finish

Plywood edges can be filled and sanded or covered with a veneer tape-type product available at your hardware store

3/4″ A-D INT or MDO for sides and ends, 1/2″ A-D or B-D INT top and bottom

Frame box with 2 × 2 lumber, including a center support

3/4″ plywood for drawer fronts, 1/2″ for sides and bottom. Nail-glue strips of 3/4″ plywood inside drawer fronts to support bottom. Purchase drawer slides

Fig. 11-12. More examples of extra storage from nooks and crannies (courtesy American Plywood Association).

318

Altering Existing Closets. One thing that can do much to improve closets is to provide full front openings to replace small doors. Doors are available in a great variety of widths, particularly accordian doors. Remove wall finish and studs to the width required for a standard accordian-fold or double-hinged door set.

Standard double doors may also be suitable. Where the closet wall is load bearing, use the same header sizes as for window openings. The header can be eliminated for a nonload-bearing wall, and a full ceiling-height accordian door can be used. Frame the opening in the same manner as other door openings with the rough-framed opening 2 1/2 inches wider than the door or set of doors.

Install closet doors in a manner similar to other interior doors. Special types of doors, such as the double-hinged doors, are usually supplied with installation instructions, making it easy for the do-it-yourselfer to hang any door, but be sure to read all directions completely before you hang the door.

Closets can sometimes be made more useful by addition or alteration of shelves and clothes rods. Usually a closet has one rod with a single shelf over it. Where hanging space is quite limited, install a second clothes rod about halfway between the existing rod and the floor. This type of space can be used for children's clothing or for short adult items.

Shelves can also be added in any manner to fit a particular need. To add either a shelf or a pole, support them by 1-×-4-inch cleats nailed to the end walls of the closet. Nail these cleats with three 6d nails at each end of the cleat and at the intermediate stud. Shelf ends can rest directly on these cleats. Attach clothes rods to the cleats that support the shelf.

Additional Ideas. The following ideas are equally adaptable to large or small existing closets, or they can be used for building new storage units that take only a few square feet of floor space.

The first step in customizing a closet is to define its storage function—sports equipment, clothing, or sewing materials, for example, Then sort out what should go into the space. Measure the vacuum, golf bag, any large piece of equipment, and plot a space for it. Think about items you need most often and whether they should be stored in drawers or on shelves (Figs. 11-13 through 11-14).

New Closets. New closets can be built in a conventional manner, or wardrobe closets of plywood or particleboard can be built at a lower cost.

Conventional closets are constructed by adding a partition around the closet area, using 2-×-3- or 2-×-4-inch framing and gypsum board or other cover material. Follow the direction provided in "Adding a Partition" and simply provide a cased opening for the closet door.

APA-trademarked plywood makes it easy to build new closets. Panels are big and smooth, and let you easily cut and install deep, sturdy shelves. Closet wall liners, if needed, may be 1/4-inch thick A-D interior plywood, which has a good paintable side and provides a solid, split-resistant nailing surface for attaching shelf supports and drawer glides.

Wardrobe Closets. Wardrobe closets require less space because the wall is a single material without framing. Build wardrobe closets as shown in Fig. 11-15. Use 5/8- or 3/4-inch plywood or particleboard supported on cleats.

Use a 1-×-4 top rail and back cleat. Fasten the cleat to the wall, and in a corner, fasten the side wall to a wall stud. Toenail base shoe moldings to the floor to hold the bottom of the side walls in place. Add shelves and closet poles where desired.

Similar units can be built with shelves for linens or other items. Any size or combination of these units can be built. Add plywood doors or folding doors as desired.

FANS

Fans have made a come back, not only because we have all become more energy conscious and wish to conserve our resources, but also because we are learning that the fan is both practical and aesthetic, providing us with old-world charm and modern decor.

When a fan is used in conjunction with your central air cooling and heating units a tremendous savings can be gained financially, as well as on

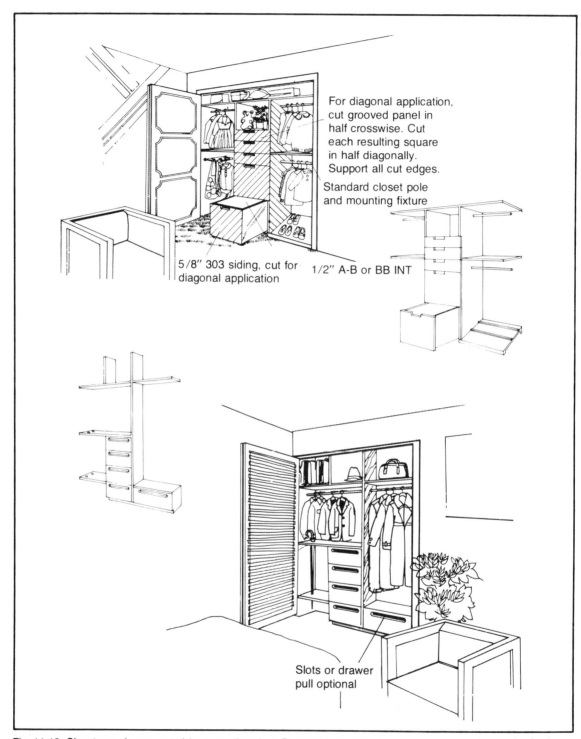

For diagonal application, cut grooved panel in half crosswise. Cut each resulting square in half diagonally. Support all cut edges.

Standard closet pole and mounting fixture

5/8″ 303 siding, cut for diagonal application

1/2″ A-B or BB INT

Slots or drawer pull optional

Fig. 11-13. Closets can be renovated (courtesy American Plywood Association).

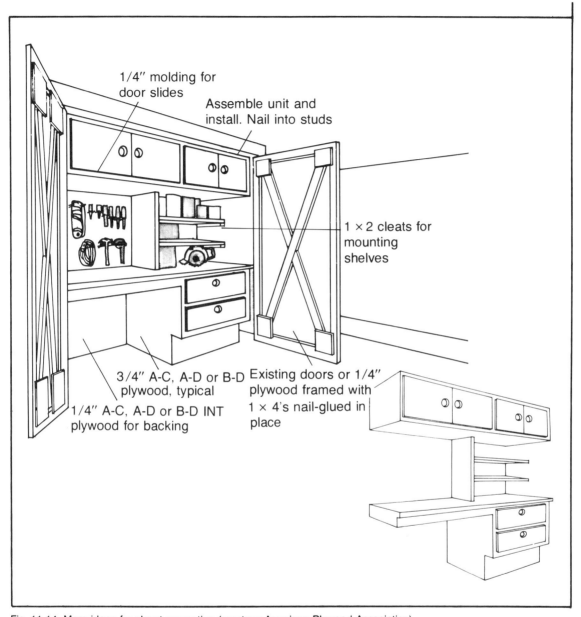

Fig. 11-14. More ideas for closet renovation (courtesy American Plywood Association).

electrical consumption. Even in the hottest climate there are many days, and especially nights, when you can turn down your air-conditioning system and let your fan keep you cool and comfortable.

Where Can Fans Be Used?

Without a doubt fans can be used in any room in the house. With the tremendous variety from which to choose on today's market, there is something for everyone and for ever decor. What better time to install one, two, or more fans in every room than when you are remodeling. Don't let the small amount of electrical work required to install a fan deter you. Fans lend their charm and their cooling

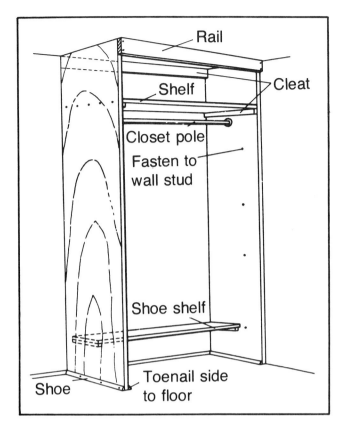

Fig. 11-15. You can make a wardrobe closet (courtesy USDA).

Rail

Shelf

Cleat

Closet pole

Fasten to wall stud

Shoe shelf

Shoe

Toenail side to floor

Fig. 11-16. The Springfield Paddle Fan (courtesy Leslie-Locke, A Quester Company).

power during the hottest time of the year, and they provide an air of tranquility with their soft whirring sound.

Purchasing

Fans can be purchased from many companies in many designs. The Springfield from Leslie-Locke, has the plain paddle fan (Fig. 11-16).

This particular design lends itself beautifully to a corner niche over a dinette area or above a sewing niche when a Classic globe is added. With a super-sturdy 56-inch sweep and a baked white enamel finish, the Springfield is designed especially for a large area. The heavy-duty motor with enclosed permanently lubricated bearings helps provide energy saving in practically any area it is used.

The Sonesta, with its 36-inch blade sweep, is compact and especially adaptable to small rooms. It provides energy savings and comfort year round. The neutral white finish handsomely accents a variety of decorator styles (Fig. 11-17).

Installing the Springfield and Sonesta

Safety Precautions. When you install your fan, be sure to observe these precautions.

—Do not wire the light kit through the controller. Refer to the wiring diagram for proper wiring.

—Minimum recommended ceiling height for mounting a fan is 8 feet.

—To avoid electrical shock, turn off the power at the fuse box before wiring or servicing. All wiring must be in accordance with national and local electrical codes.

—The support tube assembly supplied with your fan kit provides proper clearance and mounting strength. Do not modify it in any way.

Installation. The location of the hook for a hanging fan must be a minimum distance from walls or obstructions to provide minimum blade clearance. These recommended distances are as follows:

—36" fan—24" from hook to wall,
—48" fan—30" from hook to wall,
—56" fan—36" from hook to wall.

Fig. 11-17. The Sonesta Fan (courtesy Leslie-Locke, A Quester Company).

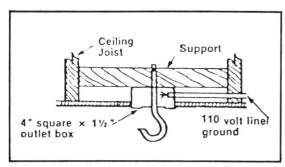

Fig. 11-18. Typical fan installation (courtesy Leslie-Locke, A Quester Company).

Greater wall clearance is recommended for improved air circulation if space permits. Avoid mounting the fan above the movement of a door.

Hook Installation. Be certain that the supporting hook and outlet box can support a load of 50 pounds. If you are installing a fan in a location with an existing electrical box, discard the hook and go onto the fan assembly instructions.

Install the hook in the ceiling with a 1/8-inch gap between the hook tip and ceiling. Drill a 7/32-inch hole into the ceiling material to ease installation of the hook. See Fig. 11-18 for typical installation.

Assemble Fan. Figure 11-19 identifies the parts of the fan.

☐ Remove the retaining screws from the lower canopy and remove the canopy.

☐ Lift the insulation paper and check the tightness of the four screws in the plastic terminal block. Check the tightness of the grounding screw.

☐ For fans with a provision for a light kit, if you are not installing the light kit, pull out the two lead wires from the motor housing. Install a decorative nut and washer on the bottom of the motor housing. Tighten securely.

☐ Place the upper canopy on the support tube bell up. The support tube is not assembled to the fan at this time. Place the lower canopy on the support tube bell down.

☐ Screw the support tube into the lower yoke until the holes for retaining the screws align.

☐ Insert all wires up the tube and out the top.

☐ Position insulation paper. Slide the lower canopy over the retaining screw holes and align the holes.

☐ Install the retaining screws and tighten securely. Screw heads must be flush against the lower canopy. Your fan is ready for hanging.

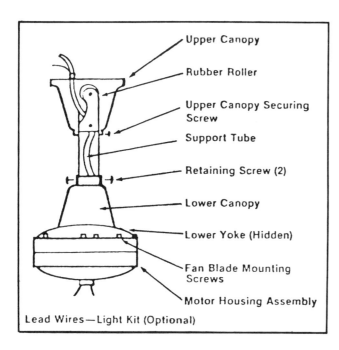

Fig. 11-19. Diagram of fan parts (courtesy Leslie-Locke, A Quester Company).

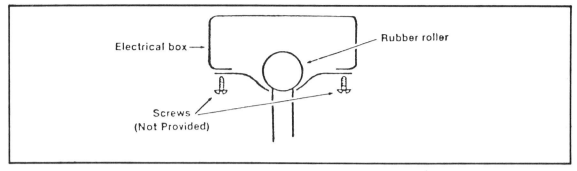

Fig. 11-20. Screw through the electrical box (courtesy Leslie-Locke, A Quester Company).

Hanging Fan. Turn off the power at the fuse box before wiring.

☐ Hang the fan on a hook by the rubber roller.

☐ If you are installing at an existing electrical box, start one screw through the bracket into the electrical box; do not tighten. Place the fan on the hanger, install the second screw through the bracket, and tighten the assembly (Fig. 11-20).

☐ Complete the wire connections for the fan as in Fig. 11-21.

☐ Install the upper canopy in position as shown in Fig. 11-22. Allow about a 1/8-inch gap between the canopy and ceiling. Tighten the locking screw securely.

Note: if a light kit is being installed, do so at this time. Remember that with this, and almost all fans, the light kit if purchased cannot be wired through the controller. Additional wiring is required.

Wiring Controller.

☐ The controller will mount to a standard wall outlet box. Remove the existing switch in the outlet box. Connect the three controller wires to the house wiring.

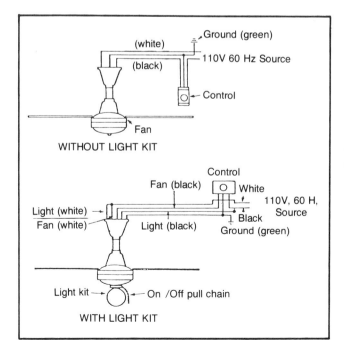

Fig. 11-21. The complete wire connection (courtesy Leslie-Locke, A Quester Company).

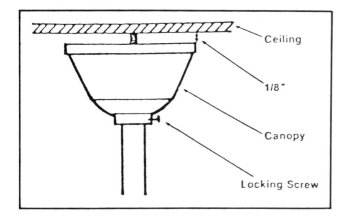

Fig. 11-22. Install the upper canopy (courtesy Leslie-Locke, A Quester Company).

□ Remove the back plate from the controller by removing four corner screws.

□ Mount the back plate to the wall through two holes, using screws from the existing switch.

□ Reassemble the control box.

Blade Installation. Remove screws and washers from the motor, and install the blades with hardware as shown in Fig. 11-23.

Fan Operation. To ensure proper operation, switch the fan on. Cycle the fan to the various control positions. The light kit is turned on and off with the pull chain.

Maintenance and Cleaning. It is recommended that you occasionally wipe the fan with a soft brush or cloth to remove dust. To remove any dirt accumulation, use only mild detergent and water. Never use strong chemical cleaners or an abrasive cleaner of any kind.

It is not necessary to lubricate the fan motor.

Bearings are permanently lubricated and sealed.

A slight wobble will be present in most fans. The mounting assembly is designed to absorb this motion. This wobble is acceptable during operation and is not a reason for safety concern. If the fan wobbles excessively, interchange the positions of two adjacent blades. This change will sometimes help balance.

If the fan sounds exceptionally noisy, check all mounting screws for tightness. A slight motor noise will be present on all units and is considered normal.

A GREENHOUSE

Many older homes lend themselves beautifully to the addition of a lean-to greenhouse. There are many shapes and sizes from which to choose. Anything smaller than 7 × 12 feet is not, however, feasible since you will quickly find that you want to

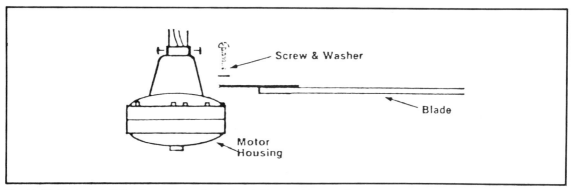

Fig. 11-23. Blade installation (courtesy Leslie-Locke, A Quester Company).

add on. More space can be added, but, of course, it will be easier if you plan ahead for your future abundance of plants.

Figure 11-24 shows Lord and Burnham's lean-to, an ideal greenhouse for those remodeling. It is easy to install and will add beauty to your remodeled structure. You will also have the joy of raising your own plants and vegetables and storing them in the winter where you can still enjoy their beauty.

Your individual structure will determine whether or not you will require footings, foundations, and sills. The following instructions are provided to assist you in this decision.

General Information About Installation

A lean-to, or attached, even-span, greenhouse requires more care in selecting an appropriate site. Plant growth takes place most rapidly in the morn-

Fig. 11-24. A lean-to greenhouse is ideal for older renovated homes (courtesy Lord & Burnham).

ing, and the ideal location faces morning sun in the winter.

In a greenhouse with a roof sash, it is not necessary to orient the ridge line in any particular direction. If you purchase automatic roof vent equipment, however, install it so it operates the sash on the side away from the prevailing winter wind. In a fan-ventilated house, it is best to face the structure with the ridge parallel to the prevailing summer wind; install the fan in the downward end.

When you are planning an attached greenhouse, make sure it doesn't interfere with anything on the face of the building to which it will be attached: doors, windows, a chimney, or the roof line of a one-story building. Cut a stick to the greenhouse ridge height, and hold it up against the building where the greenhouse will be installed to determine if any obstructions exist, and how they can be overcome.

If the ridge is too high, you can lower the greenhouse foundation and excavate inside for headroom, or you can increase the height of the greenhouse foundation, to raise the ridge over existing doors or windows. If a chimney is in the way, the depth of a lean-to can be extended with a "deck" of locally purchased lumber built around the obstruction.

If a really tricky installation seems likely, it is best to draw the outline of the greenhouse on the building face with chalk. You can also construct a framework outline of the greenhouse using 1-x-2-inch lumber held against the building to determine the exact location of the greenhouse.

If a workroom or potting shed is to be attached to the greenhouse, it should be located at the north or west end to provide protection for the greenhouse from cold winter winds.

Most municipalities require a building permit to install a greenhouse.

Assembling Your Greenhouse

Any competent do-it-yourselfer should be able to install a lean-to greenhouse without any trouble. You will need someone to help you, since some of the parts are ungainly or too heavy for one person to handle. You may also be able to do the masonry

work (if needed), the plumbing, and the electrical work. Greenhouses such as those by Lord and Burnham are prefabricated and offer the best in greenhouse design.

To speed assembly, check the shipping documents and the packing lists in each carton, to make sure all the parts are on hand before you start work. Open all the section packages, remove the parts, and sort them into like groups; open the gable packages and remove sills, corner and door casings, and sill anchors.

Obtain the proper tools before you start to work. In addition to the usual hand tools—hammer, screwdrivers, level, tape measure, etc.—a ratchet wrench with a 7/16-inch socket or an open-face or box wrench is required.

Figure 11-25 identifies nuts, bolts, and screws. Consolidate small hardware, nuts, bolts, and screws in small containers.

If you are building the type of greenhouse shown in Fig. 11-26 you will probably need a foundation and sills.

Foundation. When building the foundation, if there is a door in the greenhouse wall, leave a 2 inch ± drop in the footing for the door buck spreader. If this was not done, rest the bucks on the foundation. Determine if the bucks can be attached at the appropriate rafter holes without raising the rafter. If not, cut the bucks at the top for the proper connection. Cut back the glass over the door accordingly.

The normal wall height can be raised or lowered to suit your local conditions. If the wall is raised, increase the height of the doorsill an equal amount, and build a sloping ramp or steps as needed. You could also order longer door buck extrusions, and fabricate them to fit during construction. If the wall height is lowered, build an excavated areaway for the door or raise the door and frame and cut the glass lite over the door to fit. The door can be raised as much as 9 inches for lean-tos.

For a greenhouse attached to another building, determine the furthest projection on the building face in the area where the greenhouse is connected, and drop a plumb bob to establish the starting point for the construction of the masonry footing.

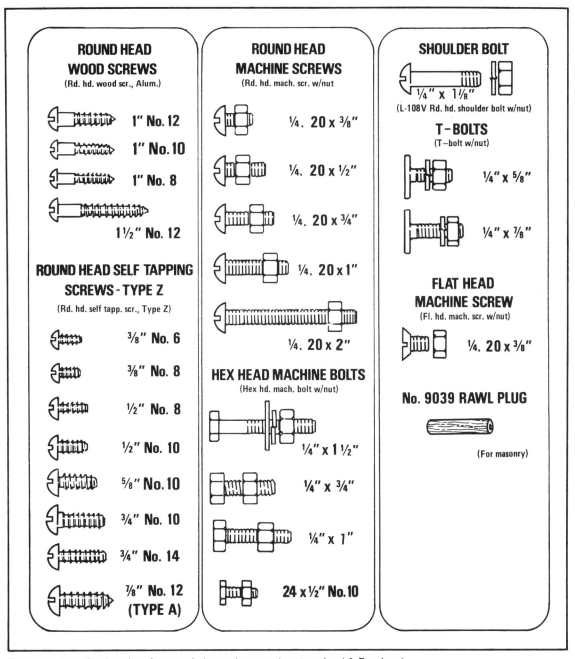

ROUND HEAD WOOD SCREWS
(Rd. hd. wood scr., Alum.)

1" No. 12
1" No. 10
1" No. 8
1½" No. 12

ROUND HEAD SELF TAPPING SCREWS - TYPE Z
(Rd. hd. self tapp. scr., Type Z)

⅜" No. 6
⅜" No. 8
½" No. 8
½" No. 10
⅝" No. 10
¾" No. 10
¾" No. 14
⅞" No. 12 (TYPE A)

ROUND HEAD MACHINE SCREWS
(Rd. hd. mach. scr. w/nut

¼. 20 x ⅜"
¼. 20 x ½"
¼. 20 x ¾"
¼. 20 x 1"
¼. 20 x 2"

HEX HEAD MACHINE BOLTS
(Hex hd. mach. bolt w/nut)

¼" x 1½"
¼" x ¾"
¼" x 1"
24 x ½" No. 10

SHOULDER BOLT

¼" x 1⅛"
(L-108V Rd. hd. shoulder bolt w/nut)

T-BOLTS
(T-bolt w/nut)

¼" x ⅝"
¼" x ⅞"

FLAT HEAD MACHINE SCREW
(Fl. hd. mach. scr. w/nut)

¼. 20 x ⅜"

No. 9039 RAWL PLUG

(For masonry)

Fig. 11-25. Identification chart for nuts, bolts, and screws (courtesy Lord & Burnham).

Your greenhouse can be erected on hollow concrete or cinder block, poured concrete, or brick foundation. The foundation should always rest on solid ground, with footings to below frost level. A depth of 36 inches is required in most areas but will vary depending on your location.

Lay out the rough trench dimension for the footing width and length. No concrete pouring will

Fig. 11-26. This lean-to greenhouse should have a foundation (courtesy Lord & Burnham).

be necessary in solid ground if the footing is dug with a narrow shovel. Wood boards are required if you have a sloping grade (Fig. 11-27). The top boards must be 1 inch above grade at the center of the door end of the greenhouse. The pouring boards should be 8 inches apart measured inside. Note that the width and length of the footing and trim inside faces the outer wood boards.

Foundation and wall details for a lean-to greenhouse are shown in Fig. 11-28. Foundation and wall details for a free-standing greenhouse are shown in Fig. 11-29.

Figure 11-30 shows that wood boards must be level the full length of the greenhouse, and level to each other. It is extremely important that the foundation be straight and square. Pour the footing and form in a continuous slot in the top of the concrete for the anchor bolts.

Nail short lengths of 1 × 3s across the wood boards, approximately 5 feet apart.

Installation of Sills. Accurate installation of the greenhouse sills is important. Place the sill on the wall, using wood block about 1-inch thick and shingle wedges for accurate leveling. Nail through 1-inch block on each side of the sill as shown in Fig. 11-31 to prevent movement of the sills while the greenhouse frame is being assembled and the glass installed. Make sure the aluminum sill is straight and level, with all corners at right angles.

Do not cement sills until the greenhouse is glazed; the nails through the 1-inch wood blocks will hold the frame in place, and allow for any required adjustment while glazing. Verify that the width between the sills is the same at the front, center, and back of the greenhouse.

Cementing the Sills. Glaze the greenhouse

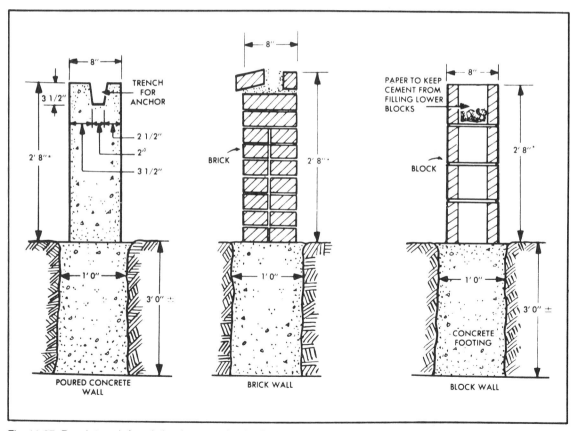

Fig. 11-27. Rough trench foundation (courtesy Lord & Burnham).

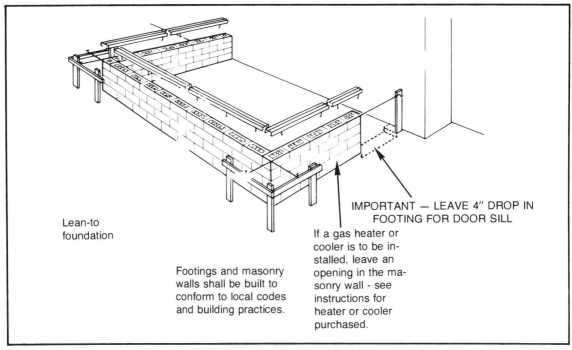

Lean-to foundation

Footings and masonry walls shall be built to conform to local codes and building practices.

IMPORTANT — LEAVE 4″ DROP IN FOOTING FOR DOOR SILL

If a gas heater or cooler is to be installed, leave an opening in the masonry wall - see instructions for heater or cooler purchased.

Fig. 11-28. A foundation for a lean-to greenhouse (courtesy Lord & Burnham).

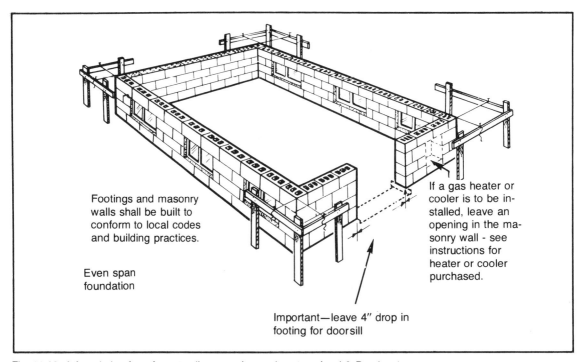

Footings and masonry walls shall be built to conform to local codes and building practices.

Even span foundation

Important—leave 4″ drop in footing for doorsill

If a gas heater or cooler is to be installed, leave an opening in the masonry wall - see instructions for heater or cooler purchased.

Fig. 11-29. A foundation for a free-standing greenhouse (courtesy Lord & Burnham).

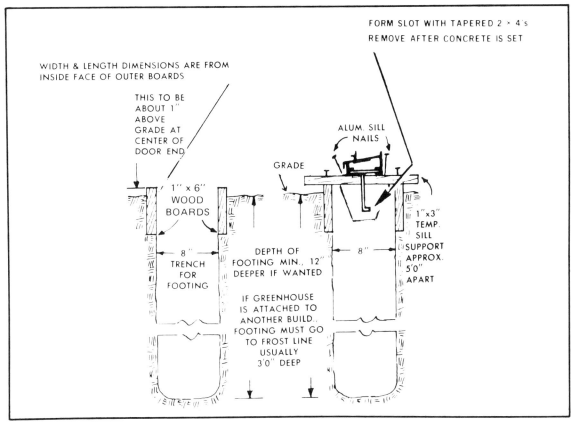

WIDTH & LENGTH DIMENSIONS ARE FROM
INSIDE FACE OF OUTER BOARDS

THIS TO BE
ABOUT 1"
ABOVE
GRADE AT
CENTER OF
DOOR END

ALUM. SILL
NAILS

GRADE

1" × 6"
WOOD
BOARDS

8"
TRENCH
FOR
FOOTING

DEPTH OF
FOOTING MIN., 12"
DEEPER IF WANTED

1"×3"
TEMP.
SILL
SUPPORT
APPROX.
5'0"
APART

8"

IF GREENHOUSE
IS ATTACHED TO
ANOTHER BUILD.,
FOOTING MUST GO
TO FROST LINE
USUALLY
3'0" DEEP

Fig. 11-30. Wood boards must be level (courtesy Lord & Burnham).

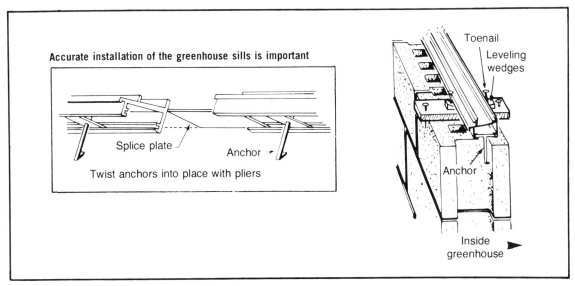

Accurate installation of the greenhouse sills is important

Splice plate

Anchor

Twist anchors into place with pliers

Toenail

Leveling
wedges

Anchor

Inside
greenhouse

Fig. 11-31. Installation of sills (courtesy Lord & Burnham).

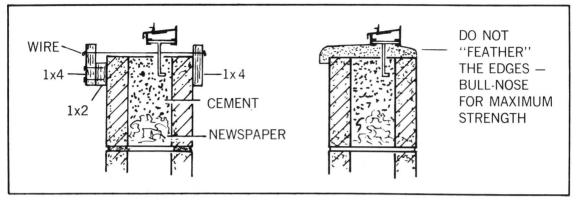

WIRE
1x4
1x2
1 x 4
CEMENT
NEWSPAPER

DO NOT "FEATHER" THE EDGES — BULL-NOSE FOR MAXIMUM STRENGTH

Fig. 11-32. Cement in sill anchors (courtesy Lord & Burnham).

before cementing the sills since the glass will square up the framework.

☐ Cement in the sill anchors. For a hollow block wall, stuff newspapers below the anchors to avoid excess use of cement (Fig. 11-32).

☐ Before cementing the sills, check again to make sure they are square and level. Stretch a taut cord along the sills from end to end to make sure they are straight.

☐ Remove the wood leveling blocks and cement in the sills (Fig. 11-33).

☐ Work the grout well up under the sills. Do not finish with a feather edge, but leave a well-rounded thickness of cement to prevent chipping. Do not work the exposed grout higher than the bottom edge of the sill both front and back. A slate or stone cap can be used instead of concrete grout.

☐ Allow the sill anchors to set for 24 hours before removing the leveling blocks and proceeding with grouting.

Framing. Set the sills on 1 × 2s on top of the wall. Level and square up to check the accuracy of the wall. Measure from the underside of the sill to establish the top line of 2 × 8 joist (Fig. 11-34).

Attach a 2 × 8 joist along the line you just determined. Check with a spirit level to make sure the joist is level. Shim 3/8 inches behind the 2 × 8 as needed. Use lag screws on wood clapboard surfaces, toggle bolts on block walls, and expansion bolts on brick or stone walls.

For a lean-to with two ends the length of the 2 × 8 is the length of the masonry wall less 7 3/4 inches. For a lean-to with one end, the 2 × 8 is as long as the masonry wall less 3 7/8 inches. Note: 2

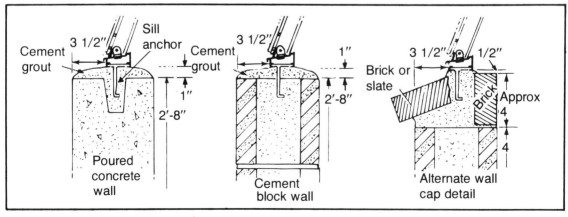

Fig. 11-33. Cemented sills (courtesy Lord & Burnham).

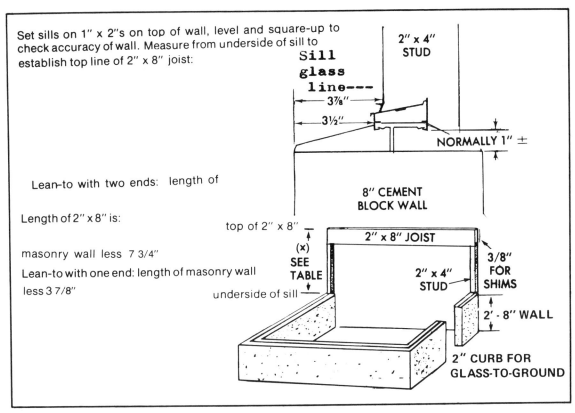

Set sills on 1" x 2"s on top of wall, level and square-up to check accuracy of wall. Measure from underside of sill to establish top line of 2" x 8" joist:

Sill glass line---

3⅞"

3½"

2" x 4" STUD

NORMALLY 1" ±

8" CEMENT BLOCK WALL

Lean-to with two ends: length of

Length of 2" x 8" is:

masonry wall less 7 3/4"

Lean-to with one end: length of masonry wall less 3 7/8"

top of 2" x 8"

(x) SEE TABLE

underside of sill

2" x 8" JOIST

3/8" FOR SHIMS

2" x 4" STUD

2' - 8" WALL

2" CURB FOR GLASS-TO-GROUND

Fig. 11-34. Framing for a lean-to (courtesy Lord & Burnham).

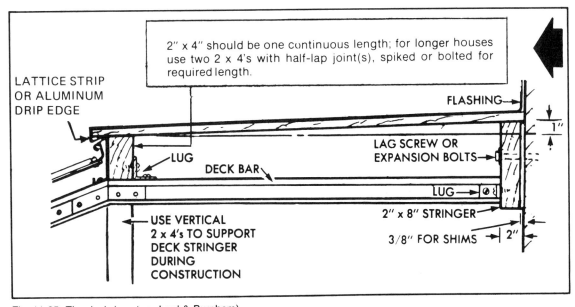

2" x 4" should be one continuous length; for longer houses use two 2 x 4's with half-lap joint(s), spiked or bolted for required length.

LATTICE STRIP OR ALUMINUM DRIP EDGE

FLASHING

1"

LUG

DECK BAR

LAG SCREW OR EXPANSION BOLTS

LUG

USE VERTICAL 2 x 4's TO SUPPORT DECK STRINGER DURING CONSTRUCTION

2" x 8" STRINGER

3/8" FOR SHIMS

2"

Fig. 11-35. The deck (courtesy Lord & Burnham).

× 4 studs could be cut to fit tightly between the masonry wall top and the 2-×-8 joist underside. Install only with the superstructure in a plumb position and the sill square and level. The studs can also be installed after glazing. Hold the outside edge flush with the sill glass line.

The Deck. The deck is built after the lean-to's aluminum frame is up (Fig. 11-35). Before building the deck, glaze at least one section at each end, so the glass will square up on the aluminum framework. If the lean-to is attached at one end, scribe and flash it to the existing building before you install the glass at the attached end.

Stretch a taut string end to end of the ridge to make sure it is level; adjust the deck bars against the 2 × 8 as necessary. Do not get up on the greenhouse roof when building the deck or to glaze the roof. Figures 11-36 through 11-38 give suggested details for extending the lean-to.

Glazing. Until your greenhouse is installed, the framework will not be completely rigid. If the first few panes, or lites, of glass do not fit correctly, rock the framework slightly until the glass squares itself in the openings.

The roof sash is glazed with vinyl "U" plastic channel on the top and both sides. Apply the plastic in one continuous piece to cover all three edges. Cut off the excess "bulge" at the two top corners with sharp scissors. Vinyl "U" shaped plastic channel is also used on the top edge only of the side glass where it fits into the eave and on the outer edge of the gable glass where it fits into the groove in the end rafter.

Glass for the sides, roof, and gable section is glazed with plastic foam tape to bed the glass and a top bead of compound. Apply the plastic foam tape to the glazing shoulder of the bars with the paper side up. Do not remove the paper or plastic back-

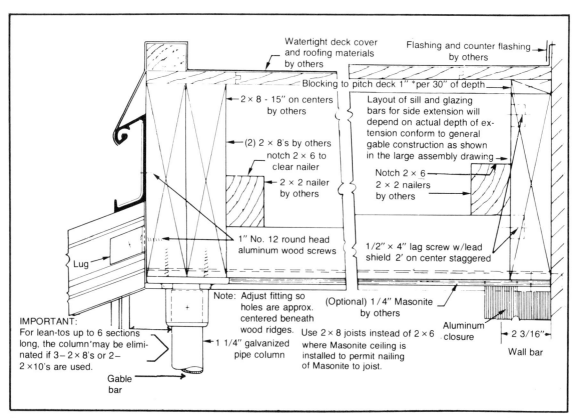

Fig. 11-36. The section through the deck at the gable rafter (courtesy Lord & Burnham).

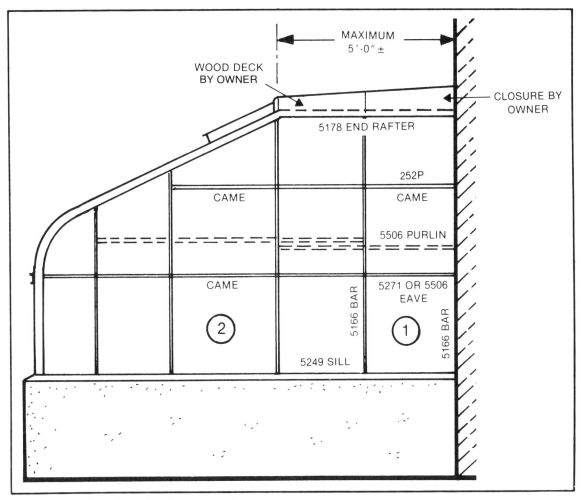

Fig. 11-37. A typical gable extension (courtesy Lord & Burnham).

ing; it provides a smooth surface on which the glass can slide to facilitate installation.

General glazing instructions are shown in Fig. 11-39. Install the vent glass first, then the roof, sides, and gables, in order. Attach the barcap as you go to keep the glass in place.

Flashing. If you plan to attach your greenhouse to your remodeled house, the glass opening next to the attached end should be glazed until the flashing work has been completed. A space of approximately 3 inches should be left between the last glazing bar in the greenhouse and the building.

Scribing boards and flashing to fill this space and form a support for the flashing materials should be made from 1 1/4 inches of 1-×-5-inch redwood or treated lumber. Cut the scribing boards as closely as possible to conform with the surface of the building. Attach them to the short lengths of lumber to act as blocking around the curve. Use angle lugs to connect them to the building.

Use flashing and counterflashing according to the suggested methods shown in Fig. 11-40. Flashing is attached to the scribing material. Counterflashing must extend up into material on the building and also cover a portion of the flashing. On clapboards or shingles, found especially on older homes, it can be pushed under the overlap. On brick or stucco, if your house is relatively new, some of

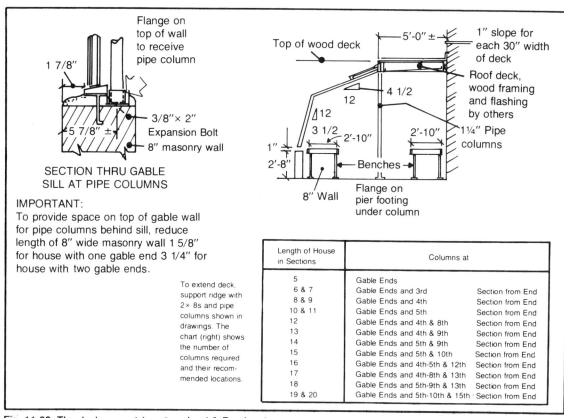

Flange on top of wall to receive pipe column

1 7/8"

3/8" × 2" Expansion Bolt
5 7/8" ±
8" masonry wall

SECTION THRU GABLE SILL AT PIPE COLUMNS

IMPORTANT:
To provide space on top of gable wall for pipe columns behind sill, reduce length of 8" wide masonry wall 1 5/8" for house with one gable end 3 1/4" for house with two gable ends.

To extend deck, support ridge with 2× 8s and pipe columns shown in drawings. The chart (right) shows the number of columns required and their recommended locations.

Top of wood deck

5'-0" ±
1" slope for each 30" width of deck
Roof deck, wood framing and flashing by others
4 1/2
12
12
3 1/2
2'-10"
2'-10"
1¼" Pipe columns
1"
2'-8"
Benches
8" Wall
Flange on pier footing under column

Length of House in Sections	Columns at	
5	Gable Ends	
6 & 7	Gable Ends and 3rd	Section from End
8 & 9	Gable Ends and 4th	Section from End
10 & 11	Gable Ends and 5th	Section from End
12	Gable Ends and 4th & 8th	Section from End
13	Gable Ends and 4th & 9th	Section from End
14	Gable Ends and 5th & 9th	Section from End
15	Gable Ends and 5th & 10th	Section from End
16	Gable Ends and 4th-5th & 12th	Section from End
17	Gable Ends and 4th-8th & 13th	Section from End
18	Gable Ends and 5th-9th & 13th	Section from End
19 & 20	Gable Ends and 5th-10th & 15th	Section from End

Fig. 11-38. The deck support (courtesy Lord & Burnham).

the masonry must be cut away and counterflashing notched into the side of the building. In this situation, a good caulking material should be used to seal the counterflashing in the wall crevice (Fig. 11-41).

Doors. Attach the door to the greenhouse by screwing the hinges in a straight line to make sure the door will open easily. Figure 11-42 shows a typical standard glass door for greenhouses.

The following steps outline the installation of a glass door; however, they are adaptable to any type of material being used (Figs. 11-43 through 11-45).

☐ Attach the gable purlin with T-bolts and lock washers. Leave two bolts loose for adjustments.

☐ Attach the door head buck to the angle purlin with 3 T-bolts and lock washers. At the center T-bolt attach the door chain lug so you can later attach the door chain.

☐ Adjust the angle purlin and door head buck

so that the centerline of the screw slot in the buck is 3 feet 9 3/32 inches from the glass set on the sill. Tighten the T-bolts.

☐ Hold the door in the Z-frame up to the bucks; make sure the door is plumb and square. Drill 5/32-inch holes into the door buck where, and if, they appear in the door frame.

☐ Remove the screws holding the door to the Z-bar. Some doors have rivets that can be removed after the door and frame are connected to the door bucks. Use a putty blade to cut the rivets.

☐ Use #10 roundhead self-tapping screws to attach the door frame to the buck.

Installing Door Chain. Attach the door chain (spring end with lug) to the door head at the prepunched holes with self-tapping screws. On doors having two sets of holes from which to choose select the holes furthest from the hinge side.

Hook the other end of the chain to the lug with

338

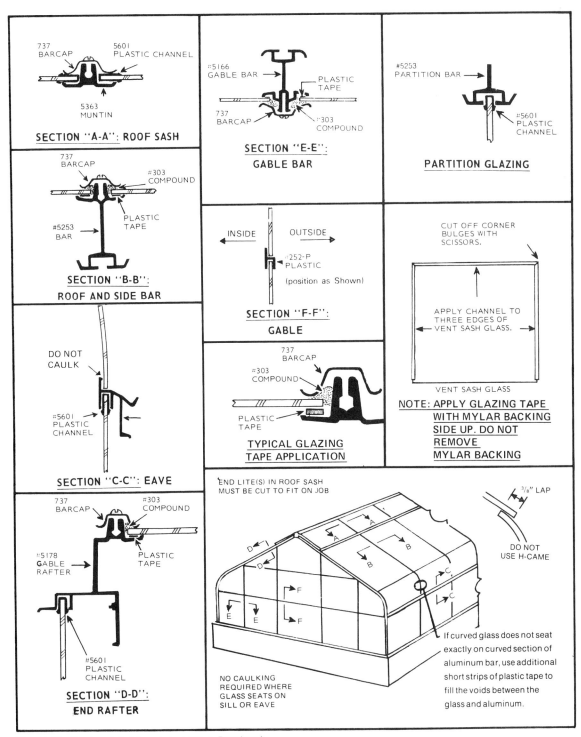

SECTION "A-A": ROOF SASH
- 737 BARCAP
- 5601 PLASTIC CHANNEL
- 5363 MUNTIN

SECTION "B-B": ROOF AND SIDE BAR
- 737 BARCAP
- #303 COMPOUND
- PLASTIC TAPE
- #5253 BAR

SECTION "C-C": EAVE
- DO NOT CAULK
- #5601 PLASTIC CHANNEL

SECTION "D-D": END RAFTER
- 737 BARCAP
- #303 COMPOUND
- #5178 GABLE RAFTER
- PLASTIC TAPE
- #5601 PLASTIC CHANNEL

SECTION "E-E": GABLE BAR
- #5166 GABLE BAR
- PLASTIC TAPE
- 737 BARCAP
- #303 COMPOUND

SECTION "F-F": GABLE
- INSIDE
- OUTSIDE
- #252-P PLASTIC
- (position as Shown)

TYPICAL GLAZING TAPE APPLICATION
- 737 BARCAP
- #303 COMPOUND
- PLASTIC TAPE

PARTITION GLAZING
- #5253 PARTITION BAR
- #5601 PLASTIC CHANNEL

CUT OFF CORNER BULGES WITH SCISSORS.

APPLY CHANNEL TO THREE EDGES OF VENT SASH GLASS.

VENT SASH GLASS

NOTE: APPLY GLAZING TAPE WITH MYLAR BACKING SIDE UP. DO NOT REMOVE MYLAR BACKING

END LITE(S) IN ROOF SASH MUST BE CUT TO FIT ON JOB

3/8" LAP

DO NOT USE H-CAME

NO CAULKING REQUIRED WHERE GLASS SEATS ON SILL OR EAVE

If curved glass does not seat exactly on curved section of aluminum bar, use additional short strips of plastic tape to fill the voids between the glass and aluminum.

Fig. 11-39. Glazing detail (courtesy Lord & Burnham).

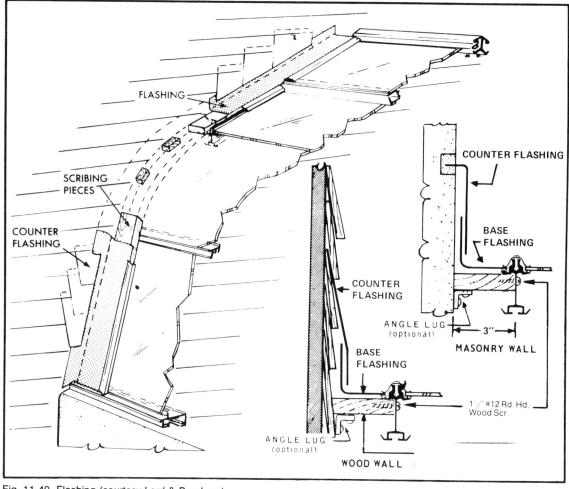

Fig. 11-40. Flashing (courtesy Lord & Burnham).

the S-hook already attached to the angle purlin. Attach the small "hold-up" spring at the door's top corner on the hinge side with a self-tapping screw and a 3/16-inch flat washer. Close the door, allowing the chain to hang vertically, and thread the chain's lowest link into the end of the spring (Fig. 11-46).

THE KITCHEN

A kitchen features specific areas for eating and working. It is also the most widely used room in the house by all members of the family. Most importantly for the homemaker, it is a room that must be arranged, not only for individual comfort during the working hours spent there, but also for the most efficiency for all household members.

There are two main areas in the suggested plan in Fig. 11-47: a kitchen area with dining space for family meals and a workroom area.

Kitchen and workroom are separated by a storage island. On the kitchen side, the island is made up of a wall refrigerator, counter, and base cabinets. On the workroom side of the island are a planning desk and shelves.

The broken "U" arrangement used for the kitchen equipment is both efficient and convenient. The break in the U between the range and refrigerator allows step-saving access to the work-

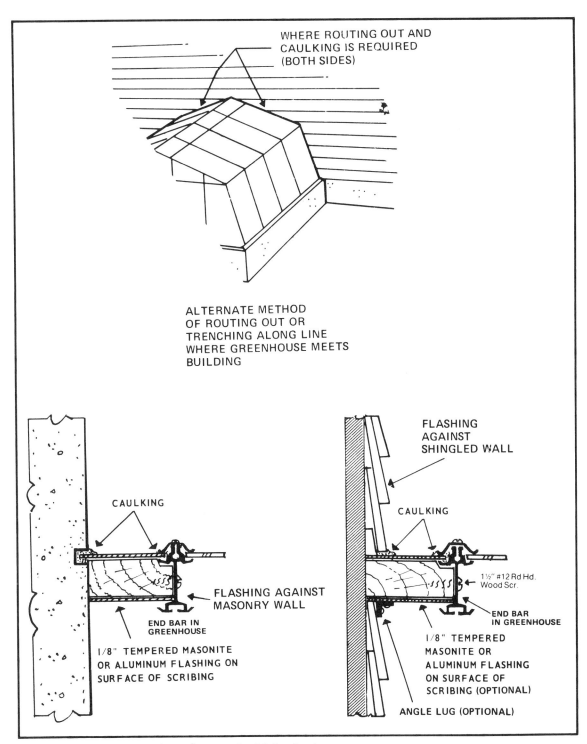

WHERE ROUTING OUT AND
CAULKING IS REQUIRED
(BOTH SIDES)

ALTERNATE METHOD
OF ROUTING OUT OR
TRENCHING ALONG LINE
WHERE GREENHOUSE MEETS
BUILDING

CAULKING

FLASHING AGAINST
MASONRY WALL

END BAR IN
GREENHOUSE

1/8" TEMPERED MASONITE
OR ALUMINUM FLASHING ON
SURFACE OF SCRIBING

FLASHING
AGAINST
SHINGLED WALL

CAULKING

1½" #12 Rd Hd.
Wood Scr.

END BAR
IN GREENHOUSE

1/8" TEMPERED
MASONITE OR
ALUMINUM FLASHING
ON SURFACE OF
SCRIBING (OPTIONAL)

ANGLE LUG (OPTIONAL)

Fig. 11-41. Caulking the greenhouse (courtesy Lord & Burnham).

341

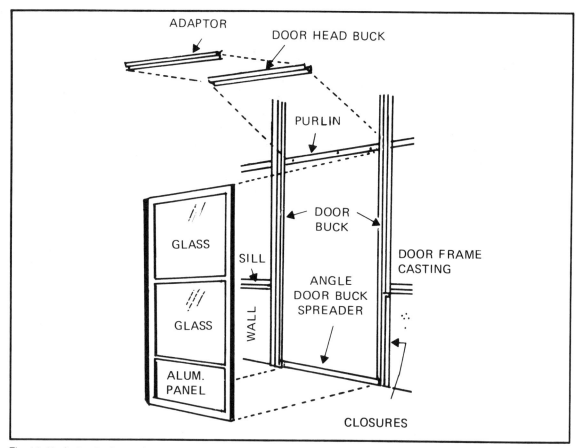

Fig. 11-42. A standard greenhouse door (courtesy Lord & Burnham).

room and dining room. The dining center has eating space for six.

The workroom includes—in addition to the desk and shelves in the island—laundry facilities, pantry, freezer, cleaning closet, and ironing closet. Workroom floor space is adequate for the varied activities carried on in this area. Small children can play safely in the end of the workroom near the dining center, within sight and hearing of the mother as she works in either area.

Perforated hardboard at each work counter provides a place to hang tools and utensils that are used often. At both the mixer counter and the sink undercounter, knee space is provided so that the homemaker can sit comfortably. An adjustable posture chair is planned as part of the kitchen equipment.

To minimize pulling and pushing doors and drawers, the dish cabinet has an accordion-type door, which can be left open without being in the way. The door of the circular supply cupboard is attached to the shelves and revolves with them. Drawers and sliding shelves can be pulled easily even when heavily loaded because they are on nylon rollers.

Light and Air

In this plan, a broad window over the sink and the counters on either side and a picture window in the dining center provides adequate daylight and ventilation.

Fluorescent ceiling fitures have been used to ensure well-lighted work areas. They are placed so

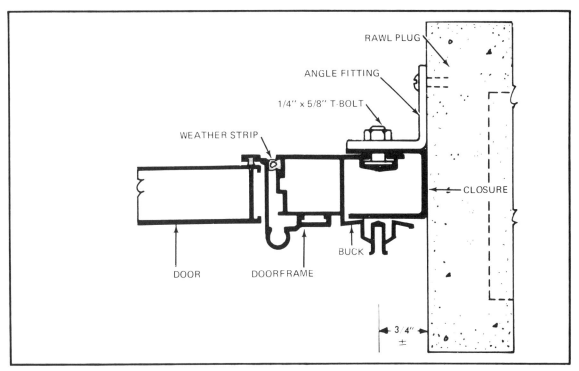

Fig. 11-43. The top view of the buck against the wall (courtesy Lord & Burnham).

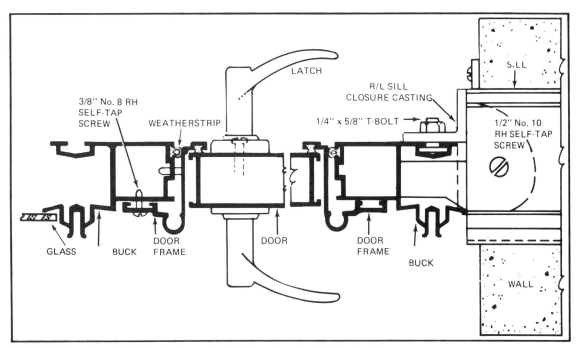

Fig. 11-44. Top view of the door buck next to latch (courtesy Lord & Burnham).

that there are no shadows on the counters. The dining table is lighted with an incandescent ceiling fixture that can be adjusted in height to provide good light for eating, studying, or sewing. The light fixture at the planning desk can be adjusted.

A ventilating fan is located in the ceiling over the ranges; however, a ventilating hood could well be installed here instead. There is space for a room

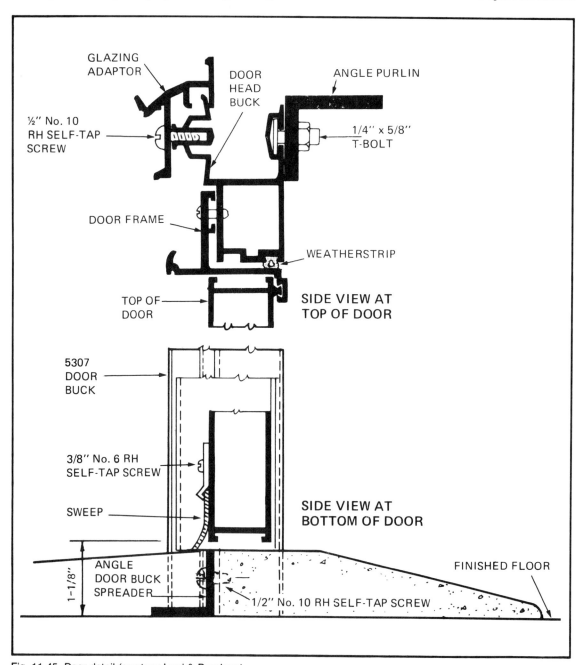

Fig. 11-45. Door detail (courtesy Lord & Burnham).

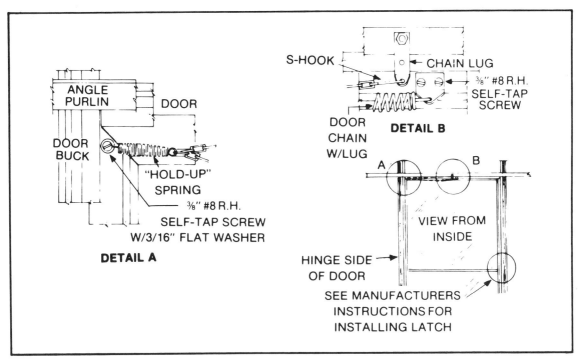

Fig. 11-46. Installing the door chain (courtesy Lord & Burnham).

air conditioner above the dish-storage cabinet in the dining center if your remodeled house is not entirely air-conditioned.

Mix Center

The counter to the right of the sink in this plan is planned for mixing jobs. There is knee space under the right part of the counter so the homemaker can sit to work if necessary. An adjustable posture chair can be stored under this counter.

In this suggested plan, whether you sit or stand to work you can reach all the supplies, tools, and utensils you need for mixing jobs without stooping or stretching.

Bins for flour and sugar are at the back of the counter. Holders for wax paper and aluminum foil are built in above the bins.

To the left of the bins is the storage compartment for the hand or table mixer. The door to this compartment folds back out of the way when it is open. An electrical outlet is located on the left wall of the compartment.

Small tools used at this counter are stored either on a perforated hardboard to the right or in drawers in the base cabinet.

All other supplies and baking pans used at this center are in the revolving corner cabinet. Shelves in this cabinet are sized and spaced so that everything stored here can be seen easily. Only kettles that are not used often are stored on the bottom shelf.

A pull-out board may be placed in one of three positions under the mix counter to provide a lower surface for some mixing jobs. With the board placed in its lowest position you can sit here to work in a comfortable straight chair. The board in the lowest position also makes a convenient working surface for children and a handy table for serving them snacks.

The Sink Center

The sink center consists of a double sink, a counter at the left with a dishwasher below, storage compartments at the counter level, and a trash bin

345

beneath the right sink bowl.

This center is located so that it is convenient to the dining center; the drawers below are a part of the storage for that center.

The homemaker can sit to work at the left sink bowl. This bowl is only 3 1/2 inches deep and has the drain set back of center, an arrangement that leaves sufficient knee space underneath. An adjustable posture chair can easily be rolled to the sink from its storage space under the mix counter.

By doing at one time all food preparation that is best done at the sink, you can sit for long enough periods to justify positioning the adjustable posture chair. This arrangement is ideal for many people who have bad backs or other physical handicaps. Onions and potatoes can be stored in ventilated bins at the back of the left counter. Saucepans used for cooking vegetables can be hung on perforated hardboard at the left of the counter. Every other tool you need for food preparation done at the sink is at your fingertips.

The trash container, which is a deep drawer at the bottom of the base cabinet under the right sink bowl, is mounted on ball-bearing casters so that it can be rolled out for emptying. It has a removable metal liner. The trash chute can also connect with a container in your basement.

Dishwashing and Refrigeration Center

In this suggested plan, the three-door refrigerator/freezer has been placed in a central location convenient to the other kitchen centers. The top shelf is about 62 inches from the floor.

There is a base cabinet which has storage

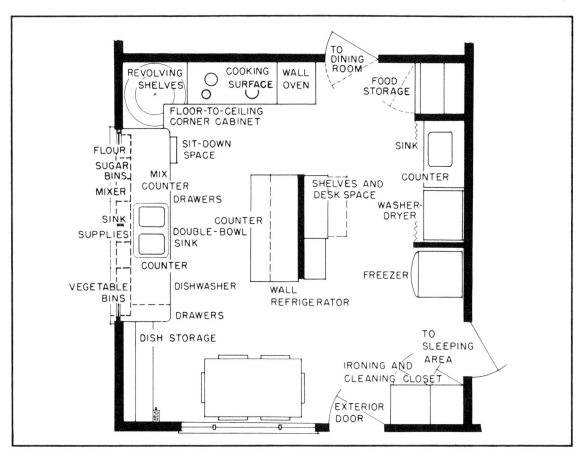

Fig. 11-47. Plan suggestion for a well-organized kitchen (courtesy USDA).

space and a drop-leaf serving cart, but an alternative arrangement would be to use a conventional refrigerator for this same center.

Range Center

The range center, to the right of the corner storage cabinet, is only a few steps from the mix counter. Directly to the right of the surface cooking top is the wall oven. Utensils used daily are hung on perforated headboard at each end of the cooking top, while others are stored in the drawers and on pull-out shelves under the cooking top.

Serving dishes are stored in the part of the cabinet above the oven that opens from the front. The back part of this cabinet, which opens at the side, provides space for extra large platters and trays.

Dining Center

A picture window in the dining center helps make this a pleasant place for meals.

Besides the combination dish-storage cabinet and serving center, an accordion-fold door can be opened with a single motion. China and glassware are stored on adjustable shelves in the top part of the cabinet. The base of the cabinet has a serving counter, drawers for silver, pull-out shelves for table linen, and a pull-out shelf for small table appliances.

It has many conveniences plus a swivel chair for the hostess, which makes it easier for her to turn to the serving counter and back to the table.

Laundry Center

The laundry center is placed conveniently near

Fig. 11-48. Potters Touch beautifies kitchen countertops (courtesy Tile Council of America).

347

Fig. 11-49. Parchment tiles on walls and countertops (courtesy Summitville Tiles).

the kitchen work centers so that if you are busy with laundry you can easily keep track of kitchen activities.

A washer/dryer, sink and counter, and shelves make up this compact center. Shelves hold laundry supplies and vases. Basswood folding doors screen the area when it is not in use.

Planning and Food Storage Centers

A drop-down desk, shelves, and comfortable chair comprise the planning center.

The food pantry to the left of the laundry center provides storage for canned goods, freezing and canning supplies and equipment, and extra household supplies.

Nine rows of canned food can be stored on shelves on the closet door. Each shelf is 5 inches

deep and is tilted up slightly at the front. A heavy caster helps support the weight of the loaded door.

Tile a Counter

Ceramic tile countertops make beautiful sense. Hot pots won't burn them; they are truly wash and wear, and they never need waxing (Figs. 11-48 through 11-50). Tile can be installed over most materials usually found on a countertop, including plastic laminates, ceramic tile, and, of course, the plywood support for a new counter.

For a new countertop installation, use 3/4-inch exterior-type-plywood. Cross braces may be needed. To be sure, check with your tile dealer. Whether the counter surface to be tiled is new or old, make sure that it is clean and smooth.

Before you tile, decide how you will treat the

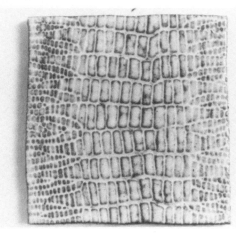

Fig. 11-50. Unusual tile designs feature burlap and reptile offered in 4″ × 8″ 1/4″ size in bone and sable. Historical Coins group productions of the world's most significant coins. 8″ × 8″ × 3/8″ ceramic tiles in bronze and pewter colors from Summitville Tiles (courtesy Tile Council of America).

countertop edge. Ceramic trim pieces that match the counter tiles are your best bet because they will give you a neat, professional tiling job as well as easier care and longer wear than any other type of trim. Most American tile manufacturers produce trim pieces to go with their countertop tile designs, but imported products hardly ever have these important items. Figure 11-51 shows three ways to trim countertops.

The Sink

To many do-it-yourselfers, the sink seems to pose a puzzle, but it needn't be if you let common sense prevail. In a new countertop installation, leave out the sink until the top is tiled. If you are remodeling your countertop, the sink must come out.

Today, most sinks are self-rimmed and lift out without a hassle. If your sink proves stubborn, call a plumber. A tiled counter is such a good improvement that the extra expense is more than justified. The tiles are cut to fit around the sink opening, and the sink, or the metal trim that attaches to the counter, rests on top of the cut tiles, covering the raw edges.

Lay out tiles in the most pleasing way with the

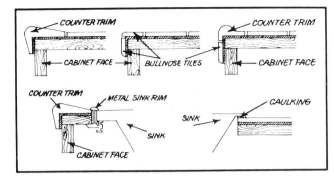

Fig. 11-51. Three ways to trim countertops (courtesy Tile Council of America).

least amount of cut tiles. Work from the front to the back, so that any cut tiles will fall where they are least noticeable. If you are tiling a counter without a sink, your starting point is the center. Measure the counter from end to end, find the center, draw a line, and lay out the tile along it, allowing for grout lines if your tiles don't feature self-spacers.

As you lay the tile up the edges, you will see what kind of cuts will need to be made. If any tiles must be cut to less than half their width, go back and shift the original lines to remedy the situation. Take your time to shift tiles around until you have arrived at a layout you like.

If you are tiling a countertop with a sink, work from the center of the sink toward the end of the countertop. Again, lay out the tile loose to arrive at the best-looking arrangement and the least amount of cuts.

Once you are happy with the layout, you can begin to tile. On a countertop first install the trim pieces along the front edges. Next, put in sink edge

tiles, corners, and other special pieces. Once the trim pieces are in place, you can move the countertop's tiles about without losing the layout. Throughout the installation, lay your carpenter's square across the top of the tiles to make sure that both courses are straight and true (Fig. 11-52). To make sure tiles are firmly set, slide a flat board across the surface while tapping it with a hammer.

Better Kitchen Storage

There are five keys to good storage:

—Weed out and sort items. Discard, or store in some other place, the seldom-used and duplicate items.

—Store the items you use most within easy reach. Make use of storage space between eye and hip level first since this height is the easiest to reach. Store heavy and awkward things at waist level or below.

—Stack like articles only. Do not put small plates on larger ones or bowls on top of pie pans, or you will have to shuffle the whole stack to get the

Fig. 11-52. Use a carpenter's square to true up tiles (courtesy Tile Council of America).

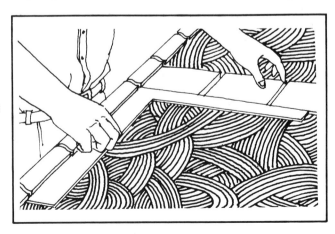

one on the bottom. Place only like articles behind each other.

—Store items at the point of first use. Utensils and foods used together should be stored together. Store the coffee maker near the sink where it is first filled with water. The coffee, a measuring spoon, and measuring cup should also be stored in the sink area.

—Plan for duplicate items which are frequently used in two places. Store flour near the range and also at your mixing center. Keep some seasonings near the range and duplicates with your foods used in baking.

Plan space to fit the items. Store supplies so that they are easy to grasp. Small food packages should be on narrow shelves, one row down, not one behind the other. Small items such as measuring spoons can be hung; knives should be stored to protect their cutting edge and your fingers.

Group supplies into work areas. To help you store utensils and supplies conveniently, think of your kitchen as three work centers. Although the work in these centers overlaps, place items where you use them most often.

Utensils stored in the mixing center include bowls, mixer, egg beater, knives and spatulas, measuring cups and spoons, casseroles, baking pans, flour sifter, and rolling pin. Supplies stored here are: flour, baking powder, cooking fats, seasonings, sugar, chocolate, cornstarch, prepared mix, nut meats, and gelatin.

Utensils stored in the cooking and serving center are: bread box, serving dishes, platters, cooking forks, frying pans, knives, spatulas, measuring cups and spoons, pot lids, tea kettle, teapot, cooling racks, griddle, meat slicing board, pressure cooker, roaster, and tongs. Supplies stored here include: breakfast cereals, flour, seasonings, pot holders, and vegetable fat.

Utensils stored in the cleanup center include: coffee maker, cutting board, towel racks, dishpan, knives, saucepans, shears, sink strainer, waste basket, can opener, and colander. Supplies stored here are: brushes, cleansers, dish towels, paper towels, scouring pads, soap or detergent, and everyday dishes.

Space under the sink is often wasted because of the location of water pipes. Following are suggestions for ways to make this area more useful (Fig. 11-53).

—Extension towel bars can be attached to the side of the cabinet, or a stationary rod can be fastened to the inside of the door.

—A rack made from wood can be attached to the inside of the door. Plastic and metal racks are available in discount stores. some also have a rod for hanging a dishcloth.

—A wastebasket can be attached to the door. Make sure it will clear the sides of the opening when the door swings shut.

—Stackable plastic bins for potatoes and onions are available in many different colors. You can also make wooden bins, but be sure to allow for ventilation.

—One or more wooden step shelves can be fitted around the pipes to give storage for cleaners, empty bottles, tool kit, etc.

—Portable vertical dividers can be used also for drain racks, wash basins, and flat items.

Shelf Storage

Most kitchen cabinets have shelves so far apart that several inches of space are wasted. You can correct this problem easily and inexpensively if you are remodeling.

When dividers are attached to fixed shelves, use cleats of plywood, wood stripping, quarter round screws or eyelet screws to hold them in place (Fig. 11-54).

Step Shelves. Step shelves are built on legs and are not attached to the cabinet. They are usually narrow, about half the width of the cabinet, or planned according to the size of articles to be stored. If the shelf is made shorter than the height of the cabinet, you can allow space to store a tall pitcher or other item.

One-step shelf can be placed on another in some cabinets where height permits. The top shelf is usually narrower so that articles below can be easily removed (Fig. 11-55).

Permanent Shelves. You can add permanent shelves, which are usually half the width of existing shelves by one of the following methods:

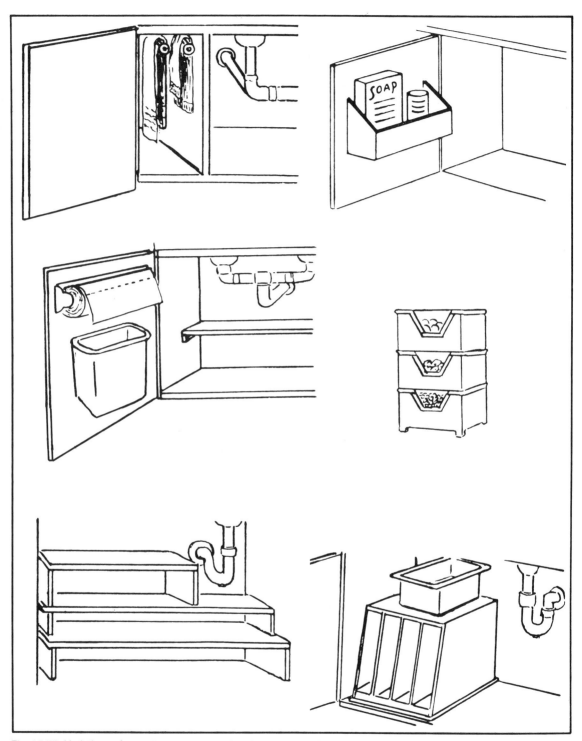

Fig. 11-53. Variations of ways to use space under sink (courtesy University of Florida Extension Service).

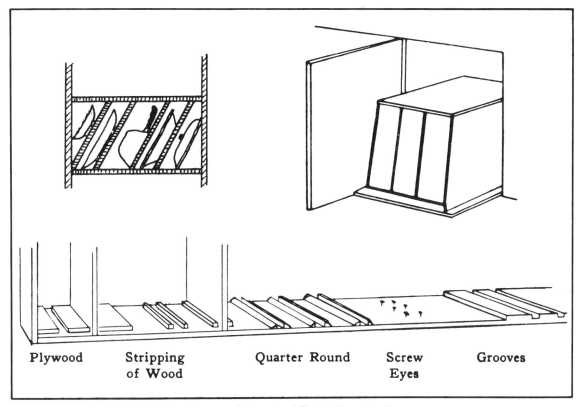

Fig. 11-54. Variations of shelf dividers (courtesy University of Florida Extension Service).

—Metal stripping is used when dividing large storage areas. It is sturdy, dependable, but more expensive than other methods. Metal stripping allows you to adjust shelves (Fig. 11-56).

—Cleats of wood attached to the sides of the storage area will support shelves. Shelf positions can be changed by adding cleats. This method requires strong side supports for the storage area.

—Metal brackets or sections of doweling may be inserted into parallel holes drilled into the sides of the storage area. A series of holes drilled 1 to 2 inches apart make it possible to change the position

Fig. 11-55. Shelves too far apart (courtesy University of Florida Extension Service).

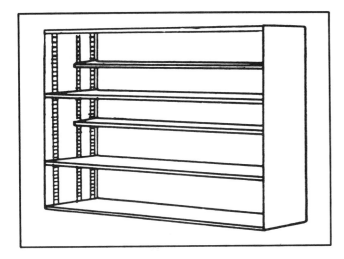

Fig. 11-56. Add permanent shelves (courtesy University of Florida Extension Service).

of the shelves. This is an inexpensive means of providing adjustable shelves (Fig. 11-57).

Vertical Dividers. File-type storage is very efficient for storing odd-shaped equipment in high or low places. Vertical dividers provide clear visibility and quick accessibility.

Make portable dividers by building a boxlike section to fit between permanent shelves. This structure can be easily moved for use elsewhere. In addition, portable dividers do not need to be the height of the permanent shelves; you can allow room for a flat article to rest on top.

Deep Cabinets. You need some deep stor-

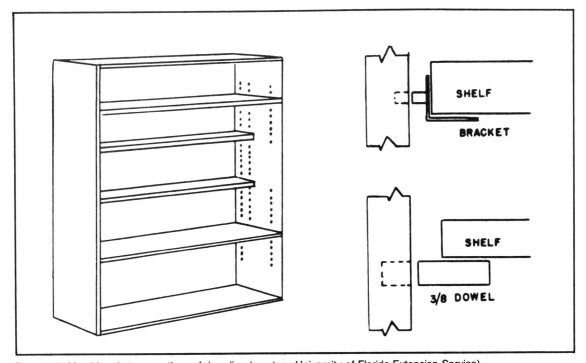

Fig. 11-57. Metal brackets or sections of doweling (courtesy University of Florida Extension Service).

age, but often base cabinets 24 inches deep provide more depth than is required in proportion to the size of the items stored.

On deep shelves keep items such as large kettles, a Dutch oven, and long-handled pans with handles extending outward because these items will probably not allow room for others to get lost behind them. To use the rest of the deep space, consider the following devices (Figs. 11-58 and 11-59):

—Sliding shelves. Particularly suited for lower areas, a sliding shelf brings all items out where you can see them and conveniently remove

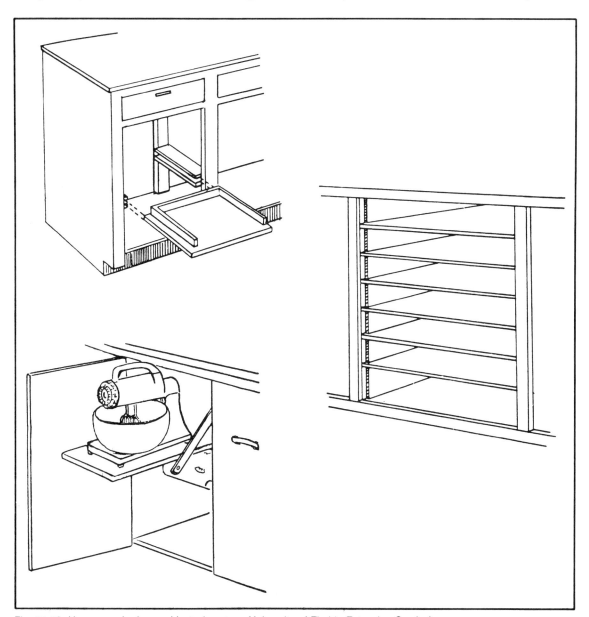

Fig. 11-58. Use space in deep cabinets (courtesy University of Florida Extension Service).

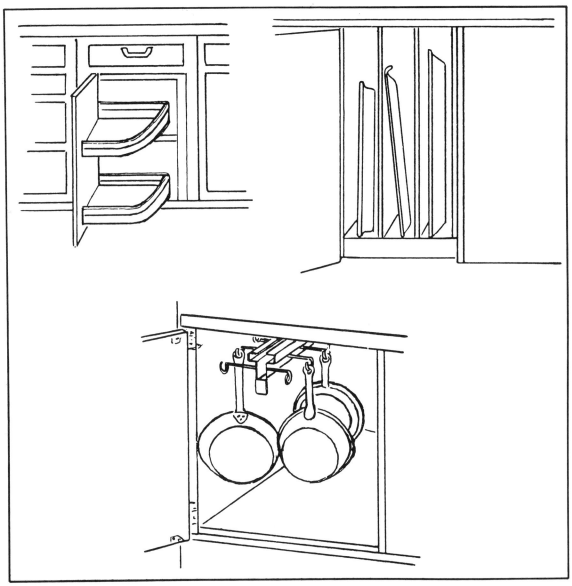

Fig. 11-59. Cabinet storage ideas (courtesy University of Florida Extension Service).

them. A guard may be used to keep articles from sliding off the back and sides of the tray. Two or more sliding shelves can be used in a base cabinet.

—Linen trays. Deep cabinets can be equipped with several sliding sheets of plywood supported by metal stripping or cleats. They are convenient for linen storage.

—Shelf for electric mixer. An electric mixer may be stored on a shelf which pulls out and upward when ready for use. Hardware for this type of shelf is available through many lumber companies. The center shelf of an existing cabinet must be removed before making this installation.

—Tray storage. Sections of base cabinets can be used for tray and platter storage by adding vertical dividers. If the dividers are high enough, some flat electric appliances, such as frying pans can be stored here also with handles pointed toward the door. For extra-large trays, the center shelf of the cabinet would need to be removed before installing dividers.

—Swing-out shelves. Shelves can be added to the doors. Be certain they are well supported and have guards to prevent supplies from falling off. The center shelf will not need to be removed if the door shelves are carefully spaced.

—Sliding pothooks. The center shelf cabinet can be removed and an extension rod with pothooks attached to the top part of the cabinet. This device is available in many stores for do-it-yourself installation.

Drawers

Drawers easily become jumbled unless divid-ers are made for small articles stored there.

To make a pattern for drawer dividers, fit a piece of paper in the bottom of the drawer and arrange items on the paper. Mark the space needed for each item or group allowing 1/4 inch for the thickness of the dividers. Remove the paper and draw dividing lines.

Heavy corregated cardboard dividers may be used for a few weeks to try out your plan before making permanent dividers. Cut slits about 1/4-inch wide 1/2 the height of the divider. Fit the dividers together by matching slits as shown in Fig. 11-60. Allow 1 inch or more space above the divider for clearance when closing the drawer.

Large drawers may need a number of partitions to fit the article stored. Plan to keep little-used equipment in the rear sections.

A wooden block with slots for knives can be

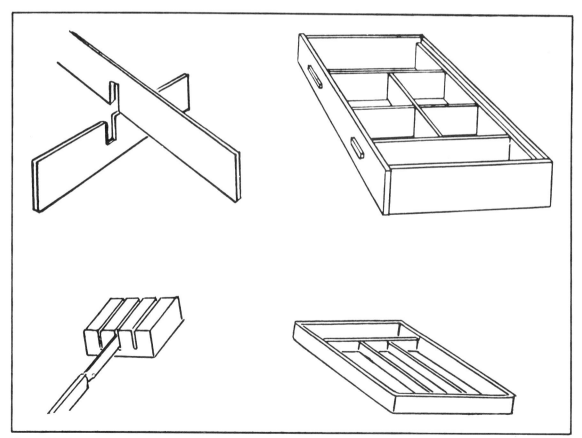

Fig. 11-60. Keep drawers orderly (courtesy University of Florida Extension Service).

glued or nailed to the bottom of a drawer. Allow 4 to 5 inches for storage of three knives, depending on the thickness of the handles. Proper knife storage helps keep cutting edges sharp and also protects fingers.

Deep Drawers. Deep drawers have a number of uses if they are located in the right work areas (Fig. 11-61). Some are equipped with metal liners for storing bread. Some bowls or pressure cookers can be stored in deep drawers without wasting space.

Make a deep drawer more usable for small items or linens by fitting it with a sliding tray. The tray helps avoid stacking unlike items. It can slide from side to side or front to back but should not cover more than half the top of the drawer.

Fit in sheet metal containers with hinged, lift-up covers to serve as canisters for flour and sugar. If the drawer is large you can use three compartments and store brown sugar, graham flour, or some food which is used less often in the back. Make certain the drawer will slide freely when the weight of the contents is added.

By adding removable dividers, deep drawers can also be used to store pie, cake, and bread pans, muffin tins, cake cooling racks, platters, trays, and other flat items. The partitions can run parallel or perpendicular to the drawer front depending on the width of the drawer and the size of equipment to be stored.

General Tips. Wax the glides of wooden drawers so that they will pull out easily.

The back of a drawer should be 3/4-inch higher than the sides to prevent it from pulling all the way out when in use.

Pegboard

If you have unused wall area over the range or elsewhere in a room, cut a piece of pegboard large enough to hold the utensils you want to hang here (Fig. 11-62). Board may be painted any color to go with the room decor.

Mount pegboard on the wall between the wall and base cabinets and use hooks to hold rolling pin, measuring cups, and measuring spoons. Hang pegboard over a desk for use as a bulletin board.

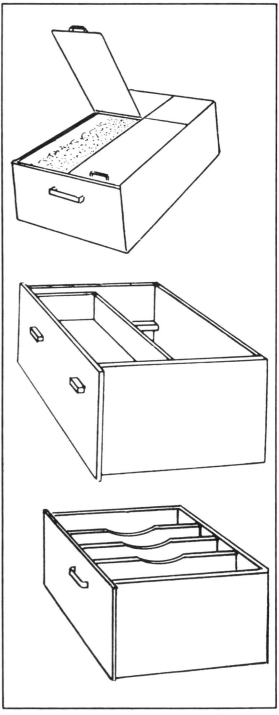

Fig. 11-61. Divide deep drawers (courtesy University of Florida Extension Service).

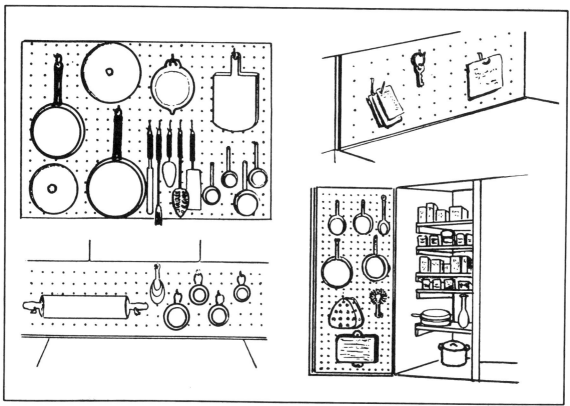

Fig. 11-62. Using pegboard (courtesy University of Florida Extension Service).

Line the inside of a closet, pantry or cabinet door. Insert the proper hardware for shelf supports and hanging utensils. A large section of pegboard behind a door is handy for hanging jackets, repair tools, etc.

Cabinet Doors

You can increase your fingertip storage by making use of the interior of cabinet doors (Fig. 11-63).

Door shelves or racks can be used for small food packages. Do not store heavy articles such as canned goods here since the door hinges may not be strong enough to prevent sagging. Place the rack high enough on the door to clear packages on the shelf inside. These shelves can be made or bought at a hardware store. Hang measuring cups and spoons on the wall cabinet door.

A rack for a cookbook consists of a shelf 1 to 2 inches wide on which the book rests. A strip of elastic near the top of the book holds it open or closed. When the wall cabinet door is open, the book is at eye level for quick reference. A flat box can be partially cut away and hung on the inside of a cabinet

Racks on the inside of a dish cabinet can be used to hold platters that are too large for a shelf. A practical depth for the rack is 3 inches. A narrow wood or metal guard at the bottom and one or two elastic strips above will hold the platter in place. For the largest platters, you may need to cut back the shelves of the cabinet about 3 inches if they come all the way to the front of the cabinet.

THE BATHROOM

You can remodel bathroom areas in your home so they provide maximum family convenience and give satisfactory service for many years. They can

Fig. 11-63. Use cabinet doors for convenient storage (courtesy University of Florida Extension Service).

be practical and pretty too. It's all possible if you plan carefully, insist on good workmanship whether you are doing it yourself or having it contracted, and use the best materials you can afford.

Even on a low budget, the cheapest isn't always the best. By spending a little more, you will find that you can stay within your budget and still prepare for years ahead. The maintenance-free time will save on your budget too!

Wood Paneling

Bathrooms can be rather bleak in older homes. To cure this problem, homeowners often think of new fixtures and new cabinets, but that is major surgery and can be expensive. You can, however, perk up your old bathroom with a face-lifting. There are many types of materials from which to choose, such as wood paneling (Fig. 11-64). This bathroom was finished in a contemporary design with West-

Fig. 11-64. Wood paneled bathroom (courtesy Western Woods Products).

ern red cedar boards and a trim of vertically grained Douglas fir.

The 1-×-4-inch cedar boards were applied horizontally, and 2-×-5-inch fir boards were used as vertical trim. On the original built-in cabinets on the end wall opposite the door, numerous old coats of enamel were sanded off.

The end walls and cabinets were repainted white inside and out, except for wide frames of natural wood left around the cabinet doors, the edges of countertops, and the vertical mirror. These parts received only a coat of Waterproof #7 coating.

A simple oval wash basin, molded of fiberglass and weighing only a pound, was the only new fixture. It was richly customized with a surrounding rectangular counter of 3/4-inch plywood covered with orange-hued formica, and fir 2 × 6s were used to frame, or box in, the countertop.

A new mirror as wide as the counter and extending from counter to ceiling, was installed; then 2 × 6s were put in. They extended from floor to ceiling and flanked both counter and mirror, also serving as a light valance above the basin.

Exposed but recessed lag screws held the framing together. Orange was repeated on the tub

Fig. 11-65. Tiled tub and commode enclosure (courtesy Summitville Tiles).

surround, and an orange pencil holder on the lavatory counter was put in to hold toothbrushes.

Track lighting in the ceiling was then installed, and new silver Mylar gave the ceiling a modern wet and shiny look.

The newly exposed end wall was paneled with 1-×-6-inch cedar boards, selected for natural color contrast and applied diagonally. The hand rail is a fir 2-×-6-inch plank.

Other Materials

If you don't want to use wood, then try ceramic tile (Fig. 11-65). A small shower-tub enclosure and commode can be treated with 2-×-4-×-4-inch Summitstones in snow white and cobalt blue, creating a fresh, crisp look.

Bifold mirrors (Fig. 11-66) allow you to enjoy front and back checking of personal grooming. Other advantages are full access to closets, smooth, quiet operation, extra-rigid steel design, and elegant styling with room-expanding full-length mirrors.

Another way to provide a quick face-lift for the bathroom is to use the bathtub itself. By using door enclosures (Fig. 11-67) you will not have to use shower curtains. Of special interest is a mirrored bath enclosure.

Fig. 11-66. Bifold mirrors (courtesy Benchmark, A General Products Company).

Fig. 11-67. Tub enclosure (courtesy Keller Industries).

Bath Arrangements

Study the arrangements in Figs. 11-68 and 11-69. The space allowances around fixtures in these plans are based on research by the United States Department of Agriculture in which both the use and the cleaning of the bathroom were considered.

Plans. Dimensioned plans for each arrangement of family bathrooms provide a choice of two sizes. The limited arrangements show one location where a mother can stand comfortably and help a child, or one adult can help another adult; the liberal arrangements show two such locations. In the one-person baths, clearance between, to the side of, and in front of fixtures, is held to a minimum. In all family bathroom plans, doors are 2 feet 8 inches wide. Doors in the one-person or minimum baths are 2 feet 4 inches wide.

Five arrangements for compartmentalized baths are shown in Fig. 11-69. Three of these areas have four fixtures; two of them have five fixtures. Three different arrangements of bathrooms with toilet, lavatory, and shower stall are also illustrated.

To plan bathroom arrangements other than those suggested, make yourself a template and place the cutouts in your desired location using the recommended clearances shown in Figs. 11-68 and 11-69.

Location of Bath Areas. Once you have decided on the kind and number of bath areas you need, the next step is to consider the best possible location for each.

Figure 11-70 provides an idea for a good location of a single bathroom in a one-story house with no other toilet facilities. The bathroom can be reached from all the rooms without going through other rooms. It is located next to the utility room for a compact, economical plumbing arrangement that requires a short run of supply and waste pipes. Another desirable feature is that the bathroom door is not visible from the living room or the front entrance.

When more than one complete bathroom is planned, the second frequently opens from the master bedroom. Such a bathroom can serve a dual purpose. Figure 11-71 illustrates an arrangement in which the master bathroom, located conveniently near the rear entrance, is also a wash-up area. Note how the family bathroom, master bathroom, and laundry area are grouped together for an economical installation of plumbing.

A single lavatory installed in a bedroom is one way to add convenience at a nominal cost. The lavatory can be enclosed or shielded by a screen (Fig. 11-72).

Fixtures

Bathroom fixtures are available in many choices. Vitreous china is always used for toilets, and can also be used for lavatories.

Fiberglass has made an impact on today's bathroom fixtures. Tub-shower units and shower stalls including the surround wall area are of leakproof, one-piece construction and are easily maintained (Fig. 11-73).

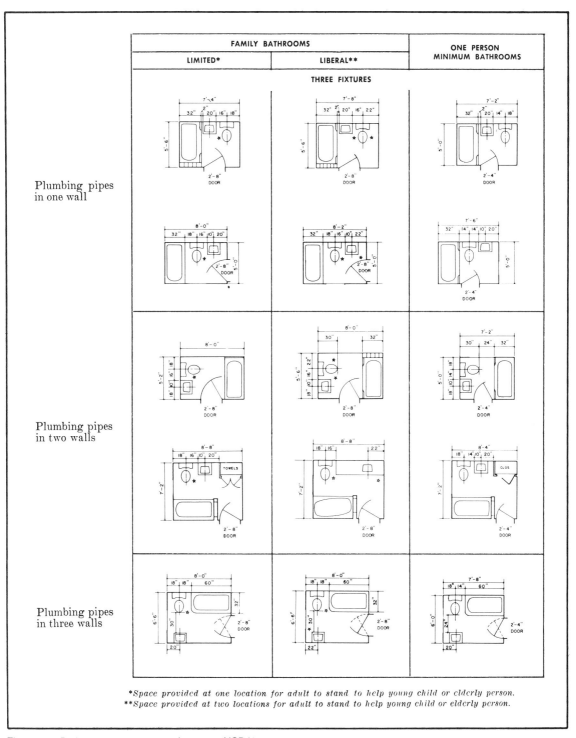

Fig. 11-68. Bathroom arrangements (courtesy USDA).

365

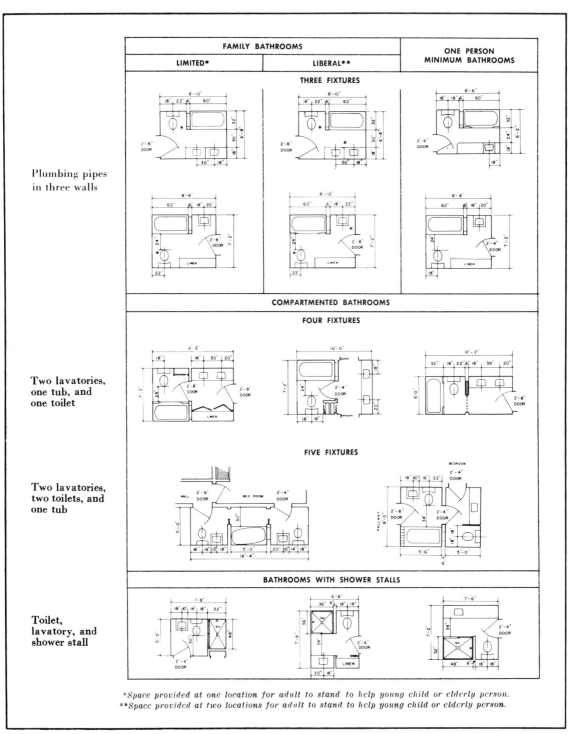

Fig. 11-69. Bathroom arrangements (courtesy USDA).

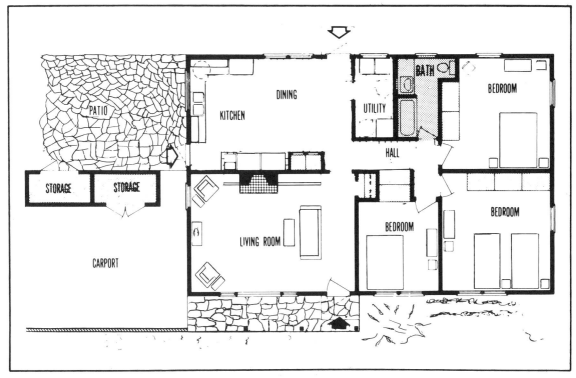

Fig. 11-70. Good location for a single bathroom (courtesy USDA).

Tub Enclosures. Tub enclosures are popular, practical, and easy to install. Recessed tubs (fit flush between two walls) and corner installations are 4, 4 1/2, 5, or 5 1/2 feet long. The 5-foot tub is the most common length. Tubs with widened rims are usually 32 or 33 inches wide; tubs with straight fronts are 30 or 31 inches wide.

Square tubs are about 4 feet by 3 1/2 or 4 feet, and are available for either recessed or corner installation. Some styles have one built-in seat; others have two. A square tub is heavier than a rectangular tub and may require additional framing for support.

Receptor tubs are approximately 36 to 38 inches long, 39 to 42 inches wide, and 12 inches high. They are most suitable for shower installations, but because they are lower, they are also convenient for bathing children and others who need assistance.

Install tub enclosures, using the following directions,

—Measure the opening at the top edge of the tub.

—Mark and cut track an equal amount from each end and 1/6 inch less than the opening dimension.

—Apply a continuous bead of caulking along the underside of both edges of the track.

—Install the track on the top edge of the tub. Be sure the plastic guide faces the enclosed area.

—Set the jambs over the track. Note: jambs are marked "bottom left," and "bottom right." Left or right is determined when facing the unit from the outside. Check the jamb for plumb with a level. Mark two installation holes per jamb.

—Remove the jambs and drill four 3/16-inch diameter installation holes (2 per wall) as marked. Note: if you are drilling into ceramic tile, be sure to use a carbide-tipped drill bit.

—Reinstall the jambs on the top of the track. Secure each jamb with two nylon anchors provided with your tub enclosure.

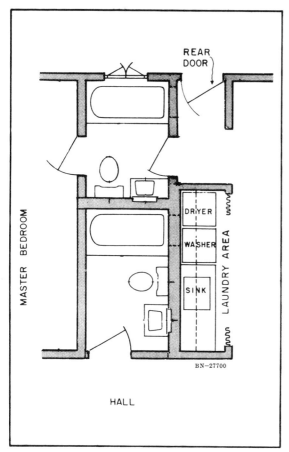

Fig. 11-71. Master bedroom bath arrangement (courtesy USDA).

Fig. 11-72. Extra lavatory in bedroom (courtesy USDA).

—Measure the opening at the top of the jamb.

—Mark and cut a header 1/16 inch less than the opening measurement.

—Install the header over the top of the jambs.

—Attach two rollers per panel on top of the panels with machine screws, which are provided with your doors.

—Lift up the inside panel by slipping rollers into the header and then down into the guide. Do the same with the outside door. Note the roller position inside the header.

—Caulk the entire unit on the inside and outside. Be sure to caulk the joint where the jambs fit over the track.

—Install the towel bar with tapped rivets and screws.

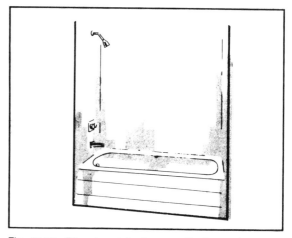

Fig. 11-73. Fiberglass tub-shower unit of one-piece construction (courtesy USDA).

368

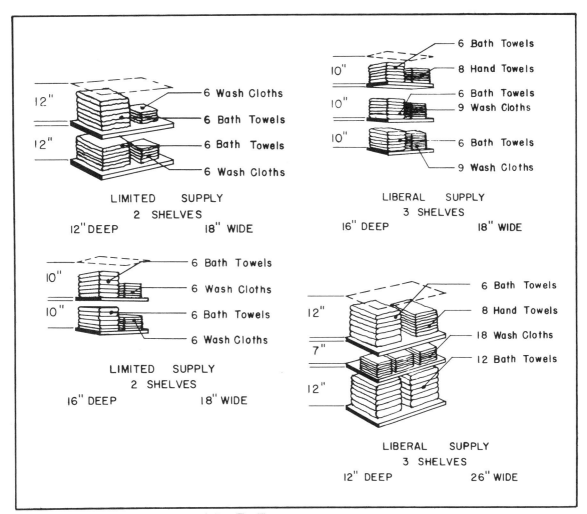

Fig. 11-74. Suggested towel storage (courtesy USDA).

Sinks and Toilets. There are a variety of sinks which work nicely in almost any bathroom; the choice is yours. If your bathroom has the space, the lavatory-countertop type is by far the most efficient since you can use the space in the cabinet area for cleaning items or for laundry or linen storage.

There are also many kinds of toilets available. The most popular is the wall-hung variety since it permits easy floor cleaning.

Towel Cabinets. You can save steps by storing some bath linens in the bathroom. Space dimensions for storing 12 washcloths and 12 bath towels and for storing 18 bath towels, 18 washcloths, and 8 hand towels are given in Fig. 11-74. If available space is deeper than 16 inches, drawers or pull-out shelves are more useful than fixed shelves.

Lighting. Good lighting in the bathroom is needed for shaving, makeup, and hair care. Figure 11-75 shows some lighting fixtures that work well in any bathroom, regardless of its individual decor. All do an excellent job.

MIRRORS

Mirrors are ideal for remodeled homes: they

369

Fig. 11-75. Excellent lighting fixtures for bathroom (courtesy Progress Lighting Company).

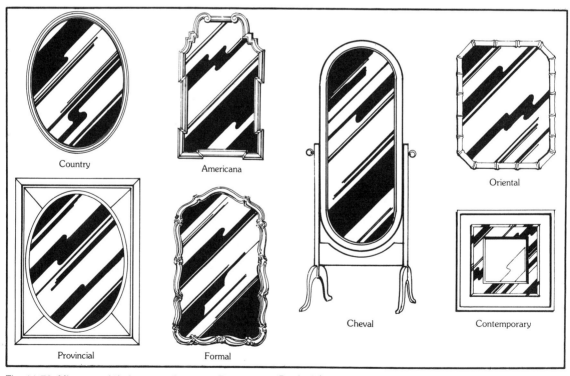

Country

Americana

Oriental

Provincial

Formal

Cheval

Contemporary

Fig. 11-76. Mirrors and their names (courtesy Benswanger Products).

Fig. 11-77. A mirror over the fireplace (courtesy Benswanger Products).

Fig. 11-78. Floor to ceiling mirror (courtesy Benswanger Products).

can save you painting and paneling; they can dress rooms up and down, and they are excellent throughout the house.

Mirrors can also add decorating impact to a room. A beautifully framed mirror is not only a great accent piece in its own right; it will also double the image of a favorite art object or a beautiful bouquet, bring stature to a not-so-important accessory, light up a dark area and add dimension where needed. Several mirrors strategically placed will multiply these effects.

Choosing the Right Mirror

For the countryfied Americana room choose simple oval, rectangular, or octagonal Regency and Sheraton frames in metallic finishes. Mirror frames boasting an oriental connection are also great for formal Americana rooms. Such frames may be lacquered or gold finished with Chinese hand-painted designs. They may feature Chippendale fretwork, or they may boast simple or ornate bamboo like curves in gloss-white finishes.

These classically oriental styles with a group of Tiffany-type stained glass mirrors are also terrific for Victoriana and eclectic rooms.

For French Provincial decors, use rectangular, oval, or octagonal mirrors in hearty wood or antique metal finishes. Ornately shaped, gold-finished mirror frames are flattering for formal period rooms, be they French, Italian, or English.

Fig. 11-79. Architectural effects (courtesy Benswanger Products).

For casual, contemporary rooms, choose wicker-framed or simple square and rectangular shapes. Frame them with suedelike material, jewel-finished gold aluminum or earthwood for more formal, contemporary rooms. There are many to choose from as shown in Fig. 11-76.

Decorating With Mirrors

A mirror in the foyer is a must. Hang one over a lowboy, bench, or shelf. A mirror over the fireplace mantel is a classic placement that cannot be faulted. You can go this tradition one better by hanging another mirror opposite the fireplace (Fig. 11-77).

Mirrors belong in the kitchen and difficult-to-decorate stairwells. They can handsomely offset a group of your favorite paintings.

Always remember that one large mirror may not be the only solution to a decorating problem. A group of smaller ones, in different shapes and styles, may prove infinitely more decorative.

Floor-to-ceiling mirror strips will heighten a room visually, so will a mirror on the ceiling. Fabulous architectural ceilings can be created with mirrors, and beams, lattice work, or molding strips. Figure 11-78 shows a floor to ceiling mirror.

Architectural Effects

Use mirror materials to chase the sameness from plain-Jane rooms, as shown in Fig. 11-79. The excitement of a fully mirrored wall obviously goes hand in hand with contemporary rooms, but since it reflects everything around it, don't be afraid to use it in a traditional setting.

There's more to mirrors than clear finishes. Antique, for example, reflects beautifully on a traditional decor. Grey and bronze are dramatic background possibilities for crisply contemporary rooms, and amber will cast a warm glow over any room. Consider the possibilities of combining panels of one of these tints with a clear mirror for the most interesting wall ever.

Sources

The various products mentioned in this book can be obtained from the manufacturers listed here.

American Home Lighting Institute
435 North Michigan Avenue
Chicago, IL 60611

American Plywood Association
7011 S. 19th Street
Tacoma, WA 98411

Birmingham Stove and Range Co.
P.O. Box 2647
Birmingham, AL 35202

Celotex Corporation
P.O. Box 22602
Tampa, FL 33622

CeramicUS
1375 Raff Rd, SW
Canton, OH 44710

General Products Company
P.O. Box 887
Fredericksburg, VA 22401

Georgia-Pacific Corporation
9000 S.W. Fifth Avenue
Portland, OR 97204

Heath Company
Benton Harbor, MI 49022

Leslie-Locke
2872 W. Market Street
Akron, OH 44313

Majestic Company
An American-Standard Company
1000 E. Market Street
Huntington IN 46750

Murray Feiss Import Corp.
860 East 138th Street
Bronx, NY 10454

Tile Council of America
P.O. Box 503
Mahwah, NJ 07430

Lordon & Burnham
Irvington-On-Hudson, NY

Progress Lighting
Erie Avenue and G Street
Philadelphia, PA 19134

Summitville Tiles, Inc.
Summitville, OH 43962

Western Wood Products Association
1500 Yeon Bldg
Portland, OR 97204

Glossary

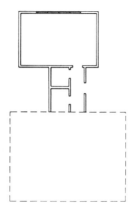

Glossary

American Plywood Association—a trade association representing most of the nation's manufacturers of construction and industrial panels.

batten—a thin, narrow piece of board used to cover vertical joints of plywood siding.

batter board—a temporary framework used to assist in locating corners when laying out a foundation.

blocking—small wood pieces used between structural members to support panel edges.

bottom plate—also called a sole plate, the lowest horizontal member of a wall or partition which rests on the subflooring. Wall studs are nailed to the bottom plate.

chalk line—also called a snap line, a long spool-wound cord encased in a container filled with chalk. Chalk-covered string is pulled from the case, pulled taut across a surface, lifted, and snapped directly downward so that it leaves a long, straight chalk mark.

collar beam—a horizontal tie beam in a gable roof, connecting two opposite rafters at a point considerably above the wall plate.

course—a continuous level row of construction units, as a layer of foundation block, shingles, or panels, as in subflooring or roof sheathing.

cripple—any part of a frame which is cut less than full length, as in cripple studs under a window opening.

d—the abbreviation for "penny" in designating nail size.

dimension lumber—lumber 2 to 5 inches thick and up to 12 inches wide. Includes joists, rafters, studs, planks, girders, and posts.

doubling—to use two like framing members nailed together, such as studs or joists, to add strength to a building.

fascia—horizontal board that is used as a facing.

fascia rafter—end rafters at the end of the rake.

footing—the concrete (usually) base foundation walls, posts, chimneys, etc. The footing is wider than the member it supports, and distributes the weight to the ground over a larger area to prevent settling.

gable—the triangular portion of the end wall of a house with a pitched roof.

gusset—a small piece of wood, plywood, or metal attached to the corners or intersections of a frame to add stiffness and strength.

header—one or more pieces of framing lumber used around openings to support the free ends of floor joists, studs, or rafters.

header joist—also called a ribbon or band joist, the horizontal lumber member that is butted against ends of floor joists around the outside of the house to add support to and tie the joists together.

in-line joint—a connection made by butting two pieces of lumber, such as floor joists, end-to-end and fastening them together using an additional splice piece nailed on both sides of the joint.

joist—one of a series of parallel framing members used to support floor or ceiling loads, and supported in turn by larger beams, girders, bearing walls, or the foundation.

kiln dried—wood seasoned in a humidity- and temperature-controlled oven to minimize shrinkage and warping.

lap joint—a connection made by placing two pieces of material side by side and fastening them by nailing, gluing, etc.

o.c.—on center. A method of indicating the spacing of raming members by stating the measurement from the center of one member to the center of the next.

outrigger—a piece of dimension lumber which extends out over the rake to support the fascia rafter.

plumb bob—a weight attached to a line for testing perpendicular surfaces for trueness.

rafter—one of a series of structural members of a roof, designed to support roof loads.

rake—the overhanging part of a roof at a gable end.

ridge board—the central framing member at the peak, or ridge, of a roof. The roof rafters frame into it from each side.

setback—placing of a building a specified distance from the street or property lines to comply with building codes.

sheathing—the structural covering on the outside surface of wall or roof framing.

siding—the finish covering on the outside walls of frame buildings.

sill—also called a mudsill or a sill plate, the lowest framing member of a structure, resting on the foundation and supporting the floor system and the uprights of the frame.

soffit—the underside of a roof overhang.

span—the distance between supports of a structural member.

studs—vertical members (usually 2 × 4s) making up the main framing of a wall.

subflooring—the bottom panel in a two-layer floor.

top plate—the uppermost horizontal member nailed to the wall or partition studs. It is usually doubled with end joints offset.

underlayment—the top panel in a two-layer floor. It provides a smooth base for carpet, tile, or sheet flooring.

Index

Index

Edited by Suzanne L. Cheatle

Acknowledgments

Special thanks are due to those individuals and organizations who aided in my research and provided photography, illustrations and knowledge which enabled me to bring to you a timely work in the "art of saving money,"—while gaining experience—to make your "house" a "home."

Heath Craft Woodworks, Heath Company, Benton Harbor, Michigan. Myron Kukla Advertising and Public Relations Coordinator for Heath Craft Woodworks, Benton Harbor, Michigan. Lis King, Public Relations, Mahwah, New Jersey who started me on the road in Chapter 11 with the wonderful information from the Tile Council of America and her other clients, Binswanger Products and National Gypsum Company, Decorative Products Division. Stacey G. Wilson, Information Manager, Building Products, Georgia-Pacific Corporation. Belden/Frenz/Lehman, Public Relations for Summitville Tiles, Inc., Summitville, Ohio and Summitville Tiles, Inc. Daniel W. Selhorst, Director of Marketing, CeramicUS, United States Ceramic Tile Company. Patricia Logan, Costitch and McConnell, Inc., for their usual help and prompt, efficient handling of any information for their client, Lord & Burnham, Irvington-on-Hudson, New York. Raymond W. Moholt, Manager Product Publicity, Western Wood Products, Portland, Oregon. Daniel J. Korman, President and Chairman of the Board, Cabell Eanes Advertising and Mary Sue Boron for their help in behalf of R. Morton Miller, General Products, Fredericksburg, Virginia. Murry Feiss, Murry Feiss Import Corp. Bronx, New York, Leslie-Locke, Akron, Ohio who are teaching all of us that "fans" have made a return in our industrialized society. Clem Moreman, Birmingham Stove Works, Birmingham, Alabama. Gregory R. Olsen, Communications Specialist, The Celotex Corporation. Marvin Pehovsky, Public Relations Manger for Progress Lighting, Philadelphia, Pennsylvania. Donald W. Minton, P.R. Specialist, Keller Crescent Majestic, an All American Standard Company, Huntington, Indiana. Harold L. Keith, Director, Publication and Information Services, Department of Housing and Urban Development. Maryann Ezell, American Plywood Association. Evert Thompson, Pacific Grove,

California, and Al Newman, Keller Industries, Miami, Florida.

To the many people with whom I spoke daily during my extensive research, especially Jim Cronley, Cronley Construction, Pensacola, Florida who is never too busy to "spare me a moment for my next book." Wayne Lovett, Escambia County Agent, Pensacola, Florida for his untiring help.

Andy Capp, Keller Construction, Pensacola, Florida who "waits for me to begin again." And for those who remain unmentioned, it is not because you are forgotten—it is only that there are so many always there.

Without all of these people, I would be unable to complete my work. Thank you all.

Bette Galman Wahlfeldt